In the Lion's Den

The Life of Oswald Rufeisen

NECHAMA TEC

OXFORD
UNIVERSITY PRESS

OXFORD
UNIVERSITY PRESS

Oxford University Press, Inc., publishes works that further
Oxford University's objective of excellence
in research, scholarship, and education.

Oxford New York
Auckland Cape Town Dar es Salaam Hong Kong Karachi
Kuala Lumpur Madrid Melbourne Mexico City Nairobi
New Delhi Shanghai Taipei Toronto

With offices in
Argentina Austria Brazil Chile Czech Republic France Greece
Guatemala Hungary Italy Japan Poland Portugal Singapore
South Korea Switzerland Thailand Turkey Ukraine Vietnam

First published by Oxford University Press, Inc., 1990
198 Madison Avenue, New York, NY 10016

www.oup.com

First issued as an Oxford University Press paperback, 2008

Oxford is a registered trademark of Oxford University Press

Library of Congress Cataloging-in-Publication Data
Tec, Nechama.
In the lion's den : the life of Oswald Rufeisen / Nechama Tec.
p. cm.
ISBN 978-0-19-538347-8 (pbk.)
1. Rufeisen, Oswald. 2. Jews—Poland—Biography. 3. Holocaust,
Jewish (1939–1945)—Poland. 4. World War, 1939–1945—Underground
Movements, Jewish—Poland. 5. Converts from Judaism—Biography.
6. Converts, Catholic—Israel—Biography. 7. Carmelites—Israel—
Biography. 8. Catholic Church—Israel—Clergy—Biography.
I. Title.
DS135.P63R848 1990
940.53′18′09438—dc20 89–27256 CIP

1 3 5 7 9 8 6 4 2

Printed in the United States of America
on acid-free paper

To my mother

Acknowledgments

I came across Oswald Rufeisen's[1] testimony in 1978 at the Jewish Historical Institute in Warsaw while collecting archival material about Poles who had risked their lives during World War II to save Jews and Jews who tried to survive the war by living illegally in the forbidden Christian world.

Intrigued by his story, I wrote him a letter explaining my eagerness to talk with him and my special involvement with the Holocaust, assuring him that, unless he gave permission, the content of our future conversations would remain confidential.

Though I received no answer, I refused to give up and eventually my journalist friend Arieh Gelblum came to my aid. He knew Hilel Seidel, a former member of parliament who was also a close friend of Oswald Rufeisen. Seidel wrote a book, half devoted to his own life and half to Oswald Rufeisen's story.[2] Arieh asked Hilel Seidel to introduce me to Oswald. Seidel, in turn, wanted to meet me first. He made no promises, saying that he had to know what kind of a person I was before mentioning me to Oswald.

In the fall of 1983, I had an appointment with Oswald Rufeisen in his church office in Haifa. When I reached the place a half-opened door revealed a small room, crowded by a table covered with papers and books. To one side of the wall was a shelf also cluttered with books and papers. Around the table three wooden chairs completed the furnishings. When I knocked at the door, a short man jumped up from one of the chairs.

Because Oswald's heroic deeds had dominated my consciousness, I was surprised by his unimposing looks and his equally unassuming manner. He came toward me with an outstretched arm and a smile that covered his entire face. His brown eyes had a special twinkle, signaling a lively intelligence and wit. Warm and friendly, his smile had a shy, tentative quality. He had to be close to sixty, yet a youthful, even boyish, spirit emanated from his very being.

On that first day, before I even settled down, gently, but firmly, Oswald told me that, after all, his life story is known and there is not much he could add. In fact, he was surprised by my wish to interview him. Then, with a sigh, he added that all these things happened so long ago and that now he concentrates on the present. Obviously, he would have preferred that I give up the idea of an interview.

I ignored his reluctance and he agreed to the interview and the use of a tape recorder.

At first, Oswald spoke Hebrew. When he became relaxed and more involved, he switched to Polish. This change of languages became a pattern, and I too would turn to Polish whenever we came to a particularly touchy issue. Occasionally, we were interrupted. People would come in to ask questions. Depending on the person, Oswald used a different language: Italian, Arabic, German, Hebrew, and others. He is fluent in eight languages.

Absorbed in the story, eager to hear more, I was unaware of the time. Oswald, on the other hand, seemed tired. After about three hours, he wanted to know if I had finished my questions. When I told him that this was merely the beginning, with a resigned smile, he agreed to see me again.

From then on, each time I came to Israel, which was at least twice a year, I would reinterview him. I also met with his family, friends, and others who knew about him. With only two exceptions, all those whom I contacted were willing to meet me. As my circle of subjects expanded, I kept checking and rechecking their stories.

While collecting information about Oswald, I continued my study of the rescuers and the rescued. Susan Rabiner, my friend and editor at Oxford University Press, was intrigued by the stories I was bringing from my interviews with Oswald and thought I should write a book about him.

Initially I intended to include the material from these interviews in my book about rescue. When I told Rufeisen that I had signed a contract for a book about him, he was upset. In a kind yet direct way, he let me know he was disappointed. He felt that I had let him down and was hurt.

By then, we had become friends. I cared about the book, but I cared more about Oswald Rufeisen. My arguments about the importance and the universal implications of his life failed to convince him. Then I reassured him that I had no intention of sensationalizing his story and promised to let him read the book before sending it to print.

Still sad, yet sensitive to my mood, he suggested that we meet again. As I was leaving, my emotions were a strange mixture of relief, guilt, embarrassment, and regret.

Our meetings continued. During one, I was moved to hear Oswald say, "If a biography about me must be written, you and no one else should be its author."

For the last five years, Oswald Rufeisen has been devoting many hours to answering my questions. I owe him an everlasting debt.

I have learned a great deal from the interviews conducted with others in the United States and Israel. For their willingness to meet with me for long hours, and often for several sessions, I wish to thank: Moshe Bairach, Jochanan Elichai, Bela Greenstein, Jacob Greenstein, Moshe Kalchheim, Cila Kapelowicz, Józiek Rakocz, Jacob Rubenfeld, Arieh Rufeisen, Hela Szippper Rufeisen, Jehuda Rytman, Stefi Schanzer, Hilel Seidel, and Ernest Seifter.

I am particularly grateful to Hilel Seidel for introducing me to Oswald Rufeisen and for the many hours he spent patiently answering my many questions.

This book has benefited from Arieh Gelblum's extensive help. Indeed, I am indebted to him for bringing about my introduction to Oswald Rufeisen, for directing me to relevant reading materials, some of which he translated from the Hebrew, for reading the entire manuscript, and for offering most valuable and insightful suggestions.

I want to thank Shmuel Krakowski, chief archivist at Yad Vashem, for a careful reading of the entire book and for his useful comments. Over the years, I have come to rely on Dina Abramowicz, the reference librarian at YIVO (Jewish Historical Institute) in New York City. Dina's eagerness to find answers to puzzling questions made such searches enjoyable. Similarly, YIVO's chief archivist, Marek Web, was always ready to direct me to new sources. The same was true for the archivist Fruma Mohrer, whose translations of various documents became a part of this book.

I am indebted to Alice L. Eckardt, professor of religion, for her patient answers to my many queries.

Though busy with their professional lives, Geuli Arad, Ilana Geva, and Ada Tal-Sima each volunteered to translate and make special materials accessible to me. To the author Sandra Brand I am indebted for her careful reading of and valuable comments about the manuscript. Similarly, Emanuel Tanay's insightful remarks helped me rethink some of the central issues.

I would like to thank Cathleen Schine for her critical suggestions that eased the process of rewriting. I am particularly indebted to Lisl Cade for her continuous enthusiastic support and helpful comments.

Whenever I searched for some hard-to-find facts that touched on Polish history or Polish literature, I knew that I could turn to Bernarda Stevenson who was always able to locate the appropriate articles and books. I appreciate her cheerful, eager helpfulness.

Susan Rabiner, my former editor, was instrumental in developing and sustaining my involvement in this project. For generous help given to me at a later stage, I would like to thank my present editor at Oxford, Valerie Aubry, and her assistant Niko Pfund.

Rosemary Wellner's special interest in my work and editorial skills improved the writing of this book while making the last stages of the job less painful. I am also indebted to Lori Somerville for her excellent secretarial assistance.

All along, my husband Leon Tec and my children Leora and Roland gave me their moral support. I am grateful to Leora for suggesting the title of this book. Whenever I found myself in a "no exit" situation, I called on Roland's editorial skills.

Though the many generous offers of help improved the end product and made the entire working process more rewarding, I alone am responsible for this book's shortcomings.

Westport, Conn. N. T.
June 1989

Contents

1

Before and Into the War

High on Mount Carmel, in a Gothic-like monastery overlooking the Mediterranean from the Holy Land, lives an enigma. A World War II hero turned monk. A Christian who is a Jew. An Israeli who wore the Nazi uniform. A Polish Jew who as an officer with a German police unit organized a ghetto breakout. A fugitive from his erstwhile Nazi colleagues who found refuge with Polish nuns and became a Catholic. A pacifist who became a resistance fighter. A priest who insists on his Jewish identity. A Zionist who chooses to live in Israel and identify with it. A fighter for Jewish survival who devotes his life to establishing bridges between Judaism and Christianity.

Among the remarkable stories from World War II, that of Oswald Rufeisen, also known as Father Daniel, is unique.

Oswald's[1] life began quietly in a world that would vanish before he turned eighteen. His father, Eliasz Rufeisen, and his mother, Fanny, lived in Zadziele, a village located at the southern tip of Poland, close to the Czechoslovakian border. At the time of his birth in 1922, Poland had regained its independence after more than a century of occupation by Austria, Prussia, and Russia.[2] Because Zadziele was in a region formerly under Austrian control, the Rufeisen family, like other Jewish families in the area, were influenced by their own Jewish culture, the larger Polish culture, and that of the occupying Austrians. The degree of influence exerted on a Jewish family by each culture depended on the size and importance of its community and how close it was to the "real" Austrian border.[3]

At the time, Zadziele consisted of a few unpaved roads lined with primitive one-room huts, practically all owned by Polish peasants who worked the surrounding fields. Unsophisticated methods of farming and the small size of the plots yielded only limited returns to these hard-working farmers. The same low standard of living characterized Zadziele's few Jewish families. Economic hardship was largely responsible for the constantly diminishing number of Jews in the countryside. At the beginning of the 1930s, not more than fifteen Jewish families lived in this entire rural area. Yet of the surrounding villages only Zadziele had a synagogue and a Jewish cemetery, suggesting that in the past it may have been home to a substantial Jewish population.

Through the early 1930s, Jews from nearby communities had come to the village for religious services. But as the Jewish exodus from the countryside continued, it became harder to find the quorums of ten men required to conduct such services.

Where were these people going? Some emigrated to Palestine, some to the United States, still others moved to larger communities nearby.

For those who chose to remain in Poland, the nearest town was Żywiec. With a population close to 10,000, Żywiec had a Polish high school, a teachers' college, and a railroad station. As a well-established town dating back to medieval times, Żywiec could also boast important historical buildings, including an ancient castle, monuments of different historical figures, paved roads, and stores. It was indeed an attractive center.

While Jews could visit the town and own businesses, they were prohibited from living there. This prohibition dated back to the seventeenth century, when Poland was ruled by a branch of the Swedish house of Vasa. During the reign of Zygmunt III, in 1626, as a special gesture of goodwill toward the citizens of Żywiec, the king issued a decree prohibiting Jews from residing there.[4] Deposited in the town's archives, this document was jealously guarded; it continued to be enforced into the twentieth century.

Because the few Jews who in the past tried to test this ancient decree had met with bitter disappointment—they had been roughly and unceremoniously removed by local authorities—the Jews who chose to live in the region preferred to leave this law unchallenged. Instead, they settled in Zabłocie.

Newer but less attractive, Zabłocie was separated from Żywiec by a river. The two communities maintained close commercial ties, with most of the industry and businesses located in Zabłocie. The major enterprise of Zabłocie was a paper factory. There were also small workshops and stores.

It is not entirely clear whether Zabłocie was a village or a town. As the period is remembered today, whenever a sign was put up identifying it as a village, someone was sure to tear it down and substitute another that used the word "town." After a while, this sign would be replaced, apparently at the direction of some area official, by one that again referred to the "village" of Zabłocie. This war of the signs continued for years. It is not surprising that the citizens of Zabłocie preferred to think of their community as a town, and it is noteworthy that they were so persistent about the issue. To this day not only do former Zabłocie residents refer to the place as a town, but some insist that it was a particularly modern town. When asked to explain what they mean by modern, they say that it was more modern than Polish towns closer to the heart of Poland.

Since no residents were engaged in agricultural pursuits, Zabłocie ought to have qualified as a small town. Zabłocie's population was almost exclusively Jewish, with about 150 to 200 families. The place had one large synagogue and a few small ones attached to private homes. With considerable pride, former inhabitants of Zabłocie point out that their community was able to support two schools: one Jewish and one Polish. Both schools were secular. Both taught the same subjects. Only the language in which the subjects were taught differed. Jews were free to attend either school.

One long paved road ran through the entire town, while most of the side streets remained unpaved. Almost without exception, dwellings were modest huts, similar to those occupied by local peasants. The closer these buildings were to the main street the more desirable they were as living quarters and businesses. For the dwindling number of rural Jews, Zabłocie became an important center and a move from any nearby village to Zabłocie was regarded as a definite step up, though perhaps more symbolic than real. In fact, none of Zabłocie's residents was rich, and most had only limited schooling.

Still, modest economic and educational circumstances did not prevent these Jews from making those invidious comparisons small-town people will make, and from classifying each other in terms of income, education, and a whole array of other concrete or illusory social distinctions. In the end, however, in Zabłocie, as in many other small Eastern European Jewish communities of the time, it was education that was most highly valued. All Jewish parents were determined to provide better schooling for their offspring. Each household, no matter how poor (and most were poor), made an effort to educate some of their children, especially boys. The amount of education achieved by children of a family very much determined that family's standing within the community.

But not all education was equally prestigious. On the high school level, points were awarded for the language in which the students were taught. Polish high schools were more desirable than those that taught in Yiddish and Hebrew, while German schools were even more highly regarded than Polish. The geographic location of a school was also important and could sometimes outweigh language in its social significance. High schools in the nearby town of Bielsko were more acceptable than those in either Żywiec or Zabłocie.

Larger than either of the two other towns, Bielsko had a mixed population of Germans, Poles, and Jews. Its size and closeness to the Austrian border reflected wider and more extensive Austrian influences. And just as residents of Zadziele and other villages looked up to Żywiec and Zabłocie, so did those from Żywiec and Zabłocie look up to Bielsko. Anything that came from Bielsko was more highly valued. Those who wanted better books, better clothes, would travel to shop there. Bielsko had a theatre, a movie house, and two kinds of high schools: German and Polish.

Those who established themselves in Bielsko felt superior to those left behind. Some Jewish residents of Bielsko identified with the German culture, an identification closely correlated to greater assimilation. A pro-German orientation influenced religious observances, though these always remained essentially orthodox.

Even now, some of the former residents of Bielsko express the pretensions and prejudices of those days. As one person recently explained with some pride, *in our town there were more German Jews than Polish Jews. We had an organ in our temple [nearly unheard of in Poland]. Only on Yom Kippur we did not play it. . . . Otherwise the organist was a non-Jew who played on Fridays and Saturdays. Still, it was an orthodox synagogue with some unorthodox features. . . . We also had a chorus, not the same that Jews had in other parts of Poland, especially the eastern parts. . . . In Zadziele, Polish was the language. In my home it was different. My parents spoke German.*[5]

Pro-German attitudes were not limited to Bielsko residents.[6] Many Jews who could not afford to live in Bielsko still hoped they might send their children to be educated in one of its more cosmopolitan high schools. But few could afford to do so. Those who could not tried other ways to make their children stand out as more cultured; the foremost was to have the children communicate in German. Even when they still lived in Zadziele, the poorest and most provincial of the four communities, German was the language spoken in the Rufeisen's household.

Oswald's father, Eliasz Rufeisen, was born in 1886. Eliasz's wife Fanny, two years older, was a distant cousin. They married in 1914, when Eliasz was twenty-eight and Fanny thirty; by local standards both were at advanced ages for marriage. At thirty Fanny clearly fit into the unflattering category of an old maid and marriage must have seemed to come as a most fortunate last-minute reprieve. Their age and the fact that Eliasz was the junior of the two, together with what we know of Jewish customs of the day, seem to suggest an arranged marriage.

Though Eliasz had already served in the Austrian army, with the outbreak of war he was conscripted once again. This time he was inducted into the Austro-German army, and then, after the establishment of an independent Poland, into the Polish forces. When he returned to civilian life in 1920, he had spent eight years in the military.

Eliasz had been a good soldier and finished his military career as a platoon comander (Zugsführer). Wounded in action, he was decorated for bravery by the three armies he served: the Austrian, the Austro-German, and the Polish. With each military distinction came a supply of interesting adventure stories, but no special skills for earning a living.

Within a year of his return home, Fanny gave birth to their first child, a daughter, who would die between her second and third birthday. In 1922 the couple had a son Oswald; he would not remember his sister. In 1923, Fanny gave birth to her last child, a boy named Arieh.[7] The Rufeisen boys were keenly aware that their parents were older than those of their playmates.

Fanny owned a house that stood on the edge of Zadziele, slightly removed from the other dwellings. Surrounded by a small lot, it was roomy and divided into two parts. One was used as a tavern; the other as living quarters. As with the rest of the houses in Zadziele, it had no indoor plumbing or running water. Each home had an outhouse and, as a rule, local peasants were glad to empty the outhouse and use the refuse for fertilizer. Water was drawn from outdoor wells.

Fanny had inherited the tavern and the dwelling from an aunt. Before the aunt died, her son, an engineer, made it clear that he was not interested in this inheritance. Fanny had several married sisters. Two lived in Bielsko and though they weren't rich, each was better off than their spinster sister. By leaving this property to Fanny, the aunt may have wanted to help her most unfortunate niece. Perhaps she also thought that a house and a ready business would help Fanny find a husband.

Still, to run a tavern, particularly in Zadziele, was not a glamorous job. The customers were poor peasants. They would order drinks but very rarely snacks to accompany them. Inevitably, one had to face intoxicated men, listen to abusive language, and occasionally deal with violence. The tavern was also unprofitable—there were simply not enough drinkers to support a family business.

At the time of their marriage, in 1914, the tavern was their only source of income. Fanny offered the running of the business to her husband. From the start Eliasz disliked the job and it soon became clear that he would be a failure as a manager. World War I and Eliasz's conscription into the Austro-German army took him away from Zadziele. Capable and energetic, Fanny took over the business and continued to run it after her husband returned from the military.

Eliasz bought a small country store. When the store also proved unsuccessful, he began to drift through a variety of occupations, all of which he handled with a minimum of distinction. One enterprise involved acting as an intermediary between peasants who wanted to sell wood from their forests and the factory owner in the village of Lydygowice who needed wood for manufacturing furniture. For this job Eliasz had to get up at four o'clock in the morning. He would walk through large forests in search of the appropriate trees. Later he would point out the selected trees to the peasant, who would cut them. Next the peasant might deliver the trees with his horse-drawn wagon, or Eliasz would rent a horse and wagon and deliver the wood to the furniture factory. For his efforts, Eliasz received a small commission both from the owner of the forest and the owner of the furniture factory. The work was hard, time-consuming, and far from profitable. Poverty was a chronic condition in the Rufeisen home.

With sadness, Oswald would later describe his father as *not successful at all. . . . He tried to do many things, he went in all kinds of directions, never making it. He was not always able to pay his debts on time. He would then send my mother to ask again for a loan. Eventually, he paid everyone back. . . . And if there were conflicts between my parents they were usually against this background.*

One quarrel in particular stuck in his mind. It happened at night when he and his brother were in bed. *Father demanded that my mother go and ask for a loan from someone to whom we still owed money. My mother refused to do it. My father became angry and said that in that case he was going to drown himself. . . . I remember that my brother and I screamed. Then I began to cry. I was convinced that he would go and drown himself as he had threatened to do. . . . I must have been eight or younger when this happened.*

Perhaps the events of that evening were particularly dramatic for young Oswald because the role his father played was out of character. A passive man, Eliasz was dominated by his more enterprising wife and willingly deferred to her judgment on all matters. For her part, Fanny carried most of the family's burdens with quiet resignation.

These problems, or Oswald's memory of them, did not prevent him from describing his family as caring and warm. Close family ties extended to other relatives; even though two of Fanny's sisters lived in Bielsko, the three were in close touch, helping each other whenever possible.

Affectionate family relations extended to the younger generation as well. One year older than Oswald, Ernest Seifter, Fanny's sister's son, became Oswald's close friend. As far back as Ernest could remember, he would spend the summers in Zadziele. The two cousins would roam the countryside, hiking and swimming in the nearby river, picking berries in the surrounding forests, and generally exploring the land. With the end of summer they would part, Ernest returning to his school in Bielsko, Oswald attending the local school in Zadziele.

A typical country place, the Zadziele school consisted of one room. Children of different ages were taught together, which meant that older students were held back. Because there were very few Jewish children, none of them received formal religious education. Shortly after Oswald's enrollment he became the school's only Jew. Though he knew he was different from the rest of the children, he succeeded in establishing friendly relations with them. He remembers that each school day began with a Catholic prayer and he participated in this activity with the rest of the pupils. Occasionally, he would even accompany his Christian friends to church.[8]

More assimilated and less orthodox than Jews living in the Russian-dominated parts of Poland, the Jews of this region did, nonetheless, follow Jewish tradition. Most homes observed the Jewish dietary laws, but apparently more out of respect for tradition than in obedience to religious law. Ernest Seifter feels that the attitude in his home toward kosher dietary laws was typical of many of the Jewish families in the area. *We had a kosher home, but my father was not following the rules. When I told my mother that I ate ham she was not mad that I had eaten it but that I had told her. It made her upset.*

When asked to describe what he remembered of Oswald's home, Ernest commented that *his parents were not religious, although his mother probably kept a kosher home. Particularly in a village, Jews had to follow the tradition. . . . Oswald was as religious as I . . . we both had a Bar-Mitzvah, but during the year we went to synagogue maybe twice or three times at most.*

Oswald would later describe his own religious upbringing somewhat differently. *I was not a pious Jew but I was deeply religious. . . . As a child I wanted to know about the truth. Already by eight or so, I began to pray to God and asked to meet someone very wise who would be able to lead me to the truth. I imagined that this wise man would look like President Mościcki. [Ignacy Mościcki was a renowned scientist who in 1926 accepted the largely ceremonious position of president of Poland. He was a distinguished looking man, tall, with white hair and a white mustache.] I was convinced that because he was a famous professor, he would know the truth. . . . I think that I was religious but I was not an observant Jew. I was religious in the spiritual sense.*

After Oswald had spent two years in the local school in Zadziele, his parents decided that the boy's inquisitive mind required more stimulation. A transfer to another school became possible only because of family support. Fanny's sister (Ernest's mother) was willing to have Oswald live with them.

At seven and a half Oswald moved to a Jewish school in Bielsko. This school was run and attended by Jews, but the instructions were in German. From then on he saw his family only on weekends and during the summers. Oswald would later comment that because of this arrangement, he did not fully belong either to his own or to the Seifter's family.

Though Ernest was one year older, the two had completed elementary school at the same time since Oswald had skipped a year. After elementary school the boys were enrolled in the Józef Piłsudski High School, a Polish state school. In this school the Jewish and Catholic children were taught religion separately, by a rabbi and a priest. For overall instructions the pupils were subdivided by age, ability, and school performance. Each class had four groups. Both cousins ended up in the highest group, Group D. As a rule, the non-Jewish children in Group D came from socially prominent families. Among them was the mayor's son, the son of a physician, children of army officers, and others of similar backgrounds.

While it was not uncommon for Polish youths to verbally taunt or even physically abuse Jews, either by stone throwing or beatings, the students in Group D did not mistreat Oswald or Ernest. They referred to them as their "special Jews." Moreover, because of the social standing of these youngsters, they were able to prevent other children from harming the two youngsters. In school Oswald does not remember feeling discriminated against or being abused. He was fond of his classmates and thinks they reciprocated his warm feelings. Yet, years later, when he tried to reconstruct his friendships with any of these Catholic boys, he said, *Only now do I realize that all my close friends were Jewish. None were Christian. The only Polish friends I had were from my class in school. But the ties between us were not very strong or meaningful. After the war, I never even tried to find any of them. I did not even think about any of them.*[9]

Neither cousin recalls ever being in a position where they had to defend themselves from physical attacks. Ernest is convinced that had Oswald been called on to fight he would have abstained—not because he lacked courage but rather because of an aversion to hurting others. Ernest describes his cousin as *very, very gentle and quiet. He felt for others. He could never hurt anybody. He was not the type that would fight . . . never did, never could.*

Oswald remembers that as a third-year high school student he had to write an essay on a subject that was of special importance to him. He invented a story about a scientist who risked his life to find cures for incurable diseases. Oswald's hero was a pacifist and a missionary who had left his own country only because he wanted to enrich the lives of less fortunate others.

According to his cousin, of the two, Oswald was *more studious and more interested in books. Unlike me, he did not waste time on girls but devoted himself to his studies. This does not mean that he had no friends. On the contrary, he was surrounded by friends and loved by them.* Rather wistfully, Ernest adds: *He had me too, but I was more like a nuisance than a friend.*

If Ernest was a nuisance, Oswald does not remember it that way. His recollection is that over time their relationship ripened and they became close friends.

By 1934 the Rufeisens were the only Jews living in Zadziele. Still poor, still struggling to make a living, but eager to be among fellow Jews, they decided to move to Zabłocie. They were fortunate to find a tenant for their house-tavern in Zadziele. Their luck, however, did not last. Soon the uninsured house went up in flames and instead of a modest income they were left with an empty lot that nobody wanted to buy.

Because of their poverty, the decision to move to Zabłocie offered few options. Eventually this meant renting a primitive hut on one of those unpaved, least desirable streets, close to the paper factory. The new quarters were much less spacious than those they had left. Still, by ending their isolation from other Jews, this change achieved what they were after. Also, because the distance between Bielsko and Zabłocie was only 21 kilometers Oswald could once again live with his family. For five years, from 1934 until 1939, he shared the family's home in Zabłocie and commuted to Bielsko by train.

These changes were not without economic hardships. Zabłocie's location made Eliasz's wood transactions even more taxing and less profitable. Once more he had to face the prospect of switching occupations. This time he bought a kiosk. But because he was always short of cash, the kiosk had little attractive merchandise and few customers. In fact, Oswald remembers being embarrassed by the place and avoiding going there.

Fanny knew that there was a market for specially fattened geese with large livers. The bigger and fatter the geese and their livers were, the more money they would bring. Resourceful and hard working, Fanny decided to raise geese in the cellar of her new home. To raise fat geese with oversized livers one had to feed them by force, which could take place only after a goose was immobilized. This was achieved by kneeling on the floor and placing a goose between one's bent legs and leaning and pressing on it. One would then take the bird's head into one hand and at the same time open its beak. The second hand would then push down into the throat a dumpling made out of a mixture of flour, corn, and water.

Understandably, the geese were opposed to this procedure and fought valiantly against it. When their attempt to free themselves proved futile, they would resort to biting the fingers that pushed food down their throat. Because a goose beak has sharp teeth Fanny had perpetually injured fingers. When a goose was deemed ready for sale, Oswald would put it into his knapsack and bring it to Bielsko. On his way to school, he would leave this extra luggage at his Aunt Mari's house, one of Fanny's sisters. Mari had the geese slaughtered and used the meat for meals that she cooked and served to special customers in her home. Whatever she did not use, she resold to local butchers. Occasionally Oswald would deliver extra livers to Jewish butchers after school hours.

Oswald elaborates. *These geese, of course, were killed by Jewish butchers in an approved ritual way. My aunt gave the geese to be slaughtered. She then separated the livers and placed them in special containers. They had to be well preserved. In those days we had no ice boxes. I think that my mother raised the geese only in the winter, when it was cool. . . . The livers were huge; sometimes each weighed more than two pounds. Those who bought them were amazed at the size. They would ask me who was capable of growing them this size . . . out of these livers the butchers made expensive sausages and pates.*

For Oswald these are bittersweet memories. On the one hand, he remembers with pain Fanny's perpetually injured fingers; on the other, he refers to his mother as *a great specialist* and a *wizard*. At a young age, Oswald was conscious of his mother's responsibilities and burdens and his father's inability to relieve her of them.

Although the move to Zabłocie failed to improve the Rufeisens' economic situation, it led to other welcomed developments. To Oswald and Arieh it provided the opportunity to establish closer ties. The family's crowded quarters forced the boys to share a bed, a common practice for that time and place. The two brothers were very different. Oswald was an outstanding student, while Arieh had graduated from the elementary school in Zadziele with an average record. He rejected his parents' offer of a high school education and instead became a locksmith. As an adolescent, Arieh worked and earned money.

The two brothers remember different events about their childhoods and attach different meanings to their parents' marriage. For example, unlike Oswald, Arieh was unaware of parental conflicts. He recalls no special quarrels and describes his parents' relationship as *correct*. He knew that his father was moving from one occupation to another, but considered this fact of less importance than his brother did. He identified his family as *lower middle class*, adding: *We were not rich but enough bread we had*. Just as he does not deplore his father's occupational failures, he does not dwell on his mother's need to supplement their income. Similarly, when he mentions the Zabłocie kiosk, he upgrades it to a *store*. As a youngster he remembers staying at the kiosk on Saturdays to attend to business while his father went to the synagogue. (In contrast to the rest of the family, Eliasz attended religious services once a week.) In this connection too, Arieh fails to mention the kiosk's poor surroundings or lack of customers. Unlike Oswald, he did not react to the place with embarrassment, but rather enjoyed being there.

Oswald's love for his parents was mixed with sadness, a sadness that seems absent from Arieh's memories. However, those who knew Oswald as a boy emphasize that he treated both parents with respect. Still, it is clear that the admiration and understanding he had for his mother surpass the kind of feelings he had for anyone else. And yet, as soon as he singles out his mother for special attention, no matter how slight, he feels compelled to match it with a favorable observation about his father. In one of those instances, for example, he says, *I was content at home. I respected both my parents, but especially my mother. We were very poor and she worked very hard. He [his father] also worked hard.*

While Oswald talks about his father with regret, he also remembers how as a little boy he was fascinated by Eliasz's military distinctions and how he loved to listen to the war stories that came with them.

Though ability, interests, and perceptions differentiated Oswald from Arieh, these differences do not appear to have generated envy or hostility between them. Arieh speaks about his brother with appreciation and affection, and Oswald reciprocates these feelings. To this day, tolerance, approval, and love seem to pervade their relationship.

In Zabłocie the two brothers became involved in the Zionist youth group, Akiva, an offshoot of the general Zionist movement. Aside from other benefits, to the two brothers, membership in Akiva gave an opportunity to spend more time together. Late in the afternoon, when Arieh finished his work and Oswald returned from Bielsko, the two would attend Akiva's daily meetings and stay there till late in the evening. They also participated in the many special trips sponsored by the movement. During frequent gatherings, the Akiva group would discuss Zionism, Jewish history, and Jewish traditions. A special teacher taught the youngsters the Hebrew language. Members were divided by age, with each group assigned a leader (madrich). Until he emigrated to Palestine, in 1937, Jacob Rubenfeld was Oswald's leader.

Rubenfeld remembers Oswald well and refers to him as *a good boy and a good friend, well behaved. He never gave rough answers; he made no trouble, was not wild, respected people, polite, pleasant . . . but I would never have predicted that he would become something extraordinary, a hero or anything like that.* When asked to explain how Oswald expressed his goodness, the unhesitating answer was: *He liked to do favors for people.*

Oswald also became a group leader. This, however, did not imply a great achievement. Unless there were some special problems, those who attended high school almost automatically assumed a position of leadership after they reached a certain age.

Though Oswald had joined the movement casually, without much thought, it soon began to play a dominant role in his life. In commenting about this involvement he states, *My life was more focused on Akiva than on my family. All evening, every evening, I would spend in the organization. I lived with and for this Zionist movement rather than for school or home. It was both a political and educational group, similar to a scout organization. It was founded by people who wanted to perpetuate Jewish traditions. It was not religious in the sense of imposing religious views, but only in the sense of maintaining Jewish tradition. . . . Akiva tried to instill in us an altruistic philosophy, an altruistic outlook that we were asked to apply to both Jews and non-Jews. It also taught us pacifist views and a certain contempt for commerce. This is how I experienced its influence.*

Contrasting his home with Akiva, Oswald says, *My home life, my parents, served as models for behavior, as examples for me to imitate. They were not offering me any education in a formal way. This I received from Akiva, and a large part of it had to do with a special philosophy of life. I had a home but I also had a second home. . . . Every day I would go out, every evening I would come back late. But I was not unique in this respect. Others lived like this too.*

Inevitably his involvement with Akiva led to a desire to settle in Palestine. Fanny and Eliasz did not share their sons' enthusiasm for Zionism, but they were not opposed to a Jewish homeland. However, if their two sons were to fulfill their own dreams and emigrate to Palestine, what would become of them? They were old. In 1938 Eliasz was 54 and Fanny was 56. At their age they could not go to Palestine as pioneers or as settlers brought over by Jewish organizations to help build the land. There existed a possibility of reaching the country as regular immigrants, but this involved large sums of money. The British authorities demanded proof of wealth from those who applied for regular immigrant visas. Even if they had the money to reach the country, how would they support themselves in a strange place? Oswald and Arieh were aware of these difficulties. Each in a different way deplored them. Oswald reacted to his parents' limited options with pain: *They were at an age that made me feel very concerned. I was afraid that they would not be able to manage. They had no prospects for future earnings. We were ready to agree that one of us should stay behind with them in order to help them, to take care of them. The problem was to decide which of us would stay with them.*

One option the family had seriously considered was for Oswald to enroll at the Hebrew University in Jerusalem. This of course required funds the Rufeisens did not have. Oswald explains: *I had relatives who had more money than we. They were not rich either, but they were ready to collect money among themselves for my ticket to Palestine and for other expenses. I was to go to Palestine as a student at the Hebrew University, my brother was supposed to remain with my parents for the time being.*

For this to happen Oswald had to graduate from high school. In 1939, at the age of seventeen, Oswald had passed the special examinations and received a high school diploma (matura), a year earlier than most. This was an important achievement, limited to a select group. His parents had always hoped that this would be just a first step toward obtaining a more advanced degree. As the entire family continued to debate Oswald's future, political events which had seemed remote took care of all the options.

On September 1, 1939, Nazi Germany attacked Poland. The southern parts of the country, close to the German-occupied Czechoslovakian border, were in immediate danger. The Germans were advancing rapidly. The distance between them and the civilian Polish population was diminishing by the hour. Panic-stricken, fearful of the enemy, many abandoned their homes to escape the advancing army. Masses of people cluttered the roads, all moving north. Many of the refugees were Jewish. On the second day of the war, a neighbor offered the Rufeisens the use of a wagon. They filled it with hastily assembled bundles. As they joined the exodus, they were not even sure where they were going. They simply followed the mass of people. A distant look comes over Arieh's face when he recalls this journey. *My mother was sickly, she was not in good shape. We put her on this wagon and we pushed it. We did not have horses. This is how we kept moving, covering slowly each tenth of a kilometer. Somewhere on the way we met my parents' friends, who had a horse-drawn wagon. They offered us a place on it. We were glad to join them and this way we reached Cracow. There we stayed one or two nights in a place where Akiva had previously trained people for emigration to Palestine. After that we boarded a train that was moving eastward. It was a freight train, very crowded, slowly crawling, in terrible shape. There were bombings on the way.*

Some people, unable to take the pressure, left the train and turned back. It was chaos. We were not even sure about the destination of this train. As we continued to move we passed ruined villages. Eventually we reached the vicinity of Jarosław. We were, in fact, told that the Germans had already taken Jarosław. At that point we left behind most of our belongings and we began to walk. We went to the village Lubaczów. I think that it is close to Rawa Ruska. There my parents broke down. They asked us to take the little money they had, I don't know how much, and continue without them. We left them near a small village not far from Rawa Ruska.

Without definite plans of their own, Fanny and Eliasz argued that they were too old to go on. They also felt that staying together would only diminish any chance their sons had of making it to safety. They hoped that without the burden they presented, Oswald and Arieh might reach Palestine. As for their own situation, the couple thought that the Germans might spare them. After all, during World War I, Eliasz had fought in the German army! He had German decorations that proved his bravery and his sacrifices. Shouldn't these facts shield them from whatever hostility the invaders might otherwise have toward the Jews? Besides, Fanny and Eliasz spoke German well and felt that knowledge of the language would also offer them some protection. More important, they were convinced that their sons were actually in greater danger than they. According to one rumor, the advancing army was forcing the young to move in front of their tanks while they attacked the Polish army.

And how did the two sons feel about this request? Sadly Arieh answered, *Who felt anything? It was happening under such tension . . . panic. We had no time to think about it.* Oswald recalls, *As we were about to part, I remember lying on the grass and crying. Maybe I had a premonition that I would not see them again. This is what happened. I never saw them again.* Numb and crying, the two brothers continued without their parents. When they reached the vicinity of Krasne, they, too, had no strength left. They entered a nearby village and asked Ukrainian peasants for shelter.

The fields were being dug for potatoes and the peasants were glad to have extra farm hands. The brothers were offered food and a place to sleep in exchange for work. This was in the middle of September, close to the high Jewish holidays, Rosh Hashana and Yom Kippur. They stayed for a few days. Just before Yom Kippur they asked the farmer's wife to give them their food allotment earlier because they had to start fasting. The woman was very surprised. Up till then she had no idea that the two refugees were Jewish. This discovery, however, did not change her attitude.

Arieh described what happened. *Next day we went to a nearby town. There on the bridge we saw strange-looking soldiers. We did not know that the fighting had stopped and that the Russians had taken over this part of the country. We returned to the village. We still had a few belongings. We parted from the peasants, thanked them and went to Krasne. Then we went to Lwów. I don't even know why to Lwów.*

In Lwów they met a group of young people, members of Akiva. All wanted to reach Palestine but knew that Russia would be unsympathetic toward such a move. They understood that if they were ever to fulfill their dream they would have to leave the parts dominated by the Soviets and go to a neutral country. For the moment, one of those countries was Lithuania, with Vilna[10] as its capital.

2

In Search of Solutions

As the Rufeisen brothers continued in the direction of Lwów they realized they were in Russian-held territories. To them Soviet occupation of Poland had come as a surprise. They had known about the signing of a Soviet-German nonaggression pact, but not that this agreement called for Poland's partition. Only a secret section of this treaty specified the division of Eastern Europe into two spheres of interest. Latvia, Estonia, the eastern part of Poland, and Besarabia (part of Rumania) were recognized as Soviet spheres, while the western half of Poland, including Lithuania, was to come under German influence.[1]

Described by the historian Norman Davies as "Poland's death warrant,"[2] these secret clauses gave Hitler a free hand and led to a swift Nazi takeover. One day after the capitulation of Poland, on September 28, 1939, Germany and Russia returned to the negotiating table. This time they signed the Boundary and Friendship Treaty that changed some of the previously specified borders. Lithuania, originally a German sphere of influence, was assigned to the Soviets, who eventually had under their control 51.6% of Poland's territory. Extending to the so-called Crouzon line, these newly acquired lands corresponded to the areas held by Russia after Poland's 1795 partition.[3] The secrecy of these and other clauses offered ample room for political maneuvering to both Germany and Russia.

A direct outcome of these unpublicized agreements was the Russian acquisition of the city of Lwów. For Jews, eager to escape from the Nazis, Lwów became a temporary haven. Among the refugees who in the fall of 1939 had reached the city 100 were members of Akiva, the Zionist youth organization. They established a center that would serve as a meeting place for new arrivals. Here the Rufeisen brothers found two of their friends, Stefi Schanzer and Józiek Rakocz. Oswald and Stefi had known each other in Bielsko and were close friends. Oswald and Józiek had met in one of the Akiva summer camps and their relationship was more casual. But in this strange city any familiar face was reassuring. Józiek and Oswald soon grew to be devoted friends.

Though a stay in Lwów represented a definite improvement over life under the Nazis, it was unpredictable and without clear prospects. An uncertain present, and a vague future, led to a continuous search for solutions. For the young Zionists, emigration to Palestine would have been ideal. They realized, however, that it was unlikely the Russians would permit it.

In the meantime, while weighing their limited options, Oswald and his brother had to support themselves. Oswald recalls, *We were very poor . . . but we managed. I would sell a few of our belongings, in the street. I don't even remember exactly what . . . maybe a watch or other things. We worked a little at odd jobs. Whatever job we were offered we accepted.* Arieh draws a similar picture: *I worked in a hotel . . . so food was not a problem. . . . Somehow I got to work in places where I could get food . . . sometimes it was a bakery, places like that.*

The Rufeisen brothers, and many young people like them, had left Lwów only after Zionist leaders arranged a transfer to a neutral country. These leaders assumed that certain neutral countries would serve as a stepping stone for Palestine. At first they considered Rumania and Hungary. But when they heard that both borders were heavily guarded they decided against such risky moves.

A set of unusual circumstances had made Lithuania and its ancient capital Vilna an accessible escape route. In part these new developments had to do with the historical animosity of Poland and Lithuania, at the heart of which was a dispute over the city of Vilna. Before World War II, Vilna had been a Polish city, legally and culturally. Lithuanians, however, felt that Vilna had been taken from them illegally, that it was rightfully theirs.

In 1921, with postwar Poland newly sovereign, after more than a hundred years of Polish subjugation, the commander of Poland's army, Józef Piłsudski, ordered the takeover of Vilna, then a part of Lithuania. Later, over the objections of Lithuania, Poland conducted a plebiscite in which the inhabitants of that city had to state their national preference. Sixty-four percent of the voters wanted to become a part of Poland. Interpreting these results as a green light, Poland annexed the city—an act unpopular with everyone but the Poles. Nevertheless, at the 1923 Conference of Ambassadors, Vilna was formally recognized as a Polish city.[4] The Lithuanians never reconciled themselves to this change and continued to claim Vilna as their capital.[5]

When Russian troops occupied Vilna in accordance with the September 1939 Soviet-German agreement the Soviets imposed on the neutral government of Lithuania a treaty that gave them the right to station troops there. In return for this privilege, the Russians transferred Vilna and parts of the surrounding territories back to the Lithuanians.[6]

This last act of generosity masked the Soviets' determination to annex Lithuania and other Baltic States. Both plans had been described in the secret clauses of the Nazi-Soviet pact.[7]

At that time, however, only the partners to these secret understandings, the Germans and the Russians, knew about these clauses. Meanwhile, on October 10, 1939, by becoming a part of Lithuania, Vilna became a neutral city.[8] The Lithuanians saw in this change an opportunity for revenge against the Poles. In one of their early moves, the Lithuanian government shut down the Polish university in Vilna. Later, the authorities made sure that there were practically no Poles among the students readmitted into the university of Kovno.[9] For about a year Lithuanian discrimination tactics focused on Poles rather than on Jews.

To the Jews, Lithuania's and Vilna's neutrality promised an escape route to safety, a promise in part supported by the vague and fluid Russian-Lithuanian relationship. Initially most contacts between these two countries were friendly. This friendliness was in turn expressed in the unstructured conditions existing on the Lithuanian-Russian border. The official law, forbidding the passage from one country to another, was only sporadically enforced. For Jews searching for places of refuge these border conditions offered unusual opportunities. A transfer to neutral Lithuania gave them a chance to reach other, more permanent and safer places.[10]

The Zionist leaders took advantage of these opportunities by maintaining a network of complicated arrangements. But even with few restrictions, border crossings were hazardous. Józiek Rakocz, who made this trip, remembers: *The transfer into Lithuania was not a simple matter. It was a hard cold winter. We were not properly dressed for that weather . . . we were without money. . . . The escape was organized in small groups. From Lwów we went by train to Lida, in Lida there was someone who, we were told, would pay for our guides that would take us across the border. We had to walk at night through the forest . . . we were caught . . . we sat in prison. Eventually most of those who came with us did pass to the other side and reached Vilna.*

In November 1939, Akiva sent Oswald to the town Grodno to arrange a transfer of a group to Lithuania. It took him two weeks to prepare the move. During that time Oswald stayed at the home of Akiva members. On a cold snowy night, his group was ready for the crossing. People felt it was safer to move in bad weather because guards were less watchful. Looking back, Oswald is convinced that luck was with them: *the attitudes of the Russians were far from consistent. They treated Lithuania as partly independent, realizing, however, that sooner or later they would occupy it. So in a way it was hardly a formal crossing of a border. Still at times they acted punitively. For example, two of my friends were sent to Siberia, each for five years, precisely because they tried to enter neutral Lithuania.* In the end, though, Oswald and his group were offered help by Russian soldiers, which was most unusual.

Arieh Rufeisen had a different experience. *When the Lithuanians caught us we showed them our documents and because they did not know how to read Polish, we told them that we were returning home to Vilna.* Without encountering the Red Army Arieh Rufeisen reached Vilna two weeks after his brother.

Gradually the border situation began to change, with most interference coming from the Russians. At first these difficulties were unpredictable and people were willing to take the risk. Later, when a few of those caught were sent to Siberia, some Jews gave up the idea of reaching Lithuania. Of those who did, a few decided to stay in Russian-occupied Poland, while others returned to their former homes in Poland. Finally, at the beginning of 1940, these borders were sealed and all illegal entry into Lithuania stopped.[11]

The overwhelming majority of the Jewish refugees who did come to Lithuania could not leave. While they waited for a country to accept them, they had to consider their present.[12] Zionist leaders in particular were eager to prepare the young for life in Palestine.[13] Representatives of each major Zionist movement joined the governing body of the Hehalutz, the federation of the pioneers.[14] With the help of Jewish organizations, their members gathered into one part of Vilna on Subacz Street. There, sorted out by political affiliation, each group was assigned to special living quarters.

Józiek Rakocz notes that *numbering approximately eighty, the Akiva group was subdivided into smaller units by age. I was 18 and so I belonged to those aged up to 21. Oswald was a member of this group. Depending on the time, there were 10 to 12 of us. We lived together and felt very close.*

Those who were there emphasize how important their friendships became. They were without family, facing an uncertain future, in a strange place. The affection they felt for each other helped alleviate some of their longings. Till this day, Oswald remembers how with all the cruelty around him, he was sustained and nourished first by the group itself and later, when he was not with them, by memories of them. The few Akiva friends from Vilna who did survive the war continue their friendships.

While they stayed together they waited for news from home. None realized the magnitude of the Nazi crimes, but they had heard about dangers and that some Jews were being murdered. They knew enough to worry.

Like others, the Rufeisen brothers tried to keep in touch with their family. For a while they were successful. They learned that their parents returned back to their home. But because the Germans annexed this area to the Reich the Rufeisens were transferred to another part of Poland, known as the General Gouvernment.[15] Arieh Rufeisen thought that they *went to Kalwaria, where they lived till August 1942. It seems that from there they were moved to Auschwitz, but I am not sure. Approximately two months before that date they were still together with our cousins in the same village. This I found out much later. Eventually, these cousins lived illegally in Warsaw as Germans. They parted from my parents in June or July 1942. . . . For a while, when Lithuania was still independent, we could send letters directly to the General Gouvernment. We also sent mail through the Red Cross. . . . In one of her last letters my mother begged us not to separate. She felt that if we stayed together we could protect each other. . . . Who knows, if we did not separate would we have both perished? . . . maybe Oswald would not have done what he did.*

Next to a longing for family was a desire to go to Palestine. And so, after Stefi finished talking about family worries, with passion, she turned to the topic of Palestine: *all our cravings concentrated on a transfer to Palestine. All our dreams, our aims centered around a move to that country. In reality very few left. Those who did were very young. They got special certificates. . . . It seems that this was organized by the Sochnut (a Jewish Agency). Oswald, at eighteen, was too old for these certificates. In fact, the overwhelming majority never made it.*

For several weeks after Oswald's arrival in Vilna, new refugees continued to come to the city. More young Zionists joined those who had already settled on Subacz Street. When the living accommodations became overcrowded, the Akiva youths were moved to a separate apartment on Beliny Street.

Moshe Kalchheim, a member of the Akiva secretariat, and eight years older than Oswald, describes their new set up. *On Beliny Street we had a big apartment with several rooms. Different age groups were assigned to each room . . . with one large living room that was used for special functions: Sabbath meetings, gatherings for discussions, and for study. A special annex to this apartment we used as a workplace. All of us worked and all gave our earnings to a common bank. In the evening we each ate in the particular group to which we belonged. . . . Stefi was assigned to the same group as Józiek, Oswald, and Arieh. Like most women she took care of the household chores.*

Stefi reports, *The men had outside jobs. Most of them became wood cutters. . . . The houses in Vilna were heated with wood, because coal was unavailable. This was a very cold winter, so people used a lot of wood.*

Like everyone else, Oswald was asked what skills he had. He remembers telling them he had *no special skills . . . they asked me what kind of a trade I would like to learn. Because I knew that we had no shoemakers I decided to become one. For five months I worked for a Jewish shoemaker and learned the trade.* While Oswald waited for a place with a shoemaker he took different jobs. One of them was wood cutting, another was construction work. Moshe Kalchheim explains Oswald's choice differently. *Because he was short, not very strong, not a man of muscles, he became a shoemaker and organized a workshop, in the annex of our apartment. This happened in the year 1940.*

The Zionist leaders viewed the hard work these youths performed as preparation for future life in Palestine. In addition to this physical "training," each group kept up its political and ideological awareness. In the Akiva ideology there was a certain tension between tradition and religion. Seidel, for example, notes: *We believed in tradition but we were not religious. . . . We followed the different rituals . . . candle lighting on the Sabbath, holidays, but we were not actually religious.*

Kalchheim sees the movement differently. *The ideology of Akiva, even though it was the ideology of the General Zionists (a secular organization), had a strong emphasis on tradition and was partly religious. We would pray on Saturdays, sometimes even in the middle of the week, when someone had to say Kadish (the prayer for the dead).*

From the ideological perspective I knew Oswald better than any other friend. Oswald was a young boy, there was one political movement in his town so he joined it. He became a devout Zionist, but this love for Zionism he could have acquired in any kind of movement. We in the Akiva had a much more traditional orientation. For example, we studied the Tanach (the bible). He also studied the bible, but in his case this study did not originate with tradition or religion. . . . Oswald was always one of those who objected to the emphasis on religion, or if he did not object he was very reserved when religious rituals were introduced into our lives. I knew him as an atheist. I referred to him as an atheist.

Life in the kibbutz was traditional plus. . . . There were many who lay "tfillim" (a religious ritual), but not Oswald. Yet, he participated in the observance of the Sabbath. He was not a rebel but ideologically he rejected religion.

Oswald knew about the strain and competing forces in the Akiva movement and thinks that later on, between 1948 and 1949, Akiva fell apart because of this tension.

Kalchheim's perceptions about Oswald's attitudes toward religion in no way diminished his approval of his young friend. Instead, he talks about Oswald glowingly: *he was loved by all of us. He was charming, with a quiet disposition, he never lost his temper, always ready to help others, intelligent, educated. He was the good one. . . . In this respect he was very different from the others. You never saw him get angry. You could do him wrong, you could scream at him, he would never do the same to you. He was balanced, in this way he was quite exceptional . . . but we did not treat him in any way as special, we did not see him as special, not then.*

Kalchheim explains that *after forty years one does not remember things unless they somehow stood out. The thing in his case that stood out was his special goodness. I told you about his atheism because this is really interesting. I thought a lot about it. I was racking my brains about how the drastic change came about. Maybe atheism is too strong an expression. But within the framework of these traditional people, some of whom were even religious, he was one of the very few who did not believe.*

All those who knew Oswald during that time were aware of an uncommon tendency to consider the needs of others and an unwillingness to hurt anyone, yet none of them saw him as extraordinary. Hilel Seidel simply says that *Oswald was not religious* and then continues talking about his other characteristics: *He seemed very quiet, a grown up boy—he was very well behaved, polite. He was always smiling. This remains till this very day . . . round cheerful face, his trademark. . . . He was in a group that was younger than I but he came to our bible class. Oswald knew a lot. He participated in all the different activities with us but we did not notice anything special about him. We did not see him as exceptional.*

Józiek Rakocz and Oswald are close friends. Józiek is glad to talk about his friend and when he does his comments are enthusiastic, full of admiration. He says: *Oswald is most interested in justice. He is honest. In my eyes he is one of the most decent people I have ever met. I believe in him fully and absolutely. He has intellectual honesty. He lives what he believes in. And despite the fact that we had all kinds of disagreements, I know that if he would not have believed in his way of life he would have had enough courage to change it. . . . It was clear to me then that he was free of selfishness. His personal interests were not important for him. He always worried that maybe someone else does not get his share . . . he never wanted to hurt anyone . . . what was most special, most typical about him was his good heart. Perhaps this was a prelude to what happened to him later. Maybe if he were harder, not as accommodating, he would not have done what he did.*

For example, when he worked at this shoemaker's in Vilna we made fun of him. He worked twelve hours but he should have worked only eight. He explained that he did it because the shoemaker was poor, he had a big family to feed, and could use the extra help. In addition, he also helped the shoemaker's children with their homework. We did not see him as exceptional, though. Not at all.

As Oswald and the others continued to wait, work, and hope, they were once more caught up in a net of political changes. The inevitable happened. On June 14, 1940, the USSR sent a sharp letter to the Lithuanian government. In this letter they protested against Lithuanian kidnappings of Soviet soldiers and Lithuania's signing of a treaty with Estonia and Latvia. The letter claimed that such agreements were in violation of the Russian-Lithuanian defense pact of 1939. Without waiting for a reply, on June 15, 1940, Soviet troops occupied Lithuania. The Lithuanian president, A. Smetona, and a number of high government officials fled to Germany.

The Russians were efficient. By June 17 they had installed a new government, headed by the Communist Justus Paleckis. All political parties, except the Communist Party, were outlawed and freedom of the press abolished. Elections to the Lithuanian parliament were held on July 14. Official results showed that the predominantly Communist Workers Union received 99.19% of the votes. Soon this newly elected Lithuanian parliament "begged" to be admitted into the USSR. On August 3, 1940, the Supreme Soviet approved the application. Lithuania officially became a part of the Soviet Union.[16]

With these changes came repressive arrests of Lithuanians, Poles, and Jews that continued for as long as the Russians were in power. As late as the middle of June 1941, members of different nationalities, among them Jews, were hastily deported to Siberia and other parts of Russia.[17]

In one of their early moves the Soviets closed down all Hebrew cultural institutions. Many active Zionists and Bundists were arrested and deported to Russia. Many were eventually murdered.[18] Zionism as a political movement became outlawed.[19] Because of these changes the young Zionists had to give up their official residence. Each movement split into small meetings and then moved into apartments rented from Jewish families. Illegal and subdivided into small units, each movement tried to retain its organization. Chaim Kermish stayed on as the official head of Akiva. At this point all members were asked to contribute 10% of their earnings to Kermish, who used it for overall organizational expenses.

Stefi notes: *All our lives became transformed. We could not live as a Kibbutz because under the Russians Zionism was forbidden. We were afraid that we could be sent to Siberia. We dispersed into small units. I was together with Arieh and Oswald, another youth from Zabłocie, Józiek Rakocz and Szaj Ginter from Lódź. I was the only girl. I kept house for all of us, I washed and cooked. Most of the men still went to work, they were cutting wood. Even in the summer wood was needed for cooking stoves.*

Oswald continued to earn money as a shoemaker. He also became the official leader of their small group. Neither the political changes nor the move disrupted the harmony of Oswald's group and their warm and close relationships continued to sustain their spirits.

For some, however, these new breakups created problems. Moshe

Kalchheim explains: *When we had to split into small units people elected to go with those with whom they could easily get along. A few people were left stranded because no one wanted to share a home with them. I and my girl friend, out of a feeling of responsibility, decided to collect those who were left out and organize them into a group. But with time the relations in our group became unpleasant. . . . Because Oswald was responsible for his group, I turned to him and asked him if he would accept me. You should have seen the joy with which he responded to my request. I was very touched when I realized how welcome I would be . . . I did not move though because soon the German-Russian war broke out.*

Though many Jewish organizations went underground and others ceased to exist, some Jewish leaders and private individuals refused to accept defeat. Largely because of their persistent efforts, even after the annexation of Lithuania to Russia, about 2400 Jews left for Japan. In addition, the British consul reluctantly agreed to honor 800 certificates for Palestine. Another 400 visas for Palestine were forged. Altogether during the Russian occupation of Lithuania about 3600 Jews saved themselves by leaving Europe.[20] Holders of visas had to submit an application for exit to the Soviet emigration office in Vilna or Kovno and most of these applications were honored.[21]

On behalf of the Zionist youths, the chief rabbi of Palestine, Dr. Isaac Halevy Herzog, appealed to Maisky, the Russian ambassador in London, asking him to intervene with the Soviet authorities. The ambassador did.[22] Among those who benefited from this intervention was Oswald's brother.

Arieh explains: *In the fall of 1940 some certificates for Palestine arrived. They were divided among the different political organizations. At that time we became even more concerned about emigration to Palestine. Eager to leave, Oswald registered at the university, thinking that this would help. I received such a visa only because I was the youngest in our group. I was not yet seventeen. It took three to four months until the Russians agreed to give us transit visas. We had to pass through their territory . . . just a little piece of paper saved your life. . . . NKVD (the Russian secret police) had to give permission. We had to go there every day and ask. The "commissar" was a Russian Jew. It was obvious that he hated us. He was supposed to issue these permits . . . I think that we received them only because Jewish organizations paid the Russians 200 dollars per permit. I am not sure, but this is what I heard had happened. We went as tourists. We stayed in a hotel in Moscow. Then we went to the Turkish consulate and got visas. Later we went by boat to Istanbul. Some Jews came to Moscow and the Turks would not give them visas and some of them were put into prison by the Russians.*

In Vilna the separation was difficult, very difficult. We did not know what would be tomorrow, we did not think. . . . If I had stayed maybe all would have been different with Oswald. Who knows?

Arieh reached Palestine in February 1941. From there he exchanged a few letters with his parents. Fanny knew that, contrary to her pleas, her two sons did not stay together. No doubt she must have realized that under the circumstances for Arieh to have refused a visa would have been sheer madness.

Still the parting was not easy. Oswald knew that he would miss his brother, but he was relieved that at least one of them would find safe refuge. His satisfaction about Arieh's good fortune and the inevitable feelings of loss came together with forebodings about a grim and shaky future. Stefi feels that such reactions were not unusual. *We all had mixed feelings. Of course we were happy for those that could leave . . . but our own thoughts were very oppressive. . . . we felt that another war was about to start. We knew that it was not finished. . . . We were determined to continue our lives. What else could we do?*

Anxiety about an unknown, threatening future turned into a concrete, painful present. On a Sunday, June 22, 1941, Oswald returned home with the news. He had been listening to the radio. At 11 o'clock the Soviet foreign minister Molotov told the Russian people that Germany had attacked their country.[23] In less than an hour bombs were falling on the city of Vilna. The timing and speed made what happened seem unreal, and the contrast between this restfully beautiful day and the glaring destruction of the attack underlined the strangeness of the situation. This quality was captured in a wartime diary: "The siren was so inappropriate to the peaceful joyous summer which spread all around us. The siren cruelly cut the blue air and announced something cruel. The evening, this beautiful evening, is marred. Bombs are bursting over the city. The streets are full of smoke. . . . People have been running bewildered. . . . The blue happy sky has become transformed into a mighty volcano which has showered the city with bombs."[24]

Like so many others, Oswald and his friends were stunned. They had expected a change and had been tense about it, but they had not quite imagined it would come in the form of this sudden onslaught. Each knew that, at least for the moment, they had to be guided by events. Choices were being made for them. They went through the expected motions. With the rest of the tenants they prepared to go to the cellar that was to serve as an air-raid shelter.

Cooler than the rest of the building, in normal times this cellar was used both as a storage place and a substitute ice box. As in most such cellars, a special space in the unfinished walls was assigned to each apartment. Each space was built like a closet with shelves, wooden doors, and locks. Here the tenants stored their belongings and in the summer kept sour milk, butter, and meat. Many of these individual storage places lined the cellar's walls, leaving a large empty area in the middle, a space that in this emergency became an air-raid shelter.

On that fateful Sunday, directed by the sirens, the tenants began to arrive in the cellar carrying covers, chairs, and food supplies. A bare, anemic bulb, suspended from the middle of the ceiling, lighted their path. This was a Jewish building; all the tenants knew each other. Usually friendly, on that day most of them were silent. They concentrated on settling down in the available spaces. Whatever little communication there was, it took place in whispers. Absorbed in thought, Oswald went through the motions of finding an appropriate place. Then, when he had assured himself that everyone was settled, he slipped out quietly.

At first, when Oswald's friends noticed his absence they thought he would reappear soon. When this did not happen they began to ask each other: "Where did he go? Why didn't he stay? What happened to him?" For some time the bombing continued. Late that evening when it was over and they returned to the apartment, Oswald was not there. He was still absent when evening turned into night, and night into dawn. At that point his friends were convinced that something dreadful occurred. Each tried not to upset the other with morbid expectations, but their fears persisted. Most found it impossible to sleep that night.

In the morning Oswald returned. He looked dirty and disheveled. His hair was in disarray, covered by a grayish powder. But somehow he seemed taller. The expression on his round, cherubic face was satisfied, even triumphant. He was showered with questions: "Where were you? Why didn't you tell us that you were leaving? Are you OK? How we worried!" Surprised, Oswald asked, "Why would you worry about me? Don't you realize that I know how to take care of myself?" His friends could not understand. "Bombs were falling and obviously you were not far from them! You could have been killed! Where were you? What did you do?"

To Oswald it was simple. He had spent the entire night working among Vilna's ruins. He was part of a rescue team that searched for those trapped in the bombed buildings. To the injured they offered immediate aid. The dead they set aside for identification and burial. Faced with the anxiety of his friends, Oswald chuckled. "Why do you make such a fuss? After all, people needed this help!"

Stefi says, *None of us thought of going out and helping. For the rest of my life I have been thinking how Oswald decided to do such a thing. We all were concerned about our own safety. He went out during the bombing, not thinking about his own life . . . only about helping others.*

Though he acted differently from his friends this did not diminish his affection for them. To this day he remembers them warmly, particularly their life together after the Russian occupation of Vilna, when his group was reduced to a handful of people. For him this was a time filled with mutual sacrifice and caring. Oswald is convinced that living with this small group made a great difference, a difference for which he is still grateful.

On June 23, in Vilna, Oswald, his friends, and most other Jews realized that time was running out. The Russians were leaving in a hurry and a German takeover was imminent. Jews knew that under the Nazis their lives would be in danger. The Zionist youths were not sure whether they should join the exodus. They had no means of transportation and didn't know if they would be able to escape from the advancing German troops. Besides, they had known already what it meant to become refugees. The prospect of once more finding themselves on roads filled with panicky, homeless people was most depressing. Some wanted to leave it all to fate and wait. Others wanted to challenge the situation and run to the Russian-held territories.

Vacillating, the Akiva youths turned to Chaim Kermish, the man in charge of their movement. Their question was simple: "Should we run or should we stay?" There was, however, no simple answer. Kermish could not decide for them. Sadly he explained, "You must choose for yourselves. Each of you, on your own, must make up his or her own mind. I don't know anymore what is right or wrong."

On June 23, many Zionist youths, among them Oswald's group, left Vilna. Altogether about 3000 people escaped from the city, most of them Jewish. They left just in time because that night the Russians had vacated Vilna.[25]

Once more these youths found themselves surrounded by desperate people, convinced that this was their last chance for safety. Due to the chaotic conditions on the road most of the youth units became separated. Oswald's group succeeded in staying together and with the throng of refugees proceeded in the direction of Oszmiana, a small town some forty kilometers from Vilna. It took them an entire day to reach the outskirts of that place. Stefi explains, *We came close to Oszmiana and discovered that the Germans had reached it before us. They had occupied the area by dropping parachute troops. We had come to the wrong place. . . . We were surrounded by crossfire and chaos.*

Discouraged, hungry, tired, they knocked at a farm house. Luck. The peasant fed them and let them sleep in his barn. The next day each of them tried to repay their host by helping with farm chores. But even though the peasant did not object to their presence, they knew that they would have to move on. After all, a small farm had no use for so many helping hands!

They wanted to stay together. Because Vilna was familiar to all of them it seemed like the only possible place to settle in. Once more Oswald and his friends found themselves on the road. Soon they returned to Vilna, a very changed city. It did not take them long to realize that whatever difficulties they had experienced under the Soviet occupation paled in comparison with what they had to confront under the Nazis. The Russians had interfered with civil liberties and sometimes their actions led to arrests and deportations. None of these, however, was accompanied by open humiliation and killings. Besides, under the Russians, Jews were not singled out as special targets.

In the summer of 1941, the Germans were well advanced in their methods of Jewish persecution and eager to accelerate the process of Jewish annihilation, the so-called Final Solution. Most historians believe that the start of the Russian-German war crystallized the policies of the Final Solution.[26]

Even before Oswald and his group returned to Vilna, violence against the Jews and specific anti-Jewish policies were common. Some Lithuanians offered their enthusiastic support for all anti-Jewish moves. From the very beginning the Lithuanians greeted the German troops as liberators. They hoped that the new conquerors would restore their country's independence. Already in the morning of June 23, while the retreating Red Army was still there, bands of armed Lithuanians were murdering Jews.[27] Then the ranks of the German special killing units (Einsatzgruppen) were augmented by 150 Lithuanians, the so-called anti-Soviet partisans. Right away these "able helpers seized, held, and shot 500 Jews, every day around the clock."[28] The Lithuanians claimed that all their victims were Communist collaborators.[29]

Hastily, the Lithuanians established a provisional government. But the Germans had different plans; they wanted to incorporate Lithuania into the Reich. And so, instead of recognizing this new government, the Nazis merely chose to tolerate a joint German-Lithuanian administration. By August 1941 the German rulers installed a civilian Nazi administration that further curtailed the Lithuanians' power. Hopes for an independent Lithuania never materialized and the Nazi control of the country ended only on July 13, 1944, when Vilna was once more occupied by the Red Army. Shattered national hopes did not eliminate Lithuanian support for the Nazis, particularly when these touched on anti-Jewish measures.[30]

Though the situation looked grim, Oswald and most others were unaware of the magnitude of Jewish murder. When Oswald and his friends returned to Vilna they had lost the right to the room they had been renting. Only with great difficulty were they able to reclaim their modest living quarters. Soon this seemed like a minor nuisance. Jews were faced with continuous new restrictions. One such decree barred Jews from gainful employment. They were forced to work for minimal pay or no pay at all.

The Akiva youths had no savings, no families to lean on. Without earnings their prospects were limited. Fortunately, a newly developed black market offered a partial, though temporary, solution. Peasants from the surrounding countryside would come into the city with their produce which they tried to exchange for watches, used clothes, and a variety of household objects. These transactions were illegal and dangerous. Still to many, including Oswald and his friends, they offered a chance to live. The Akiva youths sold whatever they could while they were searching for work, any kind of work. As usual they shared whatever food they managed to get. As they struggled for basic needs they were constantly confronted by danger and the ever-multiplying German prohibitions. On June 27, the Nazis began catching Jews in the streets. Of those caught, some were used for labor, some were allowed to return to their homes, others never came back and were never heard from again. Rumors about the missing people began to circulate. The authorities tried to counteract these horror stories by insisting that they had been sent to special work camps.

In addition to being barred from gainful employment, Jews had to shop for food in special stores and during special hours. They were prohibited from appearing in more desirable parts of the city. All Jewish property—homes, factories, bank accounts—was confiscated and Jews were asked to hand over such items as furs, radios, foreign currency, and much more. A curfew was also in effect for Jews. They were forbidden to use sidewalks and instead had to walk in the middle of the road. Finally, at the beginning of July, all Jews aged ten and over had to wear a white band with a star of David on their arm.[31]

The gradual way of introducing these decrees was noted by Stefi. *Every day there was something new. Every day there were new orders that were publicized all over the city. In one order Jews were forbidden from walking on the pavement, then two Jews could not walk together, one had to follow the other. All kinds of identifying signs were applied to the Jews. Once it was "Jude," then it was "Jud," then only the star of David. If someone did not precisely follow these orders he or she was arrested."*

Oswald accepted the official explanations for he could not believe that the Germans had a program to harm the Jews for no reason. Whoever heard of catching innocent people just to kill them? Occasional violence, he argued, could happen, but not well-organized killings. Oswald dismissed this last possibility. To accept it would have denied much of what he believed in. In the part of Poland he came from there was tremendous respect for the German culture, and his parents had instilled in him a love of anything German. Oswald clung to his convictions despite the changes. To him these anti-Jewish measures did not translate into outright mass murder. Nor was he alone in refusing to see what had in fact begun to happen.

What these measures meant to some others is described by the Jewish teenager, Rudashevski, eventually murdered by the Nazis in Ponary. A June 28, 1941, entry of his diary reads: "There is no one to take our part. And we ourselves are so helpless. . . . Life becomes more and more difficult. People do not go out anywhere. . . . We are so sad, we are exposed to mockery and humiliation. . . . Our hearts are crushed witnessing the shameful scenes where women and older people are kicked in the middle of the street. . . . I stand at the window and feel a sense of rage. Tears come to my eyes . . . all our helplessness, all our loneliness lies in the streets."[32]

Slowly this feeling of helplessness began to invade the lives of the Akiva friends. They did not know how much longer their meager belongings would feed them. Without proper work they worried about the future. Here and there some managed to find an odd job. But earnings from such sporadic employment were less than adequate. Now, like their families, they were also under the Nazi occupation, so there seemed little reason to remain separated from them. Jews, however, were not allowed to travel without special permission and traveling permits were rare.

Józiek Rakocz was one of those fortunate few who did receive such a permit. He parted from his friends with mixed feelings, afraid that they would never see each other again. He had joined his sister in Lwów. Later on he and his mother moved to Otwock, a town near Warsaw, where they lived illegally as Poles.

After Arieh's and Józiek's departure Oswald's group shrank to four, with Stefi still the only woman. One of the young men in the group was her boyfriend. Moshe Kalchheim had left for a working camp near Nowogródek run by a Lithuanian under German supervision. Kalchheim saw his work in the camp as a chance to eat and get away from the Germans. From his Lithuanian boss he received permission to recruit others. But most of those he approached refused to join him.

After Józiek's departure Oswald too began to think about joining his parents. He had not heard from them for quite a while and was not even sure where they were. He felt that if he could find them he might be of help to them. One day he read in the paper that those who once lived in other parts of Poland should register with the Red Cross. Contact with the Red Cross seemed like an opening for better things and it could, Oswald felt, lead to a permit for joining his parents. Another member of their group, Szaj Ginter, also decided to look for his parents. On July 13 the two friends set out in the direction of the Red Cross offices.

On the way they were stopped by a Lithuanian policeman, who, roughly and without any explanation, forced them into the police station. Inside, visibly agitated, the policeman shouted his accusations. "You Jewish swines, you are guilty of many crimes! Don't you know the law!?" Bewildered, the two friends looked at each other in silence. Obviously the Lithuanian was not interested in their answer. Red-faced, he continued, "You spoke Polish (Polish was forbidden). You did not wear your star of David properly! You walked on the sidewalk! And you are both Communist traitors!"

Oswald's question "How do you know that we are Communists?" was greeted with more screams and a beating. "Don't you dare contradict me! I will teach you a lesson, I will!" The two youths knew enough not to say anything else. They stood, their hands covering their faces as the only protection against the man's heavy blows. Then, for no apparent reason, the policeman abruptly left. Was he tired? Had he lost interest in the victims? Bruised, but not seriously hurt, the two friends avoided each other's eyes. The door opened. At the threshold stood another policeman. Rather indifferently, as if bored, he called out: "Follow me, you dirty Jews."

3

Imprisonment

As if it were the most natural thing, without any questions, the two friends followed the policeman. It would have been inappropriate, even dangerous, to ask for an explanation about the destination, about anything at all. Jews had no rights. No right to ask, no right to know.

Less than three weeks under the German occupation, Oswald had learned what was expected of him. As a Jew he had to take orders and not question. But knowing how to act did not necessarily mean understanding. Nor did it express acceptance. In Oswald's case the "whats" and "whys" were worlds apart. He was watchful, alert, and behaved "properly," but could not grasp why he and all the others had to act the way they did. He was puzzled and the rapidly deteriorating conditions only increased his frustrations. He was filled with questions, questions for which he had no answers. Nor was time of any help. On the contrary, as the days passed, he seemed to comprehend less and less.

Coming out of the police station, Oswald did not even try to sort out what was happening. Instead he trailed behind the policeman. First his eyes, then his mind registered that his friend Szaj had no serious injuries. He too felt only minor physical discomfort. Satisfied with these observations, he hardly noticed that they were being led into a courtyard, one of those courtyards that was a part of each large building. After they had passed through the gate, it was locked behind them. Inside, a bold sign over one of the doors identified the place as a German bakery. From the rest of the surroundings Oswald guessed that they were brought here to split wood, no doubt to feed the bread ovens.

These two newcomers were joining four other Jews who were already working. They stood in a semicircle, each in front of a stump. Each held an ax. Some were trying to split the big chunk of wood before them. Others were contemplating their task. They seemed totally engrossed in the job at hand. Of the four wood cutters not even one acknowledged the arrival of the two young men.

Oswald noticed two Germans, both simple soldiers. Each carried a thick stick. Whenever an ax failed to make contact with a block of wood, one of the supervisors treated the ax holder to a heavy blow. Depending on the position of the stick, it fell on the back or shoulders. These soldiers seemed eager for action, never missing an opportunity to hit.

The prisoners were also made to fetch loads of large wood pieces from the cellar and place them next to the stumps. After they cut the pieces down they had to put them in an orderly pile, close to the bakery's door. As Oswald was carrying the heavy wood he was engulfed by a powerful aroma of freshly baked bread. His stomach began to growl, but it was clear that his captors had no plans for feeding them.

At first the soldiers circulated among the prisoners, watching closely. Eventually, the older of the two stationed himself next to one of the prisoners, a young man. From the young man's clothes and delicate hands it was apparent that he was not used to this kind of work. Each time he tried to bring down the ax on the big slab of wood he missed his target. It was as if this ax had a mind of its own, changing directions whenever it pleased. It refused to take orders. Each time this happened, the German's stick would land forcefully on the young man's back or shoulder. The young man continued. He tried. The harder he tried, the more he missed. The more he missed, the more frequent became the blows. Under the continuous barrage of hits the prisoner's performance deteriorated further and further. A mixture of desperate attempts, missed opportunities, and blows became more and more frequent.

Helpless, raging on the inside, Oswald forced himself not to look. He saw without looking. He tried to banish the ugly feelings that clamored for expression. Such emotions were foreign to him; he did not like them. To escape from it all Oswald attacked his own wood with special fury. But he did not succeed in blocking out his surroundings. This scene has remained with him to this day. *Finally the man fell to the ground. There he remained motionless and seemingly breathless. To us, the witnesses, it was obvious that he could not go on, that he had no strength left. His tormentor thought otherwise. The soldier reached for his victim's ax, bent over him and in a threatening voice yelled: "Will you get up you dirty dog!?" When this produced no results, with the wooden end of the ax he hit the laying figure again and again. The prisoner moved. Staggering, unsteady, with an obvious effort, he got up. Once more he tried to do the job.*

The beating continued. Strangely enough this time the blows were not as intense. Was the soldier reluctant to finish the job? Or did he realize that this was the only way he could get any work out of the man? Is it possible he was guided by a remnant of compassion?

Soon the prisoners, including the young man, were told to stop working. The Germans had enough wood. The Jews were being dismissed. As they were preparing to leave, Oswald and Szaj placed the young man between them. They tried to hold him up on each side, under the arms. He could barely walk and the two friends had to drag him. It seemed that the entire group was being led back to the police station.

On the way they passed the Lukiszki prison. In front of the gate stood a few SS officers. One of them, with a slight gesture, ordered the group to come over. When they did they were unceremoniously pushed into the prison courtyard, a courtyard already filled with Jewish men. All formed orderly rows. Oswald's group had to arrange themselves behind them. Because those assembled were men, Oswald thought they would be assigned to some kind of work. This, he reasoned, would not be so terrible. For him work translated into food.

Oswald looked younger than his age, eighteen. When he realized that those in front of him were asked how old they were he wondered if it would be better to lie about his age. He had no chance to decide. When the SS man asked him how old he was Oswald told the truth.

The prisoners were pushed inside a building and from there into a large hall. Then orders to move on, to enter a room, to give information, were all delivered with frequent, random beatings. The young man from the bakery was roughly removed. He had no time to introduce himself to his helpers. No time to bid them goodbye. The prisoners were ordered to collect their documents and personal belongings, watches, money, and other valuables. These then had to be put in a handkerchief and handed over. These announcements created a flurry of excited activity. As Oswald was putting together his meager belongings, he was amazed to see the floor covered with money. People must have been afraid to admit to having money. Was it a crime to be rich? Utterly poor, Oswald was sorry that only the Nazis would benefit from all this abandoned wealth. No prisoner dared touch this dropped treasure. The men followed the orders quickly, without hesitation. When they were asked to form a line close to a door, Oswald obeyed, making sure that his friend stayed behind him. Then one of the Germans demanded Oswald's name, date of birth, and place of birth. When his answers were delivered in impeccable German, the man seemed surprised, "How come you speak German so well?"

"In my family, at home, we spoke German."

"Are you a Jew?"

"Yes."

"Is your father Jewish?"

"Yes."

"Your mother?"

"Yes."

"Your grandparents?"

"Yes."

"What a shame!"

Oswald muses, *It is possible that had I lied he would have let me go. At that point, however, it seemed to me that I had nothing to lose. Besides, I thought that from here they would send me to some place for work, where I would at least be assured of enough bread and a place to live. On the outside I had no job. Maybe I did not care?*

Soon the door opened. The order was for a single prisoner at a time to enter. Whatever was happening inside happened fast. Every minute another prisoner was asked to go in. None came out. Oswald was the fourth in line. Behind him stood his friend, an important link to life, to the real world. When it was Oswald's turn, he turned around, glanced back. For a fleeting moment their eyes met. It was the last time they saw each other.

Inside Oswald noticed a row of tables. Behind each of them sat an SS officer typing information supplied by each prisoner. Oswald recalled, *They asked my name, place of birth, date of birth, and occupation. When it came to occupation I did not know what to say. What would the Germans value most? Quickly I reviewed my skills. For a while I had worked as a bricklayer. What should I say? Hesitation meant danger. In the end I said shoemaker, thinking that after all this was what I knew best.*

The word shoemaker worked like magic. On hearing it the officer shouted: "Return to Rufeisen his documents, all the items!" As if from nowhere a German gendarme appeared with Oswald's belongings and led him to a special staircase. There the guard ordered Oswald to sit and wait. The staircase was deserted. Only loud noises kept reaching the place: slammed doors, rough curses, sounds of beatings. Then came the noises of trucks and of people, many people. The air seemed to be filled with impatience, with abuse and suffering. The least vocal were the victims. Lonely, and at a loss, Oswald tried not to feel, not to think. He was glad when another prisoner joined him. This man was also a shoemaker. Soon two more shoemakers came.

A fifth man, not a shoemaker, also arrived. But this turned out to be a mistake. He was followed by two very agitated SS men who questioned him about his occupation. He was a dentist. On hearing this the Germans became furious. Confronted by their anger, the young dentist became frightened. He began to shake. The SS men ran out. Two other Germans entered. Each carried camera equipment. They must have been journalists. They seemed intrigued by the Jewish dentist's shaking. Laughing, they made him pose for pictures. But their job was interrupted when the two SS men burst into the place and roughly pushed out the still trembling and confused dentist.

Oswald continues, *The four of us were led out of this staircase into another, larger, more crowded one. This new stairway was filled with Jewish prisoners all of whom were moving down. On each side of the stairs stood Germans with leather belts in hand. To go down the prisoners had to pass close to them. As they did, a German would arbitrarily hit them with the belts. Only the facial expressions of the prisoners registered the pain. They did not scream, they did not talk. They did not even look at the belts or those who were holding them.*

One flight above stood a Nazi (Haupsturmführer), when our group was ready to pass near one of those hitting men, he screamed, "Nicht schlagen" (Don't hit). None of Oswald's companions were touched.

Separated from the rest, the four shoemakers entered a large unlit cell. They realized that they had joined other Jewish shoemakers—together there were twelve of them. None knew why they were selected. Each wondered about their separation from the rest as they listened to the outside commotion that came in through the small window facing the prison's courtyard. Tormented, partly suppressed sounds that told of beatings were mixed with noises of moving trucks.

On July 13, 1941, the day Oswald was there, an estimated 1000 Jews perished. Among those caught and murdered were Chaim Kermish, head of the Akiva movement in Vilna, and Szaj Ginter, the friend who was arrested together with Oswald. Another Akiva friend, Hilel Seidel, was captured but miraculously survived. Of those caught fewer than twenty were spared.

The victims, as so many before and after them, were shot in Ponary, a wooded area on the outskirts of Vilna, some eight miles from the city. In the past it had served as a park for picnics and outings. During the Russian occupation huge pits were dug there for the storage of tank fuel. Under the Nazi occupation Ponary became an execution center and the large pits served as mass graves for thousands of victims, mostly Jews. In addition to the Jews, Russian prisoners of war and others whom the Nazis defined as enemies of the Reich were also executed and buried at Ponary's mass graves.[1] It is estimated that from June 1941 until December of the same year 48,000 Jews were murdered there.[2]

That first night in the cell Oswald and the shoemakers did not know about Ponary. They sensed that horrible things were happening but could not even imagine what they were. Their speculation about their own situation revealed little more. Eventually, each retreated into himself. They tried to rest on the cell's floor, half reclining, half sitting. They were hungry but did not discuss food. The only comfort their captors had provided was a pail that served as a toilet.

Oswald woke up early. A strand of light pushed its way through the small window close to the ceiling. For the first time he could recognize the features of his fellow prisoners. Some were wide awake, others were waiting with their eyes shut, still others were sleeping. Outside was silence. Compared to the night before it was an eerie kind of silence. Then close to the door he heard a rattle of keys. A German guard entered. He brought a hot brown, flavorless liquid. He called it coffee. This came together with dark bread, a thick slice for each. With no opportunity to wash, the men began to discuss their situation. Nothing made sense.

Their talk was interrupted by the appearance of a German gendarme. It was the same man who on the previous day brought Oswald to the special staircase. This time he had introduced himself as Schlesinger. Then in an unusually pleasant voice he said, "We will set up special workshops for you. You will work and live here. Do you have any questions?" There was silence. Jews did not ask questions, not of the Germans. The gendarme looked around. He was waiting. Then his eyes rested on one of the men as he said, "Don't you want to know something? Ask!" "Where will we sleep?" a prisoner wanted to know. This time the German smiled, "Right here in the cell. We will put straw on the floor to make it more comfortable. We will feed you well, three meals a day." Then he added, "All you have to do is obey the rules. Just obey and you will have a good life here. Who of you speaks German?" This time Oswald came forward. Schlesinger looked at him and then at the rest of the men. "He will represent you. You must talk to me through him." With a wave of a hand he disappeared behind the door.

As he saw him leave Oswald's first thought was "Will I be able to do something for my people?" He resolved to do his best.

Oswald's high school diploma set him apart from the rest of the shoemakers. In prewar Poland his education was quite an achievement—no one with a high school diploma would normally become a shoemaker. In Oswald's case only the unusual wartime circumstances placed him in this occupation.

Eventually, in addition to making shoes, Oswald kept track of both the raw materials and finished products. He listed how much leather, how many nails they needed for shoes, how they were used. Whenever new materials were needed, he put in the request. Oswald was both the representative for his group and the official go-between for the Germans and the Jewish shoemakers.

Before they began to work, German guards accompanied each prisoner to his home to collect worktables and all the necessary shoemaker tools. When they returned, one of the prison's large rooms was converted into a workshop with low tables and chairs for each shoemaker. Right away, as if in a hurry, the SS men began to arrive with shoe requests, for themselves and their families.

Soon each day began to resemble the next. Breakfast was served in the cell. It was always the same. It always left them with a craving for more food. Breakfast was followed by work. In the middle of the day they were given soup with vegetables, potatoes, and what were probably pieces of meat, perhaps kidneys or lungs. This soup came with a slice of dark bread. Soup was the only item on the menu that the prisoners could eat more than one portion. These men were hungry and took advantage of the opportunity to have more soup. But, no matter how many servings they had, at times three or four, these filled them up for only a short time. Invariably their hunger returned within a few hours.

Though just as hungry as the others, Oswald was glad that he could count on regular meals. He usually tried to see the positive side of a situation. Moreover, when it came to concrete things such as food, clothes, money, his aspirations were modest.

Soon an answer to the shoemakers' mystery came. The Germans had confiscated large supplies of leather from a Jewish warehouse. Instead of sending these goods to the Reich, they kept them, treating themselves to as many pairs of shoes as the Jewish shoemakers could produce. Schlesinger, the supervisor, had ordered eight pairs of boots. One day, one of the Nazis, a chauffeur, came to order shoes. As he was being measured he threatened that if the end products were not to his liking, he would shoot all the shoemakers. Oswald says, *It could have been a joke but he said it very seriously. We never knew how much power even the lowest ranking Nazi had. . . . The boots must have been satisfactory because he never complained.*

Another day a German came into our workshop, placed himself on a stool and observed us closely for a very, very long time. We felt uneasy. Anything unusual made us feel anxious and afraid. . . . For the sake of the others I looked at him trying to discern what it was all about. Finally, he turned to me and we had the following conversation. "Are all of them Jews?" "Yes, of course," "Strange. In Germany a Jew had to be at least a bookkeeper!" This German could not grasp that Jews were working with their hands rather than with their brains. He could not understand how they could be skilled laborers.

To meet the growing demand for shoes the SS men organized a separate workshop to which they brought Polish shoemakers. Unlike the Jews, these Poles were free to come and go and were paid for their labor. An additional workshop called for some cooperation between the Jews and the Poles. Oswald, the leader of the Jewish shoemakers, and a young Polish shoemaker, the foreman, whom everyone called the 'Majster,' became friends. Eventually, this new Polish friend expressed a willingness to deliver messages to the outside for any of Oswald's Jewish colleagues. Oswald contacted Stefi who sent word that she wanted to visit him.

After a while, with Schlesinger's intervention, Stefi received permission to come. On a much awaited afternoon, full of smiles, the two friends met in a small prison room. They had not seen each other for a few weeks. But to them it seemed like a very long time. On that day each realized that the other had aged. They saw a sad kind of maturity in each other's eyes. Despite the smiles, their eyes had a strained, searching look. Both were sensitive. Both were puzzled, overwhelmed by the events around them. One of the very few things they could be gratified by was their friendship—just to be able to see each other was reassuring. It gave them a taste of past stability. During that first meeting, neither spoke about being hungry or about fear. Instead, with a smile they kept repeating how good it was to see each other.

Then, as they sat across from each other, Stefi reached for her bag and Oswald for his pocket. Each took out a small package wrapped in newspaper and handed it to the other. Both had wanted to give something the other could enjoy; both had saved and cut down on their own meager food allotments to be able to offer a precious commodity: bread.

As Stefi and Oswald unwrapped the other's package, in silence, each took the other's slice of bread. Stefi insists that it tasted like the most exquisite delicacy.

Stefi told Oswald that she now lived all alone. Moshe Kalchheim came to Vilna to recruit Jewish men for his labor camp. Now more than ever before, danger loomed for them. Many had been caught, never to be heard from again. Because she was concerned about the safety of her boyfriend she wanted him to join Moshe in the camp. He did so only reluctantly.

Oswald agreed that this was a wise move, but he was concerned: "How are you managing, Stefi? All alone?"

"Oh, I still have some clothes that I can sell. Here and there I do odd jobs for people. For this they give me potatoes and bread. I manage well. And you?"

"This is a safe place. Food supply is steady. I cannot complain."

Here, away from everyone else, they almost succeeded in convincing themselves that all was well. Just seeing each other had filled them with contentment and hope. Then they had to part since Stefi needed to reach her home before curfew. She had a long walk—Jews were not allowed to use public transportation. The friends promised to meet soon. Oswald was convinced his German boss would help them again.

In this prison world Oswald had gained the reputation of being a good worker and someone who knew how to deal with people. Modest and fair, he was respected by his fellow prisoners as well as the Polish shoemakers. Even the Nazis seemed satisfied with him. They gave him additional duties. He became an official shoe polisher for SS officers. At night they left their boots in front of their rooms; in the morning Oswald would put them in the same place all polished.

Besides offering him contacts with the outside world, Oswald's relation to the Polish shoemakers resulted in gifts of food. Whatever advantages he had, he shared with others. He worked very hard, much harder than the others. But heavy work did not bother him.

One day Schlesinger decided to share some information with his Jewish workers. In confidence, he told them that all Jews who were caught with them were shot at Ponary. He also urged them not to become ill, at least never to admit to it. He explained that if any of them sought medical attention, they would be sent to Ponary and the only doctor they would see there would be a soldier with a gun. Indeed, when one of the shoemakers did report an illness he never came back.

Still Oswald could not believe what he had heard. Each time when confronted by new evidence he continued to cling to his old arguments. The killing of one Jew, even a few, might have been a whim of an individual, even a few individuals. Mass murder, however, he reasoned, was quite another matter. This last possibility he was not ready to accept. Oswald and these rumors were equally stubborn. He refused to believe them and they refused to go away.

4

Life on the Farm

Gradually, prison life took on a semblance of stability, a stability that lasted for a few weeks. Then, as if from nowhere, rumors about impending danger began to circulate. In those days there was a continuous flow of stories and any disruption of the familiar had a threatening ring to it. Frequently, an event would be predicted, the news about it would spread rapidly, and just as rapidly vanish, never to be mentioned again. Not surprisingly, attitudes toward such unauthorized information were ambiguous. People waited for news and dreaded it at the same time.

In Oswald's workplace a rumor began to circulate of Nazi reverses. The Russian army had stopped the German troops in Smolensk. Right away, enemy casualties were translated into defeat. Defeat in turn meant an end to the war and a stop to Jewish suffering. In this instance, time, the ultimate tester of reality, supported these rumors. They continued.

On one of her visits Stefi told of trains loaded with wounded German soldiers. Some stayed in Vilna's hospitals, others were sent on to the Reich. She described how little resemblance these men bore to the soldiers who only a few weeks ago were rushing to the Russian front, arrogantly and enthusiastically. Then it became an established fact that Germany was beginning to taste defeat.

Encouraging in itself, this turn of events led to other rumors that were disturbing to the Jewish shoemakers. Because of these reverses, the SS unit in charge of the prison was being transferred to the Russian front. This information gained credibility when one of the officers confided in Oswald that he and his comrades were going to the front. Schlesinger himself confirmed that preparations were being made for the SS men's departure.

The shoemakers were anxious to know what would happen to them, whether they would continue to work, whether they would be dismissed.

It was an open secret that the workshops were a semiofficial operation. The prisoners knew they were spared only because the SS men found their services useful. Their impending transfer and Schlesinger's evasive answers suggested an end to the shoemakers' protection. Dreading the unknown, unable to affect future events, Oswald and his fellow prisoners vacillated between feeling anxious, fearful, and angry.

With time, the SS men also became upset. They resented this order and seemed reluctant to defend their "Fatherland," especially when it involved risking their lives. Comfortable in their present situation, these Nazis wanted to stay as much as the shoemakers wanted them to. Who would have thought that Jewish prisoners would dread the departure of their jailers?

However, neither had the power to change the order. Neither seemed to know what effect the order would have. Only the new arrivals, those who would replace this unit, could clarify the situation.

Oswald explains, *Because a lot of leather was still left, another "Obersturbamführer" took us over. Whether he promised to liquidate us later on after the supply would be exhausted, I don't know. Initially, however, this new master of life and death seemed more humane than his predecessor. The new head collected all of us and announced that he would allow us to go home for the night. We would have to report each morning for work. This change was both good and bad. It was good to go home. But going home reduced our pay to lunch only, thus eliminating the morning and evening meals.*

This new boss must have seen this order as a special favor because he urged us not to talk about it. How he expected this to remain a secret I have no idea. Because of this new development each of us was given a special document that was to shield us from all raids and arrests.

Once more Oswald and Stefi shared a home. Even though this meant a reduction in food supplies, both were delighted with this arrangement. German wartime losses, only occasional hunger, permission to share a home with Stefi, all seemed definite improvements. For Jews, at that time any change for the better was an unheard-of luxury. Stefi and Oswald were grateful for their good fortune.

For two days the return from prison passed uneventfully. On the third day, as Oswald walked in the middle of the road, he automatically moved to one side to make way for what he knew had to be a horse-drawn wagon. As the vehicle passed, its driver turned his head and looked closely at

Oswald. He was a peasant in his forties, with a dark turned-up mustache that reached to the upper parts of his cheeks. He had equally dark bushy eyebrows that practically covered his eyes. For a split second the dark eyes of the driver and those of the young Jew met. Then with a decisive gesture the older man invited the younger one to sit next to him.

Somewhat apprehensive, Oswald climbed in. He explains, *We were afraid of everything and everybody. I had no way of knowing what his intentions were. After all, he was a stranger, the situation was strange. Any new situation, any new encounter, particularly with a non-Jew could mean danger. A Jew had no right to defend himself against anyone. None whatsoever.*

But this man seemed friendly. The peasant, the horse, and the wagon all had a prosperous air about them. And the man introduced himself as Lubomir Żukowski, the owner of a large farm near Rojstele. The "large" was mentioned without conceit, simply as a piece of information. Indeed, Żukowski did most of the talking. He said, "My farm is close to Ponary. Since the Germans came, they have been shooting Jews there. I was told that they had murdered 30,000 of them. On my farm we hear the shooting all day long, every day. Why do you stay in Vilna? You could easily pass for a Pole. You don't look Jewish at all. Save yourself!"

When Oswald reacted by saying that he had a secure job, the stranger laughed. "With the Germans that does not mean much, as long as you are a Jew. You should live as a Pole. Your Polish is good. No one would recognize a Jew in you. Besides, you can come to my farm, away from danger. You can work for me as a farm hand. Even if the war would last for years you would be safe there.

"I know a German officer who comes often to my place. He would take care of any official arrangements. You would be safe. Here they can catch you any day and then you may end up in Ponary like the rest: dead!"

Oswald remembers, *I knew and I had heard about the mass killings of Jews, but did not believe them. I refused to accept what my former supervisor, Schlesinger, had told us about Ponary. I was not the only one who had this kind of feeling. I was brought up with a certain respect for the German culture. I did not believe that one could kill people for no reason at all, 'mir nichts, dir nichts.' So I did not accept as evidence the story I heard from this peasant either. I thought that he had emphasized the killings of Jews because he wanted me to come and work for him.*

The proposition this stranger made was somewhat ambiguous. Was Oswald to come as a Pole? Was he to come as a Jew and then the German officer would take care of the formalities? Oswald was not sure about these points. Nor was he interested enough to clarify them. Still he listened politely. He was convinced that his reasons for not accepting Żukowski's offer were valid. After all, his friends and all that he was familiar with were in Vilna.

Also, though born in a village, Oswald had never worked in the fields and knew nothing about farming. More important, however, he had a special document from the Gestapo describing him as a useful Jew (Nützlicher Jude). Surely, he reasoned, such a paper gave him solid protection. For as long as the Germans considered him useful nothing could happen to him. Finally, he was not convinced that the situation was really as grim as Żukowski described it.

In the end Oswald explained to this stranger that while he himself could not accept this offer he had friends who might like to work for him. But this was not what Żukowski was after. "I like you. My invitation applies only to you and no one else. I want you to live. If you change your mind, you can come. Any time." Without making any promises Oswald took the man's address. Then with a friendly handshake they parted.

Despite Oswald's unwillingness to believe, despite doubts, the meeting with Żukowski left him with a lingering restless anxiety that threatened to plunge him into depression. Only with a special effort did he succeed in pushing both the oppressive emotions and the actual memory of this encounter into the background.

For about a week the Jewish shoemakers continued to go home in the evenings and return to their jobs in the morning. The official pay for their work was the one midday meal, consisting of plenty of soup and a limited amount of bread. Why did these men return? Why didn't they simply refuse to work for such meager pay? For Jews there were no paying jobs. One meal a day was better than no payment at all. Besides, the Germans ordered them to come. Any disobedience was followed by severe punishment, sometimes death. Everyone was registered and the Germans knew where each lived.

By working for the Nazis they were entitled to special documents that protected them against sudden raids and deportations. And if, they reasoned, rumors about Ponary were even partially true, these documents would shield them from possible death. No alternative source of income plus safety and fear of danger kept these shoemakers working. Compared to the fate of so many other Jews, they considered themselves fortunate.

A few days after the meeting with Żukowski, on his way home Oswald saw a large group of Jews, 400 to 500. They were coming through the gate of a big Jewish building on Perec Street. These people carried bundles of what looked like their personal belongings. Many were old, many were children.

Oswald was struck by the crowd's subdued, quiet resignation. *I remember distinctly how a stooped old man with a sack over his shoulder tripped and was unable to get up. He simply could not move. Two German guards noticed. They came over and dragged him by his feet like a lifeless object. The three disappeared into a nearby courtyard. There they probably finished him off. The rest continued. . . . Some of the guards were Lithuanians. From the very beginning the Lithuanians behaved toward the Jews in the most brutal ways. These guards were wearing uniforms. As far as I could see they had no weapons. Instead they carried wooden sticks. The rest of the guards were German soldiers (Wehrmacht).*

I had heard that a central ghetto was being formed in Szawle (a nearby town). On seeing these people I concluded that they were being taken there. What I found out much later was that the Germans were setting up the Vilna ghetto and were eager to reduce the number of Jews that would settle in it by simply murdering them.

When this mass of people passed, I continued in the direction of my home. Then I noticed that the Germans had blocked the street's passage. I realized that all passing Jews, with curses and indiscriminate beatings, were being herded by the Lithuanian and German guards into a nearby courtyard. When my turn came, to avoid being hit, I ran into the place on my own. Forcefully and speedily, more and more people were being shoved into the courtyard. I went over to a Lithuanian officer, showed him my special document and explained that I worked for the Germans and that they needed my services. For an answer I received a slap in the face. When no other reaction followed it dawned on me that it made no difference who worked where. I was trapped.

Oswald began to survey the situation. It looked as if the apartments in the entire house were empty. It occurred to him that in the continuous shoving, pushing, and confusion he could run upstairs to one of those unoccupied places. But he was afraid. Somehow the cellar seemed safer, less exposed. Casually, slowly, Oswald detached himself from the crowd. Soon he was moving down the stairs into the cellar. The way seemed long, endless. On each side were the usual storage places one finds in such large buildings. Searching in the darkness, Oswald felt a door made from wooden boards. It was locked. Unable to open the padlock, he removed one of the boards, creating a passage. He slid through it. From the outside, with the padlock in place, the storage room looked locked—no one would suspect that someone was hiding inside. Groping in the dark, he became aware of old furniture. He piled it up and crawled underneath.

Then he heard steps. Anxious steps. These were followed by equally anxious whispers. Other fugitives were trying to hide. Would they succeed in entering other storage rooms? Then all was quiet. After an hour or so, more determined sounds announced the arrival of German soldiers. With flashlights they began to search the place. From the cursing and beating sounds Oswald knew they were successful in locating some victims. Then the flashlights came close to Oswald's hiding place. *For the first time in my life I prayed passionately to God. At that point only prayers were left to me. . . . In the end the Germans did not find me. But I was not about to leave. . . . I waited.*

Under the pile of old furniture Oswald resolved that for the duration of the war he would not admit to being a Jew. He is convinced that in making this decision he was encouraged by Żukowski's insistence that neither his speech nor looks betrayed his Jewishness. If Żukowski were right, Oswald was fortunate indeed. This would have given him an advantage most other Jews lacked. The overwhelming majority of Polish Jews could be easily identified by their looks, speech, and a whole array of special behaviors.[1]

Oswald was also aware that shedding one's identity called for drastic steps. In Poland Christians and most Jews lived in different worlds. He was never a part of the non-Jewish world. He knew very little about the Catholic religion and was painfully aware that this would be a serious drawback in passing for a Pole.

Recognizing the many difficulties, he also realized that as a Jew he would most likely be killed. He wanted to live. Right away, Oswald had to make some concrete decisions. He took off the armband with the star of David. He would leave it here among the old furniture. This move in itself gave him a liberated feeling.

Still he knew that the authorities were continuously checking and rechecking people's papers. The documents he received from the Nazis were useless because they identified him as a Jew. Only one identification card could possibly support his claim to being a Pole. It was a student card he received in his high school in Bielsko, in 1939.[2] In it he was simply identified as Oswald Rufeisen and nothing else. Because Rufeisen was a German-sounding name, this newly created Pole decided to make up a story that he had a German father and a Polish mother. A German-Polish background would also explain his knowledge of German. He thought that familiarity with this language might come in handy. To simplify matters, Oswald would say that both his parents were dead.

In the cellar, Żukowski's farm began to seem a real haven. In fact, it was the only place he could go. Traveling in the evening would be too dangerous; his new document might not pass close scrutiny. He would have to wait until the next day.

Meanwhile, Oswald was afraid to stay in the cellar. The Germans might come back. He also felt that in the evening it might be less dangerous to slip out—after all this was a Jewish house that was supposed to be free of Jews! Then Oswald remembered the Polish foreman who had befriended him in prison. He knew where the man lived. With no one else to turn to, Oswald decided to ask this colleague for shelter. And so, without the Jewish insignia, with the student card in his pocket, slowly, cautiously Oswald emerged from the cellar.

The courtyard, only a short while ago filled with so much life, was deserted, eerie. In this huge empty space the only living creature seemed to be a lone cat. A Jewish cat?

Then Oswald's eyes were attracted to a light coming from a window next to the gate. This he knew had to be the janitor's quarters, probably a non-Jew. On the inside, Oswald saw a woman engrossed in sock mending. Except for this woman and the cat, the house seemed lifeless.

Quietly, Oswald reached the exit, but the gate was locked. It was too risky to ask the janitor for help. Only a Jew could have remained in this house. He did not trust her. In his pocket this young shoemaker carried a hammer. Noiselessly, with the help of the hammer, he lifted some stones below the large gate. His small size was a definite advantage and he slipped through the opening.

On the street Oswald was greeted by strange noises. From a distance he saw a German soldier surrounded by laughing youngsters. The children were making fun of the man, who, visibly drunk, was staggering, zigzagging from one side of the pavement to the other. Here and there he would reach for the wall to steady himself—he had a hard time staying on his feet.

Oswald explains, *I went over to him without any hesitation. Using my German I asked him where he was going. He showed me a piece of paper with an address. It was a hotel that served as a center for Germans who needed a place to stay. I realized that this address was close to where my friend, the Polish shoemaker, lived. I hoped to spend the night there. I told the boys to run along and took the soldier under the arm. Together we moved in the direction of the hotel. . . . I thought that this was a safe move, that no one would ever suspect that a Jewish man would lead a German soldier.*

Grateful for the help, the German introduced himself as a Volksdeutsche, an ethnic German. He came over from Czechoslovakia. He missed his family and did not like it here. Then abruptly he asked: "Comrade, do you know how many Jews we shot today?" Stunned, Oswald could not speak. Then, as if it was someone else's voice, he heard his own question: "How many?" The answer: "Seventeen hundred."

The soldier continued to chat, but Oswald could not hear him. All he could think of was "Here I am holding a murderer, a murderer of innocent people!" He wanted to disengage himself. An urge to run away became strong, and he felt nothing else as he delivered the soldier to the hotel.

It was past the Jewish curfew. Oswald's steps moved in the direction of the Polish shoemaker, the only non-Jew he felt he could approach. But then it occurred to him that they had known each other for less than a month. They liked each other. But was this enough?

Oswald was soon standing at the threshold of the Majster's house. On seeing the fugitive, the shoemaker paled. Oswald spoke first: "Can you put me up for the night? Just one night?"

Embarrassed, not meeting his friend's eyes, the Pole hesitated. He whispered, "It is dangerous. They are looking for Jews. Hide in the garden. I will come to you." With this he shut the door.

When later on he joined Oswald in the garden he continued to apologize: "I have a familly to think of. Who knows what the Germans would do to them if they found you!"

Again Oswald assured him that this was only for one night and that he would leave early in the morning. Besides, he could stay in the garden. Still uneasy, still hesitating, the Majster agreed. Then Oswald asked if the man would exchange some clothes with him. Oswald wanted to wear something that would more easily identify him as a Polish farm hand. After the exchange of clothes, the two men shook hands. This was the last time they met. Oswald was satisfied. *After all, our entire acquaintanceship lasted two to three weeks. We were not close friends. Yet, he was loyal. Not only did he not denounce me, he also helped me. I am grateful for what he did.*

That night, in the garden, Oswald felt safe. Some of his friends he knew were in different labor camps. He had no desire to join a camp. Unless forced to, he would not admit to being Jewish. He would live at Żukowski's farm, as a Pole. But before he would leave the city he had to find Stefi. Sleep took over as he imagined meeting her.

In the morning Oswald felt refreshed. *I had no idea of what was happening at home. I heard from my Polish friend that the Nazis were emptying only some parts of the Jewish district. . . . As I approached our house I realized that the place was still intact. . . . At that point Stefi was alone . . . maybe I should have stayed with her? On the other hand she was tied to her boyfriend who should have looked after her . . . later on they married.*

Oswald's arrival made a deep and lasting impression on Stefi. She is still able to recapture that morning down to the smallest detail. She even remembers the short peasant jacket Oswald wore, the one he got from the Polish shoemaker.

Stefi supported her friend's plans by insisting that he could easily pass for a Pole. Though she knew she would miss him, she forced herself to sound happy. In a way she was. She wanted him to be safe. As she spoke to him she tried to minimize his guilt and apprehension, emotions she saw clearly written all over his open, almost childlike face.

The two knew that the Nazis could appear at any minute. To make it easier, and to avoid danger, Stefi urged Oswald to leave. Each wanted to smile, but no smiles came.

Then Stefi heard herself say, "The war will be over soon. You will see, we will meet at happier times!"

"Of course we will. Take care of yourself, Stefi. Please don't let them take you!" said Oswald.

Gently, but firmly, Stefi pushed her friend toward the door. They had so much to say but embraced in silence. Stefi stood immobile. For a long, long time she stared at the spot where Oswald had stood. She felt alone, so utterly alone.

Oswald walked out briskly. He felt oppressed. Powerful and contradictory emotions began to invade his very soul, emotions that soon turned into a painful dialogue. "Even if I stayed I would not be able to help her. Doesn't staying in Vilna as a Jew mean waiting, waiting to be picked up?" Oswald detested passivity. He wanted to act, to be in control. Surely, he thought, "As a Pole I will be in a better position to take charge of my destiny. I have made the right decision. If I have, why do I feel so depressed and so apprehensive? Why this feeling of loss?"

He continued to be bombarded by different ideas and emotions. All those he felt attached to he was leaving behind. He was going to live among strangers. What was this new world like? Who were the people? How safe was it? And then again: "Am I doing the right thing?"

Six miles from Vilna, Oswald had no trouble reaching Żukowski's farm by foot. As he approached the cluster of buildings, he could see that this was a prosperous place. It had large vegetable gardens, horses, pigs, and chickens.

Because of Żukowski's warm welcome and the genuine pleasure he showed at seeing Oswald, the young man's apprehension gave way to a feeling of gratitude. This feeling grew stronger as he was being taken around and introduced to various people. The older man insisted that for the first day his protégé should only familiarize himself with the surroundings. Curious by nature, Oswald was eager to learn, to absorb.

He soon discovered that among the many farm employees there were two Russian prisoners of war. The Germans had sent them here to work free of charge. As all the others, they were treated very well. He also learned that one was a mason whose most recent contribution was a special cellar for storing potatoes for the winter. The mason proudly explained this last accomplishment to the newcomer. It seemed that the rest of the farm hands, quite a number, had been working on this farm for a long time.

One of those who did not work was a Jewish woman. Later Oswald heard that she and her child, a little boy, had been brought here by the German officer whom Żukowski considered a friend, the one he thought could help Oswald legitimate his stay. It was an open secret that the woman and officer were lovers. Once a week this man would come to spend a few hours with his mistress. He would usually depart without talking to anyone. No one discussed this arrangement. No one felt the need to explain. Though intrigued by this affair, Oswald refrained from asking questions. Most of what he knew, and it was not very much, he had himself observed. The rest he guessed.

On this farm people seemed relaxed and friendly. Enough food was available to all; no one went hungry. For Oswald this was quite a change. For more than two months he had been preoccupied with food. Now he could stop thinking about it. Most of the people worked hard, but without pressure and without conflict. No doubt Żukowski's unobtrusive supervision was responsible for this overall harmony. This was a protective environment with no resemblance to the chaotic and cruel conditions on the outside.

Compared to the dangerous life in Vilna, for Jews the farm was like a peaceful oasis. With so much abuse, cruelty, and persecution directed against them, inevitably some Jews had begun to feel unworthy. Perhaps because of such vague feelings they were surprised and touched by the slightest show of kindness. And when this kindness came from non-Jews it could lead to exaggerated feelings of gratitude.

Oswald's gratitude was augmented by the realization that Żukowski did not really need his services, that this was a disinterested gesture.

Though thankful, very thankful, Oswald was not feeling happy. A cloud of sadness hovered over him, refusing to go away. Why, in this protective environment, with so much to be happy with, did he feel so oppressed? What made him so melancholy?

It was probably not one thing but many. Perhaps the very absence of immediate personal danger allowed him to mourn, to feel sad, to feel out of place.

The closeness of Ponary must have contributed to his low spirits. For the first time he could not deny that Ponary was a place of Jewish executions. Here, on this farm, the shooting sounds served as constant reminders. With these noises came vivid images of dying people. Only gradually did these pictures pale. Only gradually did they appear less frequently. But they never disappeared. Both the shootings and the visions stayed on as witnesses to the Jewish plight. For Oswald, and for many others, the Jewish circumstances were incomprehensible. But there was no reason to understand. No one did. Oswald absorbed enough to feel pain.

His own personal condition might in part account for the way he felt. Unused to this kind of work and physically not very strong, Oswald found farming difficult. His body, not he, seemed to object to the work. From the start his hands were covered with blisters, and only when these blisters turned to callouses did the pain ease. But hands were not the only problem. His entire body ached. With time, the overall pain diminished and settled in Oswald's back; it remained there as long as he stayed on the farm. Even the fresh air and the sun conspired against this inexperienced farmer. He felt intoxicated by both. This intoxication made him sluggish and sleepy.

A smart man, Żukowski was aware of these difficulties. Yet he never spoke about them, nor did he push his young protégé. And if something was obviously clumsily done, he pretended not to see it. Instead, Oswald pushed himself into harder and harder work. He was eager to repay the owner's kindness and felt the only way he could was through hard work. The result was continuous physical discomfort and sadness.

To this discomfort were added problems created by Oswald's ambiguous position. Before he came to the farm people knew from Żukowski that he had met a Jewish youth whom he had invited to come and work. When Oswald arrived he was appropriately identified as this youth.

But Oswald had destroyed all documents that identified him as a Jew. In a sense, he had burned all the bridges behind him. He left Vilna as a Pole determined not to admit his Jewishness for the duration of the war. How can you pretend to be a Pole if you had been identified as a Jew? His position was awkward.

In addition, here on this protective farm, where he was hardly alone, he felt lonely. With time this need for old friends and a renewal of old times became stronger and stronger.

One day he decided to satisfy this craving by a visit to a labor camp, some 10 kilometers from the farm. Oswald knew that three of his Akiva friends lived there. When he was in Vilna, he had heard that they worked fixing roads and were given very little food.

Oswald explained his decision to Żukowski and then asked: "Could I take to them a loaf of bread and some fruit?"

"You can have these things, but I don't think that you should go."

"Why not?"

"It is dangerous. Jews are not allowed to travel and your 'Polish' document may not be good enough to protect you."

"But if I go during the day no one will suspect me."

"You can go and take food to them, of course. I am only thinking about your safety."

That was all that Oswald wanted to hear. "If they still have some things they will pay you for the food."

"Don't worry about it. I am happy just to give them food. After all, they are hungry!" said Żukowski good-naturedly. With a gesture he interrupted Oswald's thanks.

And so, in the middle of the morning, with thoughts about danger pushed into the background, with Żukowski's approval and food, Oswald set out in search of friends. He suspected that the camp inmates would be working on the road. As he came closer to the place he slowed down. There was a forest on each side of the road. Not to attract attention, Oswald walked near the edge of the forest, keeping an eye on the empty road. He had no trouble spotting the entire Jewish crew and his three friends.

The three were overjoyed to see Oswald and assured him this was a quiet road and that the guards would not interfere if he joined them during their midday break. The guards indeed looked totally disinterested, bored.

The presence of this stranger elicited no reaction at all. The main enemy of these Jewish inmates was hunger rather than mistreatment by their guards. With great enthusiasm, and at a distance from the others, Oswald's friends devoured the food. Whatever was left they divided into three parts. This they felt would allow them to pass the gate inspection when returning to camp.

They appreciated the food and the trouble Oswald had gone to. In Vilna, they had been friends who shared an enjoyment of heated debates, a love for Palestine, and dreams about a free life there. Now as they sat under the tree, in the middle of nowhere, they had so much to tell, so much to share. They all knew that Vilna's Jews, whoever was left of them, were moved to a special ghetto. They had no idea how many of their friends did or did not survive the purges.

Then, as conversation turned to their own situation, they began to think aloud. "This job will be finished in a few weeks." "Who knows what kind of work they would assign us next?" "We know how to repair roads, they will probably send us to another similar place." This made sense. They only wondered where this place would be. Broader political issues were less vague, more promising. They all agreed that the recent German losses would lead to a speedy conclusion of the war. They even tried to guess when this might be. Some claimed that by now agreements for the end of the war had been worked out. What sources of information did they have? Did they themselves believe what they were saying? For the moment this seemed not to have mattered. What mattered most was that they were together.

Oswald in particular was in a blissful mood. Giving help, providing satisfaction to others was his idea of happiness. Time passed quickly. Definite promises about future meetings made parting less difficult.

And even though traveling for Jews was becoming more dangerous, Oswald managed to reach his friends again. This time, to reciprocate, they gave him the only treasure they had: an alarm clock. It was a present for Żukowski. As Oswald took it he assured them that on his next visit he would bring a larger supply of food.

Through his trips to the camp Oswald was courting danger. When planning another visit, he refused to listen to the voices of reason. Had he listened, these voices would have told him about the increasing risks and that such trips would soon be impossible.

Not only did recent developments interfere with travel, they also threatened to destroy the protective life on the farm. Now any Jew who worked for a Christian had to have a special permit. Such permits, however, were hardly ever granted. Jews discovered anywhere other than the ghetto or camp were removed. These Jews disappeared without a trace.

One day the German officer came to the farm to take away his mistress and her child. Without being asked, he announced that he was transferring them to the ghetto in Baranowicze. In those days an unsoliticited public announcement made everyone suspicious. Through such a statement the officer might have wanted to hide their true destination. He might have taken them to a safe hiding place. No one ever discovered what happened to these two lovers. The woman's departure cut off all contacts between the German officer and the farm.

With the stepped-up Jewish persecution Oswald's situation became more perilous. Too many people knew he was Jewish. If the Germans decided to visit the farm, they could find out the truth.

Żukowski knew about the situation. He could have avoided problems by dismissing Oswald. Instead, he behaved as if the changes did not affect him. He did not raise the issue at all.

With this new wave of persecution, Oswald knew that sooner or later he would have to leave the farm. With time it became a question of endangering the others, especially his protector. By October 15, 1941, the Germans passed a law that made help to Jews a crime punishable by death.[3]

Oswald knew about the Jewish ghetto in Vilna and that some of his friends might be there. Joining them, however, would mean giving up. Besides, he heard that the Germans had issued new yellow documents to all ghetto inmates. Only holders of these documents had a right to live there. No, he could not return.[4]

Torn between conflicting emotions, with no place to go, Oswald stayed. Help came from an unexpected quarter when a cow became seriously ill. In the middle of the night, a Polish farm hand was dispatched with a wagon and instructions to fetch the regional veterinarian, Dr. Sobolewski.

As the doctor examined the sick animal Oswald assisted by holding up a lantern. Sobolewski might have been struck by Oswald's melancholy eyes and suspected that these were Jewish eyes. During the war Jews were known for the sadness of their eyes.[5] Perhaps he even heard about Oswald's Jewishness?

Continuing with his task, not wishing to frighten the youth, the older man asked casually, "Why are you so sad? What bothers you? You should not fear me, I only want to help!" No additional encouragement was necessary. All the pent-up emotions, all the frustrations could come out. Oswald poured out his life story. He explained that he did not want to endanger his host, yet he had no place to go. Without showing surprise, calmly Sobolewski said, "I come from Belorussia, a very small town called Turzec. My brother is a peasant. He, together with my parents and his family, live there. The whole area is surrounded by forests. It is a remote place.

Chances are that the Germans don't even come to the place. You would be safe there. I will give you a letter for my brother. I will only tell him that you are a Pole, an orphan. I will ask him to take you in and find you work. He will do it for me. You could live with them in peace and wait for the end of the war."

"This must be a dream" was all that Oswald could say. The man continued, "Within a few days I will bring you the letter and the day after you should be on your way."

Not only did Sobolewski give Oswald the letter but also money for the road. Żukowski approved of this arrangement wholeheartedly. "It is a smart move. This is your chance to stay alive." He insisted that Oswald take food to last him for a few days. But when Oswald expressed the wish to go and see his friends in the camp both Żukowski and Sobolewski told him not to go. A trip to the camp would be too dangerous.

This time Oswald followed their advice but felt guilty about it. He still does. He is bothered by two things: a broken promise and that he took their clock, although he gave it to Żukowski. In a way it was payment for the food they had already received. As for the broken promise, Oswald's trip to the camp would have been a wasted effort. About the time that he was leaving for Turzec, the work camp was liquidated. All inmates were executed in Ponary.

5

Becoming Someone Else

When Oswald reached the highway that was to take him to Turzec and to a new life, he felt tense and out of place. Despite past assurances that he could pass for a Christian, he was besieged by painful thoughts and doubts. In a strange, yet realistic way, Oswald feared more the native non-Jews than the Germans. He knew that the Germans, unfamiliar with and insensitive to Poland's cultural nuances, would have a hard time identifying Jews, while the Lithuanians, the Poles, and other natives, entrenched in their own culture, were conscious of even the most subtle and minute differences that separated them from Jews. Oswald knew that some of these natives willingly collaborated with the Nazis in ferretting out Jews who lived illegally in the forbidden Christian world. Nazi collaborators were a serious obstacle to Jewish survival. More often than not, recognition by a native denouncer became a prelude to death. Jews who lived illegally among Christians knew that to stay alive they had to avoid being recognized.

Still, as Oswald continued on the highway, these thoughts and uncomfortable feelings failed to defeat his determination to live. He was devising a strategy. "From now on," he thought, "I will have to convince the non-Jews that I am one of them. To do that I must act naturally, boldly. I must fight the fear in myself. Fear can betray me."

Indeed, for Jews who pretended to be Christians there was a delicate balance between physical appearance, behavior, and attitudes. A Jew could be betrayed by any one of the three and by all. In addition to mere appearance, fear, feelings of uncertainty, vacillations, or awkward behavior could be easy giveaways. On the other hand, courage, self-assurance, a relaxed posture could tip the scale in favor of a "passing" Jew. Unable to change his looks, Oswald decided to control what he could: behavior and attitudes.

Being in control meant being on the alert. And while he was convincing himself how to act and feel, he scanned the territory. He was reassured by the presence of other pedestrians, all civilians. Only a few were women. He felt certain that at least his clothes did not set him apart from the rest.

Except for horse-drawn wagons, all other vehicles were German, mostly military trucks. Occasionally one of these trucks would stop to pick up a hitchhiker. In fact, all those who asked for a ride seemed to have no trouble getting one. Most of the men hitchhiked, but none of the women did.

Oswald had a long way to go. He hesitated. "Should I try to get a ride? Is it safe?" It took him more than an hour to answer this question. When the answer did come it was a self-order: "I must act the way the others do!" His hand gesture brought a German military truck to a stop. Next to the driver sat a young man, a Polish civilian. He spoke up. "We are going to Mołodeczno, about eighty kilometers from here. If it suits you, hop in!" Nodding and smiling, Oswald climbed next to the man. A brief introduction was followed by a few casual questions and answers. Then Oswald announced that he knew German because of his German father. His explanation about Turzec and relatives was accepted without comment.

With Oswald as the interpreter, the conversation continued smoothly, in a relaxed way. It was punctuated by casual silences. As they were approaching Mołodeczno, the day was coming to an end. Because here the young men were to part from their German driver, the Polish passenger suggested that he and Oswald stop in this town for the night and continue in the morning, each in his own direction.

To do this they needed a place to sleep. An overnight stay in a small town or village required the help of someone in authority. The two travelers went to the mayor. He told them that only a few days ago the Germans had murdered all local Jews with the exception of one, a World War I hero who fought on the German side. After the killings the Nazis gave strict orders to report every Jew. Turning to Oswald the mayor said, "You are Jewish. I will not report you, but I cannot let you stay." "You are making a mistake," said Oswald. He took out his school card and began to tell his story. Unimpressed, the official shook his head in disagreement. This exchange was interrupted by the other traveler. "This is nonsense. I have known Oswald for years. He is a Pole. I vouch for him."

These words worked like magic. The mayor registered them both and directed each to a separate household. With a handshake, the two traveling companions said goodbye, and each went in a different direction. Practically strangers, this was the last time the two saw each other.

That same evening, from his hosts, Oswald found out that by coming to Mołodeczno he had taken a roundabout way to Turzec and that he was still eighty kilometers away from his destination. To reach Turzec he could go back to Vilna and start from there, or go through a less populated area, the huge Nalibocki forest.

In the morning Oswald went to the town market in the hope of finding transportation that would bring him to Turzec, or at least close to it. Right away he was spotted by two German soldiers who laughingly called him "Moritz," another word for a Jew. Shaken, Oswald vanished into the crowd, away from their view. This last episode convinced him that eighty kilometers was not very far and that he would be better off walking. He also decided to take the less populated road through the Nalibocki forest.

Part of this trip, he knew, would take him close to or through the Naliboki town, located close to this old forest. He knew that many Jews lived there. Indeed, when he reached the outskirts of the town he met a Jewish crew busy fixing telegraph wires. In Yiddish these men invited Oswald to come closer. What did he do? *I pretended that I did not understand. I knew some Yiddish, but not from home. I learned it in Vilna from the Jewish shoemakers. I spoke poorly, but understood everything. When I did not react to their calls they wanted to know why I play the part of a Pole. After all, they argued, it was written all over my face that I was a Jew.*

These men were persistent. They wanted to know where he was coming from and where he was going. Stubbornly, in Polish, Oswald gave them only the official story, adding that he had heard that all the Mołodeczno Jews were murdered. He had hoped that this news would serve as a warning and that they might try and save themselves from a similar fate. They barely reacted to this information. At the mention of Turzec, however, the crew tried to persuade Oswald to change his plans because only a few days ago all the Turzec Jews were executed. Oswald shrugged. "The killing of Jews has nothing to do with me." Without waiting for an answer he continued on his way.

Despite feigned indifference, Oswald was distressed. How easily people could recognize him! To avoid similar encounters he decided to go around the town. Later on, however, in the forest, he saw coming toward him a Belorussian policeman and a young attractive woman. When the two faced Oswald, the policeman asked, "Where are you going? Who are you?" Oswald handed him his student card, explaining, "Right now I come from Vilna. I am going to visit my relatives in Turzec." "But this is a Jew," the woman interrupted. "What kind of a Jew am I? I was born in Slesia, my father was German, my mother Polish. I am a Catholic."

Before Oswald had left the farm one of the Polish workers, a young woman, gave him a chain with a medallion of Mary and Jesus Christ and insisted that it brings luck to its wearer. At the time Oswald had hesitated. After all, Jews were not supposed to wear such things! Still, in order not to offend her, he had put it around his neck. Only later on did it occur to him that this religious object might indeed help him.

Now, to convince this suspicious woman, Oswald pointed to the medallion. "You don't believe? Look!" She was unmoved, "Anyone can put on a medal. You can hear from his accent that he is a Jew." Just as determined as she, Oswald turned to the policeman. "I am going to Turzec, and if they think that I am lying they will know what to do with me." The man agreed. "Run along!" Oswald did. As he continued, he thought how strange this episode was. He knew that as far as his accent was concerned the woman was wrong. His Polish was peculiar to the region he came from and had nothing to do with being Jewish.

Only on the sixth day did Oswald manage to reach his destination. Turzec was a cross between a village and a small town. Here, the natives not only knew each other, they were intimately acquainted with each other's life histories.

Oswald was directed to Sobolewski's home. The veterinary's brother lived in a one-room hut, with clay floors, without running water or toilet facilities. For this part of the country, such living quarters were not unusual. The room was dominated by a big woodburning oven. During the day it was used for baking bread and cooking. The oven and the space around it retained the heat for a long time and people used the oven area for sleeping.

Six children, their parents, and grandparents shared this one room. Not all could fit next to the oven. Those who did not made their beds away from the oven on the floor. Each bed consisted of some straw and a cover. Not surprisingly, the arrival of a stranger who expected to share their limited accommodations was greeted without enthusiasm. Oswald himself wondered to what extent Dr. Sobolewski had been aware of his brother's poverty. Was it possible that the veterinarian sent him here in part because he wanted to send a letter? In those days the mail was most unreliable.

As it happened, on receiving his brother's letter the peasant became suspicious. "Misha usually writes in Belorussian. How come he wrote in Polish?" "Perhaps," the newcomer explained, "because the letter was open and your brother knew that I do not read Belorussian, therefore he wrote it in Polish."

Unconvinced, the man continued, "And what will happen to us if you turn out to be a Jew? All strangers must register with the police, even if they stay for one night." "Of course I will register. Will you do me a favor and take me there?" Oswald felt that Sobolewski's letter gave him some protection and that a stay in Turzec could become his haven. He recalls, *I went to the police with bravado. . . . Now I felt that I had to have guts. I had no choice.*

Turzec was not important enough for direct German control. Before the war the place had no police station. With the Nazi occupation, part of the school was converted into a police station that doubled as offices and living quarters. Some of the policemen were Polish, the majority Belorussians. The unit received its orders either from the regional Belorussian police or from the Germans. Only occasionally did the Germans come to Turzec. The recent murder of the local Jews was one such important occasion.

Once a part of Poland, for more than one hundred years this section of Belorussia had been under Russian domination. The successive Tsarist regimes tried to erase all Polish cultural traces. In 1918 when Poland regained control, its government tried to reverse the process by vigorously supporting Polish influences and Poles were encouraged to come and live here. New settlements were established by Poles known as settlers. Protected by their government, the settlers had a higher social standing than the impoverished native Belorussians. As a privileged minority, however, they lived in relative harmony, with both local Jews and native Belorussians. Few if any Belorussians identified with the USSR. Instead, many aspired to a separate state. During the war, as a result of the Soviet-German treaty, this part of Belorussia again reverted to the Soviet Union. With the Russian takeover came large-scale deportations of actual or potential opponents of the regime.[1] The majority of the victims were Poles. From Russian-occupied Poland, including Belorussia, Poles "were deported in four vast railway convoys . . . in Febuary, April and June 1940 and June 1941. . . . The vast majority were convicted of no known offense but simply because the Polish nation was seen as the inveterate enemy of its Russian master."[2] It is estimated that more than a million and a half Poles were forcibly transferred to the USSR. Due to hardships, as many as one-third died.[3]

On November 6, 1941, when Oswald and Sobolewski came to the police station they were greeted by the secretary, a young Pole whose parents had fallen victim to Soviet deportations. He took the police position in the hope of avenging his family, thinking that by serving the Germans, who were the enemies of Russia, he would have the opportunity to act against the Soviet Union. Invariably, however, when such Russian opponents became members of the police, they were asked to perform tasks unrelated to the Soviet Union. Frequently too, police service involved the arrest and murder of innocent people, particularly Jews, and less frequently other natives. Because right away Oswald liked this Polish policeman, he preferred to think that he inadvertently became a tool for the Nazi machinery of destruction.

At that first meeting, as soon as Oswald was introduced to this amiable police secretary, he began to talk without giving his listener a chance to interrupt. He started with the usual story that he was born in Slesia to a Polish mother and a German father. As proof he presented his school card, making it clear that he had finished high school. He had rightly suspected that in this place not even the police commandant was likely to have a high school diploma. Education, Oswald felt, would in itself elicit respect and more considerate treatment.

Oswald then emphasized that he was sent here by his good friend Dr. Sobolewski. It was an unheard-of achievement for a poor Belorussian peasant to become a veterinarian, a doctor. Indeed, in Turzec Dr. Sobolewski was a legend. People who did not know him personally knew of him. Mothers would use him as an example to their children when they wanted to show what can happen to someone who tries hard and studies long. Because of Dr. Sobolewski's position, the natives thought that whoever he would send to them had to be worthy of special treatment. Except for the initial hypothetical suggestion made by Sobolewski's brother that Oswald might be a Jew, no one else mentioned this possibility.

That first time at the police office, to build up his case even further, Oswald let it be known that he was fluent in German. This fact, as usual, he explained by his German father. Appropriately impressed, the Polish secretary decided that the newcomer's superior standing required the attention of the commandant of the police station, a former corporal of the Polish cavalry. The commandant agreed without hesitation to Oswald's stay in Turzec.

While taking care of the formalities, the commandant told Oswald that he had an order to direct anyone who knew German to the German Army unit in the town of Stołpce. He explained that the authorities were short of interpreters and eager to employ them. This was an unforeseen development. The last thing Oswald wanted was to work closely with the Nazis. He explained that, after all, Dr. Sobolewski sent him here and wanted him to remain in Turzec, close to his family. Besides, after extensive travel, he was tired and must rest. He asked for permission to stay put for a while. Later on, he promised, he would seriously consider a move to Stołpce. His request was granted. It turned out that this police commandant was Dr. Sobolewski's friend.

Oswald's document identified him as a Pole whose mother was Polish and father German. A Pole who had one German parent, or even weaker German ties, could assume a special German nationality. Such a person could become a Volksdeutsche, an ethnic German. This new identity entitled an individual to many privileges. Some Polish opportunists were eager to change their nationality. Some even used fictitious German connections successfully. Others, despite clear-cut ties, were motivated by patriotism and stuck to their Polish nationality.

That Oswald chose to remain a Pole placed him in the category of Polish patriots. Strangely enough, even Poles who collaborated with the Nazis respected those who did not succumb to the German influences.

On that first day, Sobolewski's brother was impressed with the way the authorities treated this stranger. Whatever reservations he had seemed to evaporate after the visit to the police station. Without hesitation, he invited Oswald to come and share his hut. To the young man's thanks he said only, "Don't think about it. After all, my brother sent you here! We welcome you." Other members of the family went along good-naturedly with this decision.

Within a day the entire community of Turzec knew about the arrival of Dr. Sobolewski's protégé. They tried to find out all the details about him. Their imagination filled in the missing gaps, and much more. Some were convinced that this young man was the peasant's nephew. Others added in a whisper that he was the doctor's illegitimate son and that the name Rufeisen came from the mother. Convinced that such rumors helped legitimate his position, Oswald reacted with a mysterious noncommittal smile when asked to confirm or deny any of the stories. The Sobolewski connection formed a protective shield. Still this imposter knew that he had to be on guard. The end was always close by.

News of unceremonious killings of Jews were constantly arriving. Depending on the size of the community, the killers could be SS men, soldiers, or members of the gendarmerie, the "Schutzpolizei." As a rule the Germans were assisted by the Belorussian police, which had a sprinkling of Poles. More often than not, the murdering of Jews happened on the outskirts of villages or small towns, usually close to specially prepared graves.

Oswald could no longer ignore what was happening even though he was not sure about the pattern. He did not know if such killings were taking place in all parts of the country. Nor did he know whom the Germans intended to spare. He realized that what he had heard on his way to Turzec was right. A few days before his arrival the entire Jewish population of Turzec had indeed been murdered. After the massacre, the local police had been ordered to collect and sort out the victims' belongings. The citizens of Turzec were entitled to some of the Jewish possessions, including clothing. The Jews of Turzec were poor and what they left behind did not amount to much. The inhabitants of Turzec were also poor. For them such goods were valuable, welcome acquisitions.

As a Christian resident of the place, Oswald was entitled to some of these Jewish goods. Inadequately dressed for the November cold, he needed warm clothes. Yet he felt uneasy about asking for the belongings of the dead. He hesitated. In the end after considerable soul searching he joined the others explaining: *I came to feel that if anyone had a right to these Jewish goods it was I. I had a special right to these things more than anyone else. For I was also a suffering Jew! . . . Besides, I needed the clothes very much. It also occurred to me that by asking for Jewish things I would add to my legitimacy as a Pole. No one who asked for such things would be suspected of being a Jew. No Jew would have had the guts to do that. At that point I was already sliding into my new role. This was a part of the game.*

From the very beginning, Oswald was aware that his stay with the Sobolewskis burdened his hosts. This family head had ten mouths to feed and certainly did not need an extra one. Nor were the overcrowded living quarters conducive to overnight guests. Therefore, soon after Oswald arrived he started working as a shoemaker. With borrowed, primitive tools, Oswald moved from house to house fixing shoes for entire peasant families. No money changed hands. The local population was too poor for that. Instead, the shoemaker was paid with meals. This, however, was only a partial solution. Oswald let it be known that he was eager to find work that would entitle him to shelter. Within a few days, he was offered and accepted the position of school janitor. As a janitor he could move out of the Sobolewski hut and into a small room in the school. There Oswald shared a wall with the head of the local police, who continued to treat him with special consideration.

About the new job Oswald says, *I had to sweep all classrooms. I had to cut wood. Then I had to bring the wood to the classes, start a fire in all the ovens. . . . There were two of us, two janitors. My partner was a Russian prisoner of war. The school did not give us food or money. For meals we would go to the parents of the school children. Each time to a different family. This was the start. They were just beginning to organize the place and there were no funds to cover any of the school's expenses. . . . We worked long hours, just to keep the place going.*

Whenever a German came to Turzec or the police could not decipher a German letter, they would call Oswald to perform the duties of translator. These tasks he did gladly. The policemen in turn felt indebted to him—in and of itself a positive development.

Both the local authorities and everyone else knew that Oswald's qualifications entitled him to a better position. Still, this was wartime. Those who did not want to collaborate with or work for the occupational forces took whatever work they could get. Oswald's reluctance to go to Stołpce as a police translator was interpreted by some as an act of patriotism. Many other civilians refused to become associated with the authorities and were respected for it by the general population.

In no time Oswald won the support and approval of the community, but one notable exception was an old Belorussian peasant. He was an uneducated man who spent a few years in Germany during World War I as a prisoner of war. On his return to Turzec he decided to become a teacher of German in the local school. For many years, others were unaware about his inadequate knowledge of the German language. The arrival of this young janitor posed a potential threat. The Belorussian peasant was convinced that the newcomer would usurp his teaching position, that he would lose the job he came to love.

The old man began to spread rumors against Oswald, among them a suggestion that the new school janitor might be Jewish. At least this is how Oswald explained the special visit to Turzec by the Belorussian head of the regional police, Siemion Serafimowicz.

A native of this region, Serafimowicz had worked as a mill hand before the war. The owner of the mill was Jewish. Sometime before World War II, eager for adventure and advancement, Serafimowicz had enlisted into the Polish cavalry. He ended his military career as a sergeant.[4] Under the German occupation he became the head of the regional Belorussian police, with headquarters in Mir. He was in charge of four police stations, including the one in Turzec. Most of the policemen were Belorussian.

In his early thirties, Serafimowicz was a tall man with an imposing presence. To his large, but graceful frame belonged a deep voice. Those who had even casual dealings with the man knew that his physical strength was matched by a strong personality. His manner projected a mixture of self-assurance and impatience. Still, Siemion's handsome, intelligent face had a reddish complexion that betrayed signs of alcoholic ravages. It was an open secret that the head of the regional police was a drunkard, often given to fits of violence. When sober he could easily modulate his behavior from docile submission to severe commands.

Oswald describes him as *uneducated but an exceptionally intelligent man. He had charm. He had many friends and he knew how to deal with people. He had a charismatic influence over his policemen—they followed him willingly, almost blindly. He spoke Polish well, he knew Belorussian and some Russian. He never learned German . . . lack of education, no doubt, interfered with his promotion in the Polish cavalry.*

For years Siemion was in love with a beautiful daughter of Polish settlers, of the Juszkiewcz family. The family came to the area in the 1920s. Through them, as through all the other settlers, the Polish government tried to Polonize the region. As a Belorussian and a man with little education Siemion was an unsuitable match for a settler's daughter. While the Juszkiewiczs welcomed his attention and friendship, marriage was another matter. The girl's parents were opposed, and she in turn, though attracted to the handsome suitor, did not dare follow her personal inclinations. Unwilling to accept defeat, Serafimowicz continued to court both the girl and her parents. He loved the girl and admired her family. He was always ready to help them, always ready to do favors.

Impatient by nature, Serafimowicz was very patient when it came to the woman he loved. He was convinced that time was on his side. He waited. When in 1939 the Soviets occupied the region and deported many of the Polish inhabitants to camps in Russia, the girl Serafimowicz wanted to marry, one of her sisters, and her parents were among the deportees. Shaken, Siemion turned to the two remaining sisters, who had somehow managed to avoid the deportation. The older of the two, Jadwiga, in her mid-twenties, resembled the sister Serafimowicz loved. The younger one, Wanda, was twenty-three. Parental absence together with the political upheavals minimized the social distinctions between them. Besides, the two women were grateful for Siemion's protection. Eventually, the older one fell in love with Serafimowicz. The two married, and Wanda joined their household.

When the Soviets were about to lose control over the region, Serafimowicz was delighted to see them retreat in a panic. He welcomed the change. For him the Russians were the real enemies. In fact, he was eager to take revenge for what the Russians did to his beloved. Cooperation with the Germans, he felt, would give him an opportunity to pay back the Soviets for their injustices. Serafimowicz's hate of the Russians prompted him to enter Nazi service.

Serafimowicz was an impulsive man. Oswald feels that *because the Germans opposed the Russians and the Jews, Serafimowicz accepted their policies toward both. Personally he had no special resentment toward the Jews. Neither was he a pathological murderer, as some of the others were. Once he started on what to him was an anti-Communist path he continued. Once he began, he did not look for a way out.*

Three weeks after Oswald's arrival in Turzec, when he was splitting wood for the school ovens, a child rushed up to him. "The chief of police is waiting for you, come fast!" Running after the boy, Oswald soon stopped in front of a horseback rider: Siemion Serafimowicz. The tightly fitting uniform only enhanced his looks and authoritative bearing. The short, poorly dressed young man, out of breath, standing in front of this impressive looking rider underlined the very uneven nature of their relationship.

Nor did the opening remarks of the older man help equalize their respective positions: "What is your name and why are you breathing so heavily? Are you afraid?"

"I am not afraid. I was cutting wood and then I ran here. That accounts for my heavy breathing. My name is Oswald Rufeisen."

"Well 'Ruf' sounds German, but 'Eisik' is Jewish. Are you Jewish?"

"It is 'eisen' and it is a German name. My father was German and my mother Polish."

Oswald took out his document as he started to tell the same story he had already told so many others. Impatiently, Serafimowicz interrupted. "Do you know German?"

"Yes, I do."

"Well then tell me what you just said in German."

After a few sentences the older man stopped him. Jews, especially from eastern parts of Poland, had a special German accent that could easily identify them as Jews. Oswald recalls that Serafimowicz must have been satisfied with the quality of his speech because *right away he asked me if I was ready to go with him to Mir to become his teacher and interpreter of German. This was the second offer of a position somehow connected to the police. I realized with sorrow that either I would have to run away or accept his proposition. Still I tried to get out of it. I told him that I worked hard and honestly earned my bread. "At your place I will work little and will simply be fed by you." To this he said: "This is my business, not yours. I will give you until tomorrow to think it over. If you agree, we will leave tomorrow."*

Oswald was distressed. He did not want to work for or with Nazi collaborators. The idea of cooperating and being close to those who tortured and murdered innocent people was repugnant to him. Yet he also knew that if he wanted to stay in this area he had to agree to this proposition. Staying and rejecting the offer might lead to discovery. Oswald wanted to live. Jews, he felt, had an obligation to live. To live, yes, but at what price?

Had Oswald considered the possibility that by working for Serafimowicz he might be involved in killings? *I did not think about killings. No! First of all he had asked me to be his private teacher and interpreter. However, it did occur to me that it might involve more than just teaching. Let me tell you as it really was. I wanted to avoid going with him. But when I saw that there was no other way, I accepted it as a kind of providence. Somehow I felt that someone was guiding me.*

At the same time Oswald felt he could not justify his association with Nazi collaborators by his personal survival alone. The thought occurred to him that if he became Serafimowicz's teacher and interpreter he would have to do everything in his power not only to save himself but also to save others. Oswald explains, *I knew that if I would accept the job only to save myself I could not face myself or my brother . . . I did not want to be ashamed of myself.*

He had a day to think it over and says, *I could have run away, but where to? The entire area was strange to me. I came there as a stranger. I was even strange and different from the local Jews. I spoke no Yiddish, my accent was different. I was definitely out of place. I had nowhere to go. On the other hand, I knew that if I agreed to this job I myself would be responsible for all my deeds, for everything. I don't want to seem like a hero. Somehow I took the risk with the hope that I could help. Surely, had I refused the job they might have suspected me. . . . On the other hand, if I had this kind of a position I might be able to do something for people. I did not know what shape this position would take. Although not clearly, I realized that I would have the opportunity to help. First I had to gain this man's confidence. This I knew from the start.*

Toward the evening Oswald was still vacillating. *If tomorrow he meets me and asks again then I will go with him. I will try to save whomever I can. Who knows, I told myself, maybe I will succeed. I knew that I would try to save Jewish lives and non-Jewish lives. In my Zionist organization, Akiva, we pursued a pacifist philosophy. We were taught to respect life, all life, regardless of nationality, regardless of religion . . . in my home too there was the same atmosphere. I was determined to fight only in order to preserve life.*

That night, in bed, Oswald could hear disjointed noises from the other side of the wall. The local chief of police and Serafimowicz were drinking. Boisterous shouts, laughter, and loud singing continued to pour into the janitor's room. The commotion lasted for hours. But then it was followed by loud, irregular snoring. On one side of the wall, a lonely Jewish youth was imploring fate. *Because of this heavy drinking Serafimowicz may forget that he spoke to me. . . . Perhaps not all the policemen are murderers? Could it be that some of them are decent people? . . . I must let chance be the deciding force. If he still remembers tomorrow I will say yes. If I go with him, I will have to fight, not only for my life but for the lives of others. This is what I thought that night. Up to that time I was escaping the enemy, trying to save myself. Now, for the first time, I felt that I might have the opportunity to do something positive for others. There were risks. I accepted them . . . I make decisions fast and I don't regret them.* Eventually he was overcome by sleep.

Next day, when Oswald was returning from lunch, from the opposite direction he saw Serafimowicz on his horse. The horse stopped right in front of the janitor. "Well? Are you coming?"

"If you think that I could be useful, I will come."

Soon the Jewish youth and the head of the regional Belorussian police were on their way to Mir.

6

The Town of Mir

Mir, the small town Oswald was coming to, had a long history that extended for over 600 years. From the sixteenth to the nineteenth century, the town and its surrounding lands belonged to the Radziwiłłs, Polish and Lithuanian princes, known for their religious tolerance, a tolerance particularly beneficial for the Jews.

In the nineteenth century, through the marriage of a Radziwiłł princess, these possessions passed to the Russian aristocrats, the Mirskis, and remained with this family till the Nazi takeover. The last prince, Światopełk Mirski, a vigorous opponent of the Russian revolution, fled from the place in 1917. Much later, during World War II, consumed by his hatred for the Soviets, he collaborated with Nazi Germany. To escape punishment, after 1945, the prince settled in Spain and died there a few years later.[1]

When in the fall of 1941 Oswald came to Mir, the only tangible reminder of the town's aristocratic past was an ancient castle on the outskirts of town. Surrounded by a thick stone wall, it had one big gate and a number of small openings high up in the wall. The entire place had the appearance of a fortress rather than a castle. Inside this stone wall, the castle itself consisted of several buildings that hugged the three sides of a large courtyard. Since 1917 only a handful of former servants occupied a small section of this huge structure. The rest, virtually the entire castle, was empty, unattended, and thus exposed to the ravages of time. By the 1940s, partly in ruin, the place took on a gloomy and neglected appearance.

Not as concerned about political upheavals as Prince Mirski, the rest of the local population coped with the political changes by clinging to their respective traditions. Historically, Mir and its surroundings had a culturally mixed population. According to a 1921 census, almost 4000 people lived in Mir. Of this figure the Jews were a majority (55% or 2,074).[2] First mentioned in the seventeenth century, Jews were credited with making Mir an important commercial center. Twice a year the town hosted fairs that attracted large numbers of people, not only from the immediate surroundings but also from faraway places in Poland, Lithuania, and Germany.[3]

Not limiting their occupations to commerce, a large proportion of the Jews were skilled craftsmen: tailors, shoemakers, carpenters, and others. Some Jews devoted their lives to Jewish scholarship and religious pursuits. This last group in 1815 established a Yeshiva that soon became an important seat for orthodox learning. As a celebrated center of study, the Yeshiva attracted prominent rabbinical scholars and outstanding students.[4]

Mir's varied Jewish population included merchants, mostly petty merchants, different kinds of craftsmen and orthodox Jews, many associated with the prestigious Yeshiva. A few Jews who lived close to and around Mir were farmers. Some combined farming with crafts. Regardless of their occupations, most had to struggle even for a modest living.

The second largest ethnic group were the Belorussians. With a long local history, they had deep roots in this area. Strongly attached to the land, most were involved in agriculture. The majority had limited land holdings. Among those who owned no land were some tenants who leased farms from Polish landowners. Others worked as hired farm hands. Only a small minority were craftsmen or merchants. As a group the Belorussians were economically disadvantaged.

Most Poles in Belorussia came after 1918, at the urgings of the Polish government trying to Polonize these newly recovered lands. Supported by and at least informally representing their government, Poles in this part of the country enjoyed more prestige than the rest of the population. Most were identified with the so-called intelligentsia. This label applied to school principals, government officials, the clergy, and members of the minor nobility. In this last group were Polish landowners, with estates close or adjacent to Mir and their estate administrators. Usually these estate administrators owned no land. In this part of the country Poles were a definite minority.[5]

As they continued to live in relative harmony, the Belorussians, the Jews, and the Poles each had a place of their own. A lack of overt hostility, however, did not necessarily suggest the presence of meaningful social ties. Instead, each group lived in a separate world; each concentrated on perpetuating its own customs and traditions. Contacts between members of these groups were commercial rather than social.

This peaceful coexistence was disturbed by an upsurge in Polish anti-

Semitism in the 1920s during the Polish–Russian struggle.[6] Victorious Polish troops, under the command of General Haller, entered Mir, attacked Jews and their property, and encouraged the local population to do the same. Some became eager participants in these anti-Jewish moves. Soon these violent outbursts were followed by more orderly political and economic discrimination that eventually led to boycotts of Jewish businesses.[7]

One consequence of these hostile measures was a greater political awareness among younger Jews. Socialist and Zionist organizations flourished. Whereas the Socialists supported a change in Poland's political system, the much more numerous Zionists advocated emigration and the establishment of a national state in Palestine. Separated from these two positions were those associated with the Yeshiva and most other orthodox Jews. Some of them vigorously objected to such secular ideologies.[8]

With World War II, political preoccupations underwent drastic changes. From the fall of 1939 till the summer of 1941 the Soviets tried to politicize the region. For this they used two basic methods. First, they eliminated what they considered to be political opponents, deporting them to Siberia. More often, those they defined as enemies of the Communist system were innocent people, usually politically uninvolved. Second, they kept stimulating a great deal of political activity with the special show of democratic procedures. Thus, they kept introducing new measures, whose real purpose was to curtail freedom but which they presented as resulting in special benefits. Voting on all these measures was compulsory. The outcome was predictable. Invariably over 90% "voted" in support of any and all such proposals.[9]

These political efforts came to an abrupt stop when on June 22, 1941, Germany attacked Russia. By June 27, 1941, German troops were in full control of this region. For the Jews in particular Nazi occupation transformed all political issues into questions of life and death. Right away the Germans accused many Jews of Communist collaboration. It mattered little that such accusations were rarely if ever based on reality. The accused were executed.[10]

The SS (Schutzstaffel) was in charge of the region. With headquarters in nearby larger towns, Stołpce and Baranowicze, the SS came to Mir only to conduct business, usually when issuing special orders. One such early order called for the establishment of a Jewish Council, a "Judenrat" that was to include former community leaders. The stated purpose of this representative body was to serve as an intermediary between the Germans and the Jewish community. In reality, however, members of the council were expected to fulfill all Nazi demands, regardless of how they or those they were representing felt about them. Noncompliance led to severe punishments, even executions.[11]

In one of the early moves, the SS ordered the Judenrat to collect and deliver radios, furs, jewlery, gold, and other valuables. As soon as the Jews fulfilled this demand the SS came up with another and then yet another request. Basically poor, the Jewish community had a hard time satisfying the ever-increasing Nazi appetite.

In a more stable and predictable move the Germans made the Judenrat responsible for delivering a quota of laborers. This meant that each day a certain number of Jews was forced to work not only for the Germans but for local Christian civilians as well. Thus, for example, if a peasant needed a farm hand he could register with the magistrate, pay a set fee, and a Jewish laborer would be delivered to him. Officially, no money changed hands between employer and employee. It was vaguely assumed that a Jewish worker was entitled to food. But neither the kind nor the amount was specified. The offer of food was left to the employer's discretion.

The Germans gave little food; what there was was of poor quality. Frequently, German employers would physically abuse their workers. Some Jews were severely beaten; some were even murdered. When this happened no one would appeal. Jews had no rights.

Among civilian employers physical abuse was practically unheard of. They also fed their workers much better than their German counterparts. Not surprisingly, those who were sent for forced labor preferred to work for civilians. None of them could choose, however. They had to take all jobs offered. Again refusal to do so could lead to severe punishment, even death. In the region of Mir, as in all other Nazi-occupied places, many Jews clung to the idea that employment, approved of by the Germans, would shield them from danger.

Convictions about the protective power of employment refused to go away. Even when rumors and then definite accounts about mass executions of Jews from surrounding towns and villages had come to Mir, people were not ready to accept them. At first these reports were not believed at all. When both the actual events and the witnesses multiplied, making denial difficult, people wanted to know the reasons; they were searching for explanations. They could neither accept nor absorb the idea that the only reason for these killings was the victims' Jewishness. Similarly, they could not grasp that these executions were a part of an overall policy. Instead they continued to see them as exceptions and to hope that this would not happen to them.

Before Oswald came to Mir an event put a partial stop to some of these doubts and hopes. It began at dawn, on a wet foggy Sunday, on November 9, 1941. The dark stillness of that morning was interrupted by shots. People jumped out of their beds only to realize that they could not go far. Jewish houses were surrounded by German soldiers and more soldiers were approaching from several directions. As they came closer, highly agitated, furiously, abusively, they ordered the Jews out of their dwellings. Mixed in with their screams were indiscriminate, haphazard shootings. The noise level was rising rapidly, as was the overall confusion. It was as if the screamings and the shootings were locked in a competitive battle. In this strange contest the Jews were the definite losers.

Those who had come out into the streets began to run in circles, trying to avoid the flying bullets. For many these efforts were useless. Hit by ammunition, they fell. Some had wanted to get up. Some of them fell again. Among those hit, the fortunate ones died right away. The injured, unable to move, stayed wherever they happened to fall. Unlike the dead, their lives were coming to a slower, more painful end. As the chaotic screaming, shooting, and running continued, more and more bodies could be seen scattered all over.

Even in this raging confusion there was a hint of order. At one point, some of the fuming soldiers burst into the Judenrat building. Inside they kept shooting in all directions, destroying furniture and everything else in their way. The same indiscriminant wreckage took place in private dwellings where the attackers kept searching for hidden Jews. Whomever they came upon they would execute on the spot. No questions were asked. No explanations were listened to.

Later, those Jews who reached the streets on their own and had managed to avoid the bullets were ordered to assemble in the marketplace. They tried to follow these orders, moving in that direction. Many never made it. Instead, on their way they were hit by bullets that uninterruptedly poured in from all sides. Inevitably, on their way to the market, some of the Jews came face to face with their murderers who refused to budge from their determination to kill.

With guns in hand, as if drunk with their "successes," craving more prey, these soldiers easily overpowered the helpless, unarmed Jews who desperately wanted to elude death. It was an uneven match. Moreover, it had not mattered at all whether the hunted did or did not comply with the orders. The outcome was the same: more destruction, more death. The streets were covered with the dead and the dying, yet more bodies were added on.

Full daylight came. With daylight the crimes became more glaringly visible. The killers were unmoved. The slaughter continued. It went on and on.

Within this sea of devastation there were some gestures of solidarity and compassion.

At the very beginning, disregarding their own safety, the cantor and the rabbi's son-in-law ran through the streets calling in suppressed, yet weeping voices, "Jews come out to your slaughter!" This was their way of warning about the imminent danger. They wanted to alert the people to the threat, hoping that somehow some will succeed in eluding the enemy. Some did. A few escaped by hiding with or without help from their Christian neighbors. Among those protected by Christian neighbors was the rabbi's wife.[12]

Mir had a convent of the Order of the Sisters of the Resurrection where four Polish nuns lived. During the day of destruction a number of Jews found shelter there. The frantic soldiers overlooked the place, as they did all other non-Jewish quarters.

During the Russian occupation, because of the spaciousness of the convent and the Soviet persecution of Poles, the Catholic priest, the Dean Antoni Mackiewicz, and his sister had decided to move in with the nuns. On November 9 some Jewish families came to the door of the convent. Mackiewicz let them in. Inside they pleaded: "Please have mercy on us, hide us!" "Because of my position I am not allowed to lie. If the Germans will ask me if there are Jews in my house, I will not be able to deny it. But in the yard there is a stable, a pig sty, a barn. All these places are open. I am not responsible for what is in the yard. Go out there. I don't want to know about it." The fugitives understood, they scattered and hid in all those places. They were spared. A few eventually managed to survive the war.[13]

For the rest of the onslaught Mackiewicz stood close to the window that faced the main road. Bewildered, helpless, unable to move, he watched. His eyes had a faraway strange look. As if transfixed, he seemed unaware of the silent tears that kept running down his cheeks.

Outside, amid violent shoving and screaming, those who reached the marketplace were made to stand in rows. Then they were separated into two groups: able-bodied craftsmen and skilled workers, and a much larger group made up of the rest. When the Germans finished sorting them out, they turned to the larger group. In full view they began to shoot them one by one.

The rabbi was among those who were soon to die. Old and fragile, he was known for his timidity and retiring manner. But now, on the threshold of death, his shyness seemed to have left him. Concentrating only on the condemned, the rabbi circulated among them explaining in a vigorous, yet comforting voice that the approaching death was God's will. He urged the people to submit to His will with dignity and without fear. As he continued to move and speak, a spiritual strength seemed to emanate from his weak body, a gentle but sad smile accompanied his simple words. Those he spoke to listened. Some nodded in agreement. Some managed to return his smile. Others were too bewildered to react, but they too seemed to listen. None ignored him. And when a bullet reached the old man's feeble, thin body, noiselessly it fell to the ground.

When it was over 1500 Jews were dead, 850 remained alive.[14]

That day, still in Turzec, Oswald could hear shooting sounds. Careful not to appear too concerned, too involved, he asked what these noises meant. At first no one knew. But even later on, when more specific news did come, people were reluctant to discuss them. He was only told that terrible things were happening to the Jews of Mir. Nothing else was said. Much later, in Mir, from some of the policemen, Oswald heard detailed descriptions about the November 9 "Aktion." Within the context of Jewish destruction Aktion meant outright executions or concentration-camp deportations. As such, these events were not extraordinary. No doubt Oswald learned about this Aktion only because it was unusual—unusual not in the number of the dead but in the chaotic, disorderly way in which it happened.

In this case, most of the killers were German soldiers who had recently returned from the Russian front. Because these men had experienced military losses, they were angry and looking for ways to vent their pent-up frustrations. A Jew hunt seemed like an appropriate outlet. In charge of this region, the SS wholeheartedly approved of such an idea and some SS men eagerly participated in the slaughter.

After they stopped the killings the town became frighteningly silent. None of the residents ventured out. The streets were filled with dead bodies sprawled in total disarray. The sidewalks, the roads, even the walls of houses were splattered with blood. No one knew how many of the dead died right away, how many died of their wounds. No one knew who among the dead might have been saved had they been attended to. No one knew and no one dared to ask such questions. In fact, no one asked any questions at all. People were too stunned.[15]

In mid-morning the oppressive silence was broken by the appearance of a group of German gendarmes, led by "Polizei Meister" Reinhold Hein. They came to inspect. Hein was the new boss who would be responsible for keeping order both in Mir and its surrounding region. Directly under Hein's command were twelve gendarmes. In addition, his authority extended over the entire regional and local Belorussian officials. Meister Hein, a noncommissioned officer, was in turn responsible to, and had to take orders from, higher German authorities, the SS who resided in two larger towns: Baranowicze and Minsk.

Meister Hein's unit was a part of the Schutzpolizei-Gendarmerie that was entrusted with keeping order in cities and rural areas. In their case, keeping order meant adhering to Nazi policies, not only as these touched on public disturbances, but also in dealing with special groups such as Jews, Communists, and others.[16]

Unlike the men he commanded, Meister Hein was a professional policeman with twenty-eight years' experience. A dedicated policeman, his limited education kept him at the position of Meister, the highest police rank for a noncommissioned officer. Though born in Neusalz an der Oder, close to Poland's southwest border, his knowledge about Poland was limited as was his level of curiosity about that country or most other matters. He was a man of action, not a man of ideas.

In his late forties, Hein was a tall, ascetic-looking man, with a strong sense of discipline supported by an equally strong sense of duty. These two traits were topped with a deep commitment to order. Hein tried to follow commands without inflicting unnecessary pain. He abhorred the use of sadistic methods that served no other purpose except to hurt. He found equally objectionable chaos and disorder. The two most important principles that governed his life were a love for order and a sense of duty.

When on November 10, 1941, Meister Hein came to Mir he was appalled by the ghastly conditions. Wherever he turned he saw definite proof of chaotic and haphazard executions. He objected, insisting that what happened there was "eine Schweinerei," disgusting. After all, when he was responsible for an Aktion the Jews were led to their graves in an orderly fashion! They were shot in an equally orderly fashion. There was no mess.[17] What happened in Mir he felt was inexcusable; he personally would have never tolerated such undisciplined conduct.

Now in charge, he was determined to reestablish order. He was convinced that by doing away with haphazard actions he would improve the quality of life. This he hoped to achieve without having to pay too much attention to the specific content of the policies he would be implementing.

By the time Oswald came to Mir, on November 27, 1941, Meister Hein was in full control. The victims of the last massacre were buried in two collective graves on the outskirts of town. With the decomposition of the dead bodies the soil continued to settle, creating movement. To an observer the place gave an eerie impression, as if the buried were still alive.

When Oswald went to visit the grave for the first time he vowed not to go back. But he returned several times.

After Hein took care of the dead he turned his attention to the living. Jews who survived the last Aktion had to move into a special area of town that separated them more fully from the rest of the population. To accomplish this some Belorussian peasants had to vacate their huts. Those who did were assigned to vacated Jewish homes. The peasants resented the change. For them this move frequently involved leaving behind pig stys, barns, and similar structures.

True to the established Nazi tradition, these new Jewish quarters were extremely crowded, sometimes with as many as fifteen people assigned to a room. In addition, Jewish movement became limited to specific places and times. Still, the Jewish living section of town was not surrounded by walls or wires, nor was it carefully watched. Partly because of this "liberal" policy, Jews were sometimes attacked in their own homes. Some were robbed and severely beaten by policemen, civilians, or both. Such incidents were almost never reported to the authorities. No one would have done anything if they were.

On balance, however, most contacts between the Jewish and Christian neighbors were beneficial. This was particularly true for the exchange of goods. And so, local peasants supplied the Jews with farm products, while the Jews offered the peasants used clothes, furniture, and all kinds of other personal belongings. Both partners to these exchanges were poor. Both were eager to receive the goods the other had. These transactions continued. Even though they reduced starvation among the Jews, they could not eliminate hunger. And so, under extremely overcrowded conditions, with little food, often assigned jobs such as the repairing and cleaning of roads, and other kinds of manual, unwanted jobs, the Jews worked hard, very hard. They refused to give up hope and continued to cling to the idea that their labors would keep them alive.

Mir was a mixture of rural and urban conditions. Many peasants had their huts close to town which in turn were surrounded by small farm holdings. One major road ran through the middle of the community, cutting it in half. This main road continued beyond Mir, leading into the bigger town Nowogródek through Turzec. Within Mir a number of side streets converged into this one central road; these either began or ended somewhere next to an agricultural field. Thus, distinctions between peasant and town dwellings were minimal. Besides, most houses, even those on the main road, were surrounded by gardens. Close to some of these dwellings were pig stys, cow sheds, stables, and barns.

None of the homes had running water. Instead, people drew water from wells that could be easily recognized by a round or square wooden structure built over and above the ground. Not all houses had wells. Sometimes a well was shared by two or three families.

Indoor plumbing was nonexistent—people had outhouses. These were more numerous than wells, with each one attached to an individual household.

Mir definitely was a small place. On a bicycle one could move from one end of town to another in less than five minutes. On entering Mir's main road from the south, on the right-hand side, one was greeted by a house that belonged to Polish settlers, the Balickis. This family consisted of a married couple and their three daughters, ranging in age from 17 to 21. Before the war Mr. Balicki was the principal of the local public school. This job together with his Polish background placed him in the ranks of the local Polish intelligentsia.

The Balicki's three-room house was spacious when compared to most other dwellings. A garden surrounded the main living quarters and beyond it stood a pig sty for pigs and poultry.

Close to their place, in a modest hut, lived a young Pole, Karol, who earned a living by taking care of horses.[18] After the German gendarmes settled in Mir Karol ended up working for them.

Further up the major road, still on the right-hand side, was the convent. It was an eleven-room building with a garden on one side and a courtyard on the other. To the side of the courtyard was a barn and next to it a well. The entire convent was surrounded by a fence with two gates. One opened into the main street, the other into a small countrylike road, close to the fields.

When the Meister saw the convent he decided it could serve well both as a police station and as living quarters for him and his men. Though a Catholic, the only one among the gendarmes, he had no qualms about ordering the nuns to vacate their home. The women had to move to a house next to the convent. This was a Jewish house whose owners had been massacred in the November 9 Aktion. Because the new dwelling assigned to the nuns had no well, Hein offered them access to his water. At that time the priest and his sister moved back to their old place close to the church.

Farther, on the same side of the street, were the living quarters of the Belorussian police. Across from them, on the opposite side of the road, was a building reserved for German soldiers who, for various reasons, and for different amounts of time, would come to stay in Mir. In the winter of 1942 a team of communication specialists was stationed there. This group stayed longer than most others, till the very end of the summer of 1942.

Close to the soldiers' quarters was a place that housed the regional civilian administration of Mir. The regional mayor, Bielanowicz, was a greedy opportunist, ruthless in his dealings with people, particularly Jews and Poles. To the Jews he kept making wild promises, promises he could never keep. Unofficially he would receive a monthly retainer from the Judenrat. Whenever he wanted more money he would tell the Jews about a fictitious threat and then demand extra payment for averting the "disaster."

Although half Belorussian and half Polish, he resented the Poles and plotted against them. Later on it was rumored that he was responsible for a deportation of the Polish intelligentsia.[19] It seems that whatever loyalties he had applied to him alone and no one else.

In addition to Bielanowicz there was a local mayor whose authority was limited to the affairs of Mir. The offices of this local mayor were next to those of the regional mayor.

Finally, the main road led to the Serafimowicz home. It was shared by his wife, Jadwiga, his sister-in-law, Wanda, and his illegitimate son, Sasza, thirteen years old.

How did Oswald fit into his future home?

7

Becoming a Police Officer

Once more Oswald was moving into the unknown. Filled with anxious doubts he began to argue with himself: "Don't torture yourself! Let things happen. You can do nothing about it. Don't react, no matter what! Just wait and see."

Still he knew he would have to go beyond such generalities, that he would have to devise a strategy. First, he would have to convince others of his new identity. They would have to accept that he was part Polish and part German. Next he knew that he would have to establish himself as a valuable worker. But he was apprehensive; from now on he would be in close contact with the authorities and was anxious about this.

Caution, patience, self-assurance were the answer. How much of each? What was the proper proportion? Anxiety and doubts returned. Once more these emotions were ready to fight his earlier, more measured resolutions. It was as if his feelings and thoughts were locked in battle. Soon he went back to the beginning, resolving once more to be patient, cautious, self-assured. Superimposed on all this inner turmoil was a determination to succeed. But success too could mean many things. He returned to the problems of identity and work. They must come first. Perhaps, later on, all else will fall into place? Perhaps.

As emotions had given way to calmer thoughts Oswald's attention turned to the man at his side. In this impressive-looking official he recognized a potentially powerful ally. As soon as Serafimowicz's initial suspicions about Oswald's Jewish background were dispelled, the commandant transferred to this stranger the special admiration and respect he had for the Polish people.

Uneducated himself but highly intelligent, Serafimowicz appreciated education. He also recognized that this young man had qualities that went beyond mere intelligence and formal schooling. The attentiveness with which Oswald listened, the curiosity that was implied in his questions, together with his modesty, impressed the policeman.

Himself from a humble Belorussian background, Serafimowicz aspired to better things. He married a daughter of Polish settlers, someone socially above him. As head of the regional police, he had already reached a higher position than he had hoped for.

The German occupation had certainly offered unusual opportunities for advancement. He had accomplished much. But this only whetted his appetite. He continued to be frustrated and hungry for more. Serafimowicz was convinced that by excelling on the job, and, specifically, by following German orders, he would be able to fulfill his ambitions. When they wanted him to kill Jews, he did it almost indifferently. When they wanted him to find Communists and murder them, he did it gladly. All Russians, and by extension all Communists, were his enemies, for it was the Russian Communists who had deported the woman he loved. This he could neither forget nor forgive.

He was an impatient, at times violent man and he drank. When drunk, he became cruel and unmanageable. He was fortunate that after each drinking spree his robust constitution helped him recover quickly. Within a few hours he could be in full control of his senses. His job performance, therefore, suffered little from his frequent binges.

Serafimowicz was shrewd. To him problem solving was easy. His innate ability together with his willingness to take direction from the Germans made him an asset. The Nazis appreciated this eager collaborator. As a charismatic leader, he knew how to make his men follow orders. In Mir, he had twelve to fourteen policemen under his direct command. Unlike their chief, none of these men was ambitious. They saw in the position of a policeman an opportunity for steady income and easy work. The less work the better they liked it. Poorly educated, without special skills, unwilling to make an effort, these policemen were failures, described by some as social misfits.[1]

Serafimowicz knew that the youth he was bringing home was superior to any of his men. Besides, in this part of the country German interpreters were rare. Intelligent, amiable interpreters were practically nonexistent. However one looked at it, the older man had reason to be satisfied with his find.

To those who knew him, Oswald gave the impression of someone who was intelligent, soft-spoken, and eager to do things for others. Less visible were some of his other qualities, those that suggested a complex human being, not easily understood or described. Among such special qualities was Oswald's relationship to fear. When faced with danger he was able to suppress all expressions and signs of fear. Mixed in with this ability was a determination to risk and win. All were guided by caution. Oswald knew when to accept defeat, when not to risk, and when to be careful.

If and when fear did make its appearance, it came as a delayed reaction, usually when the danger had already passed. Oswald attributes this ability to seem unafraid not so much to actual fearlessness but rather to his special reaction to danger signals. Till this day, when faced with sudden threats, his responses are quick and followed closely by equally quick decisions.

For Jews who tried to conceal their identity, appearing calm and composed was a tremendous asset. Fear, uncertainty, hesitation could give away "passing" Jews. Oswald was relatively free of these burdens. The more accusations about his Jewishness he faced, the more self-assured he became and the more easily he could handle the situation. Such encounters offered him the opportunity to practice the part he had to play.

Whenever confronted by threats, Oswald's self-assurance dissolved whatever suspicions people had. In his case, most accusations were made right after the first meeting. With more contacts people gave up their initial impression. This suggests that Oswald's physical appearance rather than his behavior was responsible for the early charges of Jewishness.[2]

Probably because his speech and manners did not conform to Jewish stereotypes they in turn helped dispel the initial suspicions about his origin. A gifted linguist, Oswald's use of the Polish language was faultless, even elegant. In Belorussia in particular, where Jewish assimilation was low, people did not expect a Jew to have such a perfect command of the language. No doubt these expectations were of considerable help to Oswald.

As most other Jews who were passing for Polish Christians, he was most frequently identified by the natives, Poles and Belorussians. Sensitive to their own cultural nuances, they could easily distinguish a Jew from a non-Jew. In contrast, as strangers to this country, the Germans had a hard time deciding who was a Jew. For this task they needed the cultural knowhow of the natives. Jews who lived illegally in the forbidden Christian world were particularly afraid of those who could easily recognize them.[3] Oswald was no exception. Although fortunate because his face registered no fear, he had to be on guard.

In Mir, the first person Oswald met was Jadwiga, the Polish wife of the head of the regional police. After what seemed like a casual glance, she turned to her husband: "How come you brought this Jew with you?" This she said with genuine surprise, without malice and without anger. With a bemused chuckle Serafimowicz corrected her: "He is not a Jew. He is half German and half Polish. He will stay with us and teach me German." Outwardly calm Oswald thought, "Here it comes again!" He said nothing. The conversation moved to other topics. At least for the moment the issue was dropped. "Was she convinced? Or was it not important for her to pursue?" Oswald tried to guess as he turned his attention to what was happening around him.

From the outset Serafimowicz made it clear that he valued his teacher and asked that the room of his illegitimate son be vacated for the guest. The boy was to move into the room of Jadwiga's younger sister, Wanda. That first day Serafimowicz invited the newcomer for a family supper and announced that Oswald's job included room and board.

Shy, particularly in the presence of his strong and overbearing father, Sasza was a gentle and obedient boy of thirteen. From the moment he met Oswald he took a liking to him, recognizing that unlike his father, this stranger listened patiently to what others had to say. Sasza was also impressed by his father's obvious approval of this guest. Oswald was drawn to this quiet boy who kept eyeing him throughout that first evening. Both were outsiders; Sasza, an illegitimate child; Oswald, a passing Jew. Eventually the two became friends. In a very short time Oswald also made a friend out of Wanda. Though not as beautiful as her sister Jadwiga, Wanda had a pleasant open face. That first day she welcomed Oswald with a smile and a vigorous handshake; her whole manner was direct and unassuming.

A Slavic language, Belorussian is similar to Polish. Talented in languages, willing to learn, Oswald had already learned to speak Belorussian while in Turzec. He would have loved to continue practicing his new skills. But here, in his new home, the two women were eager to use Polish. Serafimowicz knew Polish and liked to speak it too, so Oswald's practice of his new language had to wait.

The house of the police commandant was tastefully furnished with Oriental rugs, heavy curtains, and solid furniture. Later on, from bits of conversations, Oswald had guessed that, in the past, most of what he saw had belonged to different Jewish homes. Whether the things were confiscated while the Jews still lived in their homes or after they were murdered, he did not know and did not ask.

In these new surroundings, these former Jewish possessions looked well and seemed to blend perfectly with each other. Adjusted to their new owners, fitting so effectively into this home, it seemed as if these new acquisitions had forgotten their original masters. Inanimate objects have no loyalties. When treated properly they adapt.

These objects were brought to a well-run home. The place was spotless. Each morning a servant, Shifra Czerny, arrived from the Jewish section of town. A special permit identified her as a maid who worked for important people. She wore a yellow star of David sewn on her clothes. From the moment she came in the morning until she left in the evening, she cleaned and took care of all household chores.

Sometimes Shifra Czerny was joined by other cleaning women. For altering and sewing clothes, a special seamstress would come with a little girl. There was also a gardener and a handyman. All were Jewish. All were working without pay. But this was a good place to work. They were fed properly and never abused. The women treated their employees with consideration. The head of the household ignored them. Something in Serafimowicz's attitude rather than actual treatment of these Jews suggested an absence of the human touch. Did his attitudes reflect an acceptance of the Nazi ideology? Would his indifference and the implied contempt make it easier to kill the Jews?

Serafimowicz had decided that Oswald would be his private teacher and private interpreter. The morning after Oswald's arrival the two went to the police station. On the way they saw Bielanowicz, the regional mayor of Mir. Without a greeting, from the other side of the road, the mayor shouted at the top of his voice: "Who is this Jew who is with you?" Laughter was followed by "This is not a Jew. He is a Pole, my teacher and interpreter. His father was German and his mother Polish." As usual, the accused kept silent. This time too Oswald tried and succeeded in appearing relaxed. Inside a voice warned him: "You must get used to it, you must!"

The Belorussian police were stationed in a simple building. A small hall led into a room that was used as a waiting place, one other room belonged to the secretary of the station. Another room was set aside for the head of the regional police and still another was reserved for additional office workers. The building had a special cellar that was transformed into a single jail cell. People were kept here only for a short time, before they were executed or transferred to a regular prison in one of the bigger nearby towns.

The furniture in this station was modest: simple desks and tables, filing cabinets, and hard chairs. Bare electric bulbs hung from the ceiling. During the day the windows allowed enough light, giving a naked appearance to the unlighted bulbs. The only wall decorations were maps of the region and a framed print of Adolf Hitler.

Whenever one entered the waiting room one would see a few peasants who had come to clarify matters, to inquire about the meaning of a new order. More often than not, such orders asked the peasants to deliver a large part of their farm goods to the authorities. Anyone with more serious problems went across the street to the German gendarmes. Policemen were always coming in and out of the place. Some lingering for a chat, others carrying different documents would offer news or ask a few questions, then disappear again. German soldiers and gendarmes would also come with messages and questions. It was a busy place.

Serafimowicz had until now relied on a semi-interpreter, a Belorussian youth who knew some school German. This youth was able to communicate in very simple language and for some contacts this was enough.

For more important and more complicated translations there was Rudaszewski, the head of the local police station. He was a Pole from Poznán, a former train conductor. Coming from a part of Poland that was influenced by the German culture, he knew German well. In his familiarity with the language he saw an opportunity for advancement. As a start he succeeded in changing his nationality from a Pole to a Volksdeutsche, an ethnic German. This move in itself gave him special advantages

Greatly in demand, Rudaszewski had to split his time between the Belorussian and the German stations. But Rudaszewski was much more involved with vodka than with his job. He was frequently absent from work, and when present performed his duties carelessly. However, as the only person in Mir who could translate well he had to be tolerated. Among those who had to rely heavily on his services was Meister Hein, the head of the gendarmerie.

Though Serafimowicz's authority extended over the Mir region, his men had to cooperate with the German gendarmes. Basically, the Belorussian and German authorities dealt with two kinds of problems. One had to do with regular police functions, keeping order among the local population. These usually involved personal, domestic quarrels, stealing, cheating, assault, and different kinds of crimes.

The second part of their duties had to do with so-called political matters. Here the German authorities and through them the Belorussians concentrated on the elimination of individuals whom they officially defined as undesirable. A few categories of people were singled out for such "special treatment." High on the list were Communists. This included all those who had any official position under the Soviet occupation.

Perhaps in anticipation of this policy, many of those whose lives were connected to the Russians ran away with the Soviet army. They had acted prudently, because as soon as the Nazis came to this area, whoever was suspected of Communist activities, whoever was denounced for having worked for or with the Russians was arrested. More often than not, those arrested were executed. The Nazis were merciless and only a miracle could have saved any of the accused.

In addition to Communists, their sympathizers, and Soviet co-workers, anyone suspected of partisan activities or any anti-Nazi moves was automatically placed into the category of the condemned. By extension, those who were suspected of any cooperation with Communists and partisans were subjected to the same treatment. Thus, relying on the principle of collective responsibility, many villages were partly or totally destroyed, simply because some of its inhabitants were suspected of aiding any of the "undesirables."

Different from but placed together with these political cases were the Jews. All Jews were defined as racially inferior. Every Jew, without exception, was a potential target.

Persecutions of the different categories of people were initiated and ordered by the Germans and then followed by the Belorussian collaborators. In the region of Mir Hein and his gendarmes represented all the German police factions including the Gestapo. He had absolute control, deciding on questions of life and death. One basic difference between the Belorussian and the German gendarmes was their relative power. Regardless of rank, a Belorussian had less authority than a German gendarme.

Among the social failures who worked for Serafimowicz was one exception. He was the secretary of the regional police, a young Pole from Mołodeczno, a former law student, far more educated than any Mir official. When he took the position he did not realize what he was getting into. Once he became aware of what the police were doing, he resigned.

The secretary resigned shortly after Oswald's arrival in Mir, and Serafimowicz saw in this an opportunity for Oswald. Without delay he installed his protégé as the official secretary of his police station. Unlike his predecessor, Oswald was not in a position to decline this "honor." Here people seemed to accept him. Their acceptance in turn created a protective environment. He was aware that without his newly acquired protection he would most probably be lost. If he wanted to live, and he did, he had to stay.

To Oswald's duties as a teacher and interpreter were added those of the secretary of the regional police. This position required a more extended but not full presence at the police station. When in his office, Oswald had to answer the phone, keep track of the policemen's activities, who of them had what kind of duty and where. He had to distribute salaries and keep a record of different financial transactions. He was not personally involved with political killings, but he recognized the change, a moral change, in his position.

He explains: *Once I had officially joined the police, I felt responsible for what they did. I felt an immediate co-responsibility for everything the policemen might be doing, even if personally I would not be participating. . . . For me there was a strong necessity to build a counterbalance to the evil around me.*

Though Oswald and his co-workers had little in common, he was careful to remain on friendly terms with them. These men knew that he was more educated and more intelligent. But because he never acted superior, they themselves treated him with respect and later on with affection. Always cautious, Oswald tried to keep his distance and avoid becoming entangled in personal discussions. Whenever such talks took place, he simply smiled in a noncommittal way.

Yet, at the same time, in order not to antagonize them or to arouse suspicion, he had to adjust to some of their ways, particularly their custom of heavy drinking. With the exception of two or three real alcoholics, for the rest of the Belorussian policemen heavy drinking was merely a favorite pastime. It was something natural, something they had always done, like eating and sleeping. In contrast, as a young man active in the Zionist movement, Oswald was not used to alcoholic beverages. He knew, however, that an unwillingness or an inability to drink was associated with Jews and so he participated in their drinking parties, joining in the loud singing and boisterous jokes.

While seemingly relaxed, each time this happened he was apprehensive. Unused to drinking he was afraid that under the influence of alcohol he might reveal secrets. He tried to moderate his intake of liquor, but it was not easy. Stopping before the others did could be revealing.

Oswald often felt like an unskilled acrobat who walks a tightrope. Once after one of those drinking sprees he fell off his bicycle. Alcohol was a definite adversary, one he had to cope with.

Oswald's attitude toward drinking was very different from his boss's love for vodka. At least twice a week Serafimowicz would become intoxicated. At such times he would lose self-control. At home the two sisters had a hard time keeping him from destroying plates, furniture, and whatever else was in his way.

Because they came to treat Oswald as part of the family, they turned to him for help. Oswald remembers, *Usually I would hold his legs . . . Jadwiga and Wanda would hold his hands. Once when I held his hands, he began to beg me: "Oswald let go of me, let go, I promise I will not do anything!" When I did, he slapped my face. After that he laughed and laughed.*

Always on guard, Oswald resisted becoming too much a part of a particular group or place. He explains his strategy: *I did not want to be too long in one environment. I did not want to expose myself to discussions that might go into depth, into personal matters.* About the policemen in particular Oswald feels, *I never developed any personal ties to these men. I avoided all personal talks with them. They and I had nothing in common. They were not on my level, excuse me that I say it, I was no intellectual giant either . . . but still they were not on the same level as I.*

In part what helped him follow this strategy was the fact that instead of moving into the house shared by the Belorussian policemen, Oswald continued to live with the Serafimowicz family. Fewer contacts, together with different types of duties, helped him maintain a distance without arousing suspicion.

Serafimowicz was satisfied with all the changes that came with Oswald's new position. First of all, he liked his new secretary much better than the one who resigned. Second, he continued to receive Oswald's services without incurring any personal expenses. The authorities paid.

Shortly after Oswald accepted the position of secretary to the regional Belorussian police, the Germans decided to supply the Belorussians with uniforms usually reserved for SS men. Until then, only high ranking Belorussian collaborators could wear SS clothes. To distinguish the Belorussian policemen from the Germans, the sleeves and collars of the Belorussian suits were finished with gray cloth, while those worn by the Germans were all black. In addition to a salary and a uniform Oswald also received a gun. Finally too, because Serafimowicz loved to ride, and, because whenever possible he wanted to have his protégé at his side, he gave Oswald a horse.

As a high school student in Bielsko, Oswald had a friend whose father was a colonel in the Polish cavalry. This colonel arranged riding courses for his son and for the rest of the son's class. For three years Oswald took riding lessons and distinguished himself by winning a number of prizes. Not only did he become an excellent rider but he claimed to have *felt on a horse like a fish in water.*

In Mir anyone who saw this newcomer ride was impressed by the ease with which he handled his horse. He loved riding and whenever he could he would gallop through town and through the nearby fields. After the war, one of his Polish friends, Halina Balicki, told him that initially her mother suspected Oswald of being Jewish. But when she saw him ride through town all her suspicions vanished. No Jew could ever ride like that!

Much later, a Jewish woman in Mir, who knew that Oswald was protecting Jews, also had a strong reaction. "I never spoke to him. I only saw him. For me it was a great thing. It was as if I saw a superhuman being. When we saw him ride a horse he looked like a legend. . . . He is short, but then, to me, he looked very, very tall."[4]

Only after Oswald felt secure in his position at the police station, and after he convinced himself that he enjoyed the protection and respect of Serafimowicz, did he dare ask the regional mayor, Bielanowicz, for an official identification card. By then not only did the mayor know Oswald personally, but he also knew about his powerful backing. In fact, Oswald was so closely identified with the police and with Serafimowicz that it would have been tactless to question him too closely. Bielanowicz was a smart man and not about to antagonize those in power. Presented with a school card and an official story about a German father and a Polish mother, he accepted both.

Had the authorities wanted or considered it necessary, they could have easily checked whether Oswald was Jewish since in Poland only Jewish men were circumcised. In fact, many passing Jews lost their lives as a result of such casual checks.[5] In an event touching on this issue, one day Serafimowicz invited Oswald to a public bath, an honor the young man was not in a position to refuse. With a shudder Oswald still remembers: *There, all men walked without clothes. Somehow I had to do it in a way that he should not see me where he was not supposed to. We took a bath in the same room. How I came out of it I don't know myself. Till this very day I don't understand how it happened, but somehow I succeeded.*

Whatever the reasons, without fuss, Bielanowicz supplied Oswald with a legitimate identification card. A German father entitled a son to the position of a Volksdeutsche and people with considerably less valid German connections applied for such a position and were granted it. Oswald chose to identify himself as a Pole.

I was not an SS man nor a German but remained a Pole. Later people wrote about me all kinds of things, they made many mistakes. Officially, I never became a German or a Volksdeutsche. I could have applied for a change of citizenship but did not. . . . Somewhere, somehow, I saw the light and realized that I should not do this because as a German I would automatically reach a higher rank and would become a more visible person. I would have to prove myself. On the other hand, if I remained a Pole then I would be a second-class citizen.

Had he tried for a Volksdeutsch identity, the authorities might have investigated his background. Since his school card, the basis for his new documents, placed him in his old community, any inquiries might have revealed his Jewish identity. In contrast, as a Pole, he was not important enough and the authorities were less likely to bother checking his background.[6]

Oswald's acceptance of the Polish rather than the German ethnic identity led to consequences he had not anticipated. It gained him the respect of his Polish friends, including Jadwiga and Wanda. People saw in Oswald's choice a gesture of patriotism and he gained a reputation of an honest and principled person unlikely to change his convictions because of material advantages.

Like so many others, Meister Hein was impressed with Oswald. The German valued the characteristics this youth possessed: politeness, good manners, dignity, intelligence, and an excellent command of the German language. Oswald's reactions to Hein were much more complicated, almost confused. It was common knowledge that this German was responsible for ordering executions and murders. On meeting Hein, Oswald searched for traces of criminality. To his surprise and discomfort, Oswald saw an austere man with an honest face and a certain appealingly direct, no-nonsense manner. In fact, Oswald was disturbed by the idea that had he met Hein under different circumstances, he would have been drawn to him right away.

From the start Oswald was also surprised how different his reactions were to Hein from his attitudes toward Serafimowicz. While he appreciated some of Serafimowicz's qualities, he was repulsed by his active participation in the murder of innocent people. Yet he does not remember feeling disgusted by Hein. Oswald was troubled by this uneven reaction. After all, Hein was ultimately responsible for the crimes committed by the Belorussian. How could the German appear so untouched? In his confusion Oswald also realized that the older man liked him. In fact, from the start the Meister had been asking Serafimowicz to bring along his interpreter. During these visits Hein relied on Oswald's language skills, but it was also clear that he appreciated him for much more than his linguistic ability.

Within a short time Oswald had succeeded in establishing an excellent reputation. He explains: *I think that I gained the trust of Serafimowicz and the others because I was conscientious and perhaps because I showed a certain amount of intelligence about regular police cases. When murder was committed or some other criminal action, I made a point of translating properly. With all such cases I tried to be helpful.* When Oswald's job related to the so-called political matters and situations involving Jews he tried to sabotage as much as possible. This he achieved by concentrating on the victims' welfare. To Oswald it did not matter who the victims were. As long as they were unjustly persecuted he did all he could to help them.

As Oswald's duties continued to expand, he had more access to important and sensitive information, part of which applied specifically to the Jewish plight. In Belorussia most Jews were scattered in small towns and villages. The Germans almost never deported any of them to concentration camps. In fact, often the Nazis did not even bother to assemble them into special ghettos. Instead, they would kill the Jews locally, usually close to their homes. Oswald was aware that this policy applied to the Mir region and beyond. Belorussian policemen and German gendarmes used to come to a village or small town, collect all Jewish inhabitants, and then murder them. Each killing operation resulted in ten to forty victims, depending on how many Jews resided in a specific place. The aim was to make an area clean of Jews, "Judenrein."

Oswald wanted to warn the Jews about such specific plans. But he had to be careful. He waited; one wrong move could finish it all. Soon an opportunity for aid presented itself. Oswald was sitting in his office, writing a report, when a Jewish electrician came to the police station to fix some wiring.

At first, absorbed in his job, the secretary did not even notice the man who unobtrusively worked next to him. Then *for no reason at all, I looked up. When I did I felt that I might have known this young man from somewhere, but I did not know exactly where. I was intrigued and excited. But I had to act calmly. Then, for a split of a second, we looked at each other. The tension kept mounting. I thought that he also recognized me. Then with my eyes, in silence, I signaled to him, to meet me outside the office. He understood. When he left I followed him. My heart was pounding. "What are you doing?" a voice warned. But I had to go through with it. We had little time. I had to act fast. I reminded myself that we knew each other from Vilna. In half sentences I told him who I was and that I came here from Vilna. To this he told me that he too returned from Vilna, he and two others that I knew. Mir was his hometown. Right there we arranged for our next meeting. We decided to see each other that same evening on a side street, not in a Jewish house. I never went into a Jewish house. Unless on official business, it would have been too dangerous for me to do that.*

At that time, in Mir, there was not yet a closed-in ghetto. Only a special part of town was reserved for Jews. . . . His name was Dov (Bereczke Berl) Resnik. When the two of us met I told him I would do for the Jews whatever was in my power. In return I wanted him to keep a secret. I demanded that under no circumstances should people know who I was, and only when absolutely necessary could someone be told that I, though a policeman, was helping. . . . Right there Dov supplied me with names of trustworthy people who could serve as our intermediaries.[7] *If I had to send special messages I had to have a few alternative channels. Some of these contacts were Jewish women who cleaned offices. One of them was a young boy who painted signs, by the name of Leib Ickowicz . . . another man was Yehuda Preker. He worked in the gendarmes' stable.*

Because in Vilna Dov and Oswald had belonged to different Zionist movements, Rufeisen to the political center, Akiva, and Resnik to the leftist movement, Hashomer Hatzair, they knew each other only casually. In Mir, these ideological differences lost their significance. What mattered was that two Jews met, one in need of help and the other able and eager to offer his help. But if their contacts were to bear fruit, secrecy was of utmost importance. Therefore, they both agreed that none of their trusted intermediaries would know about Oswald's past. In fact, all they were told was that this influential policeman was offering aid. The two conspirators also agreed that Oswald's true identity would be revealed only to two other men from Vilna, Israel Resnik and Shlomo Charchas.

Shlomo Charchas was considerably older than Dov, Israel, and Oswald. In Vilna he was already one of the respected leaders of the Hashomer Hatzair. Not surprisingly, on his return to his hometown, he had assumed a leadership position. According to Dov, among the Mir Jews there were about sixty members of their Zionist organization. All were willing to act against the Nazis. Except for a general desire to oppose the Germans they had little else. They had no definite plans, no resources.

What could Oswald do for the Jews? He had access to information about anti-Jewish moves. He promised to supply Resnik with these facts.

Oswald was gratified by this newly established connection. It gave him the opportunity he had been waiting and longing for. It also awoke in him a craving for more intimate friendship ties. Those who knew who he was could satisfy those needs. Only with Jews who were aware of his identity could Oswald be truly himself. Though potentially gratifying, though seemingly within his reach, more extensive contacts were out of the question. Oswald was convinced that Jews needed his help, his protection, but not his company. He knew that by selfishly satisfying his desire for friendship he might end his usefulness. Instead of enlarging, he had to limit his ties with the Jewish community. There was safety in fewer encounters.

Contrary to what others have written, Oswald has consistently denied that he ever paid a social visit to a Jewish home. And a statement that he went to the synagogue in search of Jewish company, he describes as "preposterous."[8] He insists that whatever visits he did make to a Jewish home he made in the company of Serafimowicz, in an official capacity. Throughout his stay in Mir he avoided all "unnecessary" contacts with the Jews. To do otherwise would have been an indulgence and a weakness that could only lead to disaster he and the Jews of Mir could ill afford.

8

Working for the Authorities

"Jews of the Kryniczno village and its surroundings should leave their homes." Leave? Where to? Why?

Reading and rereading these words, Krynicki, an old Jewish farmer who had lived in this village all his life, was puzzled. For an explanation he turned to the Belorussian messenger. But this man's answer was: "The Judenrat in Mir gave me this piece of paper. They asked me to bring it to you and here it is." "What does it mean?" the old farmer wanted to know. "They never told me what it said. I did not even look at it."

Krynicki consulted his daughter Ester, who some six months ago settled here with her husband and their three children. She and her family left Mir right after the outbreak of the Russian-German war. For Ester this was home. She was happier here than she had ever been in the town she had left. Realizing that as farmers they would have enough food, her husband agreed to this change. One other advantage of staying in this village was that the Germans rarely ventured into such small places. It made sense to live here.

On that day, father and daughter concluded that the message before them was strange. They also agreed that one does not leave a home without a definite cause. They decided to investigate the matter. The logical step, they felt, would be to go to Mir and ask for an explanation. But Jews were not allowed to travel. Unlike most others, Ester could easily pass for a Christian and it was decided that she would be the one to go to Mir some twenty-one kilometers from Kryniczno. Because of the distance, Ester decided to break up the trip by staying overnight at the house of one of her Belorussian friends. A day later she reached Mir where she met with Eliezer Breslin, a Judenrat official. Ester says; "Breslin told me that in Mir there was a commandant, Oswald Rufeisen, who said that the Jews in the villages should be warned because their liquidation was coming . . . When I was about to return home, Eliezer walked with me to the outskirts of town promising that if he will have news about the specific liquidation date of Kryniczno he will send a messenger with a warning."

On the way back Ester stopped over again at her friend's house.

Next morning, still in bed, Ester was visited by her brother. He brought the news: their parents, his wife, Ester's husband, their six children, and the rest of the local Jews were murdered by the Belorussian policemen and the German gendarmes. The brother was spared only because he was away on business in a nearby mill.[1]

Oswald had indeed sent the warning. This was his first effort at saving Jews. He knew that the Kryniczno Aktion was a part of a general order that came from the larger town of Baranowicze. This order called for the systematic liquidation of Jewish families scattered throughout the regional villages. The first place was Kryniczno; it was to be followed by many others.

Because Serafimowicz had full confidence in his secretary, he mentioned this order almost casually, adding that this time Oswald would be joining them. Immediately, through one of his contacts, Oswald sent the news to Resnik, who in turn delivered it to the Judenrat.

Members of the Judenrat, however, were skeptical, demanding to know how and from whom Resnik had obtained this information. They said that unless he would reveal the source they would not act on it. Under pressure Resnik told them that the policeman Rufeisen gave him the news. He did not tell them about Oswald's true identity.[2]

Somehow the urgency and the meaning of the message were diluted. Was it skepticism? A misunderstanding? Or both? Whatever the reason, Oswald's warning did not work.

As usual, the Aktion in Kryniczno was a joint Belorussian-German venture. Karl Schultz, the second-in-command in the gendarmerie, was in charge. He was substituting for Meister Hein. A baker in civilian life, Schultz enjoyed his police duties. Oswald describes this man as someone of *low intelligence, a pathological murderer and a sadist. Schultz was one of those who had the opportunity to legally kill and torture and took full advantage of it. . . . There is absolutely nothing positive that I could say about this man, absolutely nothing.*

As they were traveling toward Kryniczno, perhaps to underline his own importance, Schultz led the way in a special sleigh he shared with Serafimowicz and Rufeisen. He was closely followed by two more sleighs, each filled with policemen and gendarmes.

As soon as they arrived in Kryniczno the men quickly scattered into different directions, making sure that all the Jewish dwellings were encircled at once. Twenty-one Jews were collected. They were ordered into the Krynicki house. A part of this group were children, most were middle-aged, a few were young adults.

Trying hard not to show his feelings, Oswald watched in bewilderment. *What I saw is clear before my eyes, till this very day. . . . In this group there were two beautiful girls. One of them in particular, seventeen or so, was stunning; slim, tall with beautiful blond hair. I had a hard time keeping my eyes off her. Then I noticed that one of the Belorussian policemen, a strong tall man, took a special interest in her. He stood very close to her.*

Though absent, Meister Hein left a definite imprint on this Aktion. Events continued to move in a methodical, orderly way. The victims were made to listen to their death sentence which told that as enemies of the Reich, and in accordance with the Führer's will, they must die. Oswald had to hear from Schultz this statement aloud first in German. Then he had to translate it into Belorussian. When this was done, the man in charge of the operation stepped in with his own innovation.

Thus, Oswald recalls that Schultz *had a special note book. In it he would write the names of those with whose death he was connected. Toward the end of my stay he had eighty names in this book. . . . In Kryniczno, I had to ask the victims for their names and repeat them for Schultz. He wrote down only the names of those who were over sixteen years old. Those whose ages were less than sixteen he simply referred to by numbers: "eins, zwei, drei, vier," one, two, three, four. When it came to eight he wrote: "Acht Stueck unter 16," eight pieces below 16. That was all.*

After Schultz had entered this information into his book, once more the people were counted to see if the written figure corresponded to their actual number. Next, the victims were ordered to leave the house and go behind the barn. These moves were closely monitored.

At that point Oswald remembers being overcome by a faint numbness. He knew what inevitably had to happen and felt that he might break down. Therefore, when the Jews, led by their executioners, were leaving the house, he slipped out and hid behind it.

From where he was Oswald could hear rough cursing and swearing. Then came the children's forlorn cries. Did these children guess? In contrast, not a sound came from the rest of the victims. They were all silent, in an eerie, determined way.

Soon he heard someone call "Oswald, Oswald." Gripped by a paralyzing anxiety, he did not budge. He knew that he had no strength to come out. He waited. Shots rung out. More and more shots. Then nothing. Was it a pause or the end? Only after Oswald convinced himself that the worse was over did he venture out of the stable. When he rejoined the others no one paid attention to him. The killers were still absorbed in their job. They had not yet finished.

They were concentrating on the bodies, scattered on the snow-covered ground. There they were, lying in a disarray, in all kinds of positions, just as they happened to fall. It was as if in their death they were defying the Nazi idea of order. Against the pure white snow their blood appeared strangely alive. This blood continued to flow unevenly, soundlessly forming imaginative designs in different shades of red and pink.

Oswald looked on. The same Belorussian policeman who only a few minutes ago seemed to have taken a certain interest in the beautiful girl was standing over her. He must have been the one who shot her. And then: *To my horror I saw him bend down. Next I realized that he was busy taking off the dead girl's handmade sweater. . . . The others too continued to examine the rest of the bodies impassively, methodically. When they discovered any signs of life they shot again. . . . Inside I was a broken man. I can still see the entire scene, as if it had happened yesterday.*

On the way back Oswald once more shared the sleigh with Schultz and Serafimowicz. Once more he had to sit between the two men. Worse still, at that point, Oswald had to translate their jokes. He did that without understanding the content of his own translations. His companions seemed oblivious to his mood. In high spirits, the two killers laughed heartily. Were they rewarding themselves with jokes for a job well done? Or was their laughter a tension-releasing device? Their merriment continued all the way to Mir.

At home something inside Oswald snapped. *I went straight to my room and abandoned myself to my grief. I lost all self-control and could not stop crying. Loud sobs shook my entire body. I could do nothing about it.*

Dinner was on its way. Jadwiga called Oswald to come and eat. *I was not in a position to join them. I did not react to her call. She came to my room and asked, "What happened, why are you crying?" I answered her with more and louder crying. She called in Serafimowicz. He sat at my bed. He stroked me gently, very gently, asking what could possibly be the reason for my unhappiness. At that point I took a hold of myself and told him that I had a brother in Poland and that I heard that Poles are being treated cruelly there and today my presence at the Aktion reminded me that he too may be suffering. Serafimowicz believed me. He tried to comfort me by assuring me that these things are never done to Poles.*

For Oswald friendship was, and continues to be, an indispensable part of life. *I am made for friendship. For me friendship is as necessary as breathing.* In Mir constant exposure to danger together with exposure to cruelty contributed to Oswald's feelings of tension and utter isolation. This special situation only accentuated Oswald's need for someone to confide in, to share with, to lean on.

Talking about the same period, Hilel Seidel, a friend for almost half a century, says, *On the one hand Oswald saw the suffering of the Jews, on the other hand he had to wear the uniform of the killers that for him was the symbol of evil. He had to be in the company of the murderers of Jews. This was a difficult dilemma. Only a person that has tremendous moral strength can withstand the pressure. Every day was a day of suffering.*

No doubt Oswald could have benefited from an outlet. No doubt real friendship ties would have reduced his burdens. But in his case the need to confide and lean on someone competed with the need for safety. Safety prevented him from establishing closer ties to the Jews. Because of safety he could not be fully open with anyone else. Safety then was the definite winner and all this imposter could even hope for were only partial friendships.

Since in Mir most Poles were removed from the official Nazi machinery, and because Oswald had more in common with the Poles than with the Belorussians, he decided to cultivate his relationships with Poles. At home there were two Poles, Jadwiga and Wanda; both were fine women. Both liked and approved of him. Still their close connection to Serafimowicz put a damper on Oswald's and their relationship.

While Oswald appreciated his boss's quick intelligence and wit, he was repulsed by his direct involvement in the murder of innocent people. He therefore tried to distance himself from this man by spending as little time in the Serafimowicz home as possible. Such absences prevented him from establishing closer ties with the rest of the family.

He also made a point of staying away from the Polish priest, Mackiewicz. Contrary to what others have said, he never visited him.[3] He explains, *I did not trust the priest. I did not know him. Nor did I know that he had a positive attitude toward the Jews. This I discovered much later. Here and there, when I met him by chance, I would bow, but that was all. I never spoke to him. Maybe this was a mistake. Maybe as a seeming Catholic I should have shown an interest in the priest, but I did not. I did not go to confession because I was afraid that he might guess who I was. After all, I had no idea how a Catholic should behave in the presence of a priest.*

For the same reasons that he avoided the priest, he kept his contacts with the nuns to a bare minimum. When meeting any of them by chance he would utter the customary greeting: "Praised be Jesus Christ." His knowledge of what might be the proper behavior of a Catholic toward a nun ended with this greeting. Only much later the nuns served as intermediaries between Oswald and the Jews. This happened when Oswald supplied the Jews with blank document forms. Oswald had stolen these forms from his office. Such papers facilitated a move to the forbidden Christian world. He was told by his contacts that the nuns would deliver these items to the ghetto.

For Easter Catholics are supposed to confess and take holy communion. Around that time Serafimowicz told his protégé: "It will be your responsibility to see to it that the Catholic policemen go to confession."

Among the policemen there were only two Catholics. "Strange that these murderers had to attend to their religious needs," thought Oswald. But finding himself on slippery ground, he said nothing. Still his boss's remarks made the point. He realized that he too was expected to go through with this ritual.

I went to church and I saw there about fifteen people. They had all come to confess. They were waiting for their turn. I looked around to see who was the last in line and who came after me, and then I sat down and waited for about an hour and a half, until the person that came after me had left. I left only then. This way no one knew whether I did confess or not.

In Mir, of the Poles Oswald considered as appropriate friends was the Balicki family, consisting of the former principal of the local school, his wife, and their three daughters, Regina, Halina, and Irena.

Since Poles in this region were a definite minority it was natural for them to seek each other's company. In fact, at Jadwiga's suggestion, shortly after Oswald came to town, he introduced himself to the Balickis. At this first meeting, the oldest daughter, Irena asked, "How did you come here? After all, Jews are not allowed to move around!" "What Jews? What are you talking about? I am a Pole, not a Jew!" Oswald's strong and self-assured denial seemed to have the desired effect.

What began as a search for a partial friendship and also as a way of staying away from the Serafimowicz home turned into a warm attachment. Oswald describes his contacts with the Balicki family as follows. *I was hungry for company that could relax me, I needed to unwind, to be partly myself. The Balicki sisters had this effect on me. They made me feel at home. I would visit them almost every evening and stay in their place till ten. When I returned home the Serafimowicz household was already resting. I would then go to sleep too. For me this was convenient and pleasant. With time our affection grew, especially between Regina and me.*

Regina was seventeen and Oswald not yet nineteen. The two were attracted to each other. Oswald, however, felt that it would have been unfair to seriously court the girl. Their attachment never went beyond holding hands and occasional innocent kissing.

Oswald explains, *It would have been wrong of me to act in any other way. After all, I was a Jew. I could not be open with her. It would have been indecent of me to make more serious advances. These were fine girls, from a good family. Our mutual attraction was obvious, but it never developed into anything physical.*

In those days it was not unusual to continue a romantic involvement without it leading to sexual entanglements. Indeed lonely, Oswald valued his closeness not only to Regina but to the rest of her family, particularly to her two older sisters.

I felt least estranged in their company. When we were together I would listen to their stories. We would sing or play cards and play all kinds of innocent games. Sometimes I would tell them about our activities at the police station . . . all of it I could not tell because many of the things I had to keep secret. As much as I could I tried to share with them. I also tried to amuse them by concentrating on strange and funny tales about family squabbles. When telling them such stories I succeeded in making them laugh. I knew that they looked forward to my visits and that gave me much satisfaction.

Though the ties with the Balickis comforted Oswald, they failed to eliminate his tensions. Not only did such tensions refuse to go away, they continued to mount. And despite his many other connections within the community Oswald felt like an outsider, like someone who does not belong to anyone and to anyplace.

One day on his way from work Oswald saw many empty trucks parked on the road. He was puzzled. Under the circumstances this could mean only one thing: a move against someone. Against whom? No one had mentioned a thing. Obviously whatever was to take place was kept from him. Why? Up till now Oswald was informed about all kinds of arrests, searches, and about every anti-Jewish Aktion. Why was he left out this time? A possible answer suggested itself. Because Oswald had a reputation of being a Polish patriot, the presence of these vehicles might have to do with Poles. The more Oswald considered this possibility the more convinced he became about the plausibility of this assumption. He felt compelled to inform the Poles.

I smelled definite danger. That same evening I warned Mr. Balicki and urged him not to sleep at home. He did not take me seriously. He did not leave. At Oswald's suggestion, Balicki mentioned this warning to others. Except for one Pole, no one else acted on the information. Till this day Oswald's conscience bothers him. He feels that in giving the warning he should have been more emphatic. Had he been more insistent, the people might have followed his advice. In fact, he talks about this episode as one of his major blunders.

It is ironic that when the Russian occupation of Mir ended and the Nazis took over, the Polish priest, Mackiewicz, conducted a special mass thanking God for the termination of the Soviet occupation and the arrival of the Germans.

The night after Oswald saw the parked trucks, in the Mir region alone twenty-five Polish men and women, all defined by the Nazis as the intelligentsia, as leaders of their communities, were arrested. Balicki and the priest Mackiewicz were among them. In Mir only one Polish man was spared, the one who listened to Oswald's warning and ran away. In the vicinity of Nieświeź scores of other members of the Polish intelligentsia were rounded up.

Of the arrested all were taken to the prison in Stołpce, where they remained for about two months. From there they were transferred to the concentration camp Kołdyczewo.[4]

Like Oswald, Serafimowicz knew nothing about this raid. No doubt because of his Polish wife the Germans did not trust him either. These arrests were carried out by Bielanowicz, the Belorussian regional mayor, with the help of some local Belorussian policemen. Rumor had it that the regional mayor had initiated all anti-Polish moves. In reality, even if Bielanowicz had wanted to, he would not have had the authority to carry out such moves without German approval. The ultimate responsibility, therefore, could not have been his but the Germans'. In fact, these Polish arrests fit well into the overall Nazi policies that aimed at the elimination of the Polish elite. Many thousands of Poles were either murdered outright or sent to concentration camps, where many perished.[5]

This policy was put in effect for the entire country. In the eastern part of Poland the Nazis tried to give the impression that moves against Poles were not only initiated and executed by Belorussians but also motivated by Belorussian nationalists.[6]

Eventually all the Poles arrested that night were gassed in special trucks in the Kołdyczewo concentration camp. Among the murdered was Balicki. Besides the personal blow, his death forced the three daughters to look for employment. With time, each found a job. Regina, the one Oswald felt particularly attracted to, worked in a nearby town. From then on she came home only on Sundays. Prolonged absences undermined Regina's and Oswald's romantic fervor, without, however, destroying their friendship.

Though unsuccessful, Oswald's warning to the Poles cemented further the relationship between him and the Balicki family. Right after her father's arrest, the oldest daughter, Irena, told Oswald, "If you ever need help come to me." He thanked her casually but made a careful mental note of this offer. One could never tell! Besides, her statement validated his own feelings toward them. *I felt good with them. Their friendship was a compensation for my other painful exposures, for my feeling like an outsider.*

Soon Oswald transferred his romantic attachment from Regina to Wanda. To him the twenty-four-year-old Wanda must have seemed more intelligent and more interesting than Regina. This new relationship was a strong mixture of friendship and mutual attraction. But it too found no physical expression. In their case, too much that would have mattered to both was never discussed.

While these events were taking place, contacts between Oswald and the head of the gendarmerie, Meister Hein, became gradually more extensive. The older man came to rely and look forward to the youth's visits.

Eventually he asked Serafimowicz to give up his interpreter. Though this request was couched as a favor, under the circumstance it was an order. After only two months Oswald moved his office across the street, to the gendarmerie.

Once established, trust frequently calls for special cultivation. But Oswald had self-imposed limitations that required him to interfere with the persecution of innocent victims and forbade him to contribute to the support of the Nazi crimes. Such limitations in and of themselves made the perpetuation of Hein's trust difficult. How did this youth manage to keep Hein's confidence alive without arousing suspicion?

The Meister was depending on me for the solution to problems that had to do with theft, with disputes among neighbors, with cases involving all kinds of cheating and crimes. Especially with difficult criminal cases I had a certain intuition.

The Belorussians were shrewd, manipulative. In contrast, the gendarmes were straightforward, even naive. Although brutal toward those they defined as useless, they could be easily fooled when it came to simple theft. Fortunately, I could more easily than the Germans see through the underhanded tactics of the natives. I, therefore, knew better how to deal with some of these problems and could suggest to the Meister the direction he should be taking, saving him time, speeding up the investigation and eventually helping to bring it to a satisfactory conclusion.

With the so-called political cases, some of which involved people opposed to the Nazi regime, others simply to the annihilation of Jews, Oswald assumed a completely different posture. Here his aim was to divert, to dissuade, to sabotage. This involved constant balancing and juggling.

Oswald was in part successful because of Hein's growing affection and respect. At home the German had left a wife and a son.[7] It is quite possible that Oswald reminded him of his son. Perhaps he would have liked his son to resemble Oswald? Whatever the reasons, Hein clearly approved of and depended on his interpreter and treated him in a fatherly way.

Shortly after Oswald joined the gendarmerie, the Meister decided to legitimize this transfer to give more security to Oswald's position. He did this by dismissing the official interpreter, Raduszynski, who was also the head of the local police. This change had to go through the appropriate channels.

Oswald remembers, *The Meister showed me a letter he wrote to a colonel in Minsk. In it he said that he is releasing Ruduszynski from his position and is taking me as an interpreter, explaining that even though Raduszynski is a Volksdeutsche, he is a drunkard, while Rufeisen, though only a Pole, is intelligent and discreet, and does not drink. . . . From then on, officially, I worked only for the Meister as an interpreter and assistant without, however, becoming the head of the local police. I continued to live with Serafimowicz, but ate three meals a day with the Germans, at the gendarmerie. I was sometimes called to to the Belorussian station without being employed there. More and more, I acted as an intermediary, as a link between these two bodies.*

Located in the former convent, an eleven-room house, the gendarmerie was divided into offices and living quarters. With Oswald's transfer a second desk was moved into the Meister's room. The two desks faced each other. The wall behind Hein's chair was dominated by a framed picture of Hitler.

Each day when Oswald arrived for breakfast people were already sitting in the waiting room. The natives knew that the Germans had the real power. They would come here with what they considered to be more serious complaints. And so they preferred to bring to the attention of the Germans all kinds of political problems as well as different denouncements. The collaborators in particular seemed inhibited by the Belorussian policemen. Perhaps they were not quite sure if they had the full approval of their countrymen.

In addition to the waiting civilians, many of those entering and leaving were different kinds of officials, among them Bielanowicz and Serafimowicz. The Meister could communicate with the native visitors only through his interpreter. Surprisingly, despite his efforts, Serafimowicz never learned German. At best his command of the language was poor.

Sharing an office with the Meister provided access to significant information. This included both written materials and telephone calls. Oswald was often asked to attend to the phone, to read and write different reports. He was alert and any news he deemed important he would transmit to the appropriate channels.

Oswald would begin each working day by scrupulously translating whatever was necessary. Sometimes these translations took the entire morning. Only with these tasks out of the way would Oswald turn to the writing of official reports. Among his other duties was participation in the swearing-in ceremonies of new policemen. All newly hired policemen had to swear allegiance to the Führer. A strict observer of rules, Hein made sure that this was done properly. At such times, Oswald would be standing in front of Hitler's picture, with an outstretched right arm in the "Heil Hitler" salute, and slowly translate the oath. Each future policeman had to repeat the words after him. All participants, including Oswald, viewed it with the appropriate seriousness.

Because Oswald was busy in the office he was exempt from many of the tasks performed by the gendarmes. Unlike the Meister and his interpreter, these men spent much of their time in the field, making arrests of people accused of different transgressions. Frequently, these arrests and searches were follow-ups of vague or concrete denouncements. A considerable part of the gendarmes' efforts was devoted to guarding property. The

Germans had large deposits of farm goods, confiscated from local farms, and these goods had to be watched around the clock. Much of the gendarmes' energy was devoted to simple police tasks, ones that rarely required Oswald's presence.

The gendarmes' work did not end with simple police duties. Just as their Belorussian counterparts, the Germans devoted considerable effort to moves against real or imaginary enemies of the state. Ultimately, it was the Germans' responsibility to make the Mir region "Judenrein," clean of Jews. Here in the Belorussian part of Poland they tried to achieve this goal through executions rather than deportations to concentration camps. The Germans were also determined to eradicate all partisan activities. At least once or twice a week they would go into the field against Jews, partisans, and civilians suspected of aiding partisans.

There was, however, a visible difference in the Germans' participation in anti-Jewish and anti-partisan moves. A selected few Germans, three out of thirteen, consistently abstained from becoming a part of all anti-Jewish expeditions. Conspicuously absent from such anti-Jewish expeditions was Meister Hein. Neither he nor the other two were reprimanded for it. No one seemed to bother them. No one talked about their absences. It was as if they had a right to abstain.

In sharp contrast, none of the Germans declined to participate in activities against partisans or those accused of partisan collaboration. As a rule, all anti-partisan moves included Hein and the rest of the gendarmes. If any of them did stay behind it was because of a special reason that had little to do with the raid itself. Moreover, when this happened, each time different individuals refrained from participating in these raids.

The Belorussian policemen seemed to have fewer options than the Germans. When asked to join an anti-Jewish expedition they were expected to comply. In a way, perhaps, their full participation was due to a seeming willingness to engage in such activities. Oswald never noticed any reluctance on their part to join in an anti-Jewish move. Instead, they all appeared eager to go into the field, no matter who the victims were.

About himself Oswald says, *As an interpreter I had to go. Without me they were lost. I was the only language bridge they had. All expeditions were joint activities that included some Belorussian policemen and some gendarmes. There had to be someone who could establish and maintain communication between these two groups. I was the contact. Without me they could not perform their "job" properly. . . . Also Meister Hein made sure that during these expeditions, including the Jewish ones, I had some official translations to do.*

In addition to their joint work, Oswald's contacts with the gendarmes extended to three meals a day, all served in a dining room located in the back of the house. A large long table dominated this room. Three times a day all the Germans would assemble here for food. Oswald was the only non-German among them. Because he spoke their language fluently, the others soon began to treat him like a "Kamerade," a comrade.

Around this dining-room table each gendarme was assigned a permanent place according to rank. The Meister sat at the head of the table. Next to his right side was the "Hauptwachtmeister," Karl Schultz, the second in command. On his left side was the "Oberwachtsmeister," Rothe. Next to them on each side were the lower ranking gendarmes. There were twelve of them, and Hein was the thirteenth. The arrival of the interpreter disturbed the established sitting arrangement, and the Meister demanded that Oswald be seated at his left. But Hein's orders were never questioned—at least not openly.

How did Oswald fit into this group? *I was the only one who had a high school diploma. I also had a special standing because I was the Meister's favorite.* Did the Germans resent this newcomer's privileged position? *No, because I did not belong to their group, I was not one of them. Even though I ate with them breakfast, lunch, and dinner, I was still an outsider.*

In fact, to be different within this group was the rule rather than the exception. Beyond a German nationality, little education, and age (most were over forty), these gendarmes had little else in common. They came from diverse geographic locations. One was even a German from Holland. The only real policeman among them was their boss. The rest were assigned to the gendarmerie unit because of advanced age. They were too old to be sent to the front.

Very different from Hein was Karl Schultz, the second in command. To some he seemed like "a beast in the form of a man."[8] Schultz, a brutal man, a sadist, took great pleasure in torturing people in general, and Jews in particular. For example, when faced with two prospective victims, a mother and child, he would kill the child in front of the mother and only after a day or two execute the mother.[9] And even though heavy drinking was common among all the gendarmes, Schultz distinguished himself by being the only true alcoholic. Drinking merely increased his cruelty.

Not all the gendarmes, however, were as enthusiastic about murdering Jews as Schultz. Once, one of them approached the interpreter with the following question: *"Oswald, do you know what radio means?" I said that I did not know. "Read it backwards," he said, "o i d a r," each letter is a substitute for a word. "Ohne Juden Deutschland armes Reich." In translation this means without Jews Germany is a poor country.* It was rumored that he was a Communist who disapproved of the Nazi anti-Jewish policies.

Also different from the rest in this respect was Rothe, the German-Dutch gendarme. He looked Jewish and Oswald had some doubts about his German nationality. Perhaps for this reason Oswald felt warmly toward him. More important, this Dutch-German and the other one, Potch, never participated in any anti-Jewish Aktion.

Neither the work the gendarmes shared nor the time they would spend eating each day led to the establishment of meaningful friendships. On the contrary, it was clear that whatever ties they had stayed close to the surface. Since they themselves seemed incapable or unwilling to form close attachments Oswald was relieved from similar obligations. He felt no desire and little pressure to become more involved.

These Germans would joke about insignificant incidents that happened in relation to their contacts with the natives. As they did, they would continuously emphasize how primitive and backwards these people were. Personal feelings, meaningful observations about life or death were conspicuously absent from their conversations. Nor did they ever venture into any ideological or political discussions. How much of this superficiality was due to their limited education, limited intelligence, or something else is hard to tell.

It seemed that in their conversations they were consistently avoiding controversial or painful topics. They stayed away from any discussion of the front. Perhaps they felt ill at ease because they were not fighting? Absent from their talks were also all references to anti-Jewish moves. In contrast, they did speak about encounters with partisans. When this happened they would concentrate on successful engagements rather than failures.

Musing about these variations, Oswald notes, *It was clear that there were differences in their outlooks. I think that the whole business of anti-Jewish moves, the business of Jewish extermination they considered unclean. The operations against the partisans were not in the same category. For them a confrontation with partisans was a battle, a military move. But a move against the Jews was something they might have experienced as "dirty." I have the impression that they felt that it would be better not to discuss this matter. . . . Only very, very rarely would one of them stray into this subject.*

Oswald is convinced that, personally, his boss, Hein, disapproved of the mass killings of Jews and that such executions violated his sense of justice. Oswald says, *I never saw him hit a Jew. He never participated in any Aktion against the Jews. He was fair in his treatment of and attitudes toward the Judenrat. I was present when the head of the Judenrat, Rabbi Szulman, and the second in command, Eliezer Breslin would come to see him. Sometimes there were brief negotiations. In my presence there was no talk about bribes. Neither did Hein try to humiliate them. Of course, the Jews had to stand, while the Meister was sitting. This was the official requirement. He had to keep appearances, to follow the line . . . .*

I must say that these members of the Judenrat were dignified. . . . Also here and there when speaking to Serafimowicz the Meister tried to curb this man's excessive killing zeal.

Despite these attitudes and behavior, Hein organized each Aktion. He made sure that during an Aktion every move should meet with all the official requirements. Each part of an Aktion was orchestrated by Hein with special care. He even formalized some procedures. It was Hein who had insisted that before an execution a death sentence be read to the victims. This sentence had to be read in a language the condemned could understand.

Did Hein try to convince himself that these executions were legal? Did he really believe that an official death sentence would justify these murders? Whether he believed it or not, he insisted on such legalistic procedures. And since in Mir he had the ultimate power, this is what was done.

It is ironic that this Hein, who refused to participate directly in the killing of Jews, organized each Aktion, making sure that none of the victims escaped. It is ironic too that in his place he would send Schultz, a cruel sadist and an enthusiastic killer. Surely under these circumstances Hein's absences failed to result in more merciful deaths. He had to be aware of this fact.

Aside from their official duties what else did the gendarmes do? There were practically no organized leisure-time activities. Special lectures were rare, almost nonexistent. All reading materials were scarce. Even newspapers would reach Mir only sporadically, and when these did arrive they were already out of date. These men were probably not interested in any involved reading materials; Oswald never saw any of them read. Only some seemed to be listening to the radio. Heavy drinking was one of their favorite pastimes. Most frequently such drinking took place after work, especially after executions of Jews. A few of these Germans had established sexual liaisons with local women.

Hein had a steady mistress, a Russian woman. She was the wife of a Russian officer who left with the Soviet army. One day, toward evening, when the German and his interpreter were alone in the office, Hein almost apologetically began: "Oswald, I hope that you don't resent me because of my mistress. I hope that you don't think that I am harming her."

Taken aback, not quite understanding, Oswald asked, "Why? What do you mean?"

"Well, I have a wife at home and here this woman."

At a loss, Oswald kept silent. He scrupulously observed the rule of keeping quiet whenever he was in doubt. Soon he was even more surprised. The German was pulling down his pants and his underpants. Then he pointed to a scar near his groin and said, "I was injured during the last war. I cannot have children, so I cannot really hurt this woman."

Facing this partly naked man, uneasy, the youth mumbled, "You don't have to explain."

"But I do, I want you to think well of me. Do you?" Oswald's embarrassed nod put a stop to this exchange.

9

The Savior of Simakowo

The Belorussian woman seemed to be explaining, begging, imploring. Tears kept running down her robust cheeks. From her heaving chest came competing sounds that buried the meaning of her words. Next to her stood the arrested man. He was a Russian POW, frightened but defiant: "Why should I be leaving? What for? We are going to have a baby!" The woman listened attentively. Then she regained enough self-confidence to register her approval with a consenting nod.

The Belorussian policeman who made the arrest told a different story. He came with the prisoner to the gendarmerie because all political cases had to be brought to the attention of the Germans. He made the arrest because the couple's neighbor had filed a complaint, accusing the soldier of planning an escape to the forest, supposedly to join the partisans. A man could be executed for much less.

Visibly shaken, Rufeisen was busy writing. "Oswald, what is the meaning of this?" Hein wanted to know. Without interrupting his task, politely but firmly, the youth answered, "After I finish putting it down I will be in a better position to explain." As soon as the policeman stopped, Oswald dismissed him. With the Belorussian out of the way, now screaming with indignation, the interpreter turned to the prisoner: "Next time you get drunk and hit a woman you will pay for it! Do you understand?"

Still fuming, he told Hein, "Imagine, he beat her up and she is pregnant! All because he had a few glasses of vodka. He created an uproar, breaking things and hitting the neighbor who wanted to stop him. Then he called himself a hero and a partisan! Some hero! No wonder the neighbor went to the police."

An involuntary chuckle escaped from Hein. The expression on the German's face seemed to be saying, "Surely this is nothing of importance! Why waste time?" Out loud he said: "Oh, just give him a warning and let him go." Seemingly unaffected by the Meister's light sentence, Oswald continued to scream: "Off with you! Don't you dare hit her again. You dog!" Then roughly he shoved the man toward and then outside the door. Silently the woman followed. By now the couple understood. Without a word, they left.

Within a week the soldier committed the crime he was accused of—he ran away to the forest. Much later when Oswald was roaming the woods, he met the man. He had indeed become a partisan.

This Russian POW was one of the few fortunate exceptions. He belonged to a small minority of Russian prisoners of war assigned to work on Belorussian farms. He became a part of a program that aimed at reducing the labor-force gap, a gap created by developments that happened during the Russian occupation of Polish Belorussia.

When the Soviets took over this part of Poland, some Belorussians enlisted in the Russian army, while others cooperated closely with Communist authorities. Later, with the outbreak of the Russian-German war, on June 22, 1941, when the Soviets retreated hastily, they either took with them or were followed by many of their Belorussian co-workers. In the end, recruitment into the Red Army, together with voluntary departures, depleted the local labor supply. As a result many farms were left without male workers.

Traditionally overburdened by farm duties, the women were not in a position to perform additional jobs. The existing manpower shortage threatened the agricultural output. The German occupational forces depended on these farm products not only for themselves but also for their fighting soldiers and were considering ways of building up the depleted work force.

Nazi wartime successes in themselves offered an opportunity for such a move. Following the start of the Russian-German war, large numbers of Soviet soldiers gave up fighting. No one knows their exact numbers. For political reasons, till this day, Soviet governments have been refusing to deal with what must have been massive desertions.

Some of these deserters succeeded in disposing of their military clothes and settling down as civilians among the rest of the population. Those who originally had come from these parts of the country simply went back to their homes, where they resumed their lives as civilians.[1] Still, an overwhelming majority of these Russian soldiers after they gave up the struggle surrendered to the enemy and thus became POWs.

Nazi treatment of these Russian POWs was both cruel and ruthless. Some fell victim to mass executions, while others died a slower death, as concentration-camp slave laborers. The estimated figure for Russian POWs who perished in Nazi captivity runs into the millions.[2]

Such policies toward these prisoners of war did not prevent the Germans from occasional lapses. During the initial stages of the Russian-German war, spectacular German victories assured the winners of their military superiority. The Nazis felt invincible. As definite masters, they had little reason to fear the humiliated and defenseless Russian POWs. Instead, they saw in these captured men a solution to some of their labor problems. And so, the Germans released some of these prisoners of war "to satisfy the demands for farm hands, skilled laborers and others."[3]

Highly controlled and supervised, these selective releases of prisoners in no way implied a changed policy. Rather, these were exceptions motivated by self-interest.

Eventually, in addition to contributing to a higher agricultural output, freeing these prisoners led to other benefits. In and of itself, such moves saved the lives of some of them. It increased food production; in addition to helping the authorities, it supplied natives with more agricultural products. The Belorussian women welcomed these men, not only as laborers, but also as lovers. Some of the women became pregnant. For economic and personal reasons, these women were eager to retain such working men as long as possible. All benefited from this special arrangement.

Aware of all these advantages, Hein wanted the situation to continue. Soon, however, shifting political developments interfered with the status quo.

Like the Germans, the Soviet government was also quick in recognizing the potential benefits that could accrue from the large numbers of their captured soldiers. The Russians felt that these prisoners could help them fight the enemy from within. As early as July 1941, the Central Committee of the Soviet Communist Party urged the formation of an anti-German partisan movement.[4] This call was followed by the appointment of Ponomarenko, the first secretary of the Communist party of Belorussia, as the head of the newly created guerilla movement. With headquarters in Moscow, one of the first steps of this organization was the establishment of a school for saboteurs.[5]

Soviet control over the partisans, however, had to wait for at least two years. Scattered throughout different forests, consisting of small splinter groups, these early partisans lacked weapons, leaders, and discipline. They would rob each other of arms and anything else they considered of value.[6] Rivalry and greed would sometimes lead to murder, particularly the killing of unarmed civilians.[7]

Usually these early partisans stayed in forests close to the once-Russian borders, an area that contained huge, dense woods. Initially the majority were Russian deserters or POWs who ran away from Nazi camps. They came to the woods not so much because they wanted to fight the enemy but because they wanted to stay alive. Only when directly threatened did these fugitives retaliate against the German authorities. Still, because of their contact with the natives, their presence was well publicized. Contacts with local peasants were usually limited to food collection, particularly from farms close to the forests. Peasants who were reluctant to supply food were simply robbed.

From the start the Germans recognized the potential threat of illegal forest dwellers, and that others would be encouraged to join them. The Nazis also assumed that the most likely candidates for a life in the woods would be the Russian POWs who worked and lived on the Belorussian farms. Therefore, as a preventive measure, at the beginning of 1942, the Germans would selectively collect some of these Russian farm hands. To achieve their goal, and not create a panic, the authorities explained that a few of these POWs were needed for other jobs. These prisoners were rarely fooled by such official assurances. Instead of letting themselves be taken, many ran away. The Russian soldier who was arrested and brought to the gendarmerie was one of those POWs who realistically assessed the dangers. Others, the more trusting or timid ones, were taken away, never to be heard from again. Officially, by the end of the summer of 1942, no Russian POWs were left in the Mir region.

After a while Belorussian men began to join the ranks of these early partisans. While the specific circumstances for starting a life in the forest varied, essentially they too were motivated by a desire to escape from Nazi persecutions.

It has been argued that initially, without a strongly developed sense of nationalism, the Belorussians had no intention of fighting the Germans. Instead, they assumed a friendly posture toward their new masters.[8]

At first the Nazis were successful in recruiting Belorussian volunteers for work in Germany. Only gradually, and only after news about atrocities committed against the Jews and the Russian POWs, together with news about abuses of foreign workers by German employers, began to reach Belorussia did the supply of these volunteers begin to dwindle. Soon Belorussian laborers refused to enlist for work in Germany.

Short of labor, by 1942 the Germans used force. They started these enforced deportations in urban centers. Later on these raids extended into the countryside. Belorussian young men retaliated by running away to the forests, where they joined the already existent partisan groups or formed their own special units.

Approximately at the same time, at the beginning of 1942, the Germans stepped up their policy of Jewish annihilation. Specific measures of this policy varied with geographic location. In the heart of Poland, the General Gouvernment, all the remaining Jews were forced into urban ghettos where the policy of extermination led to starvation, mass deportations to concentration camps, and occasional mass executions.[9]

In the areas close to the Russian borders, including Western parts of Belorussia, concentration-camp deportations were rare. Here the Nazis would collect Jews who lived in the rural areas and execute them close to their dwellings. Others who lived in small towns and cities were moved into ghettos where, in overcrowded living quarters, they starved, as they slaved to support the Nazi wartime industry. Gradually, selectively, without any apparent logic, these ghetto inmates were also removed from their delapidated homes. The usual outcome was mass executions. Those who were left alive knew about these collective killings. They had also heard about men fighting in the forests. Most stories about these partisans were highly exaggerated; each painted a vivid picture about their heroic escapades.

For Jews forced into a dreary, precarious existence, tales about partisans offered a rare glimmer of hope. Particularly the young began to dream about joining the forest fighters. Little did they know—perhaps they preferred not to—that the disjointed forest bands hardly qualified for the term "movement." But, as long as the Jews continued to live in their isolated quarters, reality did not destroy their favorable partisan perceptions.

Some of these ghetto inmates tried to run away before or during Aktions. A few reached the forests. Unlike the Russian and Belorussian partisans, not all of these Jewish fugitives were young men. Some were older, some were women with or without children. Practically none of these ghetto runaways had any military training. They had no arms and an overwhelming majority did not even know how to handle weapons. Moreover, in prewar Poland most Jews (77%) lived in towns and cities.[10] No matter who these Jewish runaways were, they were unprepared and unaccustomed to life in forests.

And so, all Jewish fugitives became easy targets. Not only were they at the mercy of Nazi raiders, but they also depended on other forest dwellers who were much better equipped for this kind of life. Frequently Jews would reach the woods only to encounter different forms of persecution. Many of them were robbed, abused, and even murdered.[11] Jewish fugitives who made it added yet another category of people to the already heterogeneous forest population.[12]

Though for about two years, subdivided, poorly equipped, and leaderless, from a distance these partisans were perceived as a formidable threat. Their initially haphazard military responses led to exaggerated ideas about their actual or potential power. In the absence of clear-cut evidence rumors about their heroism continued to multiply.

The Germans reacted by devising different strategies of combat. In the region of Mir they tried to enlist the cooperation of Belorussian leaders. At the beginning of 1942 they called for a meeting of all the heads of villages and all small-town mayors. The stated purpose of this meeting was to eliminate the partisan menace. The importance of this gathering was underlined by the presence of a high-ranking SS officer from the larger town Branowicze in addition to Hein and Schultz. Their job was to teach specific ways for dealing with the largely invisible enemy. As usual, Oswald was there in the capacity of interpreter, a vital link of communication between the Germans and the natives.

While translating, Oswald noticed the SS major lean toward Schultz. Then, pointing in Oswald's direction the German whispered: " 'Sagen Sie, is das aber kein Jude? Tell me, isn't he a Jew? 'Aber woh? But no. He is a Pole and an excellent interpreter. When I scream at someone he translates and screams exactly the same way I do!' " Oswald pretended not to have heard.

A few days later one of the Belorussian officials who participated in this meeting came to the gendarmerie. He described in detail a nearby place to which next day a large group of partisans was supposed to come. All Hein understood from the man's talk was the word partisan. Aware of this fact, when translating, Oswald had substituted one word. Instead of tomorrow he said yesterday. Furious, Hein asked, "Why is he coming now to tell me? He should have come before it had happened!" One improvised translation followed another. The confused Belorussian repeated his message. But Oswald said firmly. "The partisans had passed by this place yesterday!"

Oswald had no way of knowing how many and who of the partisans were saved. All along he had been sending warnings to different fighting men. Yet he was convinced that those he had tried to save did not even know about his efforts. He was wrong.

Józef Marchwinski, a commandant of a partisan unit, knew that Oswald "warned the partisans about where and when the police would be looking for us. Such information helped us prepare. . . . For this kind of help we ought to be particularly grateful to Oswald."[13]

German concerns and fears about opposition extended to anyone with a gun. Not only was the possession of weapons illegal, but all civilian gun owners were automatically committing a crime punishable by death. Here too the Nazis appealed to the natives to denounce such transgressors.

Some took these appeals seriously. One day when together with a Belorussian policeman and a German gendarme Oswald was returning to Mir in a horse-drawn wagon, they were stopped by a forester, an old Belorussian, a resident of Simakowo, a nearby village. "I know of someone who has a gun. I can take you there now." Helpless, Oswald had to translate. For the German this was exciting news. "Show us the way!" He invited the forester to climb into the wagon.

The person accused of the crime, a sixteen-year-old boy, lived at the edge of the village. His parents, Polish settlers, had been deported by the Russians to Siberia. Somehow he managed to stay behind. He was taken in by a Belorussian peasant. The boy tried to repay this man by working on the farm.

After the start of the Polish-German war, when his parents were still with him, this boy had found a shotgun in the fields. It might have been abandoned by a retreating soldier. Though some of the parts were missing, the gun was in working condition. The boy was thrilled with his find. No one knew how and when he got ammunition. But he did. Neither his parents nor anyone else thought much about it. He was a resourceful, responsible youngster. In his spare time he would disappear into the forest to practice shooting. He never harmed anyone, not even an animal. Besides, after the deportation of his parents people felt sorry for him. They left him alone. Undisturbed, he continued his innocent pastime.

When the four men entered the boy's hut this "criminal" was at home. Frightened but cooperative, he gave up his treasure. When they arrested him he became confused, not quite understanding what it was all about. For two days he stayed in the prison of the police station in Mir. It mattered little that he was sixteen, that he had harmed no one, and that the gun was old and partially broken. All that mattered was that an important law had been violated. On the third day, the boy was taken to the execution place, behind the police station. Oswald had to read the death sentence, first in German, then in Belorussian: "In the name of the 'Grossdeutches Reich. . .' "

At first the words did not seem to reach the boy's consciousness. Only when he saw the gun point at him did he realize what it was all about. An anguished "No, no, no!" escaped from the depth of his very being. The sound of this "no" was still reverberating in the air when the body hit the ground.

That night, sleep refused to come to Oswald for a long, long time.

The Nazis continued to see in everyone who had a weapon and in those they defined as partisans a powerful destructive force that had to be eradicated. One way in which they tried to accomplish this was by searching the surrounding woods and following all leads and rumors about the enemies' whereabouts.

This enemy was in part elusive, in part nonexistent. For quite some time those who lived illegally in the countryside and forest were neither organized nor powerful. More often than not, they were made up of connected, small bands of ill-equipped Russian deserters, former POWs, and Jewish runaways. All were eager to avoid a confrontation with a superior enemy and preferred to limit their activities to finding food and shelter. Rarely would they attack Germans and only if confronted by one or a few of them. The main inducements in such cases were weapons. Ownership of a gun meant food, power, and ultimately life. And because the partisans preferred to avoid direct battles, official antipartisan expeditions hardly ever faced the enemy.

Frustrated, the Nazis continued to combat these largely invisible opponents by punishing the natives. Whenever it became known that partisans had received food or shelter in a village, or if a German was attacked in the vicinity of a village, its inhabitants were punished severely.

Through swift and vigorous punitive measures the Germans had hoped to stop or reduce partisan operations. In reality, these retaliations seemed to have had the opposite effect. Whenever an anti-German incident happened, and if people found out about it in time, some of the young men would flee into the woods to join the partisans. More men in the forests only helped expand the anti-Nazi forces.

The majority of the peasant population had no such options. Most stayed on. As they continued to take care of their families and their farms, they were caught in the middle. On the one hand, the roaming bands frequently deprived them of food. On the other, as German brutality against the natives grew, the Belorussian peasants were eager to see a German defeat. They welcomed all anti-Nazi moves. Their wish to support the enemies of the Reich was strengthened by the fact that frequently the civilians were made to pay a price for whatever damages the partisans would inflict on the Germans.

Though aware of this ambivalent situation, the Nazis demanded that the natives report all partisan moves, warning them that noncompliance would meet with severe punishments, even death. But neither these requirements nor the actual Nazi terror succeeded in eliminating the partisans. On the contrary, with time anti-German operations accelerated. With greater frequency, Germans who were alone or even in small groups of two or three were attacked.

All such anti-German moves in turn led to swift Nazi reactions. The initiators of these attacks usually would manage to disappear into the woods. The civilians who lived in the vicinity of the crime had to pay the price. In all such cases the Germans relied on the principle of collective responsibility. Thus, the killing of a German could lead to partial or total destruction of a village. Referred to as pacification, the Nazi response often involved the execution of every tenth man from a nearby village and an entire or partial burning of that place.

The Nazis had hoped that in addition to acting as a warning, such punitive measures would do away with the existing cooperation between partisans and civilians. In reality, the natives were not normally even in a position to cut their partisan contacts. When these fugitives demanded help from the peasants, the peasants had to comply. Armed, often ruthless, partisans could easily coerce the natives into submission.

Frequently, severe Nazi retaliations involved people who either could not act in any other way or whose lives were unrelated and untouched by partisan operations. However one looks at it, Nazi terror seemed ineffectual, and such terror only increased the natives' hostility. Hostile anti-Nazi feelings in turn led to more extensive support for the partisan movement. Belorussian help for the partisans increased directly with the increased Nazi terror against the civilian population.

The Soviet government, eager to see a powerful partisan movement, welcomed all the support they could get. It has even been suggested that sporadic killings of Germans were sometimes orchestrated by the Russian authorities to elicit severe Nazi retaliations against the civilian population, who, they knew, would in turn react by supporting the partisans.[14] The same historian also asserts that "the claim that the Soviet agents had created the movement (partisan) is unwarranted, and in fact the credit should be given to the Germans themselves."[15] In this vicious cycle of actions and reactions the partisans and ultimately Russia were the winners, the Germans and the civilians the losers.

In 1942, on a summer day, in the Mir region, in the village Simakowo, a German was shot. The dead man was a soldier, one of those communication experts stationed in the area. When this incident occurred the victim and another Wehrmacht soldier were repairing telegraph wires. Oswald reports: *One of the soldiers was shot. The second one escaped. While the second soldier was running away he looked back and claimed to have seen peasants show to the partisans the direction in which he ran. The partisans chased him and shot in his direction. He escaped. . . . Such incidents were not unusual. By the middle of 1942 partisans were more likely to attack Germans if they considered them to be easy targets. In this case there were only two soldiers and both were busy working.*

In this particular instance the army demanded action. The authorities reacted swiftly. They descended on the village in large numbers. This time, in addition to the gendarmes and Belorussian policemen, the entire Wehrmacht unit of the murdered soldier, some 250 of them, arrived and surrounded the village. Some began to search each hut, while the rest collected the able-bodied men, more than two hundred. These men were brought to a field on the edge of the village where they were ordered to sit on the grass in a semicircle.

The official head of the expedition, Hein, asked to see the chief of the village. Through Oswald the German communicated to the visibly shaken official that all those who had tried to help the partisans catch the second soldier must be identified. Unless this is done, of the assembled men every tenth one will be shot. If carried out this would result in the death of about twenty-five men. Hein added that the village will be burned to the ground.

The head of Simakowo denied there had been any witnesses to the crime. How can he produce people if no one was present when the incident happened? Oswald had no answer to this question. All he wanted was to avoid a mass execution. How should he proceed? Time was running out. Here was Oswald, with Hein and the village head—these three men were the center of attention. They were surrounded by many German soldiers, Belorussian policemen, and gendarmes, all fully armed. On the ground sat more than two hundred natives. They watched carefully. These peasants knew how threatened their lives were. Besides, they were close enough to hear. It was clear to everyone that this event would inevitably end with killings. The only unresolved question was: how many and who? The air was oppressive, full of anticipation.

Oswald was convinced that Meister Hein was unhappy with the prospect of shooting people who had no direct connection to the murder. Still, Hein was under pressure to act. The Wehrmacht, the victim's comrades, came to avenge his death.

Oswald recalls: *I decided to exploit the more or less humanitarian feelings of Hein. . . . I turned to him and said: "This is not the front. Here we are 500 kilometers away from the front. You are the only legal power, you are the one that is responsible. One cannot kill every tenth man because of the shooting of one soldier. You should punish the guilty party." To this he answered: "So find the guilty, or at least those who helped the partisans." He wanted a way out. I had to do something. I turned to the head of the village and said, "The situation is as follows: either every tenth of the men will be killed and the entire village will be burned down or tell me who were the people who were present when the German was shot. If you cannot do that, give me two people of whom the village would want to be rid." He understood. He brought two men. One of them was a retarded youth who did not know what was happening. The other was the local forester.*

It was the same forester who had earlier denounced the Polish boy for possession of a gun. The boy had paid with his life. Oswald feels that as far as this man was concerned, *it is quite possible that the natives knew about many more such deeds about him and they wanted to be rid of him.*

To the forester the case was clear. He realized that he had to appeal to the translator. Oswald remembers: *This man got to his knees and turned his head up to me with his hands folded, as if in prayer: "Sir, tell them that I am not guilty, that I did not do it and I will bring them to the partisans' hideout in the forest!"*

In a split of a second I had to translate, recognizing that since he says it in front of the entire village, the partisans will finish him off anyway, should he be spared by the Germans. Everyone heard his promises. He spoke Belorussian. I realized that if this is what he says he will perish anyway. I also knew that by following the wishes of the head of the village I would be saving not only many of the local men but also partisans in the forest. It was a tragic game about which I am reluctant to talk, but this was the situation. Here I was not yet twenty and I had to decide in a split of a second a matter of such magnitude.

The Meister kept asking: "What is he saying? What does he say?" I looked at the kneeling figure in front of me. He was again and again promising that he would take us to a special hiding place of the partisans. Again everyone heard it. And I? What did I do?

I was translating. In this translation I had to include the word "partisans." I did, as I explained that he did not kill, that the partisans killed the soldier. This was hard to do. The whole thing lasted three or two minutes. It was an inhuman situation. . . . But I repeated again: "He says that he is not guilty, that the partisans shot him. He was only working in the field at the time."

Hein was not rushing. He wanted to be sure. He repeated his question several times. My answer was always the same. Finally the German gave the order. The forester was shot at close range by one of the Wehrmacht soldiers. The Wehrmacht insisted on doing the job. Without a sound, the kneeling man tumbled. Not understanding what it was all about, the retarded youth was shot next. That day another young peasant lost his life as he tried to run away. The expedition ended with the burning of the forester's hut.

The events of this day left on Oswald a deep, long-lasting impression. When it happened, he had to think fast. He did. He did not hesitate. At the time Oswald was convinced that the head of the village had the support of his people and that the selected two had to die. When it was over this initially clear determination was becoming hazy. Oswald's thoughts and even more so his feelings were invaded by doubts, doubts that threatened to disturb his equilibrium. On the one hand, Oswald felt good that he saved so many men from a sure death. Some of those saved were local peasants. The rest were an unknown number of partisans. If surprised in their bunkers, these partisans would have perished. This was the reality. These were the facts.

But did he have the right to decide who would be sacrificed for whom? True, the village head brought forward these two men, but he was the one who suggested it in the first place. The forester was a father of eleven children. The man's death must have caused much suffering for his entire family. In one day this family lost a father, a husband, and a home.

Till now when asked to talk about events of this day Oswald vacillates. Depending on the time and mood, he has different insights into what he had done.

He elaborates, *If I may say so, if you allow me to say it, this was the most heroic of my deeds . . . out of all my wartime activities. Because the whole thing I did in a totally disinterested fashion. Jews were not involved here at all. I had no obligation or special interest in these partisans. I had no obligation toward this village. I did it for people who were for me total strangers. Nor did I act out of hate to the Germans, but simply out of a desire to save human lives. . . .*

I could have said that these people should not concern me and just translate as I was supposed to do. But mine was a struggle to save people. From the start I had reached a decision to rescue anyone I could, regardless of who they were. This was the line I followed. . . . The risk was that among the German soldiers who were there some might have been from Silesia. Some of them might have known the Polish language which is similar to Belorussian. This was a terrible risk. There were too many witnesses. All were standing around. . . . Under the circumstances perhaps I ought to be proud about this incident? Proud because I never exposed myself to a greater danger. At least not when it had to do with people who for me were total strangers. I had nothing in common with them. They were just human beings.

Maybe at the time this was the only way out? But now I ask myself if I had the right to designate as guilty and sacrifice for the others even the retarded youth. Still, under the circumstances, I had to decide right away. I could not have hesitated.

Today my conscience is not clean. The truth is that the forester did not deserve mercy. He was a collaborator. . . . But even this does not give me the right to decide about his death. Particularly since I knew that he had eleven children. . . . As you know his house was burned. I am not sure whether I realized that they would do this.

I would have preferred if this event had never happened. But it took place. And so now I am not sure whether I should be proud of it or ashamed. I don't even want anyone to tell me how I should feel. . . . No one can enter into the situation as it was then at the time.

The Nazis continued to apply swift and severe retaliatory measures against the natives even though they knew such measures increased the hostility against them. They also knew that this hostility could interfere in their struggle against the enemies of the Reich. Without abandoning their punitive policies they wanted to neutralize some of the negative effects. For this purpose, particularly in the rural areas, the Nazis dispatched emissaries to instruct local officials how to create good will among the natives.

One day such an emissary, a secret serviceman of the Polish police in

Baranowicze, arrived in Mir. Originally from Cracow, he came to teach the Belorussian policemen how to behave toward the natives, how to curtail their antagonism. Always the perfect host, Serafimowicz invited the man to stay in his house. The guest was to share Oswald's room.

Oswald remembers, *We slept in two beds in my room. Before we fell asleep he began to talk about Zionist organizations in Cracow. He knew the different groups thoroughly, the left and the right. I listened, pretending to be interested. Perhaps he had wanted me to show him some sign? . . . At one point I felt that either he would reveal himself as a Jew or he would begin to investigate me as a passing Jew. I became apprehensive. He was one of the very few people who inspired fear in me.*

He looked like a typical Pole. But his knowledge of the Jewish organizations and Jewish life was exceptional. Or maybe he knew it all as a member of the secret service? Because he had to know it? His job consisted in moving from place to place and lecturing.

Through his teachings the Germans wanted to make sure that the Belorussian policemen behaved "properly" toward the local population, and would learn how to avoid unnecessary hostility. By engaging this man, the Nazis tried to impress upon the policemen that one of their functions was to protect the people.

Judging by the stepped-up partisan activities and the growing support they received from the natives, such lectures had only a limited effect. Gradually, the Germans seemed to be losing their battle against the partisans. Only when it came to the destruction of the clearly defined, isolated, and humiliated Jews could the Nazis claim spectacular victories.

10

Involvement with the Ghetto

As Oswald continued to help people, time acted as a double edge. It cemented his position at the office, offering more and better opportunities for aid. Oswald's greater experience and more privileged position facilitated his defense of prospective victims. He was also confronted by an ever-increasing Nazi tenacity to destroy. Inevitably, this interfered with Oswald's effectiveness. His life turned into a continuous battle, a battle to save people.

How did Oswald feel about the nine months he spent in Mir, working for the Germans? When asked, he tries to distinguish himself from a righteous person. The latter refers to someone who selflessly protects the needy, without rewards and regardless of cost.

He explains: *I saw myself as a soldier rather than a righteous person. All soldiers fight. Every soldier has to be ready to sacrifice his life for an idea, for others. . . . By coincidence I found myself in a special situation. . . . In my youth I was impressed with the image of Konrad Wallenrod.*

Konrad Wallenrod was a knight in Medieval Prussia, who discovered that he was kidnapped from the Lithuanians during a battle that took place between the Prussians and Lithuanians. Although of Lithuanian parentage, he was brought up as a Prussian knight. When Wallenrod learned about this, he identified with his Lithuanian background and decided to aid his country by leading his order into defeat. In Poland the name Wallenrod continues to suggest a number of images and interpretations. It may refer to a person forced to choose between conflicting loyalties. It also suggests that the traitor hero can only resolve his agonies in an act of noble self-sacrifice.[1]

Who knows, perhaps I used him as a model? But no one would consider Konrad Wallenrod to be a righteous man. My behavior, like his, was soldierly. In some way too it was also an adventure. I was nineteen, twenty. I was constantly under tension. . . . Fortunately the tension did not prevent me from being true to myself. I was watchful, but I was also in control.

In addition to seeing himself as a soldier he remembers feeling like *someone who was sent with a special mission, someone who did not like the mission but had a duty to perform. No matter how I reacted and what I had to do I was convinced that it would have been wrong for a Jew to save himself passively, without using the opportunities he had. For me, not to help others would have been inexcusable.*

But with all the tension and danger my life continued to be exciting . . . what I did for others was a sort of a play, an adventure and a duty. I did what I had to do. It was not heroism. Mine was a battle of a soldier. One fights one way, another fights another way. Do you understand me? . . . I am not a holy gentile who saved Jews, even though he did not have to. I had to do what was right!

It so happened that I found myself in special circumstances. If I had not done what I did I would not have been able to talk to you or look into my brother's eyes. Because what I did was natural I can talk about it freely . . . I must confess, that in some way I also liked the role. I was gratified by it.

Oswald was keenly aware then and continues to be now of his limited power. He explains: *When I saw no possibility to save I kept quiet. There were cases where I simply had to shut my eyes and make believe that I don't see.*

Still I was convinced that to rescue a Jew, at the time when we were being exterminated, was a big achievement. My main aim was to save myself and in this process to retain a Jewish soul. Actually, any way of protecting a human being is all right, if it does not hurt someone else.

I know that few Jews had the opportunity to be active in this way. I think that there were some who had the opportunity and who acted on behalf of others, but who did not succeed. We probably don't know about them.

Though these sober thoughts and decisions continued to influence Oswald's actions, the day-to-day reality proved more complex. And it was this reality that had to accommodate and juggle between rational reasoning and emotions. It was easier to make rational decisions than to control emotions. He knew that he had to be on guard. Frequently his emotions demanded success even though his rational self knew that success was not plausible. And so, no matter how many times he had witnessed executions he felt overwhelmed, emotionally wounded. Similarly, when confronted with the suffering of others he could not avert feeling pain. At such times he became acutely aware of his powerlessness.

Yet he also knew there was much he had to be grateful for. He had a gun, but was not forced to use it. Those who were with him must have guessed that he did not approve of the killings. Perhaps those who had participated in mass murders would have liked to see him do the same? Perhaps they would have liked to see the difference between him and themselves disappear?[2]

At the beginning of 1942 Oswald's position of noninvolvement was challenged. It happened during an Aktion in the village of Łukowo. This village had one Jewish family of seven. Among them was an old couple, one of whom, the man, was unable to walk. During the Aktion the old man was ordered into a horseless sleigh.

This event stuck in Oswald's mind. *Two young men, probably the grandchildren, were made to push the sleigh up the hill. It was a strenuous task. As they worked their way up on the snow-covered path, they were dripping with sweat. It occurred to me that the age difference between these two was the same as between me and my brother. I wondered. What goes on in their heads? Do they know? I knew, and because of it, felt numb with pain. The uselessness of it all!*

At the top of the hill Schultz ordered the party to stop next to a big hole, only partially covered by snow. Without a murmur the condemned obeyed. Oswald continued to search their faces. He found no fear. He found nothing at all. No expression. It seemed as if these people had already departed to another world.

Then, with guns pointed at the victims, the executioners ordered them to lie down on the ground. They obeyed. Eager for action, a few of the killers darted into the direction of the victims. Schultz stopped them: "Halt!" He turned to the interpreter: "Oswald, bitte, schiessen Sie. Oswald, please shoot."

What happened? *I still don't know whether this was a favorable gesture or an attempt to provoke me. I was there as an interpreter, not just as a common policeman. I felt that I had a right to refuse. I said, "Nein danke ich werde nicht schiessen. No thank you, I will not shoot."*

Without a word, Schultz pushed his men aside. Then, systematically, one by one, he shot the seven people on the ground.

As soon as they convinced themselves that the bodies were motionless, the Germans and the Belorussians became impatient to get away. Oswald welcomed their haste. Without a glance back, without a word, he climbed into the waiting sleigh. After that they kept moving from one village to another, from one hamlet to another, collecting Jews. At each stop, a few more victims climbed into a sleigh. Eventually, there were forty-one, among them many children.

The final destination of this strange caravan was a large Polish estate, Dołmatowszczyzna, where the victims were to be shot. The signal for shooting had to be translated from German into Belorussian: "Achtung" Attention, "Feuer" Fire. The translator was performing his duties mechanically, trying not to see, not to notice. Mercilessly, defiantly, his mind was registering every detail.

As usual, here too all the steps were orchestrated from a distance by Meister Hein. He ordered that each victim be shot in the heart. In practice, this was not always possible.

On that late afternoon, among the prospective victims was a barber. He had come from Warsaw. During the Russian occupation he reached the Mir region, hoping to escape from the Nazi menace. He was immediately recognized as the best, most talented barber. Eventually, even the Germans took advantage of his rare skills. All of them became his customers.

Still, on this wintry day, neither his talents nor his past services made a difference. With the rest of the Jews, he was shot in the chest. The bullet refused to do the job. On the ground, wounded and visibly in pain, the barber moved his head. He eyes searched for the man whose hair he used to cut: "Herr Schultz, bitte noch eine Kugel im Kopf! Please, one more bullet for my head!" Then, in Polish, in an almost apologetic way, he added: "I don't want to suffer any more." The German heard him. Without fuss, as if he has just received the most simple request, he put a bullet into the barber's head.

Among these victims were four ravishing teenage girls. Schultz asked them to stand to the side and wait. He was attending to the killing of others. Only after everyone else in this group was shot did he turn his attention to the four beauties. Without ordering them to lie down, he personally shot them, one by one. He was precise. After a single bullet, each was dead.

Because of their exceptional looks, did he feel more powerful? Did this ability to destroy something of rare value create a feeling of omnipotence? He was an eager, enthusiastic killer, particularly so when faced with the extraordinarily beautiful.

Oswald had been informed about this Aktion ahead of time and transmitted the news to the proper channels. Warnings reached all the communities that were singled out for liquidation. The Jews were urged to hide. Some found shelter with non-Jewish neighbors. Others created their own hiding places. Still others left for the surrounding woods. The official date for the Aktion came and passed. Nothing happened. After several days, and still no sign from the authorities, the people decided that the message must have been one of those frequent false alarms. Spectacular unfounded rumors were not unusual in those days. Those who had listened to the warnings returned to their homes.

Then, suddenly, without prior notice, the policemen and gendarmes were ordered into the field. The big Aktion was to begin. As Oswald was leaving, at the last minute, he passed on the information to his contact. It was too late. The Jews of Mir could not send out the message in time. The victims were taken by surprise.

When it was over, those responsible for the operation had reason to congratulate themselves. Pleased with themselves, Schultz and Serafimowicz were happy to accept an invitation for dinner from the Polish manager of the Dołmatowszczyzna estate. The two asked Oswald to join them.

In the dining room, the estate manager and his three guests were joined by a Jewish physician, Dr. Lefkowicz, and his family. Originally from Vilna, the doctor studied medicine in Switzerland. His German was impeccable. Because he was the only physician in the area, Schultz was instructed to leave him and his large family alone.

At the table, excellent food, vodka, and a variety of wines were continuously being served to this strange assortment of diners. The drinks, in particular, led to a more relaxed mood and lively conversations. Oswald noted that *after the second and third vodka, the discussion turned to the Jews and Schultz became very talkative, very gay. . . . But then the doctor began to defend Jews. Exchanges became loud, heated.*

More intelligent, a smooth talker, the physician used logic and easily showed how absurd the German's position was. With quite a few drinks behind him, Schultz was becoming more and more agitated. His color changed. With a raised voice, he was on the verge of an explosion. In another minute he could be reaching for his gun.

Conscious about the situation, I tried to catch the doctor's eye. When this was not possible, under the table I kicked his knee several times. I continued to kick it vigorously until he understood my signal. The doctor changed the tone of his voice and agreed with Schultz. . . . The German calmed down. . . . Try to explain to someone that with a kick of a knee you can save a man's life!

Within a few months, the physician and his family ran away from the estate. For a while they were protected by a Belorussian peasant. When they were compelled to leave his place, they went into the forest. There, except for the doctor's wife, all were murdered by Russian partisans.

Years later, after the war, the doctor's wife[3] visited Oswald. She reminded him of the story and thanked him for his effort to save her husband.

In the spring of 1942, Oswald was elevated to the position of a noncommissioned officer. It was both a recognition for past services and an attempt at giving more authority to Hein's orders. Indeed, because most of the

Meister's orders were transmitted through his interpreter, the German felt that these would have more weight if delivered by a noncommissioned officer.

Oswald's job was not affected by this change. He continued to work as Hein's interpreter and secretary with little or no official autonomy. However, to some, those on the outside, Oswald's promotion seemed more important than it really was. Because of it and because his new rank was the same as that of the local police commandant, some called him "commandant." Others even confused his position with the position of the regional commandant of the police, Serafimowicz.

In this connection Oswald comments, *I was certainly not the regional commandant, but in a practical sense, I was the only one who was the intermediary between the Meister and all the local heads of police. I was never officially nominated to be the regional commandant. I was the acting regional commandant for only a few weeks. . . . De facto, I transferred all the information to the Meister and from him to others. Because of this, at times, I did perform important functions. Of course, I was never independent—what I did was through the Meister.*

Oswald remembers a day when he walked through Mir in the company of Schultz. Without much warning, the German became enraged. According to a Nazi law, Jews were supposed to use the middle of the road instead of the sidewalk and greet the passing German. That day, Ephraim Sinder was guilty of a "crime." He was moving along the pavement and did not greet Schultz. Yelling and cursing, Schultz ordered the man to come with him to the gendarmerie.

This Nazi was not about to miss an opportunity to degrade and inflict pain. Nor was there any way in which he could be dissuaded from following through with a punishment. It would have been useless, even dangerous, to try to intervene. Oswald could not afford to antagonize this powerful, brutal man. Without a word, he followed the two into the gendarmerie. Inside, still excited, Schultz was telling Hein that this Jew had the audacity not to use the middle of the road. A law was obviously broken. Hardly overjoyed, the Meister said nothing. His silence meant agreement. Twenty lashes had to be administered for this crime.

It was Oswald's duty to translate into Belorussian the reasons for the arrest and the form of punishment, while Schultz was ordering the victim to pull down his pants and lean on the table. Impatient, before the prisoner had the time to obey, the German was already waiting with a thick leather belt in hand. Oswald had to count. The belt started its job. Wherever it fell, it left a red mark. The victim, a grown man, did not scream; only here and there an involuntary groan would escape him. These brief noises were followed by self-imposed silences. Soon these sounds stopped altogether. Oswald continued to count, careful not to miss. He knew, from experience, that an error would give Schultz an excuse to start from the beginning. When he reached "twenty," the beating stopped. "Dress and go home," Hein ordered. With shaky hands, Sinder pulled up his pants. He seemed dazed. Staggering, without as much as a glance or a nod, he disappeared behind the door. Oswald felt tired, very tired. Yet he was also grateful that Hein was there. He knew that without the restraining presence of his superior, Schultz might have killed the man. As far as Oswald knows, Schultz never paid for his crimes. In 1944 he disappeared from Mir just before the Red Army came.

When alone with his boss, Oswald could afford to be less passive. He knew that although responsible for all the executions, the Meister basically did not approve of cruelty. In a strange sort of way, in this sea of destruction, Hein tried to retain a sense of justice. And it seemed to Oswald that this man often looked for excuses not to harm. Whether his assessment was right or wrong, Oswald knew how to appeal to Hein's special sense of fairness. He remembers one such appeal.

The Germans caught a young woman near Nowogródek, with a small child. She was accused of being Jewish. Because she claimed to be Russian, and with a woman it was hard to determine a Jewish origin, the authorities were sending her from one police station to another to be investigated. She insisted that the town Minsk was her permanent home.

Fluent in Russian, the woman refused to change her story. After many interrogations and moves from one station to another, the woman was sent to Mir with the request that she be transferred to the nearby town of Stołpce. The order specified that from there she should be delivered to the authorities in Minsk who would be in a better position to check out her story. Each move required the presence of a guard.

One look at this prisoner convinced Oswald that she was Jewish. During the interrogation he turned to Hein, "I am sure that she is Russian. Why should you waste your valuable time on such a case?" "Well, what do you suggest I do?" the German asked. "Let her go, she will have to return home to Minsk. If she is Jewish, they will find out and they will know how to deal with her."

But Oswald did not stop at that. *I also tried to persuade him that, after all, the war has been won and that it makes no sense to waste the time of a special policeman to accompany her to Stołpce. I urged him to free her instead.* He let the woman go. She left without a word, behaving as if the whole incident was a terrible mistake.

Much later, in the forest, the same woman identified Oswald as her savior. Only then did she have the opportunity to thank him properly. She and her child survived the war.[4]

In Nazi-occupied Europe, including Western Belorussia, time was running out for Jews. In the Mir region, a constant reminder was the selective mass execution of Jews from the surrounding communities and hamlets. Despite such mounting evidence, some Jews continued to cling to the idea that somehow, in some way, they would be spared. In Mir in particular, these hopes were supported by the absence of large-scale disturbances. Whatever loss of life there was, and there was some, it happened in a haphazard, unplanned way. Only occasionally when German soldiers would visit the town, through the windows of their moving vehicles, would they shoot at the passing Jews. Sometimes their bullets killed. Sometimes they missed. Sporadically, too, Jews in Mir were punished or executed for a variety of transgressions: black market dealings, curfew violations, or for improperly greeting a German. All such instances were infrequent. Compared to the total liquidation of entire communities, these were only looked on as unfortunate accidents.

But things did not stand still. In May 1942, the Jews of Mir were ordered to move to the Mirski Castle on the outskirts of town. Neglected, partly in ruin, the castle seemed more like a prison than a place of residence. This large, run-down structure was surrounded by a massive stone wall, with a river running next to one of its sides. The stone wall had one gate and a number of hard-to-reach openings that served as windows. Before the castle was transformed into a ghetto, the Germans had placed barbed wire on top of its walls.

The castle had to accommodate 805 individuals, inevitably leading to unbearable overcrowding. Similarly, because the wells were not built for this size population, there was a shortage of water. For the same reason, toilet facilities were practically nonexistent.

In these new surroundings, however, the ghetto inmates showed an extraordinary capacity for accommodation and adjustment. By mutual consent, they decided that the young would occupy the top floors while the old and less able would stay on the lower levels. The Judenrat, with Rabbi Szulman as head, was responsible for the establishment of guards that would prevent all unauthorized moves in and out of the ghetto. This was an important accomplishment supposedly achieved by bribing the administrative head of the Mir region, Bielanowicz.

Concretely, this meant that the watch over the ghetto would be kept by Jewish policemen who were in favor of food smuggling. Smuggling kept starvation in check. The Jewish police was also responsible for sanitary conditions, which prevented punitive actions that might have come from the outside.[5]

About the wartime Jewish authorities in Mir, Oswald remarks, *All the things you might have heard or read about the Jewish police and Judenrat do not apply here. The Mir policemen were all right. They behaved properly. The Judenrat simply selected a few young men who watched the gate, the entrance to the ghetto. They were particularly concerned with seeing to it that no one came in to hurt them or bother them. Whatever other tasks they had to perform, they never abused their fellow Jews. Instead, they tried to protect them as well as they could.*

Oswald knew the Judenrat from its dealings with the Germans. In this capacity, he never saw them engage in any wrongdoings. On the contrary, whenever the head of the Judenrat, Rabbi Szulman, did come to the gendarmerie with a request, he managed to retain his dignity. The man's sense of responsibility was mingled with a permanent sadness, a sadness that verged on depression.

With very limited power, more often than not the Jewish representatives could do little for their people. Most of their requests, particularly when they had to be presented to someone other than Hein, met with cynical rebukes. Thus, for example, a standard reaction to their pleas to be permitted to build outhouses was: "Don't eat so you will not need outhouses."[6]

The ghetto inmates reacted to their plight in a variety of ways. Some were convinced that if they continued to comply with the German orders their lives would be spared. Others felt that no matter what they did, their destruction was inevitable. Some of those who felt this way, without considering any options, waited for the end. Others in this category wanted to fight. They refused to be passive. In turn, this desire to fight was also based on a variety of motivations and different aims.

Dov Resnik, Oswald's main contact with the ghetto, claims that after the transfer to the castle, the young began to organize into a resistance group. He writes: "We started to organize our friends. Most of them were members of the Hashomer Hatzair (Leftist Zionist Youth Organization) because we trusted them most. We had gathered about eighty people. They were divided into groups of five. We intended to fight, if and when the Germans would come to liquidate the ghetto. Every group of five had its special area of operation. For that eventuality, we prepared stones, sticks, semi-arms. We had no real arms."[7]

Shlomo Charchas, a former leader of the Vilna Hashomer Hazair, acted as the official head of the underground in the Mir ghetto. He maintains that their resistance group accepted all whom they could trust, regardless of political affiliation. Judging by Resnik's comments, those they did trust came mostly from their own political party.[8]

Oswald was detached from the internal life of the ghetto. He notes: *I did not know the people in the ghetto by name. Consciously, I did not want to know their names. If I know some of the names now, it must be from a later period.*

It was much safer this way. Knowledge about ghetto life would not improve his ability to help and could interfere with his freedom to act. Such knowledge was potentially dangerous. If caught, under torture one never knew what information one might be forced to divulge. Besides, Oswald's increased contacts with Jews could have led to discovery, hence to danger. Such contacts had to be kept at a bare minimum. Inevitably, Oswald's overall detachment from the internal affairs of the ghetto and his ignorance about its affairs extended to the Jewish underground as well.

I was outside. I never participated in the organization of the underground. Only by chance did I find out about it. I do not know whether it was a resistance group, in the sense of being really organized. You see, they never left the castle. Probably there were no special exercises. In the ghetto, there were some ex-soldiers from the Polish army who knew how to use guns. But I know that they had no real weapons. At least none for quite a while . . . I never asked them whether they had an underground or not. I did not want to know. It did not interest me. It was better for me to be ignorant about this.

In fact, the first time Oswald heard about a Jewish resistance group was indirectly through a denouncement by the Belorussian peasant, Chudoba. A ghetto inmate in Mir, a young man named Ben-Zion Szimonowicz knew this peasant.[9] One day he approached him with a request for arms. Actually, their meeting turned into a social occasion in Chudoba's home. The two men ate and drank vodka and discussed Szimonowicz's need for weapons. Under the influence of alcohol, the young man confided in the older one that the ghetto underground had sixty members planning to fight the Germans. They needed arms and were willing to pay a good price.

Chudoba expressed an interest in this important deal. The two agreed that, as a first step, the next day Chudoba will deliver one gun to the ghetto. Szimonowicz promised to arrange access to the castle with the Jewish policeman at the gate. At this ghetto meeting, a gun was to be exchanged for money.[10]

Next day, instead of searching for a weapon, Chudoba went straight to the head of the regional Belorussian police, Serafimowicz. There he told the story about the Jewish resistance group. Serafimowicz and the Belorussian peasant came to the gendarmerie where the denouncer repeated the news in front of Hein. At that point Serafimowicz ordered Oswald to render only a partial translation. All he wanted Oswald to say was that the young Jew Szimonowicz wanted to buy a gun. For the rest of the facts Serafimowicz wanted to take credit later on. An unauthorized possession of a gun was a crime punishable by death.

Though there was enough evidence to convict, the Meister preferred to catch the guilty in the act. What happened? *The peasant was waiting for instructions. I was the go-between in the entire exchange. We decided, with the Meister, that we will give Chudoba a broken and useless revolver. With this gun,*

Chudoba was to go to the ghetto. The two of us, Serafimowicz and I, were to go to the ghetto too. But instead of entering, we were supposed to stay in the bushes and wait across the entrance to the castle until they would let the peasant in. Only after a short while were we to go into the ghetto to make the arrest as the illegal transaction was taking place. We had some time left. Serafimowicz said: "Let me go home and take a coat." When he left, I left on my bicycle for the ghetto. I decided that I had about ten minutes, no more. The ghetto was a kilometer and a half from town. Excuse me for focusing so much on my own personal actions. It would be better if someone else had told about it. But I say it because this is how it was, well, to this I have witnesses. I went by bicycle to the castle. One of the three men from Vilna, Israel Resnik, was keeping guard. I told him: "I forbid you to let anyone come into the ghetto. Whoever would come, you are not to open the gate. This is an order!"

After this, Oswald jumped on the bicycle and rushed back to the gendarmerie. *In the meantime, Serafimowicz returned, he also brought my coat and on bicycles both of us went again to the ghetto and sat in the bushes as planned. Chudoba arrived. He came to the ghetto gate. No one opened.*

He shouted for someone to open, began to pound on the door, with more and more vigor. Nothing happened. Furious, he went to meet the two men hidden in the bushes. At that point, the peasant knew only the name of this one Jew who approached him for the deal. In no way could the Jewish police refuse access to the head of the Belorussian police. That same day, on the basis of Chudoba's information, Serafimowicz arrested Szimonowicz. The arrest took place toward the evening. With the prisoner locked up in a special cell, Oswald and the Belorussian head of police parted company.

Thus far, Hein knew nothing about a Jewish resistance group. All he heard was that one particular man wanted to purchase a weapon. Oswald is convinced that the Belorussian *arrested Szimonowicz with the intention of starting an involved investigation. He wanted to show what a gifted investigator he was. No doubt, such a successful investigation would have led to an important promotion.*

For the third time in one day, Oswald went to the ghetto. Israel Resnik was again the policeman on duty. This time, Oswald came to warn of the impending danger. He told them that most probably the next day Szimonowicz will be interrogated and under torture might break. Should he reveal the names of the resistance group members, they too will be executed. Oswald advised those who might be implicated to hide and stay hidden until the completion of the investigation. After that, a new decision would have to be reached.[11]

But the least expected happened. *The same evening, Serafimowicz was riding his bicycle, I don't remember where to. He had around his waist a small revolver. The gun went off and a bullet hit him on the upper part of the leg close to his groin. He was taken to the hospital in Baranowicze and stayed there for six weeks. He was operated on. I remained with the Meister. Because Hein knew that the prisoner wanted to buy a gun, I could not defend him. He was shot the next day, in my presence. So this way, no one could find out about the sixty other Jews that supposedly were involved in the underground operation.*

Hein was convinced that Oswald was the only one who could step into the shoes of the flamboyant, powerful Serafimowicz. Indeed, during this man's absence, Oswald became the acting head of the regional Belorussian police. The newly appointed acting commandant once more contacted his ghetto friends. For those who might have been implicated in the affair of the gun, the danger was over. At least, for the time being, the ghetto inmates were not threatened.[12]

When after six weeks Serafimowicz left the hospital, he was promoted to a high ranking officer. By giving this kind of a promotion to an uneducated man, the Germans might have been showing how little meaning the high rank of a Belorussian had. No German would have been elevated to as high a position with as little schooling. Though in absolute terms Serafimowicz's new rank was higher than Hein's, he was still subordinated to the German. Being German was more important than having a high rank, any rank.

Even before the Jews were ordered into the castle, like the rest of the population, they had been exposed to all kinds of tales about partisan activities. In their case in particular, the stories assumed a very special meaning. Marchwinska, who eventually survived as a partisan, explains: "We were desperate. We were like someone who is about to drown and tries to cling to anything that promises life. The idea of joining the partisans gave us hope. In reality we had no contacts. None whatsoever. What we heard came from peasants who would tell us that there were partisans. We Jews exaggerated their presence and their power. We know now that at the time, in 1942, their numbers were insignificant. For us, however, the dream was important and not the reality. This dream told some of us that our salvation depended on the partisans."[13]

Rumor had it that the partisans accepted only able-bodied men and only if they were armed. Not surprisingly, those eager to join were looking for weapons. In the ghetto, four young men approached Charchas and Resnik with a suggestion that they try and organize an escape to a nearby forest to join Russian partisans. The four, Velvel Rabinowicz, Baruch Fikus, Ben-Zion Pisner, and Alter Bulocki, said that they knew a Russian prisoner of war and a Belorussian peasant who promised to sell them arms and establish contacts with Russian partisans. Charchas and Resnik rejected the proposition—they preferred to rely on Oswald.[14]

The four youths decided to act on their own. After some initial negotiations, they were set to finalize the deal. They were to meet both the Russian and the Belorussian at a farm. It was isolated and their meeting was to take place in a barn. All the parties agreed that at that time a transfer of money for guns would take place, followed by a meeting with the partisans.

When the four youths came to the barn, they were taken by surprise. The Russian and the Belorussian attacked them with an ax. Three of the Jews were murdered on the spot. The fourth, Velvel Rabinowicz, escaped. Unharmed, he reached the ghetto, where he told the story to the head of the Judenrat.

In the meantime, the two murderers stripped the dead of their money and buried them in the barn.

A day after the event, the head of the Judenrat came to see Hein. Oswald remembers that *without explaining the reasons for the youths' visit to the farm, Szulman simply informed us that three Jews went to the countryside and failed to return, and that he believes that they went to this particular peasant.* His name was Chulidoba.[15]

Hein did not like it when others assumed the position of judges, self-appointed judges . . . I went with the Meister, maybe even Serafimowicz, to the farm to investigate. The peasant and the Russian confessed without any hesitation and showed us where they buried the bodies. They did not think they had committed a crime. After all, these were only Jews! The Meister thought otherwise. He shot both of them right on the spot. They were buried in the same place. I was present when this happened so I remember it well.

Except for the two Resnik cousins, Israel and Bereczke (Dov), and Shlomo Charchas, for quite a while no one else knew that Oswald was a Jew. Sinder, the man who Oswald watched being lashed by Schultz, is convinced that "no one thought about it. Who would think that a Jew would be a Belorussian policeman?"[16]

Without suspecting this imposter's true identity, the ghetto inmates knew he was different. Cila Kapelowicz recalls that *All of us knew that Oswald was good-natured, that he would not beat people. When he rode the horse or walked around holding a whip, he would say that there is no point in fearing him, he does not hit people. He never did. Of course, we did not know that he was a Jew. We knew nothing at all about that.*[17]

Eventually, Fani Bilecki was added to the three who knew the whole story. She explains: "Shlomo Charchas was my friend. He came and told me the secret, that there is a boy here who was with them in Vilna and he promised to help. The story was so fantastic that at first I thought that it might be someone's imagination. Still these were not ordinary times—anything could happen. He made me swear not to tell it to anyone. This was the biggest secret I had ever kept."[18]

For the ghetto inmates anyone in authority who would help Jews without taking bribes was under suspicion. Oswald was aware of this. *They were talking about me in the ghetto. In a way I was too good. That is why someone made up a story that I took from a woman a bottle of milk she bought illegally and broke it on the pavement. Even if I had done such a thing, it would not have been so terrible and maybe it would have had a purpose—to show that I was not as good.* His friends, who knew who he was, tried in other ways to make him more believable. One day, he met Resnik in front of the ghetto.

I think that I was on my horse, and my friend, Dov Resnik, asked "Maybe you could use a watch?" I am not even sure if I had one or not. But I told him "no." I told him that if he will give me a watch, I will throw it into the water. This is how it was with bribes—and that was all.[19] Someone also spread the rumor that Oswald slapped Eliezer Breslin, a Judenrat member, in front of other people.[20]

The strongest, most virulent opposition to and suspicion of the interpreter came from members of the Judenrat. From the very beginning, when Oswald was sending warnings about future Aktions, the Jewish Council refused to act on them unless they were informed about their source. Out of necessity, the Judenrat was told that Oswald, because of the goodness of his heart, was supplying this information. Eventually, the Judenrat had many opportunities to convince themselves that his warnings were genuine and that, if followed, they could have saved lives. Sometimes, in fact, they did. But the Judenrat's distrust lingered. This young interpreter definitely did not live up to their stereotyped expectations. Nor did the evidence before them disperse their doubts. On the contrary, they were convinced that eventually only trouble would come from the ghetto's association with this Pole.

After the war Fani Bilecki said: "When Oswald was the head of the police, he told us: 'You don't have to hurry. I can promise you one thing, I will most probably know ahead of time about the date of the liquidation. I cannot promise to save you, I cannot change the laws.' "[21]

Oswald was aware of the Judenrat's attitudes. But this in no way changed his determination to help. One day, in June 1942, on entering his office, Rufeisen saw Hein talking on the phone. From the Meister's subservient "Yes, sir, of course, I have the date, the 13th of August," Oswald knew that someone of high rank had to be on the line. Then, an attentive silence was followed by a vigorous yet deferential: "Total liquidation. It is clear, the 13th of August. Jawohl!" Whoever was on the other end hung up.

Hein's distracted, uneasy manner told that he would have preferred if his interpreter had not listened to the conversation. Surely, this youth needed no explanation.

And so the older man said, "Oswald, you are the only one here besides me who knows. I am sure that you have guessed. There will be a total liquidation of the Mir ghetto on August 13. If anyone finds out about it, I will know that you supplied the information."

"Yes, Meister."

With this exchange barely finished, Oswald was already wracking his brains about the possibilities for rescue. "Don't lose your head, slowly, carefully" a voice kept urging him. Momentarily, this voice of reason was overpowered by a strong impulse to get away. To do something. He could not afford to lose time. But he had to. Caution won. Caution forced him to wait and to act on this information in a careful and systematic way.

11

Organizing the Escape

Hein sat behind his desk. He had been listening to the man standing before him. As a Jew, Rabbi Eliachu Szulman, the head of the Judenrat, could not be asked to sit down—this was a Nazi law. Next to Szulman stood another Judenrat member, Eliezer Breslin. This second visitor took no part in the conversation. Only his eyes spoke.

The rabbi's request was simple, yet important. "We would like you to preserve our community. Surely, Herr Meister, you can see to it that our ghetto continues as is?"

The German seemed awkward, uneasy. "I can make no promises."

"Don't we work hard? Don't we contribute to the Reich's war efforts?"

Looking more uncomfortable, the Meister nodded in agreement. Still a refusal followed. "I would be lying if I told you that I am going to preserve the ghetto."

Then Hein excused himself and left the room. When he returned, he noticed jewelry and watches on his desk. Szulman explained, "This is a gift from our people to you."

The German shook his head. "It would not be right. You must take it with you. You see, I can give you nothing in return." Almost apologetically, he made a parting gesture.

But Szulman had another request. "Herr Meister, will you see to it that we die a humanitarian death?"

A brief silence, then Hein's voice. "I will try to. I can promise you this."

The meeting was over. In an unusual show of respect, the German escorted the two Jews to the door.[1]

Oswald does not remember this visit. He is convinced that it took place in his absence. These officials might have requested a private audience. After all, they had come to discuss sensitive matters, including a bribe!

At the time of this visit the Judenrat had no idea about the actual liquidation date for the ghetto. Oswald thinks that *they came because they could not help but realize how all over the region entire communities were being destroyed with most of the area Jews falling victims to mass executions. The obvious conclusion was that they might be next in line. . . . It is also possible that the administrative head of the region, Bielanowicz, told them that the ghetto would be soon liquidated.*

It was to Bielanowicz's advantage to scare the Jewish leaders. He knew that to avert death they would pay him well. All along, for exorbitant sums, this Belorussian official had been offering all kinds of "services" to the Jews. More often than not, these services were of dubious value. Usually they took care of nonexistent, imaginary perils.

Later, Oswald heard from Resnik that Bielanowicz approached the Judenrat. *The Belorussian promised to prevent a liquidation of the ghetto if the Judenrat would pay him 20,000 German marks. They agreed that this sum will be paid in four installments: 5000 each. The first was delivered in late June 1942. The second was to be paid sometime in September. Because I knew that the date for the annihilation of the ghetto was August 13, I realized even more fully how fraudulent Bielanowicz's claim was.*

For the time being, however, Oswald and his Vilna friends decided not to divulge the liquidation date to anyone. Had the authorities realized that others knew about the final Aktion, this might have endangered Oswald's life. More important, spread of this information might have interfered with the anticipated rescue. In short, the August 13 Aktion, and all the plans designed to hinder its success, had to remain secret.

The need to deal with this future event raised many issues. Some had to do with the determination to fight. The very idea of a struggle led to questions of how, when, and where. Inevitably, a fight with homemade, improvised weapons, the kind the ghetto Jews had, would have quickly turned into a suicidal gesture. Ironically, this suited the mood of some ghetto inhabitants. Fani Bilecki explains, "We did not think about life, we only thought of how to die—how it would be best to die. Some thought that we should commit suicide. Some thought that we should run and let the enemy shoot us from the back."[2]

For some, this preoccupation with death was paralleled by a determination to fight. Those who wanted to fight insisted that a battle with knives and other improvised weapons, no matter how desperate and uneven, would be better than passive submission.

The strongest supporters of a battle were the ghetto underground leaders. They felt that because the ghetto was, in effect, a fortress, they might succeed in defending it for a while. They dared to hope that before their death they would inflict some losses on the enemy.[3] The ideas of death and struggle were in turn dominated by a desire for revenge.[4] This desire became an obsession. They knew, however, that without arms it would at best turn into a desperate move with no real results. Trapped, feeling frustrated, they turned to Oswald who could not ignore their pleas. He supplied them with weapons.

About his offer to give them arms, Oswald talks as if it were the most natural thing. *Because the ghetto had no guns, I had to do it. . . . At the gendarmerie we had an assortment of arms and ammunition. Some of it we had confiscated directly from the natives, some we had collected during raids in the forests. Also, whenever the natives found weapons, they would bring them to us because this was the law.*

We cleaned all these items . . . our policemen did. When they were in usable condition they would give some of these pieces to me. I then carried them into the attic or placed them in a special cupboard in the room I shared with the Meister. The cupboard was locked. But I had access to the key. They trusted me.[5]

When transferring arms to the ghetto, Oswald took special precautions, particularly with bigger items. Often, he would take one of those treasures to the garden and put it in the raspberry bushes, close to the fence. This fence had a few removable boards. When ready to bring the gun to the castle, he would remove the boards and then carefully replace each. Sometimes he would hide a large gun in the garbage from the stable. At night, when going horseback riding, he would retrieve it.

Between Oswald's possession of a weapon and its final destination was an important additional step. *Whenever I took weapons from the closet or from the attic, that same day I would notify my people that I will be meeting them. They waited for me in a shed close to the castle wall. At the designated time I would push in the weapons through a little opening in the ghetto wall.*

To ease Oswald's burden, his friends recruited a helper, Leib Ickowicz, a Jewish youth who seemed to have all the necessary qualifications: courage, good judgment, and enthusiasm. Ickowicz worked outside the ghetto. He was an excellent painter, known for creating beautiful signs. He also helped with the gendarmes' horses. After work, Leib would meet Oswald in the gendarmarie. He would enter the place with an empty briefcase and leave with it filled with ammunitions and explosives. To camouflage these transfers, the two conspirators would cover the goods with food.

Toward the end, when time was becoming a problem, the two youths made daily deliveries. At that stage, they had established a routine. The resistance leaders made sure that each evening a trusted person came to the gate to relieve Oswald of his load. Whoever received the arms was responsible for hiding them inside the ghetto.[6]

As the only arms supplier, Oswald brought to the ghetto eleven rifles. Two were automatic, bigger than the rest, each capable of holding ten bullets. In addition, he also delivered eight pistols, six grenades, and thousands of bullets.[7]

This gift of arms, and the anticipated ghetto uprising, did not quite fit into Oswald's scheme. He explains. *By promising them weapons I entered into, what was for me, a strange, unexpected realm of activities. I had no intention of becoming involved with armed resistance. To me it was very obvious that a battle within the castle, no matter how well planned, could only lead to the destruction of the entire Jewish population. I knew, just as anyone else, that under the circumstances, a victory over the Germans was out of the question. Unlike my ghetto friends, who craved revenge, I was only interested in saving lives, ... But when I realized how desperate for arms these young men were and how much they wanted to resist the Nazi onslaught, I could not refuse them and gave them what they asked for. . . . What else could I do?*

Still, he was convinced that only by escaping from the ghetto in time would some of them stay alive. This was an issue he felt deeply about and was determined to act on.

Gradually I convinced my friends that they should give up the idea of fighting within the castle. I see this as one of my most important wartime achievements. . . . After all, I was very young. Yet I understood the value of life . . . I felt that at a time when all Jews perish, heroism was necessary, but more necessary than that was the saving of lives, Jewish lives. I felt that live people were preferable to dead heroes! . . . Had they insisted on fighting inside the ghetto, they might have killed three or even ten Germans, but after that they would have all died.

With the willingness to give up a ghetto fight came an opportunity for a ghetto exodus. If successful, such a move contained a promise of partisan activities and, therefore, armed opposition against the Nazis.[8]

Mass departure from the ghetto, to be effective, required arms. Few illegal groups could survive in the countryside without weapons. Oswald reasoned *that even for self-defense, or for the purpose of obtaining food, arms were indispensable, a simple necessity.* The change of plans from an internal fight to a mass exodus did not alter the need for arms.

The partisans were still an elusive, largely invisible enemy. Fearing their potential power, eager to destroy them, the Germans were ready to listen to any evidence that might lead to a partisan defeat. In part because of this receptiveness, Nazi collaborators and denouncers would frequently offer false reports about the whereabouts of these illegal fighters. Presented as hard facts, in reality most of the intelligence about these groups was based on hearsay and unsubstantiated rumors. The authorities were used to frequent unsuccessful expeditions.

In planning an escape from the castle, Oswald took advantage of the Nazi fervor for pursuing all anti-partisan leads. In a fictitious account, he wrote that a large armed band was expected to pass through one of the forests in the Mir region. The designated place required abut half a day's travel. Specifically, Oswald's report claimed that these partisans were expected at night on August 9. Timing and patience were important ingredients of such raids. In this case, the way Oswald described it, it was advisable to reach the place ahead of time, hide, and take the enemy by surprise.

The interpreter wanted to allow the Jews enough time to prepare for the escape and get a safe distance away. His report suggested that the authorities leave a day earlier for this important encounter. As usual, the castle was being guarded by Jewish policemen, a fact that could only facilitate a mass departure.

Oswald specified to the resistance leaders that the runaways should go in the opposite direction from the expedition of the fictitious partisan raid. They were to move toward Stara Miranka, several miles from Mir, a wooded and relatively safe area. In the past, partisans had occasionally come there. Oswald had hoped that some of the Jews, those with arms, would be accepted into these fighting units. Finally, Oswald and his friends agreed that after the escape he would continue to supply them with news about Nazi raids into the surrounding forests. Once the runaways had become adjusted to the outside conditions and less dependent on Oswald's support, he would join them. Oswald knew that he would have no problem "losing his way" during one of the official forest expeditions.[9]

When the plans about the ghetto breakout became more definite, Oswald supplied the underground with maps and more precise instructions. Not all aspects were clear. Not all could be anticipated. Moreover, even if anticipated, for most of the problems there were no solutions. Thus, for example, the arms they had could at best suffice for fifty people, which meant that more than one person was assigned to a weapon. Without knowing precise numbers, the underground members and those trying to join them definitely amounted to many more than fifty individuals.[10] The majority of the ghetto escapees would remain unprotected.

Fearful about interferences and premature disclosures, the organizers agreed to keep as much of the information secret, for as long as possible, and from as many people as possible. Almost till the last day, and beyond, even the underground members knew none of the specifics. This included the plans for departure and the date. Similarly, most were not told about the source of guns and the identity of their rescuer. In fact, of the resistance group, less than a handful knew who Oswald was and what part he had been playing in the arrangements for their future.

Those few who knew who Oswald was and that he was helping them were comforted by this knowledge. One of them, Fani Bilecki, says, "The period in the ghetto was not as hard for me because I knew that Oswald was protecting us, that he was behind us. Every word he told us we felt was the absolute truth. It was a ray of hope in all the disaster."[11]

Even though most of the underground members were unfamiliar with the plans and timing of the escape, they thought they would be taken care of by their leaders. What about the rest? After all, more than 800 people lived in the ghetto. At the "proper time," with all the potential guards out of the way, they could all leave. But would they? What about the old, the children, the mothers with children? What would most of the Jewish runaways do on the outside without arms and without any means of survival?

Oswald recalls that *compared to the rest, the resistance group was well-organized. They were most eager to take care of their own people and felt that during a ghetto breakout, the children, the women and the old would be in their way.*

In the castle, almost from the start, the diversity of groupings, opinions, and interests led to many conflicts and crosscurrents. Thus, for example, some of the young women who had been working as chorewomen for the authorities had acted as intermediaries between Oswald and the ghetto. Despite their risky involvement, the resistance leaders, all men, denied equal underground participation to these women. Only very late, and under considerable pressure, did these leaders grant the privilege of becoming full-fledged underground members to these women. Within the ghetto, however, none assumed a leadership position.[12]

Not all ghetto inmates could run away. Not all had the will or the courage to do so. Oswald feels that *an escape from the ghetto carried with it responsibilities and burdens. It is understandable that only some felt strong enough to take them on.*

Perhaps in part an unwillingness or inability to run was related to an absence of adequate information. Almost till the very end the ghetto population was receiving inadequate and often faulty information. Without clear evidence, many opinions were even at odds with each other, leading to confusing signals and equally confusing expectations.

There were those who, out of a feeling of apathy, depression, and indifference, were convinced that there was no point in doing anything, that nothing mattered anyway. Among those who felt this way were some who got used to the idea of committing suicide. They wanted to find peace in death. Suicide, they agreed, would prevent them from falling into the hands of the enemy.

Others believed it did not matter how they died. Thus, for example,

Ephraim Sinder tells of one such young man: "He was a friend of my brother's. He said, 'Why do you want to run away? It is only a minute and all is finished—what for are you running—you get a bullet in your head and it is over.' "[13]

Still others believed that the liquidation of the ghetto could be averted if everyone continued to comply with Nazi demands.

But rumor had it that there was an organizing hand that brings arms into the ghetto. Those who equated safety with conformity began to watch those whom they had suspected of involvement with arms.

The ghetto's divisiveness and apprehension were bolstered by the appearance of Goldberg and his teenage son, two fugitives from the nearby town of Nieśwież. The two managed to escape during a final ghetto Aktion and an uprising.[14] For more than a week they had been roaming the countryside, looking in vain for shelter and food.

They came to Mir in tattered clothes, dirty, disheveled, and dejected. They told anyone who cared to listen that no Jew can survive on the outside, that there are no partisans, and that to Jews no one is willing to extend a helping hand. They warned that anyone leaving a ghetto can expect either a quick death from a bullet or a slow one caused by total rejection and starvation. The appearance of these two fugitives had an oppressive effect on the Mir Jews. Even those who up till then would have been eager to run away, if given the opportunity, had second thoughts.

The Judenrat's policy was to comply, not to rock the boat. They were cautious, watchful. Some Judenrat members knew that in the past the police interpreter had been warning Jews about impending dangers. By and large accurate, his warnings failed to eliminate the leaders' suspicion and distrust. In the summer of 1942, they rightly suspected that Oswald was continuing his ties to the ghetto. They were convinced that these connections would end in tragedy.

Two separate incidents helped support their fears. The leader of the ghetto resistance, Shlomo Charchas, shared a room with a Judenrat member, Michal Pinsecner. One day, Pinsecner found a rifle. When questioned, Charchas admitted it belonged to him.

The Judenrat viewed the presence of this weapon as a scandalous provocation and Charchas had to appear before their self-appointed court. What did these leaders want to know?

"Do you and your friends have more guns?"

"Yes, we have."

"Where are they kept?"

This question was met with silence.

The older men persisted. "Don't you realize that whoever gave you these weapons is a provocateur who wants only to bring disaster upon all of us?"

"Not at all," was Charchas' answer, "I am sure of this person. He is trying to help us live. You must trust me because I believe in him fully."

"Who is he?"

"I cannot tell you. You will know at the proper time."

They tried to guess. "It is Oswald?"

The absence of an answer supported their suspicions while Charchas' earlier assurances failed to convince them.

"You must tell to one of us where exactly all the weapons are being kept. Tell it to Sally Czerne and we promise not to question him about it."

The meeting ended with Charchas' consenting nod and was followed by a private conversation with Sally Czerne.

Charchas sensed that the Judenrat would calm down if they thought that the arms were placed outside the ghetto. Therefore, he told Czerne that they were buried at a cemetery outside the castle. With this obstacle out of the way, the resistance leader added, "We know that our ghetto will be liquidated on the 13th of August and we are organizing an escape before that date." The Judenrat member refrained from probing any further. Instead, he said, "When the time comes, please take me with you!"

Charchas assured him that at the appropriate moment whoever would want will have the opportunity to leave.

In sharp contrast to Czerne, who was relatively young, the majority of the Judenrat members, and particularly Rabbi Szulman, were conservative. As a body they continued to reason in the accustomed ways, in terms of cause and effect. Implied in their kind of thinking was the idea that the Germans would not destroy the ghetto unless provoked. While clinging to this belief, the Judenrat was willing to disregard facts. After all, ghettos were being liquidated and Jews were being executed for no reason at all. The Judenrat had to be aware of this. Why then did reality refuse to invade the consciousness of the Judenrat? Why this persistent denial?

Logical patterns of thinking are inflexible. They die hard and do not take into account new and contradictory evidence, no matter how otherwise convincing this evidence is or how realistic. In a conflict between established thought patterns and unexpected, hence, unfamiliar facts, the established patterns are usually the winners.

The apprehension about arms did not end with Charchas' case. Those who shared the Resniks' room found a rifle, hidden under the cupboard. This discovery was communicated to the Judenrat. Dov Resnik confessed to the "crime"; the gun belonged to him.

Unlike most others in the ghetto, Resnik still had a part of his family, a mother, a sister, and a cousin. In his case, too, because of his past connection to Oswald, the Judenrat suspected that the gun was delivered by the interpreter.

This time, Rabbi Szulman approached Resnik's mother. "Your son is going to cause the ruin of the entire ghetto. He gets arms from the policeman, Oswald, who is surely a provocateur."

"Why would Oswald want to do that?" Resnik's mother inquired.

"Once the Nazis discover guns, they will have a reason to destroy us. He will be promoted for helping them with this discovery."

Not only did the mother agree, but she and the Rabbi figured out that the guns offered by this official must be defective and therefore useless. Following Szulman's visit, Mrs. Resnik begged her son not to trust this policeman who must be an anti-Semite and a troublemaker. She argued that by continuing this association, Dov will bring death to all the Jews and shame on his family. Unable to withstand the pressure, Resnik told her that Oswald was a Jew and swore her and his sister into secrecy.[15]

Not surprisingly, this revelation transformed the family's attitude, both toward Oswald and anything related to his plans. Now his mother and sister were in favor of the ghetto exodus even though they themselves decided to stay. They argued that, unlike the young armed men, they would not make it on the outside, and if they did try to run, they would only become a burden to others. Having made this decision, they proceeded calmly to collect food for the departure of the two cousins, Dov and Israel Resnik.

Because of a chronic absence of facts, the ghetto became a fertile ground for rumors. Fantastic stories about Oswald began to circulate, none of them flattering. Most of these tales told about this policeman's need and desire to ruin the Jews in order to advance himself. In part because the underground leaders refused to reveal Oswald's identity, they too continued to be suspected of wrongdoings. As it was, their presumed connection to Oswald met with hostility.

Perhaps, too, the arrangement the Judenrat had with Bielanowicz interfered with a more favorable attitude toward Oswald. Oswald himself was tolerant about these reactions. *The Judenrat did not know whom to trust, me or Bielanowicz. With the Belorussian, there was a question of money, he received only one-fourth of the sum. He claimed that he had special contacts with the Gestapo, I reported that on the 13th of August there will be an "Aktion." But he was supposed to receive the second part of the money after that date. Whom should they have believed, him or me?*

To the Jewish elders, Bielanowicz's behavior made sense. There were valid reasons for his actions—he agreed to save the Jews for a profit. This fit into normal expectations. In sharp contrast, Oswald's protection was incomprehensible. Why should a Pole, a stranger, probably an anti-Semite, want to endanger his life for Jews? Why should he do it without asking for anything in return? Surely, there was something in his behavior that was not clear at all. They concluded that it would have been foolhardy to rely on such a person.

Perhaps for the Judenrat it was more comforting to believe the Belorussian's version of the future than the Pole's. One offered hope and survival. The other spoke of doom and destruction.

Possibly for the same reason Szulman and others refused to draw the inevitable conclusions from their recent encounter with Hein. The German as much as told them that their ghetto could not be spared. Bielanowicz promised to preserve it. They preferred to believe that the Belorussian was in a position to influence Hein's superiors. Finally, they chose to ignore the news about August 13, which one of their own, Sally Czerne, must have conveyed.

When, less than a week before the August 13 Aktion, Resnik once more mentioned the liquidation of the ghetto, Szulman said, "We are paying a lot of money to Bielanowicz. He promised to protect us. A liquidation of the ghetto is out of the question!"

Even at that late stage, only a few underground leaders, Resnik's family, and probably a select few Judenrat members had been told about the August 13 Aktion. Of those familiar with this date, few knew that the information was supplied by Oswald and that, at the appropriate time, he would take on the responsibility for removing obstacles for a ghetto breakout. Fewer still were aware of Oswald's Jewishness.

On Thursday night, a week before the fateful day, for the last time, Oswald met Dov Resnik at the gate of the castle. He came to say goodbye and to give last-minute instructions and assurances. *Sunday evening you may start leaving. We will be gone earlier. Whoever wants and can should be given a chance to escape.*

Looking up at the friend who sat erect on his horse, the ghetto youth was torn by powerful and conflicting emotions. Their situations were so different. What did it mean? Then, without much thought, Resnik said, "You know what they are telling about you in the castle? They are sure that you are bringing disaster to all of us and that you are giving us useless guns."

"I know all this. I have heard these rumors before. But why are you mentioning them now?"

A question came up in reply. "How do we know that the guns you gave us are fit for use?"

Taken aback, Oswald sighed. "If I were able to open my heart and show you the pain that is stored there, I would do so. But even this would not help you. Time is short. You must do as I tell you. Save yourself and as many others as possible."[16] He seemed to have no time for further conversation. Expertly, the rider turned his horse around and disappeared into the night.

A few of the ghetto inmates were former army men. They showed the rest of the underground members how one would use a gun, how to hold it, load, and unload it. But this was not the same as actually trying it out. The Jews had no opportunities to test their weapons outside or inside the castle. Resnik's parting question reflected their ignorance about the quality of these arms. More important, however, it also showed that even those who knew Oswald well might have become contaminated by the ghetto atmosphere of suspiciousness.

Till this day, Oswald refuses to dwell on memories that accuse others of injustices directed against him. By now, Oswald must have forgotten Resnik's unpleasant question. When asked directly if the Jews became convinced about his good intentions, if they had learned to depend on him, he tends to gloss over their distrustfulness. Yet, at the same time, wishing to be truthful, he does not deny that some did doubt him. He notes, *It is hard for me to say. Most probably, the boys trusted and believed in me. Mir ghetto had no contact with Poland. They did not know that there were Jewish collaborators—that one could also not believe a Jew. I was a Halutz. Of course, I came from another section of the country. You know that Jews tend to be suspicious of each other. I did not speak Yiddish. Still they knew me as a member of the Zionist organization, that I wanted to go to Palestine. I think that they trusted me fully. In their case, there was not even a trace of suspicion.*

After Oswald's last meeting with Resnik, the underground began to prepare in earnest. They began to collect food, clothing, and the hidden arms. The overcrowded conditions robbed these preparations of secrecy. Some ghetto inmates, those who had no intention of leaving, felt that later on they would pay a price for these illegal departures. They refused to become the scapegoats. Some tried to forcefully interfere with the ongoing preparations. Others restored to verbal abuse. Quarrels and name-calling became common.

Partly to put a stop to these disputes and abuses, the underground leaders decided that the time had come to disclose to Rabbi Szulman that Oswald was a Jew. They also told him that Oswald, by organizing the police exodus and leaving in town only four policemen and gendarmes, all of whom were ordered to keep an eye on the interior of official buildings, made a ghetto breakout safe.[17] They emphasized that the entire town was unguarded and that all ghetto inmates would have a chance to run. Finally, they explained that to avoid meeting the Mir authorities, people should proceed in the opposite direction from the anti-partisan expedition. With this revelation came a plea not to divulge Oswald's Jewishness nor his involvement with the breakout.

But Oswald sees this disclosure differently: *my boys told to one member of the Judenrat that I was a Jew. They did not want to run away from the ghetto without the consent of the Judenrat.*

Whatever the reasons, for the Judenrat the news about Oswald's Jewishness put in place the pieces to the puzzle. Only now did it all make sense.

Friday night the tension in the ghetto continued to mount. By Saturday, it turned into chaos. People began to run in circles, asking questions, questions to which none had answers. Should they all leave? What will happen on the outside? Was the liquidation of the ghetto set? When? How? Rabbi Szulman called for a meeting of the entire population and announced that no one should interfere with those who are about to leave the ghetto. Then he asked his people to fast and blow the Shofar, just as they used to do on the day of atonement, the holiest of holidays. He told them to expect a miracle. But the miracle did not happen and the restlessness of the crowd grew.[18]

The majority decided to stay. They would not leave, even though they knew that death would come to them soon. Rabbi Szulman fit into this large group. When asked by Eliezer Breslin to leave with him, he smiled sadly. "My place is here. I would not make it on the outside anyway."

Another smaller, unarmed, unprepared group refused to give up hope. Exposed only to vague rumors, one of them, a young girl, Cila Kapelowicz, remembers that fateful time. *On Saturday, I went into the courtyard and saw that people were getting ready for departure. I did not know a thing. No one told me. Before that, we have heard that the Judenrat was arguing with the young people whether the ghetto will be liquidated or not.*

Even as some were getting ready to leave, there were those who doubted that there will be an Aktion. . . . No one explained to us a thing. Nothing was clear. But I sensed that there will be an end. I knew it in my bones. . . . All over it was "Judenrein," and we knew that we had to leave if we wanted to avoid death. I did not know that Oswald arranged it, only that around us people were being executed and that our end was coming.

That evening Rabbi Szulman walked among the crowd saying leave if you like. Then I heard that people will be escaping on the 9th of August, Sunday night. I knew that death was close by, so I decided to run away with some boys and girls. I escaped in order not to give myself up, to avoid death.[19]

Still, when the actual moment came for the breakout, members of this unarmed, unorganized group became panic-stricken. Some began to ask, "Where are we going? What is happening? There was a lot of crying and screaming. Yet, we knew that we should be leaving."[20]

The Judenrat told the people to avoid certain places. Without understanding why, they tried to follow these instructions. Other than that, they did not know where they were going, how they would manage.

With the resistance group, it was different. They had been living with the idea of a breakout. With the departure set, most were not burdened by choices and decisions. Without knowing any details, those in the underground knew enough to feel better than the rest. Sinder remembers: "Saturday afternoon, there were rumors. I belonged to the fighting group that had to run away—so they told me that Sunday night we are leaving—Sunday during the day the gate was closed. No one left the ghetto. In the afternoon we knew that at night whoever wants should leave."[21]

Before they left, the underground tried to subdivide into smaller units of five. Later, some of these units were led by people familiar with the countryside. They had been instructed to meet outside the ghetto at the Tatar cemetery.[22]

The hardest hit were those who could not make up their minds and those who had to tear themselves away from their families.

It is Sunday. One must decide. To go? To stay? Here is a mother, one of the few women who still has a small child. She runs in circles, begging, searching for shoes for her child. "Soon it will be fall," she says. She wants to protect her child from the cold. Some cannot help wondering "What for?" Does she expect to run away and make it? How unrealistic can one be? Then, there is a father, an "older man" of fifty. He urges his children: "Run, children, run. The world is big. In it you may find a place. Try it!"

Some religious Jews are waiting for a miracle. Among them is the Rabbi from Ostrolnik, who insists that sometimes miracles happen without revealing their presence. Sometimes it may seem that they are not there but they really are.

To the side one can see a young man about to leave his son and wife. The child asks, "Are you going away from us? What will become of us?" The mother is silent. She looks vacantly into space as she clasps the boy's hand. The man bends his head. Resigned, he whispers into his son's ear, "I will stay with you." He places the modest bundle close to his wife. The woman offers a tentative smile, a smile devoid of happiness, devoid of life.[23]

Time is short, night comes. The night has no feelings. It does not respond to the surrounding tragedy. The night is cool, indifferent. Unfeeling, this night nevertheless offers a chance, the only chance. And so it happens. Under the cover of darkness, those who made up their minds are departing. Some leave through the small windows after they cut the iron bars. Others push through the gate. Some others jump over the high stone wall. The noises these runaways make are subdued.

Others, the majority, are resigned. They see no point in going anywhere. They stay. Those who refuse to leave might be overcome by a feeling of unrest. Perhaps they are envious and resentful of those who left. Perhaps they keep wondering why they did not go along.

What has been happening on the outside? Were the conditions as horrendous as some had anticipated? Cila Kapelowicz survived to tell a small part of her story: *I pushed myself through the window as did some of my friends. They told us that the gate was locked. Later on, I found out that this was not true. I checked it out . . . I run with a few boys and girls. We lost our way. Many of the girls did not know the way. Some of them returned to the ghetto. I knew the area well, but we were running around in circles. I lost all the others and roamed the countryside by myelf, alone. This lasted till Thursday, August 13, the day of the mass execution. I went to the Christian woman who hid me during the first big Aktion in November 1941. She took me in and told me that on that day all Jews were shot.*

Afraid, not trusting this woman, Cila left after two days. In the country, near the forest, she met her brother, his wife, and two other friends. They decided to join forces. During the day, they stayed hidden in a hole in the forest. At night, they ventured out into the adjacent peasant huts to beg for food, often in exchange for their few belongings. The food they received was meager. One day, Cila went to see a Christian friend with whom she had left some clothes. While in her friend's hut, Cila heard shots from the direction of her hiding place. When she went to rejoin her group she discovered they were all dead. They were shot by Russian partisans who had expected to find valuables. A small group of Jews hidden not far from Cila's place accepted her. Eventually, Cila and a part of this group reached the Bielski family camp where they survived the war.[24]

Those who were a part of the underground arrived at the Tartar cemetery. They were followed by many unarmed runaways, who felt more secure near people with weapons. All decided to move on under the cover of darkness and hide during the day in the forests. With few exceptions, most were unfamiliar with their surroundings. Dejected, some wanted to go back. Where are we going? they asked. Why did we start? Most continued as planned to Stara Miranka.[25]

Among these runaways were about ten children aged twelve to fourteen, orphans who lost their parents in the November 1941 Aktion. Against all odds, they managed to stay alive until August 1942. Around that time, the children sensed that something was about to happen and banded together.

How did they react? "We heard about the killings of the Jews in the surrounding towns. We knew that the grown-ups brought some guns, but they did not tell us about it. They felt that we were too young to become a part of any illegal activity. We understood. We knew that something was being prepared. We saw how the grown-ups were overcome by fear. . . .

Sometimes we would notice a pistol under a coat . . . and so we prepared a little food and clothes for the road.[26]

"We wanted to go with those who had arms, at least to follow them, to be close to them. We wanted protection. We followed them at a distance. The grown-ups wanted each group to move separately. As we got nearer to them, they shouted at us to stay away. . . .

"But we followed anyway. When we reached the Tartar cemetery, some of us returned to the ghetto. Some of us could not stand the fear, the loneliness, and the lack of protection. When we reached the Miranka forest, there was again an argument. They (the adults) told us that a large group could be easily discovered. Those who were armed demanded that we leave them alone and not follow them."[27]

The children who did not choose to return to the ghetto were not about to give up. Although they were being chased away, they continued to follow the armed grown-ups, from a safe distance. Eventually, some of these children were accepted into partisan units as fighters. Some died fighting. Some were shot either by Germans or by partisans. Only a fraction made it till the end of the war.[28]

As for the official anti-partisan expedition, all proceeded as scheduled. Oswald introduced his fictitious report as a rare opportunity for the destruction of a powerful enemy unit. Hein found the suggested move attractive. Oswald recalls that *except for four men who had to be left behind, all the other policemen and gendarmes joined this "important" raid. I initiated the expedition, and organized it, making sure that our group would go into the opposite direction from that of the runaway Jews. . . . I only organized the move. Meister Hein was at the head of it. He was the leader. We came to the specified forest on time. We sat there all night and returned to Mir briefly before dawn.*

At 8 o'clock in the morning, on the 11th of August, I was already back at the gendarmerie at my desk working. Soon after that, Bielanowicz burst in screaming: "Juden weggelaufen! Juden, gehen weg! Jews run away!" The Meister asked: "Wieviel, how many?" "Driehundert, three hundred." "Ach nicht viel! Im Nieświź sind tausend weggelaufen" "Ah, not many! In Nieświeź a thousand escaped!" This is probably what he had heard. Actually, hardly that many succeeded in running away.[29]

On hearing the news, Meister Hein wanted to know why the Jews escaped. Bielanowicz explained that peasants came to the castle to buy furniture and told about Nieświeź and other Jewish communities that were being liquidated. The Jews of Mir must have concluded that their turn was about to come.

Oswald was translating Bielanowicz's explanation. To Hein, this made sense. He did not seem unhappy or surprised. In sharp contrast, the Belorussian official was shaken by his own news. To him this meant that 15,000 marks, money he felt entitled to, would not be paid.

12

Exodus and Confrontation

Three hundred Jews ran away and a little over five hundred remained in the castle (505).[1] These were the figures—cold, impersonal. Can they be translated into feeling, thinking, human beings?

On August 11, 1942, at his desk in the gendarmerie, Oswald was trying to pour life into these statistics. Images of different persons, some vivid, some blurred, kept appearing and vanishing. These were visions of a few isolated individuals, of people he had known. The rest, the overwhelming majority, were lost. They presented themselves only as detached numbers.

Ideas about these numbers began to clamor for attention. Three hundred escaped. They have a chance to live. How sad that not more of them got away. But then a comforting thought returned. His friends might be far away. How many of them will make it? Superstition kept him from guessing.

Then he was once more overcome by sadness for those left behind. Their future was doomed. Meister Hein was not about to "lose" them. In fact, as soon as he learned about the breakout, he ordered his men to surround the castle. From then on, no one could slip out.

Oswald felt tired. His mind kept wandering. He was surprised to see how much of his work was unchanged, even though an event affecting hundreds of lives had occurred.

While Oswald had a hard time concentrating, those around him seemed untouched. On those rare occasions when the ghetto breakout was mentioned, it was treated like a curious incident. Some natives, those who were politically minded, chuckled maliciously, as if to say "Some super race! Even the poor, miserable Jews were able to outwit them." The suffering, the efforts, the courage, so much a part of this escape, were absent from these comments.

Lunch came as if it were an ordinary day. During the meal the runaway Jews were barely mentioned. No sooner did the topic come up then it was immediately dropped. No one was interested. Instead, the gendarmes spoke about their last anti-partisan expedition. Someone suggested that news about their move must have reached the enemy before they ventured into the field. The rest agreed. Not discouraged by this recent failure, they spoke about more fruitful future raids. Trying hard to act casual, Oswald could hardly follow the conversation. He was relieved when the meal was over.

Oswald returned to the office. In part to see for himself what had happened, in part to reestablish order Meister Hein went to the castle. He tried to calm the Judenrat, then asked them to collect the people into the courtyard. Faced with a frightened, anxious crowd, Hein spoke softly, explaining that there was absolutely no reason for a breakout. He told them that he was surprised by this kind of an irrational event. After all, he is the one who knows that their lives are by no means threatened. On the contrary, the runaways are in danger. But he would accept them into the castle. If they want to come back, they can. He is not going to punish them. They had made a mistake and he was willing to forgive them.[2] Some did return to the ghetto, but not because of what Hein said. They came because they were discouraged by the hardships on the outside. For those who stayed inside it made no difference whether they believed his assurances or not. They were trapped.

Standing before this crowd was a man who not long ago refused to accept watches and valuables because in good conscience he could not promise the continued existence of the ghetto. On August 11 the same man was denying that they were being threatened, knowing well that those he was talking to will die in two days.

How does one reconcile his earlier refusal to accept a gift under false pretenses with this direct open deception? Could it be that when he rejected a gift he was acting as a private individual? Perhaps when he was denying that the ghetto was threatened he was acting in his official capacity. Was he making sure that an order, in this case to execute the Jews, should be carried out, according to schedule, in the most efficient way?

That same day, in the early afternoon, Oswald saw his boss return in the company of a Jewish man. Without greetings, without an explanation, the two disappeared into an empty room.

Oswald recognized the man as Stanisławski. Until the ghetto breakout he had worked in the stable, at the gendarmerie. Like the other Jewish employees, he had performed different manual tasks all designed to keep the horses and the stables in good condition. Unlike some other workers, who acted as Oswald's contacts with the ghetto, Stanisławski never did.

Who was he? In his forties, the man settled in Mir during the war. He was a native of Lódź, an industrial city of Poland. Here he lived all alone, without a wife, without a family, without friends. He never became a part of this community. At once a stranger and strange, he was an outsider, a person the Jews did not trust. Oswald thinks that Hein and Stanisławski met only on August 11, 1942. Before that time the German might not have even known about this man's existence.

On that day, this unlikely pair stayed for a long time in a room. It was unusual for Oswald not to have been included in the Meister's lengthy, official conversations. He notes, *In fact because this never happened before, I had a feeling that something ominous was going on. I thought that this visit had to do with me, but I was not absolutely sure. On the other hand, I became apathetic. I saw no point in running away. I was just waiting. At that stage I saw little reason for saving myself. Perhaps I stopped caring? Was I leaving things to fate?*

Two hours later, through the window, Oswald saw Stanisławski leave with a gendarme. Then Hein entered their office. He stopped in front of his interpreter's desk. The youth stood up. For a moment the two men were facing each other. Oswald knew that this was not going to be a casual, ordinary encounter. He noticed that Meister Hein had changed. Gone were his usual self-assurance, his military bearing. Each was replaced by a diffused kind of sadness, mixed with a vague tiredness.

Taller than Oswald, Meister Hein had been looking down at the youth before him, scrutinizing his face, as if seeing it for the first time. He seemed to be searching for clues, for answers. For the last nine months he spent more time with Oswald than with anyone else. Hein valued the boy and treated him in a fatherly way. All along he was convinced that beside mutual affection they had much else in common. Religion, Hein knew, was one of their common links. Both were Catholic. They had a similar way of looking at life, a basic decency. And now? The older man was at a loss. Then in a strained voice he said, "Oswald, you are being suspected of treason. Is it true that you told the Jews the date of the Aktion?"

To Oswald it was clear: Stanisławski had denounced him. What else did he say? What else did the Meister know? For a moment he kept silent and then replied, "Yes, Herr Meister, it is true."

Visibly shaken, more hurt than angry, the German shouted, "Stupid! Stupid! Why did you admit? I would have believed you rather than this Jew!"

Many years later, as I listened to Oswald, I too wanted to know why he had admitted. He explained, *I think very quickly. I react fast. I realized right away that if Stanisławski knows, others must know too, many others. If people in the ghetto know, it makes no sense to deny. I could prolong the agony for a bit, but eventually Hein would find out. But he does not have to know that I am a Jew. This is how it seemed to me, at the moment. That is why I confessed to what his question contained and about the rest I kept quiet.*

Without waiting for more answers, Hein continued, "How could you have done this to me? I trusted you so! How could you have betrayed me? Why? Why?"

Oswald said, "Out of pity. I felt sorry for them."

"But," Hein spoke again, "I know something else. I want you to admit it by yourself!"

Oswald was puzzled. *What was this 'something else'? I had no idea what he had in mind, the anti-partisan expedition? Arms? What? I tried to protect myself. There was no point in rushing things. . . . I told him about Bielanowicz, that he was taking money from Jews and promising to protect them. I emphasized that the man has been cheating on a large scale and that he was a fraud. He really did not know the fate of Jews and took money from them on false pretenses, insisting that he was delaying the Aktion indefinitely.*

Satisfied with this news, Hein said, "Excellent, excellent. For a long time I have been looking for some evidence against this man!"

Right away he dispatched a gendarme to Bielanowicz's home. There the gendarme had found foreign currency . . . probably the money he received from the Jews. That afternoon, Bielanowicz was arrested and put into prison.

With this case temporarily out of the way, Hein returned to the more pressing business before him. He asked Oswald to sit down. Too nervous to do the same, he continued to pace. As he did, he kept repeating, "Why did you do it to me? Why? Why?"

What happened next is imprinted in Oswald's mind. *Suddenly the Meister stopped in front of my desk, looked at me intensely, and said, "And how was it with arms? Is it true that you supplied the ghetto with weapons?" I was quiet for a moment, then I said, "Yes, it is true." He again asked, "Why did you give them arms, for what reason?" Stubbornly, I repeated "because of compassion."*

Then I told him that these people were not Communists. They were simple laborers, poor and hard working. They were not harming anyone. I felt sorry for them. I had to help them.

For Hein, these were inadequate answers. He thought that something was missing. Dissatisfied, he continued. "What should I do with you? I trusted you fully and you betrayed me. If it were someone else . . . but you! I have to think it over, at least for a day or so. Right now I must arrest you."

Oswald described what happened next. *I felt that if he would arrest me, he would have to explain why. This in itself was already an accusation. Therefore, I gave him my word of honor that I will not run away, if he will leave me free till tomorrow. I had all the intention of keeping my promise. He said that he cannot do this because if I would run away, he would be responsible.*

Faithful to the official regulations, Hein disarmed this youth who meant so much to him. Then, perhaps making sure that he will go through with it, he immediately asked Oswald to follow him. The prisoner was being taken across the street to the Belorussian police station. This was a makeshift prison and all the arrested had to stay together in one cell, in the cellar.

On the way to the station, Oswald and Hein met Siemion Serafimowicz. The Meister stopped him, glad to have someone with whom he could share his problem. Oswald notes that *this time Hein spoke in broken German, the only kind of language he thought Serafimowicz could understand. "Wiessen Oswald Juden Aktion verraten? Wiessen Waffe geben, was denken? You know that Oswald betrayed to the Jews the date of the Aktion? Do you know that he gave them arms, what do you think?" Serafimowicz turned to me with a question, "Have you really done this?" I said, "Yes." I explained that these are his former friends, people that worked with him before, not Communists. There was no reason to kill them. As I spoke, the Meister next to us continued. "Warum, was denken warum? Why, why do you think?" Serafimowicz hit his forehead with the palm of his hand and said, "Young and stupid!" Then the Meister ordered: "Siemion nach Hause laufen und Mantel bringen. Run home and bring a coat!" He was obviously concerned that I will be cold. Right away, Serafimowicz returned with a coat, a Russian military coat.*

Here they were, two men, both powerful, both in a position of authority, both betrayed by a much younger subordinate whom they had treated very well and from whom they expected loyalty. Despite their inevitable disappointment, each continued to treat the traitor with consideration and understanding. Oswald was puzzled. This was something he would not have expected. Indeed, at the police station, as Hein was taking leave of Oswald, he said, "Don't worry. Get a good night's rest. I will speak to you tomorrow." Taken by surprise, confused, yet grateful, all that this unusual prisoner had offered was a smile.

Oswald knew how the cell looked. He had been here before. Still, when in the past he had entered the place it felt different—he was a free man then. Now he realized he was joining three more prisoners. Two were natives accused of partisan collaboration; at dawn both were to be executed. The third man was Bielanowicz. After Oswald had denounced him, the case slipped his mind. Preoccupied with their own plight, they limited their contacts to a silent greeting. But there was no animosity between them. The older man had no way of knowing that this unusual prisoner was responsible for his arrest. Oswald says, *Bielanowicz knew that Jews had run away. He might have thought that some of them had denounced him. He could not have guessed that I did it.*

Later on, Bielanowicz was transferred to the camp Kołdyczewo. This was the same camp to which the Polish intelligentsia was sent earlier. It seems that Bielanowicz was in part responsible for these deportations. Presumably, he had the power to decide who of the Poles should be arrested. Like so many of these earlier prisoners, he too never returned.

How did Oswald feel about the part he played in Bielanowicz's arrest? *At the time I did not know that he will die. I thought that he will be removed from his post. On the other hand, he was ruthless and manipulative. In his case, there was absolutely no excuse for his behavior. . . . My conscience does not bother me and I never felt that I had committed a crime. I still don't.*

Unlike Bielanowicz, Stanisławski might have had some valid reason for acting the way he did. Till this day, however, neither his personality nor his motivation for denouncement are clear. One can only speculate about each. Oswald muses about some of these possibilities. *I don't know why he did it. Perhaps he wanted to save himself. . . . He was killed three days later. Maybe he did it to save the rest in the ghetto? It could be that someone in the ghetto demanded that he do it. Maybe they thought that by putting the blame on me, the rest will be saved? I cannot understand this man. But I don't hate him.*

Sometimes I think that the Judenrat sent Stanisławski to Hein in the hope of saving the remaining Jews. But I have no proof for this, it is only my speculation.

Some former ghetto inmates from Mir think that Stanisławski denounced Oswald to save his own life. They say that Hein announced that whoever would tell him about the person who helped arrange the ghetto outbreak will be protected by the authorities.[3]

I believe that the Judenrat had no part in Stanisławski's intervention. Rather, it was an attempt, an unsuccessful one, at saving his own skin. The man was an outsider. He was not well liked by the rest of the Jewish community. Why would the Judenrat select him of all the people to represent their cause? Nor is it likely, given the man's position among the Mir Jews, that he would have cared enough about the community to do it. Had the Judenrat wanted to save the ghetto by sacrificing Oswald, they would have selected another, more appropriate representative.

Moreover, at the very end the Judenrat knew that Oswald was a Jew. It seems they had never divulged this secret. If they thought of sacrificing Oswald for the rest of the ghetto and had done it through Stanisławski, they would have told him that Oswald was a Jew. Oswald says that *Stanisławski most probably did not know that I was a Jew. But if he did not, it is worse, much worse.*

Oswald feels that a Jew had an obligation, a duty, to save other Jews regardless of risk. In contrast, for a Pole to have saved Jews was neither a duty nor an obligation. A Pole who risked his life for Jews was acting above and beyond the call of duty. Such a rescue would then be on a higher moral plane, hence a betrayal of such an act would be particularly despicable.

Years later, Oswald saw the Stanisławski episode in a different light, explaining, *Today when I think about Stanisławski, I am grateful to him for denouncing me. Why? Because this was a way of finishing this period in my life. It was a proper ending. By forcing me out of the place, Stanisławski was saving me from some possibly terrible future entanglements. . . . If I stayed I might have complicated my life and my conscience as well. There were no great opportunities left to rescue people. Maybe I would be able to save myself, maybe not.*

In the prison cell, on August 11 to 12, different ideas dominated Oswald's mind. *I thought that if there is a God, he will forgive me. I did not remember sinning against anyone. And if there is no God, then it makes no difference anyway. I was unhappy that I will have no opportunity to ever see my brother. But I was glad that he was safely in Palestine. . . . I decided that, next morning, when alone with the Meister, I will grab his gun and shoot myself, to put an end to all my suffering. This decision allowed me to sleep calmly. Next morning, however, I woke up thinking differently. "Why should I kill myself? I might as well wait."*

His determination to live was soon replaced by a desire to end it all. As he was vacillating, there was a noise at the door of the cell. A gendarme came for Oswald. With his gun behind Oswald's back, the German led the prisoner across the street to the gendarmerie. On the way he saw the Polish girls, the Balickis, standing on the pavement, waving. Later on, he heard that these girls were praying for his release.

The gendarmerie was swarming with people. Most of the daily business could not be attended to without an interpreter. Oswald explains, *I was put to work. I began to translate. I wrote reports. The Meister requested a payroll. I followed his order.*

Then Bielanowicz came in. He had to be interrogated. Hein was asking the questions and Oswald acted as the interpreter. Inadvertently, Bielanowicz himself admitted to much of his wrongdoing. He could not imagine that it would have been a crime to cheat Jews. After all, they were only Jews! The head of the gendarmerie had different ideas. The case was finished quickly.

Time moved in the accustomed way, unaware that this was a special day. Lunch came. Oswald was invited to eat with the others. He took his usual seat next to the Meister. The other gendarmes knew that he was a prisoner. Yet they also realized that he had been working. Clearly, the Meister had made no decision.

Without addressing him in public, Hein treated his interpreter with consideration. The meal continued in silence. It dragged on. As soon as it was over, the Meister and Oswald returned to their office. In a tired, subdued voice, the older man began, "All night I have been thinking about you. I have been a policeman for twenty-eight years, but I never came across a case like this. I find it impossible to believe that you could have done it only out of compassion. You might have told the Jews the date of the Aktion because you felt sorry for them, because you pitied them. But arms, no. One does not supply weapons out of compassion. Besides, someone must have been helping you. I am convinced that there is much more to this than you told me."

"I can assure you that I took no money for it," Oswald said.

"I know, I know. Otherwise, I would be talking to you differently."

"No one was helping me, I swear to you that I did it all by myself."

"Where did you take the weapons from?" the Meister wanted to know.

Oswald told him the truth. Describing some of the special steps, he asked, "Do you remember when you were sitting in the garden on the bench with Yelena and I passed?"

"Yes, I remember."

"Then, too, I took out a gun that I had hidden before in the bushes close to the fence. You just saw me pass. But I had the gun with me."

Hein nodded, surprised, then somewhat relieved, he said, "So you did it all alone? All by yourself!"

After a long pause, the German continued, "I came to the conclusion that as a Polish nationalist you took revenge for what we did to the Poles. It was a Pole acting against the Germans. An act of revenge. Am I right? I want to hear it from you!"

To this unexpected twist Oswald replied, "No, you are not right. I will tell you the truth on condition that you give me a gun so that I can shoot myself."

"Oh no, no, this I cannot have. Not here."

"I will do it in the garden away from the window," said Oswald.

"You have time. You are too young for that."

"Promise me that you will give me a chance to kill myself later on and I will tell you the truth."

"All right, we shall see, we shall see. Just tell me."

Hein was becoming more eager. He seemed excited by what he was about to hear.

"So I will tell you. Herr Meister, I am not a Pole. I am a Jew."

"What?!"

"Yes, Herr Meister."

"Really, Oswald?!"

"Yes."

Why did Oswald tell the truth? *I thought that for him and for me it would be better this way. But particularly for him, it would be easier to accept my rescue of Jews if he knew that I was a Jew, that on my part it was a positive and not a hostile act. I told him the truth because the truth, as far as Hein was concerned, put me in a proper light. . . . He behaved always decently toward me. It would have been hard for him to accept that I betrayed him because I wanted to take revenge. I think that it ended the way it should have ended.* Besides, Oswald reasons that *as a Prussian policeman, Hein was trained to keep order. But all that was happening around him was the reverse of what order really meant. What was happening had to do with moral disorder. In a sense then, and as someone who is used to keeping order, he had failed. Deep down, he must have known that he did not act the way he should have acted. He must have somehow realized that as far as the two of us were concerned, I was the one who followed some kind of an order. . . . In Mir Hein received work for which he was not suited at all. His Christian conscience demanded that he help and not destroy. But I did it in his place. Perhaps that is why when he knew what I had done his attitude to me was very mild, very open. He took away my weapon. But he treated me with consideration.*

All along Hein had warm, fatherly feelings toward Oswald. But how did Oswald react to Hein? Looking back, his answer is *I was a good actor. I entered fully into my role, this probably persuaded people. As for the Meister, perhaps I liked him. For nine months we were constantly in each other's company. I might not have been able to play my part so well. Had I really disliked him he might have felt it. For I doubt that I could have been such a consistently good actor. He would have removed me from his office had he suspected or thought that I did not like him. . . . So, in a way I might have been fond of him. . . . Whenever someone tried to convince him not to follow a destructive path he listened. He preferred to compromise. He wanted to find solutions. I suspect that he wanted to be persuaded to save. He was not eager to destroy. Several times I succeeded in convincing him that he should release people who were accused of different crimes.*

On that summer day, the meeting between Hein and Oswald continued with the older man sighing and saying, as if to himself, "Also die Schutzleute haben doch Recht gehabt! The gendarmes were right after all!"

Oswald thinks that *most probably his co-workers were telling him something about me, but I don't know when and what. "This is a tragedy. Now I understand." He said. His eyes got red. He was close to tears. Then he asked, "Why didn't you tell me this earlier? You could not have worked for me, but I would not have hurt you."*

Was he disappointed that Oswald, toward whom he had so much affection, did not trust him? Was he trying to tell him that he could have counted on him? Not quite, not fully. After all, there was this "You could not have worked for me." Yet he tried to salvage something from their relationship. He cared.

Oswald remembers that *next, in a sad and almost pleading voice, Hein asked whether in other matters I was honest. I told him that I was. What could I have said? In reality I was. There were situations where I was very straightforward. For purely criminal cases, I had a certain gift. I was a good detective. And in criminal matters, I tried to be helpful to him. I became his ears and his tongue.*

In part to make it easier for him? For me? For us? I told him that my father was in the Austrian Army, a noncommissioned officer, that he lived for eight years with the Germans, that I did not come here on my own. This is how it happened, and that twice I managed to escape from death. And when the circumstances brought me here, I felt that it was my duty to save lives. I could not act in any other way . . . I emphasized that I came from the part of Poland that was influenced by the German culture. In my home this was the spoken language. In my family no one ever felt or acted badly toward the Germans. On the contrary, we valued the German culture and its people.

To all this Hein said, "Personally, I never killed a Jew and never will. But what could I have done? Someone had to do the job! I had to follow orders!" Oswald did not react. He stopped pretending. All was lost anyway. He refused to agree.

From the Meister's earlier comments, it seemed that others had suspected that his interpreter was a Jew. The Meister never acted on this information. Oswald explained, *To work with a person for long, long hours every day, for months, and to tell that person: "Take off your pants, I have to check who you are" is not very pleasant so Hein did not do it.*

On that day, an oppressive, accusing stillness set in. It was interrupted by Hein's order. "Write your story down. I want a report." While the youth sat writing, the older man once more paced nervously around the room. He did not interrupt. He too seemed to be concentrating.

Oswald recalls, *When I finished writing, toward the end, I added with a bravado that I had no regrets—that I am ready to die having done my duty—I signed the report. The Meister sat down to read it through. Then he stood up from the table, called the gendarme, Wachtmeister Martens, and asked him to watch me so I would not hurt myself. The gendarme was supposed to remain with me. Hein left. Most probably he went to the ghetto to check if they knew that I was a Jew.*

With the Meister gone, Oswald tried to prepare for the end. He knew that he would surely die. The question still to be decided on was how? He was not at all certain that his boss would help him with this task. Oswald did not want to be shot by the enemy. He preferred to do it himself.

But first he wanted to say goodbye to his brother and to the world. He sat down to write a letter to Arieh. When he finished, he wrote another letter to Wanda, Serafinowicz's sister-in-law. He explained to her that his life was coming to an end and that after the war she should send the enclosed letter to his brother. He remembered the address in Palestine and carefully wrote it out. Somehow he hoped that before his death he could place these letters into the proper hands.

Hein returned around five o'clock. When he entered his office, he dismissed the guard. He looked even more worn out. Now it was Oswald who spoke first. "Herr Meister, you promised to give me an opportunity to shoot myself. Tomorrow they will be executing all the Jews. I prefer to do it myself."

Distractedly, as if he did not hear or understand, Hein looked at this youth before him, and then placed a hand on his shoulder, saying, "There is no need for that. After all, you are a smart boy. You succeeded twice, you may succeed a third time."

Oswald recalls, *At that moment, I felt that something was beginning to stir within me. Did he try to comfort me? Was he hinting at an escape? Was he giving me a chance? I did not know how to react. I offered him my hand and I said, "I thank you, Herr Meister." He, in turn, hesitated whether to accept my hand or not. In the end, he both shook and squeezed it gently. Then, as if in a hurry, without a word, he turned around and left.*[4]

The gendarme came in. The two did not speak. Oswald felt excited, but unable to formulate definite thoughts or plans. At dinner, he was escorted to the dining room by the guard. At the table, the gendarme left his side. Once more, Oswald sat next to the Meister. His report was on the table. They probably read it; if not, they must have been familiar with its content. Once more, they ate in total silence, an embarrassed, tense kind of silence. The only sounds one could hear were coming from the chewed food and the silverware as it made contact with the dishes. Those present avoided each other's eyes, and especially the eyes of the man who was the cause of this tension.

When Oswald finished eating, he got up from the table to deliver his letters. He went into the hall calling, "Karol, Karol." This was the Polish stable boy. Karol, he thought, would surely bring the letters to Wanda. But there was no answer. Still calling "Karol," Oswald stepped out of the building and into the courtyard. Close to the well a nun was turning up the handle with a bucket full of water. The convent was next door and the nuns had a standing invitation to help themselves to water. The woman was too absorbed in her task to even acknowledge his presence. Not far from her were three gendarmes. They stood in a triangle talking. Oswald did not know any of them. They were a part of the enforcement that came from Stołpce to help with the ghetto liquidation. This was August 12. The Aktion was scheduled for the next day. Even the disappearance of three hundred inmates could not change the initial plans.

Oswald realized that no one was following him. Quickly, he turned toward the gate that led into a back street, passed through two side streets, and then ran into the fields.

This was the middle of the harvest. The day was coming to an end and people were winding up their jobs. Part of the wheat was cut and arranged into sheaves; part remained uncut, standing tall.

Behind, a commotion—shouting, screaming, running—told Oswald that he was being chased. These noises became mixed with the peasants' helpful hints about the runaway's whereabouts.

Determined to make it, he pushed his body inside a sheaf. Though convinced that a part of him was exposed, he nevertheless remained immobile. All around, and quite close, he could hear loud cursing, the stomping of heavy boots, and sounds of horseback riders. He estimates that more than forty men were after him.

Suddenly, the sheaf he was hiding in collapsed. Totally visible, he jumped to the as-yet uncut part of the field. Someone must have seen him. The pursuers were closing in. Then Oswald heard shots and more shots. Bullets whistled by. Not only did he hear the men next to him, but he could practically touch their boots. Yet these boots chose not to step on him.

The wheat was hospitable, protective, behaving like a caring good friend. Despite this cover, he knew that the slightest move could mean the end. At this point he began to pray: "God help me! God!" He could think of nothing else. The search party circled around and around. Several times different feet were almost touching Oswald who remained flat on the ground.

The sun continued to sink. Frustrated and angry, without finding what they came for, the men were leaving the field.

Oswald waited. He craved peace, rest. Where should he go? Who will help? Then he remembered that one of the Balicki sisters, Irena, told him that if he would ever be in trouble, he could count on her. Oswald went to the home of the Polish stable boy, Karol, and asked him to contact Irena.

Glad to be of help, Karol left to bring Irena Balicki. Together the three decided that it would be safer if Oswald were transferred to the nearby pigsty, close to the Balicki house.

In the past, this place was filled with pigs and poultry. With the German requirement that the natives deliver such animals for slaughter, the Balickis stopped raising them. The pigsty was in part empty, in part used as a storage shed.

By then, the entire town knew what had happened and therefore there was no need to explain.

When on August 13 the runaway Cila Kapelowicz reached the hut of a Belorussian peasant who offered her shelter, she too was told that Oswald was a Jew and that he had escaped. She also heard that an official announcement was posted all over town, offering a big reward for information leading to his capture. It seemed that to the authorities he was worth a lot.

That evening, though aware of the situation, Irena did not speak about

Oswald's "sins." She was only concerned about helping and advised him to remain in the pigsty at least for a day. She promised to return next evening with a letter that would recommend him to a friend of hers, a manager of a Polish estate, some ten kilometers from Mir. When Irena left, she shut the door from the outside with a wire.

Left alone, Oswald noticed a ladder leading to the attic. He climbed up. There he found straw and hay scattered on the ground. He piled up the hay and straw close to the wall and slipped underneath, leaving only space for his head that was close to the small opening in the attic wall. Too tired to think, he was soon overcome by sleep.

At dawn, loud shooting reminded Oswald of his predicament. He knew what those sounds meant. This was August 13. The executions were taking place two or three kilometers from Mir. For this, special trenches had been prepared ahead of time. Eventually, the shooting was replaced by loud singing. Obviously drunk, the killers were trying to march to the rhythm of their songs. Their job was finished.

From above, Oswald saw a Belorussian policeman circling the pigsty, as if looking for some footprints. As he came closer, the man seemed particularly big and healthy. He was armed. When he reached the door, he removed the wire and stepped inside. Frightened, Oswald did not dare move. He kept wondering: "Did someone direct him to this place? Does he expect to find me?" He could think of no solutions.

Then Oswald could hear the policeman climbing up the ladder. At the edge the man stopped. He seemed annoyed. He murmured something under his breath. Was he thinking? Deciding? What must, in reality, have been a brief moment felt like a very long time. Then the same heavy boots began a noisy descent. Soon, through the opening in the wall, Oswald saw the policeman replace the wire on the door. He was still muttering under his breath. When he disappeared from view, something inside Oswald snapped. He felt as if the entire weight of Jewish suffering was on him. He burst into tears and then, still crying, began to put questions to God. He wanted to know why the Jews were the targets of destruction. He kept asking, over and over again, Why? Why? Why? These "whys" and tears refused to stop. Indeed, Oswald had spent most of August 13 crying and arguing with God. Toward the evening, exhausted, he fell asleep.

He was awakened by Irena. This time she brought him bread, fruit, and a letter to her friend. She was hoping that he would give Oswald shelter. After she explained how to reach the place, she said, "Come back if you need help." She made the sign of a cross and left.

Encouraged by her concern, Oswald moved on. He arrived at his destination late at night. In the main house, the light was still on. Oswald tapped gently at the window. A door opened, revealing first a head and then a man's tall, slim body. It was the Polish estate manager. After listening to a brief explanation, he took the letter and read it next to the lighted window. Then, with a sigh, he said, "I feel badly, but I must refuse you. It is too dangerous." Crushed, Oswald said nothing. The man continued, "Only the other day the Germans murdered forty-five of the Polish intelligentsia. I simply cannot keep you. Tonight you may sleep over in the barn. But you must leave very early in the morning. Let me show you the place."

They came to a spacious barn, clean and airy. Then the man left and came back with bread, milk, and sausage. At that point Oswald thanked him. But the Pole interrupted, saying, "I am truly sorry." With a wave of his hand he disappeared into the darkness.

When Oswald woke up, the night was about to retreat and the morning had not come. Even the dogs were not up. No one registered the presence of the stranger who, with a bundle of leftover food, ventured into the nearby forest.

Oswald was alone. There was both safety and threat in this absence of people. Where should he go? Whom can he turn to? The strength that helped him pretend and play a special role for such a long time was gone. He was afraid of the partisans; he knew how ruthless they could be. Besides, he had no gun. He could have looked for the runaway Jews from Mir, but was not sure where he could find them. He did not feel like searching for them.

All day long, Oswald continued to roam the countryside, crying and asking God, Why? Why has he been abandoned? In this agitated state, he came close to the village Simakowo, the village he had saved from destruction. There he sat down to rest on a big tree stump. He could hear shots but did not care enough to move on. He fell asleep. He dreamt that he was with the nuns, who lived right next to the gendarmerie. As a rule, he did not trust the clergy, but these nuns he knew quite well. After all, in the past, he gave them blank document forms that they had delivered to the ghetto. He knew they were trustworthy.

What happened next? *In this dream, I spoke to the Mother Superior of the Convent. . . . Maybe it was half a dream—maybe not quite a dream—I doubt that a person in the condition I was in is capable of knowing whether it was a dream or not. It lasted five to ten minutes, and in this state, whatever it might have been, I asked her to notify the Balicki sisters that they should find me another place. The Mother Superior agreed. I woke up. In a totally different mood, without crying, without despair, I went in the direction of the convent.*

13

Conversion

It was Sunday, August 16, 1942, five o'clock in the morning. Except for an occasional animal sound, the stillness in Mir was complete, a stillness soon interrupted by the pounding of wooden clogs against cobblestones and by a dangling batch of keys. The shoes and the keys belonged to Sister Nepomucena Kościuszek, who, still absorbed in her morning prayer, had come to open the convent's gate.

Suddenly through the half-opened space a man jumped into the courtyard. "Jesus Christ" escaped from the nun's lips, as her hand made the sign of the cross. She barely recaptured her composure when she recognized Oswald. She knew that the authorities were looking for him. Oswald was guilty of two crimes: he was a Jew and he had betrayed the Germans. Each required a death sentence.

Confronted with this dangerous runaway, the nun quickly relocked the gate and then asked him to follow her into the house. Inside, Oswald met the Mother Superior, Euzebia Bartkowiak, and the only two other inhabitants of the convent, Andrea Głowacka and Laurencja Domysłowska. Of the four Laurencja Domysłowska, in her thirties, had as yet not taken her final vows.

Except for the Mother Superior, the rest of the women seemed frightened by the sudden appearance of this dirty, somewhat confused youth. They knew that his mere presence was endangering their lives. Speechless, they looked at their leader. The unspoken question each seemed to be raising was: "What are we going to do with him?"

As Oswald stood there his own reactions were at best ambiguous. He remembers, *I was in a resigned mood. I was in a situation with no exit. All my strength had left me. But maybe not quite, maybe it was even an act of courage to come here? After all, the gendarmerie was right next to the convent! The threat was obvious. So perhaps mine was not a mood of resignation? Maybe I was more exhausted than resigned? Quite possibly the tension of the last nine months had to find an outlet. Still in some way, somehow I was also pleased with myself, excuse me for saying this, it sounds so very immodest. For the last nine months I had been under tension, but it was also a battle, like on the front. I fought to save. I was constantly active. I must have become very exhausted. Yet, at the same time, I had a tremendous satisfaction.*

Consciously I had come to the convent with a request that they help me contact the Balicki family. For me it would have been more dangerous to approach them directly because we were known as friends. . . . I thought that the Balicki sisters would know about other places for me to stay at. . . . When I explained this to the Mother Superior she said "no." For the time being she forbade any outside communication, stressing that these young girls may not be able to keep a secret and thus others could learn about my whereabouts. She insisted, "No one should know that you are here. We must pray to God to tell us what to do with you!" Then she explained that because this was a difficult and complicated situation only God can settle it. Instead of deciding by themselves they must wait for a sign from God.

But Euzebia Bartkowiak's reliance on God in no way interfered with her activities. She was enterprising, full of energy and determination. She concluded, "Until we know how to resolve this problem, we cannot send you away. You must wash, eat, and rest. After that we shall see."

It felt good to have someone else make the choices, someone else take over the responsibility. This was a welcome change from what he had been accustomed to during his service at the gendarmerie. He was glad to be passive, relieved to be leaving his future in the hands of someone else. Especially when this someone else was as competent as that Mother Superior.

The convent Oswald came to belonged to the Order of the Sisters of Resurrection, an order established in the nineteenth century by the Polish intelligentsia who lived as emigrants in Paris. Oswald explains that its founders identified *the resurrection of Christ with the rebirth of Poland as a nation. Today this group has gradually become universal. Initially it was Polish, in the spirit of Polish messianism. There was such a movement in the literature. The idea was that the suffering of Poland will save other nations, just like Christ saved the world through his suffering. This was a way of finding a reason, a justification, for the terrible fate of the Polish nation under the different occupations. In short, symbolically, the founders of this order connected the resurrection of Poland to the resurrection of Christ.*

Originally from the region of Poznań, in 1936 Euzebia Bartkowiak came to Mir to establish a convent, located in a spacious fourteen-room house. Only in 1941, when Hein decided to make a gendarmerie out of this building, did he ask the nuns to move next door. The new convent, previously owned by Jews, used to be a modest inn for those who came to the Mir fairs.

In addition to the main building, this former inn had a barn, a pigsty, and a storage shed. Though the main house and these lesser structures were separated by a courtyard, they were all connected by a single roof. This roof in turn created a semienclosure, offering privacy. Except for the back of the main building, the rest of the property was surrounded by a fence. Close to the fence was a garden. The garden and the fence prevented anyone on the outside from seeing what went on in the fenced-in space.

The new convent had two entrances, with one main gate that could admit a horse-drawn wagon. This gate, as in the next-door gendarmerie, opened into a side street close to the fields. The second entrance, from the main road, led directly into the living quarters: five small rooms, one spacious living room, and a large kitchen. From the kitchen a door led into a courtyard. On the other side of the courtyard adjacent to the gendarmerie were outer buildings.

The nuns kept one cow, pigs, and poultry, all helping to support them. The convent also owned land, part of which was rented to an old Pole who worked the fields and shared the profits with the nuns. This man lived alone in a hut that belonged to the convent.

Part of the land was used as a meadow for feeding the cow that was either in the meadow or the barn. The pigs only rarely ventured outside the pigsty while the chickens were left to roam all over the place, the yard, the barn, the shed, and sometimes even the house. One could find eggs in all kinds of places, but especially in the hay and straw scattered over the barn.

On that Sunday, the Mother Superior concluded that, for Oswald, the safest place would be the attic in the barn. When they reached it, she began to arrange the straw into the shape of a mattress. Then, as she took leave of this uninvited guest, she smiled, assuring him that God will show them the right way.

Left alone, Oswald noticed that the small opening in the attic offered a full view of the gendarmerie compound. Wasn't it too daring to stay that close? Still, those who were so vigorously pursuing him would probably never guess that he would hide next door. Oswald had no alternative. The nuns did. For the moment they chose not to act on it.

Since the arrest of the local Polish elite, one of whom was Dean Mackiewicz, Mir was without a Catholic priest. This meant that in town no Mass was being conducted—the nearest Catholic services were in the village Iszkoldź, about ten miles away. Each Sunday two of the nuns would walk to the church in Iszkolodź. The day Oswald came it was the Mother Superior's and Sister Andrea's turn.

Every Sunday during Mass the priest reads a special message from the Gospel. On that particular day he read about the good Samaritan. This is a story about a Jew who was robbed and wounded and left on the side of the road by his attackers. A priest passed next to the suffering man but did not bother to help him. Neither did a Levite. Only a traveling Samaritan took an interest in the helpless Jew. The Samaritan first attended to the man's wounds and then moved him to a nearby inn where he generously paid the innkeeper for keeping this stranger. Before the Samaritan left he assured the innkeeper that he will be coming back to check the condition of the patient. The story finishes with Jesus saying, "Go and do as he has done."[1]

Listening to this sermon and particularly the last sentence, the two women felt that God had spoken to them. Euzebia Bartkowiak was especially convinced that God wanted them to save Oswald. Of the four nuns, two were less than enthusiastic about keeping him. They objected. But the Mother Superior would not be dissuaded. When it came to moral issues she followed her own conscience. Firmly, she overruled their opposition.

About this decision and the events leading up to it Oswald did not hear right away. Exhausted, he slept on and on, perhaps for twenty-four hours, perhaps longer. He describes his rest as an "endless sleep." When he did wake up, next to him he found a Carmelite publication, a magazine containing articles about miraculous healings in Lourdes, France. These utterly incredible recoveries were attributed to the interventions of Mary.[2] Oswald became intrigued by these accounts and asked for more readings about similar cures.

With free access to Mackiewicz's library the nuns could easily satisfy his request. More readings about such supernatural healings convinced Oswald that they were sufficiently verified and that they really had happened. He thought that a religion that had to do with such events deserved closer study.

And so, after I read about these miraculous cures I asked for the New Testament and began to study it. I also read different Hebrew books that I found in the attic. . . . I was full of questions. I kept asking why such tragic things were happening to my people. I felt very much like a Jew, I identified with the plight of my people. I also felt like a Zionist. I longed for Palestine, for my own country. . . .

In this frame of mind I became exposed to the New Testament, a book that describes events that were taking place in my fatherland, the land I was longing for. This, in itself, must have created a psychological bridge between me and the New Testament. . . . Strange as it may seem, I had a Polish high school diploma but I never read the New Testament. No one demanded it of me. About the church I knew only negative things. I was prejudiced against the church.

In the convent, all alone, among strangers, I created an artificial world for myself. I pretended that the 2000 years had never happened. In this make-believe world of mine I am confronted by Jesus from Nazareth. . . . If you will not understand this, you will not understand my struggle for the right to my Jewish nationality. . . . And so I am faced with Jesus from Nazareth. . . . You must realize that not all history about Jesus is the history of the church. The history of Jesus is a fragment of Jewish history. Then I follow the exchanges of ideas and arguments that took place between Jesus and some of the Jews, different kinds of Jews. Soon I begin to lean more and more toward the position taken by Jesus. I find myself agreeing with Jesus' approach and view of Judaism. His sermons appeal to me strongly. In this process I somehow disregard all that happened later in the relationship between the Jews and the Christians.

At the same time I needed a teacher, someone that would show me the way, a guide . . . someone strong. . . . And so I come to the stage where Jesus dies on the cross and then is resurrected.

Suddenly, and I don't know how, I identify his suffering and resurrection with the suffering of my people and the hope of their resurrection. I begin to think that if a man who is just and pure dies, not for his sins but because of circumstances, there must be a God, because it is God who brings him back to life. Then I think that if there is justice toward Christ in the form of resurrection there will be some kind of justice toward my people too.

I was cut off from my Jewishness almost for a year. I was separated from all that was Jewish. I felt then that for the Jew in this church there must be a reserved place, I am not wrong about it. I became convinced that perhaps I have some special function to perform in this church, maybe to improve, to fix the relation between the Jews and the Christians. . . .

In the end my move to Christianity was not an escape from Judaism but, on the contrary, a way of finding answers to my problems as a Jew. . . . When I realized that I stood before a decision to embrace Catholicism the psychological battle began. I myself had all the prejudices about Jews who convert to Christianity. Aware of these prejudices, I was afraid that my people, the Jews, will reject me. Actually, they did not. At any rate, my psychological battle lasted for two days. During that time I cried a lot, asking God for guidance. . . .

It was not an intellectual battle. . . . Intellectually I accepted Jesus. The entire problem was what will be my relationship to the Jewish people, to my brother, possibly my parents if they lived.

At this point I asked Oswald, "If you were afraid that the Jews would reject you, how come you converted?"

His answer was, *Because my intellect overpowered my emotions. . . . Aristotle once said, "Plato is my friend but the truth is stronger than friendship." Do you understand? If God approved of this man so it is my duty to follow what I see as right. This is stronger than my ties with my people. . . . After all, human ties are also created by God! If God calls into a certain direction, one cuts ties with the family and moves into the direction of God. I knew all this. I also knew that I was taking a risk. I risked thinking that I will be able to persuade my brother and the others. . . . I hoped that I will succeed in convincing them that I did not betray the Jewish interests. . . . For me the acceptance of Christianity was a Jewish step. It was a move of a Jew toward a certain historical period of the Jewish people.*

Eventually I told myself that, even though my people, because of tragic circumstances, did not accept Jesus, this does not mean that I have to be always faithful to their decisions.

To my question on how he intends to deal with the traditional Christian-Jewish antagonism he said that Christian religion per se *has no connection to anti-Semitism, only the Christian education, the interpretation does. Christ's teachings as such are basically Jewish, not Roman, not Greek, not Polish. The New Testament is Jewish, written by Jews for Jews, almost the entire New Testament. . . . Just because at this moment the inheritors, the administrators of this Testament, are not Jews does not mean that I have to remove myself from it. On the contrary, I should bring back into the New Testament the Jewish elements, myself being one of those Jewish elements, and others like me. There are many people like I, Christans who see themselves as Jews.*

Besides, I have already become a fighter. For the last nine months I was all alone. I had to struggle for everything by myself. I thought that somehow I will explain this to my brother and if they survive the war, to my parents, and friends as well. I had reached this decision on my father's birthday and wanted to be baptized right then.

That day when the Mother Superior came to see me I told her, "I want to be baptized today."

"Why today?" she asked.

"Because today is my father's birthday. I want to show that there is continuity, that I am not rejecting Judaism but accepting its special form."

Then she said: "But you know nothing about Christianity."

"I believe that Jesus was the Messiah. Please baptize me today."

Oswald claims that he had accepted Christianity through the church because he had no other choice. He explains, *I did not want to receive religious instructions. I did not want the nuns to teach me about Christianity. My aim was to receive Christianity from its original source. Its real source was the New Testament, a Jewish source. . . . Only after sixty years or so did the Jewish Christians stop being a part of the Jewish religion. I understood this from the beginning.*

On that day Mother Superior reacted to Oswald's wish by saying, "It is strange, I heard a voice telling me that I should pray and that you will become a Catholic priest. When I heard it I was moved. I did not want to accept it. I argued with myself that the man is a Jew but the voice kept returning again and again."

Oswald thinks that *because of this set of circumstances she did not object to my request. That same day, in the evening, I was baptized by one of the nuns. . . . Since that day Judaism and Christianity have been always at the center of my very existence.* In less than three weeks after Oswald's arrival in the convent he was baptized.

Significantly, Oswald insists that in the convent Christianity did bring him closer to Palestine and hence closer to his national Jewish identity. At that point he began to reason that if, for example, a Frenchman, a Pole, and an Italian can be Catholic, so can a Jew. Issues related to the separation between religion and nationality, in his case Jewish nationality and Catholic religion, continue to preoccupy him.

In addition, and perhaps more important, he claims that the life of Jesus helped him cope with the Holocaust. In the life of Jesus and his resurrection he saw an analogy to the martyrdom of the Jewish people.

Oswald asserts, *In Jesus I found an answer to the Holocaust which I could not find in Judaism. In Jesus I see a crucified Jew who through his crucifixion offers redemption.*

To clarify, I asked, "Symbolically, you see the Holocaust as another crucifixion?"

He answered, *Yes, of course. For me the Holocaust is the Golgotha of the Jews, a road to redemption.*

I wanted to understand and inquired, "Why should God do that?"

I do not know. I cannot ask God, I have no right to ask God was Oswald's answer.

I continued to probe. "What makes you think that? What gave you the idea that this is so?"

Oswald tried to explain. *If a man like Jesus, without sins, the most beautiful man we had on earth, according to what we know about him, if he was crucified and God accepted this sacrifice, why would he not accept the sacrifice of millions of others?*

My comment was, "Jesus was willing to be crucified. None of the Jews that were murdered and gassed went willingly; they did not want to die!"

He reacted by saying, *I understand your objection. Maybe I should answer you with Cardinal Lustiger's words. He said, "Jews have been crucified by us Christians for many centuries. We failed to see in them the brothers of Christ. Jews were condemned to follow the same path that Jesus did. Christians did to the Jews what was done to Christ without realizing that they were continuing to crucify Christ." Then as we sat across from each other, just like you and I, he said, "We, the Jews in the church, have an obligation to make the Christians aware of what they have done to the Jews." This happened in Paris, after I saw the Pope. I met with Lustiger.*[3] (Cardinal Lustiger is a French Jew who converted and who identifies himself as a Jew.)

I told Oswald that I have difficulties with this kind of reasoning and that in a sense it may justify the World War II murder of the Jews. It may justify future Jewish persecutions as well.

He disagreed. *No. At the moment virulent anti-Semitism does not exist. Right now anti-Semitism has to do with political issues. . . . You must understand that what I say is not a part of my faith, it is an interpretation. I cannot even persuade the Christians that this is how they ought to see their relationship to Jews. I have been looking for the meaning of my existence, for the meaning of what had happened during the war to my people. My common sense, even after the horrors I had witnessed, could not conclude that there is no God. If God exists, then I must somehow save his image, for myself. I felt that from all the possible solutions, this one maintains God's place within the context of this world and preserves my relation to the Jewish nation. . . .*

All this is speculation. But this kind of reasoning brought me to Christianity, because it sees in Jesus the savior. Through the crucifixion he became the savior.

I asked, "You want to explain the Holocaust?"

He said *yes,* adding, *I want to explain all suffering, Biafra, Cambodia, etc. No one explained suffering better than the one who voluntarily went to suffer.*

I found myself raising the same issue. "But during the Holocaust and in the other instances you mentioned, in all the other places, people have not voluntarily chosen suffering."

Oswald again tried to explain. *I understand, but I am not sure that in order for suffering to lead to redemption there has to be acceptance. We cannot measure or apply to God human criteria. I don't want to say that I love the world that is full of suffering, but maybe there is no other way out. Maybe this is how it always was in the world, but we did not see those Holocausts? . . . This is not a rational kind of reasoning. I don't know how else to believe in God's justice, even in His very existence. How else can I believe in God as someone who intervenes on this earth?*

"You give God a lot of responsibility," I said.

He agreed. *Yes, I do . . . just think, isn't it strange that three years after the Jews were almost totally annihilated, the Jewish nation came into being? Don't you see in this an expression of higher justice?*

This question I left unanswered.

Aside from Oswald's religious transformation, for him life in the convent represented a change from constant exposure to people and uninterrupted activities, to isolation and partial inaction. In the gendarmerie Oswald's Jewishness was a well-guarded secret; during his stay in the convent it was a well-publicized liability. Whereas before, in case of discovery, only he himself would have paid a price for his crimes, now those who were protecting him would be subjected to severe punishment, most likely death.[4]

Oswald's new situation was further compounded by the fact that two of the nuns were openly opposed to his presence. He had realized that he remained in this place only because the Mother Superior overruled their objections.[5] This made Oswald feel superfluous and hurt—he was not used to personal rejections. Usually people would become easily attached to him and, once formed, such affectionate ties were not easily cut.[6] Though initially the head of this convent acted out of a sense of moral duty, her attitudes soon turned into something else. Not demonstrative, the Mother Superior had developed a special liking for this lonely renegade. Perhaps to lift his spirits, she agreed to visits from Wanda, the sister-in-law of Siemion Serafimowicz. This young woman had an important and potentially dangerous connection to the local authorities, but the nuns trusted her more than the Balicki sisters. They never had any reason to regret their confidence.

When the romance between Regina Balicki and Oswald died down, he had transferred his affection to Wanda. In this new relationship there was a double bond: a deep friendship and a strong attraction. Eventually Oswald and Wanda believed themselves in love. And though their contacts never moved beyond hugging and kissing, the couple was engrossed in each other's feelings. In the convent their emotional reunion reconfirmed that the revelations about Oswald's origin did not destroy their mutual attachment.

From Wanda Oswald heard that the authorities were still energetically searching for him. Not only did his name and picture appear on different lists of wanted criminals, but a high price was being offered to anyone who would help capture him. Official eagerness to apprehend him was very different from the reactions of single individuals, even those who had been directly affected by his actions.

Thus, for example, Oswald is convinced that *Hein was happy that I succeeded and that I escaped. Meister Hein, in fact, paid a price for this affair. He was moved from Mir, probably as punishment, because the new position was not better at all. In this new place during a battle with the partisans Hein was severely wounded. The partisans carved a Soviet star on his forehead and left him in the forest. He died because of loss of blood, on the way to a hospital. Serafimowicz was probably pleased that I escaped.*

Oswald also heard from Wanda that her sister, Jadwiga Serafimowicz, continued to feel warmly toward him. Once when cleaning closets, Jadwiga came across his sweater. As she held it in her hand, she burst into tears. Then between sobs she spoke about his lot, imagining him roam the country, all alone, poor and hungry, finding it hard to elude danger.

True to her promise, Wanda did not reveal Oswald's whereabouts even to her sister. On another occasion, when no one was around, she took the sweater and returned it to its owner.

Unlike Oswald, his girlfriend took her Catholicism for granted. She also found all religious discussions boring. Not surprisingly, Oswald's piousness created a wedge between the two young people. Wanda was interested in her boyfriend, not his religion. Besides, with Oswald's baptism came a vague realization that he might dedicate his life to religious pursuits. Gradually he began to detach himself from his affectionate ties to this young woman. He notes, *I let Wanda know that I had no intention of marrying. I told her that I might become a monk. I felt strongly that I should not lead her on. In the end I was convinced that I had an obligation, even a duty to terminate our romantic involvement.* Wanda's visits became less frequent, though they never stopped. Till the very end she kept Oswald's secret and remained his loyal friend.

Conversion also led to other more concrete changes. *The two nuns, who initially opposed my stay in the convent, accepted me completely. Their approval coincided with my baptism. . . . Soon not only did these nuns tolerate me but they were even happy to have me there.*

Despite such developments, despite greater inner peace, Oswald became convinced that he ought to go away. He did not want his protectors to think that he had become a Christian in order to remain in the convent. Still, there is a difference between a decision to leave and an actual departure. It took him at least ten days until he put these ideas into practice. As he was about to leave, he was glad that the nuns were sad to see him go.

What did he intend to do on the outside? *I thought that I would go into the forest. But something kept me from doing this. I was afraid. I felt that the partisans may hurt me because I had worked for the Germans. Besides, I knew that they were not interested in Jews, nor in rescuers of Jews. I knew that much.*

Actually, he could think of no one to turn to, of no place to go to. On the outside, wherever he went he was recognized. He slept in the fields hiding from people, trying not to show his face. At one time he found a ruined hut and decided to rest there. In the morning he heard voices of peasants working in the fields. Feeling protected inside the ruins, he decided to stay. Then he fell asleep, but not for long. *I was awakened by a man who entered this hut. When he saw me he seemed shocked. He must have recognized me. When he had sufficiently recovered, he ran away making some scary sounds. Knowing that a report about my presence might bring him a big price, I too ran as fast as my feet would carry me. I felt like a hunted animal. I had reached a dead end and returned to the convent.* Oswald's absence had lasted four days. His protectors eased his dejection by welcoming him warmly.

When Oswald first came to the nunnery he would stay in the attic of the barn. Out of the straw he built an easy chair. He sat there looking through the opening. This way he could follow some of the activities in the next door gendarmerie. He also read extensively, something he had not done for a long time. To break the monotony, the nuns gave him the task of searching through the straw and hay for freshly laid eggs. Still, reading, staring at the gendarmerie, gathering eggs, left him with much too much free time.

How did he cope? *Soon I realized that in this place all alone, isolated from life and everyone else, I might lose my mind. I wanted to become more active. This is when the nuns taught me how to knit.* Knitting was more than just a pastime. These women supplemented their income by taking orders for sweaters, gloves, stockings, and dresses. Their customers were mainly Poles who lived in the vicinity. Sometimes they would pay with goods: eggs, meat, wheat, and other farm products. Such payments were just as welcomed as cash. In no time Oswald became an expert knitter, so proficient that he began to knit dresses. Eager to contribute to his upkeep, he would spend a large part of the day at this job.

Eventually his contributions to the household continued to expand. Except for his involvement with knitting, all the other tasks were strictly male jobs: splitting wood, starting fires, fixing things around the house. Despite these activities Oswald continued to spend a great deal of time in the attic and ate all his meals there. Later on the nuns invited him to join them in the dining room. This change was not without danger. Whenever he came to the dining room, they had to make sure that both the front door to the house and the gate in the courtyard were locked. During meal times Oswald would tell stories about his former life in Mir and about his childhood. He would also sing songs, especially Zionist, religious songs.

Because Mir was without a Catholic priest, many natives would bring their personal problems to the nuns. When together, the five companions would talk about ways to alleviate the suffering of these people. Frequently, after evening meals, they would take turns reading passages from the Bible. They also read different religious magazines that they had found in the priest's library. After Oswald became baptized, he spent a great deal of time praying. He notes that *with the Christening came greater familiarity with prayers, talk with God. This occupied much of my time. I was not bored.*

Grateful, Oswald was not surprised by the nuns' decision to shelter him. For him to save another human being was not extraordinary. Used to rescuing people, he had expected the nuns to do the same. Still, when he speaks about his four companions, he is full of admiration. He has a great deal of respect for their courage and is convinced that they were not concerned about the risk they were taking in sheltering him. Invariably, when referring to them he says that *they were wonderful women, they looked upon my stay there as a duty. There were no fears in that house, except during certain moments. They were definitely not scared, if they were they could not have allowed me to take my meals with them. . . . They were like soldiers, for whom saving me was a duty . . . they also had open tolerant attitudes toward Jews.*

Actually Oswald's constant presence in the convent broke many of the house rules. When it was all over, in 1946, the Mother Superior went to the head of their order to discuss these transgressions. She wanted to know whether it was right for them to have disregarded so many established regulations. The head of the order, an old woman, said, "If we had created the Mir convent only to save this one man, we would have something to thank God for. Be assured that human life is much more important than all the rules."[7]

With time, contacts between Oswald and the nuns became more extensive although they did not develop into deep friendships. One possible exception was the Mother Superior. Euzebia Bartkowiak had a rare combination of attributes: strength, warmth, tolerance, and an endless amount of curiosity about people and the world around her. Strong affectionate ties developed between Oswald and this woman, usually reflected in the favors these two friends did for each other. About his relationship to all the nuns Oswald says, *It was not an intimate, deep friendship. I always maintained a distance. It was not so simple. I never entered into the internal business of the home. I tried not to become too nosy. I made an effort at being helpful, but I did not want to interfere. Actually, almost all day long I was alone, I read, I knit, I prayed a lot. I was in my protectors' company only during our meals. Rarely at other times. We lived in the same house but they had their life and I had mine. . . .*

In October there was a lot of rain, it was windy, freezing. It was too cold to stay in the attic. This is when the nuns invited me to sleep in the house. At that point Oswald was offered one of the small rooms.

This arrangement called for greater caution. They always had to be prepared for unexpected guests. Sometimes Oswald had no time to disappear into the barn or any of the other safer places.

How well prepared were they for such sudden eventualities? *It would happen that I would be in the living room talking to them and there was no time to run away. In this living room there was a big closet that contained the nuns' clothes. I had a chair in this closet. When there was danger, I would jump inside and sit on this chair. I would wait until the danger would pass.*

I was not supposed to sneeze or cough. This could give me away. It was good that in my youth I had boy scout training. I was taught how to act when one feels like sneezing, but should not, where to squeeze the nose, etc. I had all kinds of tricks when my nose tickled.

Because the nuns were respected both by the civilians and the authorities, visits to their place were quite common. As Oswald sat in the closet, he recognized many of the guests by their voices. Some were policemen who came to tell about partisan threats and about other official or semiofficial business. Oswald had a special liking for some of those who came. At times he was tempted to make his presence known, to talk to them, to enjoy their company. But it was far too dangerous to follow his impulse. He never did. Instead, he continued to stay in the closet, glad that no one had discovered him.

The presence of outsiders, however, was not always as uneventful. Among the frequent convent callers was a peasant woman, a Catholic and a Nazi-collaborator. Everyone knew that part of her income came from spying on civilians and denouncing them to the authorities. The nuns were unsuccessful in dissuading her from these devious ways. Still, they encouraged her visits, hoping that in the end they might lead her away from her sinful path.

One day, unaware that the woman was in the convent, Oswald, carrying a batch of wood, entered the living room to start a fire. When this guest noticed him, startled she stood up. She had recognized him—most local people would. It mattered little that Oswald disappeared quickly. The damage was done. In a split second, impulsively, she ran out of the house. In no time she returned, threw herself on her knees in front of the Mother Superior, and swore she would tell no one about this dangerous encounter. Oswald feels that because of the possible peril, *right away the nuns should have asked me to leave. They did not. The Mother Superior chose to believe this untrustworthy person. She proved to be right. Although a Nazi collaborator, the woman told no one that she had seen me.*

In Belorussia and in other parts close to the Soviet borders, the Russians were determined to dominate the different, often disjointed, partisan groupings. Soviet efforts were directed from Moscow. They succeeded only gradually, and these successes were closely related to Soviet victories at the front. As the Germans were losing the war, the partisans were gaining in strength. Eventually, nightly partisan attacks began to penetrate into towns, among them Mir. With these incursions becoming bolder, the Nazis began to look for more countermeasures. In Mir the authorities were concerned with the safety of their official buildings. To them one obvious solution was to surround these structures with barbed wire. If done, this would transform the heart of the town into a police area. But before this plan could be put into effect the Germans had to decide what to do with the convent located in the middle of their official buildings. This decision, in turn, called for an inspection of the place.

The formal visit to the convent occurred on a Sunday, when three of the nuns, among them the Mother Superior, were away in church in Iszkoldź. Only one nun stayed home to protect Oswald. For him, indeed, this event was memorable. *Two policemen knocked. The nun opened the door but forgot to warn me. The men began to enter into the different rooms. Soon I could hear their heavy military boots quite close to me. I had a room two by six meters, a long and narrow place. When these threatening sounds reached me, I was near the window, reading or knitting. My room had the usual wash basin. In front of it was a screen that was supposed to hide anyone who was washing.*

At this wash basin was a shawl, a big, black shawl. The nuns gave it to me to keep warm. When I heard the heavy boots and the loud voices, practically in my room, I quickly jumped behind the screen and threw the shawl over it. This suggested that one of the nuns might be behind it. The men came in. They stopped not far from the screen. Amused, they commented that a nun must be behind it. They chuckled. Then I heard them leave the room. When they were out of the house, the nun appeared, pale and shaking all over. All I could do was pray.

After this official visit the Nazis ordered the convent to move to Stara Miranka, a few miles away from Mir. The transfer had to take place by March 1943.

The new house consisted of four rooms and a barn attached to the main building. Because Oswald was well known in the area, he could not show his face. The actual move, therefore, had to take place in a number of steps. *As the nuns emptied the different rooms they locked me into one of them. On the last day, one of the nuns left for the new place very early in the morning, before anyone was up. That same evening, I, dressed as a nun, walked with the other three nuns to our new home.*

The new convent was not only smaller but also more exposed, without a garden, without a fence. At this time the Germans were becoming more and more nervous. Night searches for partisans were common. It would have been too dangerous for Oswald to sleep in such an exposed place. The barn became Oswald's sleeping quarters. This barn, although attached to the new convent, was used by the Germans as a storage place for food confiscated from peasants. To avert partisan attacks, at night it was guarded by policemen. Each evening another group of policemen would come and watch the barn till dawn. Because of this watch, no Germans would dream of searching inside the barn.

In principle, those buildings belonged to the parish-church of Mir, but were being used by the authorities. In a small hall opposite the entrance a ladder served as the way to the attic of the barn. Every evening the Mother Superior, Oswald dressed as a nun, and a cat would climb up this ladder behind the standing guard. As they climbed the nun spoke to the cat, pretending that she was bringing it there to keep away the mice. Since the attic contained all kinds of food, the presence of a cat protected the food from mice. And so the guard never considered interfering with this nightly pastime. Each morning after the policeman had left, Oswald still dressed as a nun, would sneak down and into the house.

Watchful, anxious to protect their "invisible" tenant, the nuns divided their activities between work and prayer. In this new place, because of its smaller size and greater exposure, they tried to keep contacts with the local people to a bare minimum. Their own close group continued to hope and pray for calm. But peace was becoming progressively more elusive. In fact, the Germans were becoming more cruel and more violent. It was as if the loss of battles created a special need for victories against vulnerable civilians. The smallest crimes, often imaginary ones, were met with severe punishment.

Thus, for example, in a nearby town, twelve nuns, suspected of feeding partisans, were executed. Raids into private homes became more frequent. As the terror grew, more natives joined the partisans. Escapes into forests, in turn, led to more violent Nazi retaliations. As usual, the losers were the innocent people who had little or nothing to do with such moves.

With this increasingly threatening situation, Oswald became concerned about the nuns' safety. He was convinced that he could avert disaster by leaving the convent. But he had no place to go. Relying on God, he waited for an inspiration, for a sign. As he hoped for a change, two distinct needs were combatting for attention. One demanded that he consider the nuns' safety. The other had to do with his own protection against death. He vacillated, but stayed. Though aware of the potential threats, and the difficult choices, his companions never suggested that he leave.

Summer came and passed without Oswald's making a move. With the approach of winter there was a severe gasoline shortage. Rumor had it that the Germans were searching private homes in the hope of finding gasoline. Actually, this was a strange report because in this part of the country private ownership of cars was practically unheard of. And even if any civilian had a car, it would have been confiscated by the Nazis a long time ago. Whether true or not, for Oswald, this news acted as a final push. God, he felt, was giving him a sign to free the nuns of their burden.

And so, on December 3, 1943, in the evening, dressed as a nun, Oswald left the convent in the company of the Mother Superior. In a nearby forest he took off his robe. As he handed it to the nun, she cried, saying, "Come back in case of difficulties. Be sure to come back." Too upset to speak, Oswald nodded, knowing full well that this time he wouldn't be returning.

Still crying softly the nun blessed him and left. She did not look back. Speechless, motionless, Oswald continued to stand, watching long after she had disappeared.

Oswald's plans were vague. He was going to approach the old Pole who was renting the convent's land. This peasant lived all alone in a small hut that also belonged to the convent. Oswald knew him as a hard working, honest man who had a reputation of a recluse. In fact, the only people he had dealings with were the nuns and officials. In each case these contacts were indispensable. In each case the man kept them to a bare minimum.

The nuns had thought that their tenant might offer shelter to Oswald. His hut was relatively safe because it stood away from all other dwellings. Also, the peasant's reputation as someone who preferred to be left alone made him an unlikely target for partisan visits or German raids.

When Oswald knocked at his door, from within came the sound of a rough voice: "Who is there? What do you want!?"

"Oswald from the gendarmerie. I need your help, please let me in."

The door opened. Angry, the man spoke in part to himself, in part to the uninvited guest. "I cannot keep him. You know that they could kill me for that? Come in." Inside Oswald was told that the would have to leave at dawn. The peasant was obviously frightened. Oswald felt sorry for this man as he assured him, "I will go away early. Don't worry, I don't want to make trouble for you."

He kept his promise. The next day, when the moon and the stars were still in full charge of the sky, Oswald left.

14

Moving to the Forest

On December 4, 1943, Oswald was once more searching for a haven. Almost sixteen months had passed since his escape from the Mir gendarmerie, yet time failed to erase the memory of this event. It was too unusual to be forgotten and people continued to talk about it. Lingering recollections made Oswald's safety elusive. To evade being recognized, he tried to change his appearance. Oswald grew a big mustache while the nuns found some civilian clothes: a worn-out warm jacket and an equally worn-out pair of pants. These gifts allowed him to discard the upper part of his SS uniform. The pants he slipped over the SS black ones. Because military boots were unlikely to reveal their original owner, he kept them. Under the circumstances, with the prospect of having to stay in the open fields and forests, boots were a most valuable possession.

In the end neither Oswald's mustache nor the changed wardrobe modified his looks. Those who had known this former interpreter would have had no trouble recognizing him. Only a nun's robe and the special face cover he put on when leaving the convent might have done the job. But Oswald could not roam the countryside in this disguise. A nun with a man's face could hardly approach people for food or shelter. And so he had to rely on a partial, imperfect camouflage, and the intangible entity called luck. He had little else.

When he was leaving the convent, the nuns wanted to give him money. Knowing how poor they were, he refused the offer. All he accepted was bread and cheese, a small-sized New Testament, a Hebrew Psalm book, and a few holy pictures.

On the fourth of December Oswald had behind him one night's rest, an open country road, and only vague plans for the future. Considering his limited resources and the ever-changing circumstances, there was no point in designing a definite course of action. He could only anticipate broad moves. Still, in some way he had to sort out and rank the possible threats and dangers.

As a sought-after fugitive, he could be a target of persecution for various groups. The Nazis were eager to catch an imposter, a Jew, and one who had betrayed their confidence. By deceiving them, by escaping, he had challenged their judgment, their power, and, in a way, their self-respect. Only through the capture of such an offender could the Nazis restore some of their lost "honor." Thus, even more than a year after the event the Germans were still offering a substantial price for evidence about Oswald's whereabouts.

Some civilians had to be tempted by such an easy profit. However, one could not predict who or how many of the natives would be ready to hand him over to the authorities. This uncertainty made all those who could identify him a potential threat. Oswald had to stay away from possible denouncers, while seeking out prospective helpers. The further removed he would be from the Mir region the likelihood of being recognized would lessen. Oswald's first priority was to increase the distance between himself and the place he had lived in for over two years. As he was acting on this decision he had few illusions. All he was hoping for was an occasional gift of food and permission to stay overnight. His expectations were correct. People would extend their hospitality for a day. Not for longer. Not surprisingly, Oswald became convinced that acceptance into a partisan group would be the best solution. In addition to offering protection, membership in a fighting unit would provide an opportunity to battle the Nazis, an agreeable prospect.

Oswald knew that in his case joining the partisans was not simple. No gun was a definite disadvantage. Forest fighters were reluctant to recruit unarmed men. It was also likely that some fighters knew about his experiences, especially his past association with the Mir gendarmerie. They might be suspicious of his German connection. He was aware of the unpredictable and often violent ways of some of the armed forest dwellers who called themselves anti-Fascist soldiers. Thus, partisan encounters could be risky and an eventual acceptance into their ranks was at best questionable.

On the other hand, there was the possibility of meeting Jews who had escaped from the ghetto in Mir. They would be eager to repay what Oswald had done for them. He expected that many of these fugitives had become partisans and that they would be scattered among different fighting groups. Because they would ease his acceptance into a partisan group, Oswald decided to search for them.

Much of Western Belorussia is covered by old, thick forests. Those eager to escape from the Nazis found these huge, almost junglelike wooded areas hospitable havens. Particularly toward the end of 1943, these forests sheltered thousands of refugees. Many of these illegal runaways were transformed into better organized and more effective fighters. With time too, partisan control over these forests spilled into the adjacent small towns and villages. As a result, by the end of 1943, it was not unusual for the Nazi authorities to avoid partisan enclaves. Not only were the Germans and their collaborators reluctant to enter into the forests, but they often stayed away from their surrounding communities.

Oswald was right in assuming that he would be exposed to less danger the closer he came to one of those wooded areas. He wanted to reach one of those forests, the Nalibocki forest. Also, in these partially liberated places the incentive to hand him over to the authorities would not be there. It was perhaps less likely that in these parts the natives would be punished by the Nazis for sheltering runaways. Finally, in such partisan-dominated areas, Oswald's chances for meeting some of the Mir Jews were better, as were his chances for being accepted into one of their units.

When Oswald was approaching the Nalibocki forest, all underground activities, including the different partisan operations, were more orderly.

Oswald notes that *at the time the Communists succeeded in establishing in the Belorussian forests a civilian and a military hierarchy. In a way, the party, the political arm of the Russian-dominated forest fighters, was just as important as the military segment.*

However, even though the Russians had a better grip over the partisan movement, this did not mean they established complete order, or that they did not have to bow to some local demands. At best the Soviets created only a partially integrated fighting force. They continued to tolerate a variety of subgroups, with distinct, at times, even hostile aims. Sometimes the mutual opposition of these subgroupings led to outright battles. Some could be traced to political sources, others to the ethnically mixed composition of these underground units. In Western Belorussia, though dominant, the Russian partisan movement was an ethnic mixture of Russians, Belorussians, Ukrainians, Jews, Poles, and Lithuanians. Each ethnic group was politically and socially heterogeneous.[1]

Oswald was familiar with the traditional Polish-Russian split. He also knew about the hostile position of each toward Jewish runaways. He comments about the Russian-Polish divisiveness: *As I was approaching the forest I felt that I would have to make a decision whether to go to Polish or to Soviet partisans. I had no relationship or contacts with either group. All I knew was that there were separate Polish and Russian fighting units.*

Predictably, most Poles resented the Russian domination of this area's partisan movement. Still, this did not prevent some from joining Russian ranks. Poles who became a part of the Russian groups were under direct Soviet domination. Some were Communists, while others found themselves there by chance. The majority of Poles, however, refused to be under a direct Soviet command and insisted on forming their own fighting units. Oswald notes that *those who became a part of such special groups were local people, old Poles, settlers and others who recently arrived from the Warsaw region. They did not want to be ruled by the Russians. They wanted to be under the authority of the Polish Government in Exile in London.*

Before the summer of 1943, a local Pole, Lieutenant Miłaszewski organized a separate fighting group. His men identified themselves with the AK (Home Army), the official fighting force of the Polish underground, that was under the command of the Polish Government in Exile in London. Miłaszewski, although an AK man, cooperated with the Russian headquarters, coordinating his anti-German moves with theirs. Under his leadership the Polish fighting group grew to several hundred. Politically, these Poles were heterogeneous, ranging from the left to the right with some affiliated with the Fascist part of the underground, the NSZ.[2]

The Jewish-Russian partisan Jacob Greenstein explains why the Russians tolerated an autonomous group of Polish fighters. *Here the head of the Nazi puppet government, a prominent Belorussian, Ostrowski, was successfully enlisting Belorussian youths into the German army and for labor in Germany. This, of course, backfired against us. We tried to respond by collecting men before Ostrowski could get to them. We wanted to prevent this kind of recruitment of Poles. At the same time, we knew that Poles would more readily follow their own people. In short, we were willing to support the autonomy of Polish partisans because we knew that it was easier for Poles to enlist their youths than for us (Russians). We also knew that these Polish fighters would cooperate with us only if we gave them some freedom. In the end, even though they had a great deal of autonomy, they were dependent on us. We outnumbered them. There were 30,000 of us and only 400 of them.*[3]

Toward the end of the summer in 1943, the situation changed. A small group of Polish officers came to join this Polish unit. They were sent by the Polish Government in Exile, with instructions to undermine the Soviet power in this area. Some of these officers belonged to the Fascist NSZ. Throughout the war the NSZ had waged multiple battles: against the Germans, the Russians, the Jews, and Poles who disagreed with them politically. Only in 1943 did a part of the NSZ agree to join forces with the AK.[4]

The arrival of these officers disturbed the existing Polish-Russian equilibrium. When a fighting group of twelve Jews came to the forest from the Nieśwież region they were attacked by the Polish partisans. All but one were killed. These Poles also ambushed another group of Jews on their way to collect food.[5]

Such unauthorized killings were in direct opposition to the policies of the Russian command. At the Russian partisan headquarters, a decision was reached to disband the Polish fighting group. Greenstein thinks that rather than to kill, *the Soviets wanted to deprive the Poles of their autonomy. We went out, 200 of us, I was a part of the group. We surrounded them at night and in the early hours of the morning, without one shot, we took them prisoners. There were about 400 of them. Only 50 or so of their cavalry men were missing. They were in a nearby town, Iwieniec. When they heard what had happened they united with the Germans and fought against us.*

To be sure, not all Polish partisans favored the anti-Jewish moves. Some felt that they should be fighting Germans, not Jews. Still they were unable to prevent these actions. Greenstein continues, *When we took these Poles prisoners, the soldiers among them we divided into small groups and sent each group into a different Russian unit. Many of them had come from the surrounding villages and towns. Soon most of them ran away. The rest stayed with us and fought against the Germans. With the officers we dealt differently. . . . I was present when they were being interrogated. We could get nothing out of them. They refused to tell why they were sent here, by whom, and why they had concentrated on attacking Jews. I have heard later that some of them were sent to Moscow. I don't know what happened to them there. Some were supposedly put on trial in Poland, after the war. Maybe the Russians tried to brainwash them, who knows? . . . I know that when we disarmed them and when we took them prisoners we did not kill them.*

About these Polish fighters Oswald tells a different story. He denies that they had murdered Jews. He points out that after the Poles were overpowered by the Russian partisans they were scattered in small numbers to different Soviet-dominated groups and that eventually most were murdered. This Polish-Russian confrontation had happened before Oswald came to the forest. He notes, *When I entered the forest the Polish partisans were being liquidated, disarmed, subdivided, and placed into different units. I don't know if the purpose was to finish them off or simply to subordinate them to the Soviets. Perhaps only later on someone gave an order to liquidate them. After they were dispersed they could not have become Russian enemies because they were disarmed. The few I had met in our unit were shot in the back, in an underhanded way. This happened when they were supposedly being transferred to another place. Someone who sat behind them shot them, one by one. . . . This was not decent. I think that it was a part of a conscious effort to liquidate the Polish underground. . . . This was a dirty job of the Soviets, the same way as Katyn was or the Polish uprising in Warsaw.*[6]

Oswald sees the Soviet move against the Polish fighters as part of a deliberate, overall attempt to gain control over postwar Poland. Thus, he thinks that the Russians *were opposed to the existence of any group that could have had some claims to victory over the Germans.* Russian hostility to the Polish Government in Exile is a historical fact, as are the Soviet efforts at suppressing all evidence about the part that the non-Communist Polish underground played in opposing and weakening the Nazi occupation. The destruction of an independent Polish combat unit therefore fits into the overall Russian plan to subjugate the Polish people.[7]

When Oswald came to the Nalibocki forest the choice was made for him. At that point the independent Polish fighting unit ceased to exist. The Soviets had established a firmer grip over the area and its partisans.

Compared to any other ethnic group, Jews who wanted to stay in the forests were in the most vulnerable position. Up to, and even past 1943, Jewish runaways were hunted by the Nazis and everyone else that happened to live in the woods.

Oswald feels that Russian persecution of Jewish fugitives can in part be traced to their own shaky position. He notes that *at first these Russian partisans were poorly organized. Among the runaway Jews many were older people, children, and women. The Russians were afraid that when the Germans would catch such people they might in turn tell about the Russians' whereabouts. To prevent this from happening, and for their own safety, the Russians would deliver to the authorities the unarmed, helpless Jews, or they would themselves kill them. These were the laws of the jungle.* The murder of Jews by Poles fits also into the overall situation.[8]

The partisan Jacob Greenstein explains that in the forest, unlike the non-Jews, *we Jews felt that it was a great achievement to save a woman, a child. We knew what would happen to them. But the Russian partisans did not understand that.*

Only by 1943 did the Russians show an official willingness to accept the able-bodied Jewish men. At that time orders were already arriving directly from Moscow advocating the establishment of a uniform anti-Nazi force. Still, acceptance of some young Jewish men failed to take care of those unfit for combat. Soviet opposition to older Jews, women, and children persisted. Some Jewish partisans became preoccupied with the protection of their own people, particularly those who had no chance to survive as fighters. Concern about these helpless fugitives was a direct reaction to the ever-increasing Nazi persecutions. Eventually this concern led to the establishment of special family camps. The two biggest, best known were the Bielski and the Zorin camps. The aim of each was to protect all Jews regardless of age, women, and children. In 1943 each was located in the heart of the Nalibocki forest. Each was surrounded by a ring of fighting groups.

Of the two camps, the Bielski was larger and better organized. By 1944 it included over 1200 people. This group was created and led by Tuvia Bielski and his two brothers.[9] Oswald comments about this camp: *I admired how in the forest they were able to create a "Shtetl," a little town, where people lived in dignity. They all worked. It was a town in the middle of the forest. On both sides of the streets there were structures that contained many different workshops: shoemakers, tailors, workshops for fixing arms, slaughter houses, mills, and others. In this camp one could find people from Belorussia and other parts of Poland. I have a tremendous respect for this man, Tuvia Bielski. He created an almost normal atmosphere under abnormal conditions. In his unit the overwhelming majority were "weaker" people: families, older people. There were proportionally fewer able-bodied young men. They belonged to the fighting group. Their job was to defend the rest.*

Each of these family camps had a long and stormy history. Their emergence and eventual semitolerance by the rest of the partisans has been gradual and not without problems. The beginnings and continuity of each camp was due to the presence of charismatic leadership.

When Oswald was moving toward the Nalibocki forest, he had not known about family camps. He had assumed that most Mir Jews would be dispersed within different fighting groups. But at first, instead of finding any of them, he met a group of Russian partisans, the kind he would have preferred to miss. What happened? *Without any preliminaries, without any greetings, these fighters announced that I was their prisoner. Next they took me to a nearby estate. This band was known for its brutality. . . . After they brought me to the estate they interrogated me in an abusive rough way, cursing continuously. When they realized that I could not be intimidated they were surprised. Who knows, maybe they even respected me for it? At one point they asked where I was going. I told them that I was searching for the people from Mir and that I wanted to join a partisan group. "Why not our group?" they asked. I explained by telling them about myself and also about my conversion. The only thing I did not mention was my stay in the convent.*

These men searched their prisoner thoroughly. They were looking for something of value. But instead of weapons, or money, they found the New Testament and some holy pictures. Irritated, puzzled, they continued the questioning. Sneeringly, they threatened that Oswald's life would soon end.

In contrast, the employees of this estate were impressed by the prisoner's piousness and courage. The young women, in particular, begged the partisans for mercy. After a night's cross-examination, without any explanation, Oswald was told that he was free to leave.

These were violent men, known for their impulsive and cruel behavior. In the past each person they had captured was murdered. When the local priest was told that Oswald was released he called it a miracle.

Less traumatic was Oswald's next partisan encounter. *I met four Russians, former members of the Red Army. It so happened that one of them was a Russian prisoner of war whose life I had saved when I worked at the Mir gendarmerie. He recognized me right away. He thanked me publicly, explaining to his companions that he was alive because of me. I must say that I was gratified by this turn of events. These men were friendly toward me but they wanted me to hand over my weapons. When I told them that I had none they did not search me.*

Even though Oswald had saved this man's life, and the man acknowledged the deed, he made no effort at repaying the debt. Oswald did not even stop to think about this fact. With the other partisan experience behind him, he was glad to be on his way, free and unharmed.

Oswald was approaching those parts of Belorussia that were officially under the German occupation but in reality were free from their interference. In this area one could see Russian partisans move about freely and fearlessly. In one of those partially liberated small towns Oswald came to a large Catholic parish. He explains, *I was naive then. . . . I thought that if I tell them that I am a Catholic they will automatically help. . . . At this place there were three or four priests. When I spoke about my conversion they listened. They fed me, but made it clear that I could not stay with them. They refused to keep me even for one night. . . . Maybe it was worse when there were three or four of them. It was harder to keep a secret. Besides this was a responsibility. If the Nazis would find me, then all of them would die.*

Actually, since German control over this section was minimal, to shelter a fugitive could not have been as dangerous as Oswald suggests. Perhaps by exaggerating the existing risks Oswald, the Catholic neophyte, was trying to find an excuse for the priests' refusal.

In Rubierzewicze, the next town Oswald came to, he was more welcome. Here on the outskirts, in a modest hut, a Belorussian family offered him shelter. Next day these simple and kind peasants extended their hospitality for another night. At dusk Oswald stood at the window of this hut. Outside he saw a horse-drawn sleigh with partisans. As the sleigh was passing close to the hut, one of the men looked up at the window. For a split second their eyes met. The partisan hesitated. Oswald too felt something stir in him. He did not quite know what it was. Then the horses came to an abrupt halt. The man jumped out of his seat. He ran into the hut shouting, "Who are you?"

"I am Oswald."

"Oh my God, you are alive!" was all he said as he threw himself at his neck.

Oswald recognized Ephraim Sinder, the Mir Jew he had watched being lashed by Schultz because he walked on the pavement instead of the middle of the road.

This meeting became engraved in Sinder's memory. "In the window I saw a man. I felt that I knew him but I was not sure who he was. . . . He had a mustache—a reddish one—I never saw him with a mustache—then to my question he said, 'Oswald.' I believed that he had perished long ago. After all, who had thought about him? He told me, 'I was all the time in Mir, now there is no place there. I had to leave. Where are the Mir partisans, I want to go to them?' I said, 'Stay here, on my way back I will take you and from my unit we will somehow get you in touch with the others.' "[10]

True to his word, next day, Sinder came to fetch the youth who was responsible for his ghetto escape and ultimately for his being alive. Oswald recalls. *The partisans were supposed to come for me on the 8th of December. This is a church holiday: Immaculate Conception. I felt it my duty to go to church and I did. Sinder came there with a gun hanging off his shoulder and took me away. I felt good about it.*

Because Sinder had to do some errands, by the time he and his companion climbed into the sleigh it was getting dark. The partisan recalls their trip. "All the way we talked. We did not believe that we were actually alive. This was unreal. The same evening, I don't know how it came about, he took out a book and told me that this was the New Testament. It was dark, I could not see. But later I noticed, by the light of the cigarette, that in his hand he had a picture of Mary—and Jesus Christ—so I said to him, 'Now you can throw it away.' To this he said, 'I believe in this.' I said again, 'There you had to believe but here you don't have to.' He began to tell me the story of his conversion. When he finished I told him, 'You are dealing with silly things, leave this, now you are free.' "[11]

That night Sinder brought his companion to the headquarters of the Russian partisan brigade, in the Nalibocki forest. Many different rumors were already circulating about Oswald's extraordinary deeds. All these accounts identified him as a commandant of a German police station who had risked his life to save Jews and non-Jews. The Russians, however, were unimpressed by his protection of innocent victims. They were interested in his connection to the Nazis. Suspicious of Oswald's unexpected arrival, the head of the Russian brigade, Colonel Dubov, ordered his arrest. The colonel considered this case important enough to personally conduct the investigation. To Dubov, and to the rest of his cross-examiners, Oswald spoke freely about his life, his work with and for the Germans. He also readily described his conversion to Catholicism, telling everyone who cared to listen that this in no way affected his Jewish identity.

Though open about different aspects of his life, he never mentioned the stay in the convent. He was afraid that if he revealed that the nuns hid him, the news might travel back to Mir and eventually lead to the punishment of his protectors. The hiding of such a sought-after criminal would no doubt carry the death sentence. Others were executed for much less serious crimes.

Because of Oswald's concern about the nuns' welfare, those who listened to his story were faced with a time gap of about sixteen months. He simply refused to talk about that period. Threats and accusations had no effect. Whenever his interrogators came to that missing time, his answer was always the same: "I cannot tell you where I was."

The Russians were suspicious. They were convinced that this fugitive must be engaged in anti-Soviet actions. After all, what other reason could there be for such a concealment of facts? In the end, his examiners concluded that the prisoner had spent the unaccounted for months in a German school for spies, and that the Nazis had sent him to gather intelligence information about partisan moves. Spying for the Germans called for the death sentence. Oswald was sentenced to die.

Sinder, the man who brought Oswald to the partisan headquarters, describes what happened. "After we came to the camp, in the middle of the night, they woke me up. I had to go to the head of the NKVD.[12] He was a friend of mine. He and I used to drink together. That night he spoke to me as if I were a stranger. All his questions were about Oswald. I realized that the Russians were very suspicious, particularly about the sixteen-month gap in his story. When I told this man Oswald's extraordinary life story, he wrote everything down. I insisted that Oswald was innocent and that I guaranteed for him with my own head." Sinder thinks that his guarantee saved Oswald's life.[13]

It is true that the partisans were executing people with ease. It is also true that the shooting of suspected individuals, or people who were simply in the way, was common. The murder of Jews by partisans has been repeatedly reported.[14] Oswald was in a most precarious situation. But the fact that he was not shot does not necessarily mean that Sinder guaranteed for Oswald's innocence or that Sinder's intervention had saved his life.

Oswald was very secretive about his relationship with the nuns. His secretiveness extended to more than just his interrogators. Asked if he told Sinder about his stay in the convent, Oswald hesitated but then said, *I am convinced that Ephraim Sinder did not know where I have been from August 1942 till December 1943.*

When I raised the issue of Sinder's guarantee, Oswald was silent. Then came an embarrassed, reluctant answer. *I am not so sure. Of course he claims that he fought all night with those high in the partisan hierarchy, trying to convince them that I was OK. I don't know if he had the courage to do it. I am not sure if he himself was convinced that I was innocent. But let us leave this. Maybe you should accept what he says? He says that all night he tried to persuade the Russians of my innocence. It could be. . . . Still I doubt it very much, that I spoke to him about the nuns. I told him that I was a Christian, that yes. But I did not tell him that I stayed with the nuns. And so in a way, he could not have guaranteed for me if he did not really know. I suspect that for the missing time, the time that I was in the convent, he washed off his hands and that he was reluctant and unwilling to expose himself. . . . Now it is hard for me to contradict all those who insist that they are telling the truth about things that I know never happened. This Sinder claim is not the only one. . . . You see when Sinder met me right after the war he never even mentioned that he guaranteed for me with his head.*

Whereas at that time in the Nalibocki forest the Russians were concerned about Oswald's intentions and suspected him of pro-Nazi leanings, the Jewish partisans kept telling and retelling stories about his extraordinary deeds and courage. Some of these accounts had no basis in reality. Some relied only on wishful thinking and little else. For example, till very recently, one of the Jewish partisans who was at the Nalibocki headquarters to which Oswald came, Jehuda Rytman, did not know that his hero was accused of espionage and that his life was in danger. When I interviewed Rytman, in 1983, he told me that a group of partisans went to the convent because they had heard that Oswald lived there disguised as a nun. He continued the story by informing me that it was those partisans who brought Oswald to the headquarters. He also assured me that there Oswald was treated like God, in recognition of all the courageous deeds he performed on behalf of the Jews.[15]

In reality, Oswald was kept at the headquarters for two days. During that time he was being interrogated around the clock. He was then transferred to the Ponomarenko "otriad" with a recommended death sentence. An otriad is an independent partisan unit. Five or six otriads become a brigade. The Ponomarenko otriad was in the Nalibocki forest, a few miles from the headquarters. Greenstein, a member of this group, notes that *the head of this otriad was a former captain of the Red Army, Kajdanov. During the war he was injured and taken prisoner by the Germans, but succeeded in running away. We, the Jewish underground from Minsk, brought him to the ghetto. We took care of his wounds and then transferred him back to the forest. Kajdanov came from the northern part of Russia. He was free of anti-Semitism. He was a good commandant, highly respected by his men.*

Commenting about his move to the Ponomarenko otriad and Sinder's intervention, Oswald says: *It is possible that Sinder spoke to Dubov at the headquarters and that the results of their conversations were not transferred to Kajdanov and therefore I once more had to defend myself.*

But why and how could anyone withhold such important information? On the other hand, if Sinder had guaranteed for Oswald's innocence, and this guarantee had an effect, this would have ended the investigation. Since Oswald was sent to the Ponomarenko otriad as a prisoner, whatever Sinder might have said in his defense failed to convince.

Oswald's first impression of Kajdanov was much less favorable than Greenstein's description of the man. When Oswald entered the commandant's office, he noticed on the table a gun. Pointing to the weapon the Russian shouted, "You son of a bitch, you see this, look at it closely and remember that ammunition is cheap. If you won't talk, one of those bullets will end up in your head! Where were you from August 1942 till December 1943?"

"I cannot tell you. All I can say is that I have done nothing wrong."

"Admit that the Germans sent you here! Where have they been training you for the last sixteen months?"

"I was not with the Germans. I was hidden but cannot tell you where."

"You have already been sentenced to death. Only the truth may save you!" Kajdanov was pounding the table. He took the gun in his hand and pointing at the prisoner repeated the questions over and over again.

Oswald knew that time was running out. He shuddered at the thought of being executed as a Nazi collaborator. This was definitely an unexpected twist. And yet, he also felt helpless. He could not act differently. The investigation continued.

Oswald recalls: *Then a doctor arrived. He came to examine some patients and also to check the health of the rest of the partisans. In the forest doctors were scarce. The few that were available moved from place to place, offering their services to as many people as possible. This particular doctor was Jewish, a cultured, pleasant person.*[16]

As a gesture of friendliness, the commandant invited this honored guest to attend one of Oswald's interrogations. He was also given the opportunity to question the prisoner. The two, Oswald and the doctor, spoke Russian, then switched to German, and finally to Polish. When Oswald's life story reached the still unaccounted for sixteen months, the older man told him that he must fill in the missing information, otherwise he will be shot. Somehow this physician inspired confidence. Oswald agreed to divulge his secret to the doctor, but only on condition that he in turn would keep it to himself.

The man agreed and kept his word. At the same time he searched for a solution. He approached Kadjanov and told him that he had learned the truth and that the prisoner's story had nothing to do with the accusations. Moreover, the doctor insisted that if at anytime they would have reason to doubt the prisoner's innocence, they can punish him together with Oswald. In effect, the physician did guarantee for Oswald's innocence.

While the negotiations between Kajdanov and the doctor continued, two partisans arrived. Oswald notes, *Both of these partisans were Jews from Mir. . . . They came at the very moment when my case was being discussed and clarified by the doctor and Kajdanov. They came from far because they had heard that my life was in danger. They were sent by Sally Czerne, a former member of the Judenrat in Mir. In the forest Czerne became the chief of staff of an otriad. In the Russian partisan hierarchy he had a high position. Grateful, he was determined to save me.*

These new arrivals together with the physician succeeded in persuading Kajdanov of the prisoner's innocence. Later, a formal petition was sent to General Platon to annul Oswald's death sentence. Platon was the head of the Russian partisan movement in the Baranowicze region in Western Belorussia. In no time Oswald became a full-fledged partisan.[17]

The arrival of these two Jewish partisans from Mir was only a prelude to similar visits. Fani Bilecki described her own reaction and the reaction of other Jews to the news about Oswald. "Suddenly someone comes and tells us: 'You know Oswald is in the forest.' We were so excited. We wanted to arrange a trip right away. We knew where he was. We went. We met him. We did not know yet that he converted, nothing of this sort. In the pocket he carried a small book. This of course was the New Testament. But we were not interested in anything. We saw him alive. We loved him. He saved our lives. Other things were not important."[18]

15

Life as a Partisan

For me being a partisan was worse than staying at the gendarmerie. When I worked for the Germans my aim was to help and save others. But I was in the forest because I wanted to live, and, as I did, I was robbing innocent people. . . . To be a partisan was not simple. It was something between a hero and a robber. We had to live and we had to deprive the peasants of their meager belongings. These natives were punished by the Nazis and by us. . . . At least if they were pro-German it would have been easier. This usually was not the case. Most of the time we took by force from poor peasants who were not even pro-Nazi.

For Oswald to take away by force from harmless people what rightfully belonged to them, and what they could ill afford to part with, was unacceptable, something he strongly disapproved of. Oswald's opposition to this aspect of partisan life would often overshadow other features of his forest existence. Being a partisan involved more than just robbing people. Oswald knew that. And once he had finished talking about the injustices committed against the natives he would turn to these other facets.

Oswald remained in the Ponomarenko otriad. Under direct Russian control, it consisted of Russians, Ukrainians, Belorussians, and a handful of Jews. For a while, this unit had an additional six Poles, all captured during the anti-Polish attack. Depending on whose version of this event one accepts, within a few weeks these Poles were either murdered or escaped. Their disappearance made the Ponomarenko otriad once more free of Poles. Of the 150 to 200 members most were able-bodied men younger than thirty, with a sprinkle of "older" men, usually in their forties. The rest, less than 20%, were women.

Some of these women were married to partisan fighters. Others were single. Though some were eager to participate in all aspects of forest life, they were usually relegated to lower level tasks. No matter how devoted to their jobs they were, the men treated them like second-class members.

Toward the end of 1943 the Ponomarenko otriad, as most others in the area, became better organized, stronger, and partly inaccessible to the Germans. This meant that the Nalibocki forest did offer both protection from the Nazis and a more permanent shelter. The partisans had reason to believe that they would not be chased away by the enemy. When building their forest dwellings, they took advantage of both the changed conditions and the available materials.

The age and size of the Nalibocki trees created special building opportunities. For example, already in August, the bark of the trees would come off in a single piece. These large sheets of bark were used as roof coverings for their dwellings. Built in a tentlike shape, half of the structure was buried in the ground. The rest, mainly the roof, was on top of the soil. The upper part consisted of wooden sticks and branches that touched each other, forming a triangle. These sections of wood were in turn covered by the bark sheets.

Both the soil and the bark gave these dwellings protection from cold and wetness. Standing in rows, these units were used for different purposes. Those assigned for living quarters each had two long beds, made out of wood. Other structures were used as a first-aid clinic and a hospital, the headquarters for the otriad, the kitchen, a dining room, storage places, and whatever else the camp required.

By and large, members of the otriad were assigned to jobs they seemed best suited for. The majority of the people spent their time working inside the camp. Even in otriads identified as fighting units, active engagements against the enemy were less common than usually assumed. In fact, Oswald insists that by far the most central function of any partisan group had to do with feeding its members. And because this was an important and difficult part of the forest existence, most members, regardless of their other duties, took part in food expeditions.

Greenstein, a member of the Ponomarenko otriad, describes the process: *We had to be careful when we collected food. We did not want to antagonize the natives. We needed their support. Therefore, we tried hard to make this food collection less painful for the peasants, especially to those that were supporting us. We were not allowed to take provisions from villages next to our camp. The order was to go to farmers who lived far from us and close to the German garrisons. Usually, those who lived near to the Germans were also pro-Nazi and, therefore, we were allowed to confiscate their food.*

We took advantage of some of the special situations. Peasants were required to supply the authorities with a portion of their farm products. In every village we had our people who spied for us. When a transport of food was going to be delivered to the Germans in town, we would attack it, confiscate the provisions, and bring them to our camp. This way we would divert the goods that were supposed to go to the Nazis.[1]

Oswald paints a different picture of this food-gathering process. *For me, one of the worst things was the plunder. The peasants were anyway robbed by the Germans. They were poor. It was horrible to see how they were deprived. . . . Yet we had to do it. The peasants would not have given us on their own. We were in a predicament. . . . Sometimes we would take away the last cow, or the last horse. I had no choice in the matter.*

True, Oswald could do little. But he tried. Whenever partisans came to a village to collect food they followed certain procedures. For safety, two people had to keep guard at each end of a village. In case of an approaching danger those who kept an eye were responsible for signalling. The rest of the men, with guns in hand, went from hut to hut helping themselves to whatever they wanted. To avoid becoming a part of this activity, Oswald tried to take the job of watchman. Even as a watchman, he still felt responsible for what was taking place. He notes, *Just keeping watch while others were looting did not save my conscience.*

Oswald had no permanent claim to the position of guardsman. At times others were assigned to the job. When this happened, he had to go with the rest inside the village. Oswald's friend Greenstein remembers, *When we came to a village we would go in and help ourselves to whatever we wanted. But Oswald would approach the owner of the place and say, "Maybe you have a piece of bread?" "Would you like to give me something to eat?" If the peasant did not give him, he would not eat. This behavior just did not fit with the role of a partisan. After all, he had arms.*

Through this kind of action Oswald was violating basic partisan rules. Yet he was not condemned for it. People continued to treat him with respect and affection. When commenting on these strange actions Greenstein notes that *Oswald was definitely involved with the good side of Christianity.*

Although less central than food gathering, fighting the enemy was highly valued. Those who were permanent members of a combat unit were definitely the elite. Greenstein belonged to this select minority. Occasionally fighting groups would leave the camp to engage in anti-Nazi moves. Usually such expeditions involved the derailment of trains, the destruction of bridges, or simply attacks on German garrisons. Particularly in the late stages of the war, the aim of these operations was to demoralize the enemy and interfere with its war efforts. Oswald was included in one such combat expedition. The purpose of this outfit was to derail military trains and destroy a bridge. Oswald performed his duties well, but without enthusiasm. He himself mentions combat participation only in passing. Greenstein, who was with him, emphasizes that *whenever possible, Oswald avoided killing. He would shoot and become a part of a battle when ordered to. But he preferred not to fight.*

Though opposed to the Nazis and eager to see them defeated, Oswald found it hard to use violence. His unenthusiastic attitude toward combat set him apart from the rest of the partisans. Most would have liked to become a part of fighting expeditions.

Women were kept away from most combat units. Eagerness to participate, or special fitness, rarely tipped the scale in their favor. Instead, they were assigned to service jobs that had to do with the kitchen: cooking and keeping the place clean. Because Oswald was willing and able to follow instructions, he had a variety of duties. One of his more steady assignments was a job in the kitchen, which he did not mind at all. Oswald would start each day at five o'clock with kitchen work. After that he would take a cow or cows to the pasture.

Guarding the camp was another of Oswald's more permanent duties. An otriad had to be constantly watched. One never knew how and where an enemy might sneak in. Even during the late stages of the war the Nazis would periodically send spies into the forest. Surprise moves by the enemy, no matter how seemingly trivial, could have far-reaching consequences. A single individual, by collecting sensitive information or throwing one grenade into a camp, could create havoc. The partisans tried to counteract such possibilities by keeping close watch over their places. The duty of a watchman was to warn about impending danger rather than to defend the place. Those who were assigned to this job were not required to have special fighting skills. In the Ponomarenko otriad the women were often assigned to watch duty. Guarding the place was a day and night activity. Oswald approved of this job, noting that *I had no problem with standing guard. I did not mind getting up in the middle of the night. I also liked to help women in this and other tasks.*

Jacob Greenstein's wife, Bela, points out what guarding the camp meant, and how Oswald would ease her job and that of other women. *We women had to keep an eye on the place. . . . You slept two hours and then they woke you up again to keep watch for another four hours, and over and over like this. It takes a long time to fall asleep after a watch. No sooner you shut your eyes you are being awakened again. So under the circumstances some of us would fall asleep while we were guarding the camp. If they caught us sleeping, we would be shot. . . . Oswald was sensitive to our needs. He knew that we were constantly fighting exhaustion. He would come to check if we were awake. He would ask how we were, making sure that we don't fall asleep. He would bring us hot water, so we would not be so cold.*[2]

Oswald's concern for others is also remembered by Jacob Greenstein who says that *within the otriad he did all he could to help. He would come and substitute for the women guards and send them away to rest. Oswald would also come to the kitchen when he was not supposed to work and do the job for others, also women.*

Because Oswald does not like to dwell on his good deeds, the stories I have heard about him come from others. For example, once when Jacob Greenstein was away on a fighting expedition his wife Bela became seriously ill. She had a high fever and the nurse did not know what to do. Oswald took over. He asked the commandant of the otriad for permission to take her to the Bielski camp, where he knew the medical care would be better.[3] To him the effort and danger involved in bringing a patient on a more than ten-mile road did not matter. What mattered was that a human being's health would improve.

In the forest Oswald became preoccupied with the idea of becoming a monk, which in turn shaped his attitudes to women. He stopped seeing them as possible targets for attraction. For him they were human beings who could benefit from his help. He tried to meet their needs, never expecting or wanting anything in return. Oswald's behavior was in sharp contrast to that of most other men. In the forest in particular, where the future was uncertain, and when every day could bring death, men would think of women only as sex objects. Whenever a partisan did a favor for a woman he expected to be paid with sexual favors. Oswald registers the difference between himself and other men by saying, *I had an honest approach to women. I did not look at them in sexual terms. I intended to join a monastery. The women were aware about the difference between me and the other men around them.*

Conscious of Oswald's unexploitive giving, women would honor him in special ways. March 8 is a Soviet holiday dedicated to the woman. Because of the pervasive Russian influence in the Ponomarenko otriad, this day became a holiday with planned festivities.

A board of women was elected to decide on the kinds of celebrations. With a satisfied chuckle, Oswald remembers, *Of the men I was the only one chosen to become an honorary memeber of the board in charge of the woman's day celebrations. In our otriad it was obvious that I was the one who had a very close, warm relationship to the women. I was flattered by their attention and affection.*

Because Oswald had the courage of his convictions, he did not hide what he believed in. Nor was he bothered by the fact that in a Communist otriad some might consider his religious involvement inappropriate, even strange. He prayed often and talked about his religious beliefs.

Oswald recalls, *Once we were on the road, taking part in a special assignment. We stopped at a house. I lied down while the others were drinking. They wanted me to drink with them. But one of the Russians said: "Leave him alone, this is a Polish monk." Whether he had heard about my plans for the future or whether he deduced it from my behavior I don't know. I also don't know if he meant this as a compliment or a condemnation.*

To Greenstein this comment would mean an expression of respect and approval. Again and again he emphasizes that *Oswald was special and very different from the rest of us. . . . Life among partisans was not easy. No matter how psychologically strong you were, you could still fall apart. There were too many hardships, too many temptations. But Oswald was exceptional. He was quiet. He spoke softly, as he does now. He fulfilled all orders. He did what he was asked to do. He never tried to get out of a job; there were those who did. To dislike someone he would have to do something bad to you. But Oswald helped whomever he could. . . . Everyone loved him. . . . The Russians would swear at God. When they did, Oswald would tell them that they should not be doing it, that it was wrong. They never got mad at him. Instead, they would laugh and they continued to love him. . . .*

He worked hard. But every free minute he had, he spent praying. This was most unusual for our place. He was the only pious person among us. Others made fun of him because he prayed so much. At the same time they respected him. They knew that he was very special.

At this stage the Russians did more than just send military and political men into Belorussia. They were also supplying the forest fighters with arms, ammunition, clothes, medicine, and other necessities. Usually such cargo was dropped by plane. Occasionally too, a Soviet plane would come to pick up wounded men who required more extensive care. Sometimes planes would also bring people from Russia for special consultations with the partisan leaders.

Any contacts with Soviet planes required well-coordinated arrangements. The partisans had built special "airports" that were in effect clearing areas. Not surprisingly, such illegal airports had to be continuously watched and protected. In addition to keeping an eye on the place, those assigned to airports had to signal the approaching planes in a specific way, making signs with fire or light. The particular sign was prearranged either in the form of a square, a triangle, a snake, or any other shape. If a pilot's mission called for a landing, these signs would inform him where to do it and whether he could safely land.

Pilots would drop their cargo only when notified with the appropriate signs. At such times the partisans would collect the goods and bring them to their base.

Keeping watch over an airport and communicating with planes was Oswald's favorite pastime. The first airport expedition cemented Oswald's and Jacob Greenstein's friendship. The two had met when Greenstein returned to the otriad from a fighting expedition. This seasoned partisan remembers being intrigued by the presence of the newcomer. Greenstein notes: *He was very different. I had little in common with the others. They and I could not talk about anything. Oswald looked to me like an intelligent man.*

Soon after they had met, Greenstein was sent out again. This time his mission involved watching an airport. The otriad was expecting important deliveries. Oswald was included in this expedition.

Greenstein recalls: *For a month we sat together. We argued and talked the entire time. He was, of course, a Catholic. I thought that because he was such an intelligent man, I would be able to convince him to give up Christianity. First I told him, "If you want to believe in God and be religious you have the original God. Why do you have to go to the son when you have the father?" This argument did not work. In vain I tried to win him with Marxism. Then I became convinced that although he was intelligent, he did not grasp some basic things. He was a fanatic. He really believed in miracles; these were things that little children would not have thought possible.*

We decided that we will remain friends and not talk anymore about religion. It took us a month to come to this understanding. . . . Actually I was not so insistent or eager to have him return to Judaism because I am not religious. I only felt that it was a shame that such a fine person should remove himself from Jews and Jewishness.

With him, however, one thing was very different from others who had converted to Christianity. He emphasized that he was a Jew with a Christian religion. In our place the Russians ruled. Yet he said openly that if he will survive the war he will go to Jerusalem. None of us would have said it. He had guts. He identified himself as a Zionist, as a Jew, and he was not afraid to say it. . . . At one point he wanted to convince me with the following example. "We are in Paris, I am at the top of the Eiffel Tower and you are at the bottom, who sees Paris better, you or I?" I told him that this argument failed to do the job. . . . We remained friends till this day. But we never touch on the subject of religion.

In addition to keeping watch over airports, Oswald also liked to visit villages for the purpose of educating the peasants about Nazi perils. Enlightment of the natives belonged to the propaganda section of the movement. Such educational expeditions into Belorussian villages had at least two purposes. First, they aimed at gaining political and ideological support for the partisans and for Russia. Second, through these contacts the authorities had hoped to stimulate opposition toward the Nazis and indirectly create help for the partisans.

Greenstein feels that Oswald's talents were especially valuable for propaganda purposes. He describes such moves: *In every village we gathered the peasants. I spoke about the cruelty of the Germans, how they murdered people. Oswald knew exactly what the Nazis were doing to the Christians, how they killed priests, how they destroyed convents, how out of a church they made a barn, etc. . . . He knew all the details. He would tell it to the peasants and he would urge them to take revenge and fight the Nazis. He would argue with them that by helping the partisans they would be destroying the German oppressors.*

If his talks had the desired effect they would have led to fighting and ultimately to the destruction of lives. Greenstein notes that *toward mid-1944 we were catching Germans. According to the law we were supposed to hand them over as prisoners of war. We were not eager to do that. Once we got a group of SS men. We knew exactly what they did with our people. Our commandant wanted to do with them what they did with the Jews. We decided that they should dig graves for themselves and then we shot them. Oswald knew German better than anyone else. He was the intermediary between the commandant and the Germans. He translated word for word.*

A refusal to participate in this kind of a punitive action would not have resulted in any punishment. But Oswald did not object to this treatment of the German prisoners. Instead, together with the others, he was dispensing justice, a special kind of justice. In this case his religion in no way interfered with avengeful actions.

And yet, Oswald is reluctant to talk about his partisan experiences. When he does, he is overwhelmed by the injustices he had witnessed. Though wistful that it was in the second-class category he still cherishes his partisan medal. Similarly, when describing his activities in Mir he refers to himself as a soldier. To save others, he feels, was a fight against evil. As a young boy, he remembers being intrigued by his father's war medals. He liked to examine them. All along, one senses a subtle flirtation with the idea of war. Somehow tied in with a struggle against evil is even an approval of revenge.

While others appreciated Oswald's contributions to the otriad, he himself only says, *I was a self-disciplined partisan, but that was all.* Though he never actively sought out praise, when it came his way he welcomed it. Indeed, till now his first visit to the Bielski camp remains a valued memory. *One day I was asked to bring a cow to this Jewish otriad. Our partisans had confiscated a cow. They wanted to have sausages. So they sent me to the Jewish division. I was supposed to leave there the cow and bring fifty kilos of sausage.*

No sooner did Oswald enter the camp, the word got around that he was there. People begun to gather from all directions. Some shook his hand, others, weeping with joy, threw themselves at his neck, still others laughed and shouted as they called him their savior. Their number continued to grow. The object of this joyous attention together with his cow was encircled by the expanding crowd, barely able to take a step. Of those present some were former Mir ghetto inmates, some were different individuals who had benefited from Oswald's generosity. Still others were curious onlookers, lured by the many stories they had heard. Tales about Oswald's deeds had circulated among Jewish fugitives. Jews needed heroes and he certainly fit the image. Among these emotional greeters Oswald recognized Dov Resnik, the man who had served as a link between him and the Mir Jews.

Oswald stood speechless, overwhelmed by this outpouring of affection. His face expressed contentment through a shy, embarrassed smile. When the crowd enabled him to move it followed like a huge emotional wave. Oswald remembers, *They were taking me through the camp. I had difficulty walking. . . . I didn't mind it at all. I was surrounded by my people, warm excited people and they led me to the headquarters. This was like a triumphant parade. It was an expression of their gratitude. As I continued slowly on the path, suddenly a woman with a little child threw herself at me. She recognized me, screaming that I had saved her life.*

He in turn recognized the Jewish woman who had tried to pass as a Russian Christian and whom Hein had been persuaded to release at Oswald's insistence.

In the forest, together with the crowd, the woman accompanied Oswald to the headquarters. When they reached the place, Oswald was met by Tuvia Bielski who also was aware of his story.

Bielski, an imposing, tall man in his thirties, looked down at this unusual visitor with a playful, surprised smile. No formal introduction was necessary. Amused by the timidity of this young man, perhaps to ease his awkwardness, perhaps to satisfy his own curiosity, the older man asked, "Tell me, how did the idea of organizing, of arming and then of arranging a breakout from the ghetto come to you? What made you do this?"

The quiet answer was, "What else could I do?"

But Bielski pursued, "Still, what made you act the way you did?"

Reluctantly, Oswald said, "The opportunity was there, I did what had to be done."

Bemused, even awed, the commandant shook his head. Clearly the youth before him would not tell much more. Bielski finished this brief exchange by inviting the visitor to a special meal.

A witness to this meeting, Moshe Bairach, still remembers, *The unassumed simplicity of Oswald's answer impressed me no end. It became engraved in my memory till this very day.*[4]

As for Oswald's reaction to Bielski, he was, and still is, full of admiration for his deeds, his ability to organize a well-run town in the forest, and for his saving of so many Jewish lives. But because it was their only meeting, he refuses to give an evaluation of Bielski the man.

When more than forty years later I asked Bielski what he thought of Oswald Rufeisen, he said, *What is there to think or talk about? He is a convert, drunk with religion.* I countered by pointing out that he had saved many lives and inquired again if he would care to tell me about his impression of

Oswald. Already an old man, Bielski was impatient. *There is no point to talk about him at all! So he tried to help a few Jews, so what? One can count them on one's fingers. It is not a big deal. Many people now tell stories. So?*[5]

Before this visit, when Oswald had been cleared of all wrongdoing, he was given a chance to join the Bielski otriad. He declined. Instead he stayed in the Ponomarenko group with total strangers. Greenstein explains that *he did not want people to give him special privileges, he was very modest. He stayed in the Ponomarenko otriad because no one knew him there. No one made a fuss over him.*

When asked directly, Oswald said, *I already had my place. The people from Mir were spread all over. Only some of them were in the Bielski camp. I was not especially interested in being with them. Those from Mir were very useful to me when it came to saving my life, to guarantee for me. I am talking about the two partisans who came to the Ponomarenko otriad to save me. Other than that I did not have much in common with them. They were dispersed. Resnik, for example, was with Bielski. Charchas was in a Russian group. . . . Also, in a partisan sense it would have been a step down to be in the Bielski camp because it was not a fighting unit. I think that I am telling you as it was.*

Behind this decision other less obvious motivations might have also been involved. Possibly as a Christian, he might have felt uncomfortable in a purely Jewish environment. Perhaps too he feared that in this kind of a setting he would be under pressure to give up his new religion.

Oswald's own explanations leave some unanswered questions. Why would it matter to him that the Bielski otriad was not a fighting group? In view of his preoccupation with the protection of human lives, his admiration for Bielski's efforts to save people, his reluctance to kill, his commitment to religion, one would have expected that he would be delighted to join a noncombat unit. Could it be that, as suggested by Greenstein, modesty kept him in the Ponomarenko otriad, but he was too modest to admit it? Could his mention of the fighting aspect of the otriad be an expression of Oswald's ambiguous feelings toward partisan life?

Oswald was, indeed, preoccupied with the inconsistencies of the partisan existence and kept returning to the same issues by saying, *For me a partisan was at least three things: someone who was hiding in the forest, a bandit, and a fighter. . . . I would not describe each partisan as a robber. Nor can I say that all went to the forest only to hide from the Germans. No doubt there were those who fought against the Germans, there were battles. . . . This was a struggle under difficult conditions and people were in moral and physical dangers. Moral dangers were great. One could kill people and this way settle personal counts.*

At stake in the operations against farmers were moral issues. I am thinking about the forceful confiscations of goods that belonged to other people. Sometimes partisans would take a horse in one village and then sell it for vodka in another village. I would have understood had they taken a horse in one place and sold it for wheat in another place. But often this was not the case. These men were fond of vodka.

There were also military actions against the enemy. No doubt there were acts of heroism. . . . Toward the end of the war, when we were leaving the partisans, the Russians were distributing titles, medals, and orders, even the highest kind of distinctions. Some of those could be bought with vodka. Also, whoever had good connections could count on receiving a medal.

But there were also interesting and important situations. Examples of these would be the cargo we were receiving from Moscow that was thrown from planes. These were inventive different ways of undermining the enemy. . . . There was such a mixture of everything. I would not like to give to the partisans a totally negative evaluation. . . . I would like to give you a balanced view.

In August 1944, the long-awaited Red Army came to Belorussia. The civilian population and the partisans rejoiced over their arrival, and with few exceptions, the victorious troops were greeted as liberators. On their part too, these soldiers, anxious for the support of the natives, behaved in a friendly and accommodating way. At first the relationships between the civilians, the Russian soldiers, and the partisans were good.

As Oswald and his fellow partisans welcomed the victors they were delighted with the continuous Nazi losses. But the war was still on. When the Polish uprising in Warsaw began, in August 1944, the Red Army stopped advancing and watched Poland's embattled capital from Praga across the Wisła River. The Russians did not budge, when in those last stages of the war, in Warsaw, the Germans had ravaged the city and its inhabitants.[6]

August 1944 was also a time when trainloads filled with Hungarian Jews and other victims were rolling into Auschwitz. The crematoria ovens of the biggest death factory were operating nonstop, day and night, burning gassed bodies.[7]

No announcements about the Warsaw uprising or about the continuing Jewish extermination process were reaching the Russian-occupied parts of Poland. The liberated partisans, including Oswald, remember the days that followed the Red Army's arrival as a time when they felt elated and free. In this special mood a large group from the Ponomarenko otriad, with the Greensteins and Oswald, came to the town Iwieniec.

From here Jacob Greenstein left to join the Red Army. Oswald was determined to enter a monastery. For this he knew that he would have to go to Poland. He was also aware that the Russians were not about to return the parts of Poland they had occupied in 1939.

Oswald recalls that *in Iwieniec the partisans were being assigned to different military formations. Soon Dov Resnik and Ephraim Sinder arrived in a horse-*

drawn wagon from Mir. They brought with them an official order from the NKVD, the Russian Police. I was to go with them to Mir for a special assignment with the police.

He had no desire to become involved with police activities. For the moment, however, he was forced to temporarily set aside his plans. Though agreeing to the official assignment, he privately registered his objections. *In the German police I worked because I had to, but at the NKVD I did not want to. Those who had arranged for me the job had good intentions. They probably did not know that they were doing me a disfavor.*

On arrival in Mir Oswald was once more transformed into a policeman. This time he was given a Russian uniform and a gun. His job involved informing the authorities about wartime Nazi collaborators. The Russians assumed that because Oswald had worked in the German gendarmerie he would have all the information they wanted. They gave him a private office and ordered him to write reports.

As far as the Russians were concerned his work was disappointing. Oswald explains, *During the Nazi occupation there were not many anti-Communist police cases. People had few opportunities to show their hostility to the Soviets. In this respect I could be of little help to the Russians. Personally, I was interested in actions that were committed against the local population. But the authorities were concentrating on political cases.*

By writing about Nazi collaborators Oswald tried to help apprehend those who had cooperated with the Germans. Asked whether this kind of a task interfered with his Christian values of forgiveness, he denied that this was the case, saying, *I think that it was a problem of justice. It was a question of making the counts, of evening out. The church is not opposed to this. . . . While the Russians were interested in the political anti-Communist activities, I was concerned with the persecution of Jews and other people regardless of politics. I had no problems with it, I wrote what was, about people who did not behave decently. I did not see in it a conflict with my religion.*

With my luck those who had an unclean conscience ran away with the Germans. They did arrest only one, the peasant Chudoba (the man who had denounced a Jew for wanting to buy weapons). He might have been arrested even before my arrival. I think that Jews who had returned to Mir from the forest, who knew about him, told the Russians about his collaboration. He was taken away. What happened to him I don't know. . . . So in reality I was not denouncing. Of course if they had found those I was writing about they would have had material against them.

Oswald supplied information about Nazi collaborators, yet he considers himself "lucky" that they all ran away with the Germans. He seems to contradict himself when he says, *It is a duty of every person to see that justice is done. What I did then in Mir was trying to do just that. It was not denouncement.*

Eager to move into the next phase of his life, Oswald was impatient about staying in Mir. Perhaps this desire to get away made him forget much of what happened during that period. He is not even sure where he lived. He knows, however, that most of the people he had known well were not there. Many of the Poles, including the Balicki family, ran away as the Germans were retreating. Some must have remembered the 1939 Soviet persecution of Poles. Others escaped because of their connection to the Nazis. For example, all the Belorussian policemen and Serafimowicz were gone, as was his wife Jadwiga and her sister, Wanda Juszkiewicz. It has been rumored that Serafimowicz ended up in East Germany. Wanda married, settled in the United States, in California, and continues to live there.[8]

A few of the Mir Jews came back. They all rejoiced at seeing Oswald. None objected to his conversion. Though Oswald says that he welcomed their warmth and approval, he did not seek their company. Perhaps he was afraid that they would try to dissuade him from his future religious plans. The only people he did feel comfortable with were the nuns. Except for seeing them, he kept to himself. Usually he sat in his office writing and thinking about how to get out of his job. After three weeks his special assignment was coming to an end.

As a policeman in the secret service Oswald was responsible to the Russian commandant of the station and his two assistants. One of these assistants was a Russian, the other a Belorussian, a former partisan. Both had the rank of lieutenant. Of the two the Belorussian felt threatened by Oswald. He was afraid that this newcomer was aspiring to his position and that he might succeed in getting it.

Oswald took advantage of the man's insecurity. When the commandant and his Russian assistant were away he approached the Belorussian. *I asked him for permission to move to the West, closer to the front, explaining that since I knew languages I could be of more use there. Pleased, the man gave me a letter to a major of the secret service, NKGB, in Baranowicze. I don't even remember his name.*

Soon Oswald was facing this major who, without offering him a chair, began to read the letter. When he finished he looked up, "Rufeisen, Oswald, Illytch, what nationality are you?"

Oswald hesitated. He was afraid that if he would say Jewish the Russian would engage him for work. The Soviets, he thought, preferred to employ Jews than Poles. They distrusted the Poles. On the other hand, if he would identify himself as Polish he might be accused of giving false information. He decided to bypass the issue, and said: "I am a Catholic."

Irritated, the major slammed the table. "I did not ask you about your religion! What is your nationality?"

The answer was, "I am a Jew."

This news was greeted with a cynical half smile. Then sneeringly he said, "Sorry, the quota is filled."

"What do you suggest I do?" Oswald asked.

"You are free."

Not believing in his good fortune, Oswald asked if he could go to Vilna. Impatiently, the major nodded as he stood up behind his desk. The meeting was over.

With this experience behind him, on his way to Vilna, Oswald decided to visit the farm he had worked on during the war. Before Oswald had left for Belorussia, he gave to the farm owner, Lubomir Żukowski, his high school diploma for safety. Now he wanted to see his former boss and get the document.

Oswald's arrival at the farm created a commotion. Żukowski received him with open arms and cried with tears of joy. Not only did he return a well-preserved diploma, but he insisted that this unexpected guest stay for a festive meal. Though touched by the attention, Oswald was eager to get away. With the special reception barely over, after an emotional and friendly parting he was once more on the road. This time his destination was the Carmelite monastery in Vilna, near Ostra Brama. Ostra Brama is a religious shrine and anyone passing near acknowledges it by making the sign of the cross, removing a hat, or both.

At first the head of the monastery listened attentively to Oswald's story. But when he discovered that his visitor was a former partisan, a member of a Russian otriad, and a Jew, he refused to hear the rest. Shaking his head, he interrupted, "You must wait. You cannot be accepted into this monastery. We have enough problems as it is. Your stay with us is totally out of the question! Our order in Cracow may take you. They may have provisions for novices, we don't." The older man did not even ask the visitor to stay for a rest or a meal. Bewildered, Oswald left.

With the war still on, Oswald had few options. Travel to Cracow was prohibited. He returned to the convent in Mir. This time too the Mother Superior was ready to help. She knew a priest in Nowa Wilejka who was willing to employ Oswald. He was accepted into the parish as a semi-handiman, semi-farm hand. It was hard physical work: carrying water, chopping wood, and anything else that had to be done in the house or garden. Oswald was determined to stay away from police stations, from investigative work, from political or criminal accusations and punishments. He wanted to be with himself and his religion. The job he had accomplished just that.

One day, the Mother Superior from Mir brought him the news that special trains were repatriating Poles. This was the opportunity Oswald had been waiting for. By March 1945, this aspiring monk arrived in Poland.

16

Becoming a Carmelite Monk and a Priest

I went to Poland with the intention of finding my parents. As the train was approaching Cracow I changed my mind. I had decided that if my parents survived the war they will manage without me. I thought that if I found them they would stand in my way. . . . And so, I did not go to search for them. The fact that I did not look for my mother and father was a weakness. Maybe I was not human enough . . . maybe it was fanaticism. . . . Now I would have acted differently.

Impatient and anxious to immerse himself into religious life, Oswald refused to be distracted even by his close family. He was obsessed with the idea of entering a monastery. What did becoming a monk mean to him? *Some feel that Christ's life was one continuous sacrifice. This is how it has been interpreted. . . . I don't know if this is the historical truth, but this is how we see him. A monk wants to imitate Christ, that is why he gives up all, he sacrifices. I felt that now after all that happened, I somehow had to sacrifice myself to God. I hoped that God will accept my offer. In the passion of my belief I thought that this was what I should do. I wanted to give up all my rights. . . . This is how I thought then. I am not sorry that I elected this path. Whether objectively I was right or not, I cannot decide.*

In 1945 Oswald came to Cracow with a letter of introduction to Father Jósef Prus, the Provincial of the Carmelite order in Poland. When he reached his destination he was told that the man he came to see was in his monastery in Czerna, some fifteen miles away from the city. Oswald walked to Czerna.[1]

Father Jósef rewarded Oswald's efforts with a warm welcome. The forty-seven-year-old man made it obvious that the letter he read only aroused his curiosity. He asked for a fuller account. When telling his story Oswald soon came to his conversion and the readings about the miraculous healings in Lourdes. Noting that he found these articles in a Carmelite publication, he explained that these writings put him on the road to Christianity. Excitedly, Father Jósef interrupted, "But I am the author of these articles! Strange, rarely in my life did I find it as hard to write as I did about these miracles of Lourdes."

The part these publications had played in Oswald's conversion created a special bond between the two men. In their meeting both saw God's hand. At the close of this first encounter the older man suggested that since Oswald had been like Daniel in the lion's den and survived, as a monk he should take the name Daniel. This is how Oswald Rufeisen eventually became Brother Daniel and, as a priest, Father Daniel.

At Czerna for Oswald, as for others who aspired to become monks, each day was divided into separate duties: prayer, work, and study. Every minute was filled with activities. Even so-called free time was devoted to prayers and contemplation. With the others Oswald would wake up at midnight and spend an hour praying. This was followed by a few hours of sleep, with each day starting at five in the morning.

In this, as in all other monasteries, the Polish postwar government confiscated most of their properties, leaving to each only a small lot. The inhabitants of these institutions had to contribute their labor, making the land alotted to them as fruitful as possible. Never an agricultural wizard, Oswald joined the others by devoting many hours to rigorous farming.

For Oswald, life at Czerna was divided into three broad phases, each corresponding approximately to his particular position. The first was the period of probation. After that he became a novice. In the third and final stage Oswald was a student of theology and philosophy, in Przemyśl and Cracow. Acceptance into any of these phases was by no means automatic, nor were they neatly separated from each other. For years, involved in the different monastic pursuits, Oswald was shielded from the outside. Whatever contacts with the external world he did have were indirect and usually related to his past.

Oswald had committed his brother's address to memory. During the war to keep a piece of paper with an address from Palestine would have been dangerous, even foolish—it would have been incriminating evidence in case of arrest. He wrote to Arieh soon after his liberation and by 1945 established communication with Palestine. He had also heard that two of his cousins survived the war and lived in the city of Bielsko. From them he learned that his parents were murdered by the Nazis. No one knew exactly how they died and where. One likely possibility was the concentration camp Auschwitz at the end of August 1942. Their death saved him from waging a battle over his conversion. He must have been thinking about this hypothetical conflict when he remarked that news about his mother's and father's fate came as a "relief." As for his brother, the distance between them reduced the effectiveness of pressure that could have been applied to Oswald's religious fervor. For years, their contact was limited to letters.

Arieh Rufeisen lived in a settlement near Haifa (Moshav). Right after the war he married a young woman from Cracow, a former member of the Jewish underground, Hela Szipper. During the war Hela was both a fighter and a courier who carried messages between the ghetto and the forbidden Christian world.[2]

At first Arieh Rufeisen recalls being puzzled by the mere appearance of his brother's letter. At the corner of the paper he noticed the words Pax Christi and a sign of the cross next to it. The content of the writing was also strange. Much of it was devoted to thanking God for saving his life. Communications that followed were more explicit. Soon Oswald notified his brother about his conversion. He wrote about the miraculous cures in Lourdes and how these led him to Christianity. Parts of one of his early letters read as follows: "I know that you trust your brother. I have no intention of leading you into misunderstandings. If I had the smallest doubt about these things I would not have written to you. These miraculous healings in Lourdes led me into the desire to learn more about Christ's healings. . . . The New Testament is a holy scripture, written almost exclusively by Jews, the disciples of Jesus Christ, and almost in its entirety, without changes, preserved till our time. It was not easy to believe it, but now I am ready to give my life for this truth."

Parts of another communication read: "What I wrote to you is the honest truth, not exaggerated at all. Rather understated. These are ideological convictions that could be subjected to debate. This is the essence of my entire spiritual life and it dominates all I do. Here in the monastery instead of suffering, I found inner peace. This is the basis of a human being. This is the real and only truth. I don't have much time for writing. I am subordinated in everything to the superiors of the monastery. I would have liked to see you, to personally convince you. But this is not what God wants right now. Yet, I believe strongly that one day we shall see each other. When? God knows."

Arieh reacted with a mixture of competing emotions. He was happy that Oswald managed to survive. He was also proud about his brother's selfless protection of innocent lives. At the same time, he was disappointed and hurt by Oswald's Catholicism and what looked to him like religious fanaticism. Yet in no way did his brother's unexpected religious preoccupation reduce Arieh's affection and concern. It never even occurred to Arieh that he might cut their ties. On the contrary, he was eager to keep up their correspondence, dreaming about their future reunion. This longing was sustained by Oswald who often expressed the desire to settle in the oldest Carmelite monestary in Haifa, Stella Maris. Significantly, at these early stages Arieh clung to the idea that Oswald would return to Judaism. He had hoped he could be prevented from becoming permanently attached to monastic life. Arieh Rufeisen had expected that friends and others, with direct access to his brother, could be effective in returning him to Judaism, or at least to the secular world.

A few of those who had shared the Rufeisens' life in Vilna, members of the Zionist Organization Akiva, survived the war. They and others who knew Oswald, or even some who had only heard his story, were eager to intervene. They were anxious to visit this aspiring monk, hoping to persuade him to return to Judaism.

One of the first visitors was Ernest Seifter, a cousin in whose house in Bielsko Oswald had lived for several years. The two had attended the same high school and shared the same school bench. As students, they were inseparable. About their relationship Oswald says that they were like "Siamese twins." They had not seen each other since 1939.

During the war Seifter ended up in Russia where he stayed till 1945. With other Polish citizens, he was repatriated to Poland. Their mutual cousins in Bielsko told Seifter about Oswald. One day he simply appeared at the Czerna monastery. *I rang the gate. They asked whom I wanted to see. I said that we, Oswald and I, were brothers. We looked alike. I was afraid that a cousin they would not let in. As it turned out, the Superior knew about me. Oswald mentioned names of people for whom he and others prayed so that they would return safely. I was among those they had prayed for. . . . I had just come back from Russia. In this place where he was it was so quiet, so peaceful, you were cut off from the world completely, you did not know what was going on on the outside. . . .*

When we met, we embraced. I felt strange, bewildered. . . . Oswald brought me into a room. It was a guest room with a big cross on the wall. I felt uncomfortable. I asked him: "Are you happy here?" "Yes," he said, then he explained: "I could have gotten out before. My brother begged me to, but I refused. I decided to stay. I can do much more from inside than I can do from the outside. I can help the Jewish people from here. These people know nothing about Jews. Anti-Semitism came about because they did not know who was a Jew. . . . I promised that I will stay in the monastery, and I will. If I left they would not trust another Jew." These were his own words. . . . I think that an important issue was the question of honor. He gave his word that he would stay so he did. He felt that if he will leave they would not trust another Jew. So I did not inquire further. I told him: "If this is what you want I am not against you. I am happy that you are alive!" He told me: "I like to go to the main monastery in Israel. I want to be closer to my brother!"

Then and now Seifter has been supportive of his cousin. He explains, *I am not interested in religion or no religion. All I wanted was for him to be happy. If he was content, that was good enough for me. He was always an idealist, a Zionist. In his heart, he remained a Zionist and he does not think that he left Judaism. At that time he thought that the messiah was Jesus. In our religion we had many messiahs. They were usually revolutionaries. . . . He himself is a revolutionary. I imagine that this must get him in trouble with the church. I care only about him. His religion does not matter.*

Seifter's visit to the monastery lasted three days. Soon after that he left Poland. The two cousins continued to exchange letters. They met again only in 1972.

Józiek Rakocz also came to Czerna. During the war, in Vilna, Józiek and Oswald had shared a room. Both had belonged to the Akiva organization. They became close friends. After the outbreak of the German-Russian War, Józiek ended up in Warsaw where he survived hidden by his mother who pretended to be a Christian. He remembers, *One day as I was walking on the outskirts of Warsaw, wagons with people were returning from Russia. Someone shouted from the wagon, Józiek! Józiek! This was Hilel Seidel. He told me: "Do you know, supposedly Oswald is alive but he is in a monastery, we must look for him." Later on we looked for him.*

As soon as Rakocz found out where Oswald was, he went to see him. *It was not simple to enter the monastery. At the gate they ask to whom I came. I told them. The monk in charge received me warmly. It turned out that he knew about me from Oswald. When Oswald and I saw each other we were very emotional. After we calmed down, he began to tell me his story. We sat for hours. I tried to convince him to come with me. But he was a passionate believer, very strongly involved. Now with age he speaks differently, but then . . .*

Does he think that with time Oswald became disappointed in religion? *I am not sure . . . no! He sees now things more realistically like everyone else. I think that every idealist changes somewhat, regardless of what the basis for this idealism is . . . I think that even today he believes. I am convinced that he is not able to play a comedy. I am sure that he is very honest.*

At the time the two met, Oswald had not taken the vows. He could have left without much difficulty. At least this is what Rakocz thought. He therefore set about to persuade his friend to give up life in the Polish monastery. He tried appealing to Oswald's love for his brother and how wonderful it would be for the two to reunite. Then Rakocz pointed out that eventually all his old friends would be leaving for Palestine and Oswald would be here all alone without close Jewish ties.

When Rakocz realized that his listener was unimpressed, he continued by pointing out that after all there were churches in Palestine too. No one, he assured Oswald, would interfere with his religious pursuits there.

Rufeisen was attentive. He did not contradict his guest. Instead, he tried to assure him that he remained a Zionist and a Jew. He admitted that he was longing to be close to his brother and his old friends, but this had to wait. He was convinced that such a reunion will take place. However, this had to happen with the official approval of his Carmelite superiors and ultimately God.

Looking back, Oswald remembers their talk as warm and unpressured. Rakocz recalls in turn its final phase as follows. *In the end he told me: "Tomorrow I will give you an answer!" They gave me a small room and I slept there. The next day when we met Oswald said, "I prayed all night for guidance. I decided to stay here." Then he explained that for himself he sees the monastery as a way of life and that in Christianity he saw a continuation of Judaism.*

Whatever regrets Rakocz had, they did not change his warm feelings toward Oswald. For years their friendship was kept alive through letters. Indeed, later on Rakocz was delighted to hear *that Oswald was going to study philosophy in Cracow. He finished. He is very intelligent, knowledgeable, open to new things, interested in all. Today too he feels a part of the Jewish nation. He emphasizes his belongingness to the Jewish people. This he does not want to give up.*

Though Oswald's Jewish friends were concerned about his fate, they were not always able to come to see him. This, for example, was the case with Moshe Kalchheim, who survived the war as a partisan. Eager to reach Palestine, he decided to go there via Italy. In Italy he heard that Oswald was in a monastery.

In a way Kalchheim was not surprised by the news. *Oswald was always a serious person, he had a sense of humor but he was very serious. If there were Jewish monasteries, he would not have converted. He did not find his place in society. He was very sensitive. Somehow he did not fit into this world.*

Despite this evaluation, Kalchheim burst into tears when he read Oswald's letter informing him that he had become a full-fledged Carmelite monk. Perhaps, along with so many others, Kalchheim had hoped that in the end Oswald's religious path could be reversed. It was the finality of the event that shook him up.

When he had first heard in Rome about Oswald he tried to do something. He sent a cable to Poland to their mutual friend Hilel Seidel.

Hilel lived in the city of Lódź. He had become a leader of the Zionist Youth Organization, an offshoot of Akiva. Seidel in turn did more than just tell Rakocz about Oswald. *I thought that maybe Oswald is hiding in the monastery. I thought that there might be some pressure upon him, that he is being kept against his will. I gave an announcement in a Catholic paper saying that his brother is looking for him, this is how I found him. Brother could be a real brother or a monk.*

Seidel claims that in response to this advertisement a nun came to see him. He says that this was the Mother Superior from the Mir convent. He also says that from her he heard for the first time Oswald's story and that when after hours they were about to part company the nun said, "He will not return to you, he is a Christian."[3] Oswald does not think that the Mother Superior ever met with Seidel.[4]

Unlike some others, Seidel never went to the monastery at Czerna. Those who did, without exception, tried to convince this ardent Catholic to give up, if not his new religion, at least the monastic life. Of those who came some were even strangers. One, for example, was an official messenger from Palestine. He was probably urged by Arieh Rufeisen to try to dissuade his brother from making a permanent commitment to the Carmelite order. About all such visitors, including this stranger, Oswald talks with a tolerant, bemused smile. *His name was Wicek Lichthauser. He came to see me in the hope of taking me with him. I felt honored that he came because I knew that he was a prominent member of prewar Akiva. But even he did not pressure me. His approach was gentle, refined. In general, no matter who came, when I made my position clear they respected my judgment. Only one of my visitors was very insistent, wanting me to leave with him immediately. This man was Siunek Weiss. We knew each other from my hometown. He was determined to get me out and would not even listen to my explanation. Siunek arrived at the monastery, armed with a revolver. I guess he was afraid that someone will kill him*[5] *(chuckle). He insisted on smuggling me abroad through Czechoslovakia. He was the only one who pressured me.*

Though these guests must have disturbed the order of the monastic life, Oswald never objected to any of the visitors, not even to this very aggressive caller. On the contrary, he welcomed all who came to see him. Perhaps their efforts at removing him from his chosen path and his ability to resist gave him strength? Perhaps the arguments he had to use over and over again showed him that he was "right"? After a while these visitors stopped coming.

In 1946 Oswald received a monk's robe. As Brother Daniel he took special vows in which he obligated himself to continue the life of a monk for another three years.

As a monk, in 1948 Oswald decided to visit his birthplace and its surroundings. The timing and the reason for this trip had to do with psychological changes. He explains, *I felt stronger. I knew that my parents were dead. I loved my native places, the mountains and forests. These are the most beautiful parts of Poland. While I was growing up, I used to hike and ski in these mountains. Though I wanted to live in Israel, I was attached to these places. They were close to my heart . . . I also wanted to see my cousins in Bielsko. I had written to them before, so they were prepared for what they saw . . . I came to them dressed as a monk. They received me warmly. Already my head was shaved in a special way, leaving one part of the scalp exposed. With this kind of a hair cut one had to wear a monk's robe . . . otherwise it would look strange.*

Shortly after this trip, in 1949, at the age of twenty-seven, Brother Daniel took the final vows. This meant he would remain a monk for life.

During the war a large proportion of the Polish clergy had perished. For this reason, and also because the political climate of the country was not conducive to religious occupational pursuits, postwar Poland experienced a shortage of Catholic priests. In part to fill this gap, Oswald was asked to prepare for priesthood. Seeing in this request, as in everything else, God's hand, he accepted.

Preparations for priesthood took six years. The 1946 decision was followed by concentrated learning of theology and philosophy. The first five years in particular centered on intensive study within different religious institutions. Only during the sixth year public appearances were added to this program.

He describes the process. *The sixth year of preparation for priesthood required actual work that had to do with lectures and sermons for student groups, religious institutions, and parishes. Because there was a great demand for my appearances, I spent much of my time traveling, giving speeches and sermons. When a parish priest ordered a number of sermons he would pay me. The pay was good. I would take the money and give it to my monastery. Personally I had practically no expenses.*

Because of the ever-growing requests for Oswald's appearances, his sixth year was more demanding than any of the previous ones. His time had to be carefully divided into sections devoted to different activities: prayer, study, physical work, preparation for sermons, and other public appearances. Later he would make about sixty speeches per month.

In 1952, at the age of thirty, Oswald was to become a Catholic priest. A special ceremony marks an individual's entrance into the priesthood, and the new priest conducts his first Mass, the Primicium Mass. Traditionally, ordination takes place in the family parish. The elaborate ceremony associated with this important step helps all who are familiar with the priest to recognize him in his new position. In addition, his very presence in the community serves as a model to be emulated by the young.

Oswald regarded Zadziele, the village he was born in, as his home. His attachment to the place was strong, even though when still a child he and his family had moved away. Over the years, he had practically no contact with any of its inhabitants. Still, he remembered that his parents loved the place. He knew that they left Zadziele reluctantly and did so only after they became the single Jewish family. He also knew that the relations between his family and the local people were warm and supportive. For these and perhaps other reasons Oswald felt that his ordination should take place in his native village.

Oswald's mentor, Father Walerian Ryszka, the prior of the Cracow monastery, felt differently. For Jews postwar Poland and particularly its provinces were unsafe. Hundreds were murdered by Poles after the war.[6] This older and experienced monk felt that Zadziele, a backward community, might be dangerous for a former Jew. And if not dangerous, perhaps unpleasant. He had expected that, at best, the natives would look with suspicion at a Jew who was to become a priest. Father Walerian tried to dissuade Oswald from holding this important ceremony in Zadziele. The Mother Superior from Mir echoed his objections.

This time, however, Oswald would not listen. Perhaps it was his way of emphasizing the continuity between his Jewishness and Catholicism. Possibly he was trying to show respect for the memory of his parents. His cousin Seifter recalls that the actual announcements for Oswald's ordination were printed in two languages: Hebrew and Polish.

Oswald's decision prevailed. Contrary to what others had feared, he was received warmly by the parish priest in Stary Żywiec. In fact, the priest invited Oswald to stay at his place. The rest of the natives did not remember ever having one of their sons initiated into priesthood and were eager to participate in such an event.

The highlight of the ceremony, the Mass conducted by the new priest, took place in a quaint church some three miles away. This meant that a huge religious procession moved from Zadziele to this special place of worship. According to Oswald's estimate, some 6000 people came, but only a small part could fit into the church. The rest waited patiently outside until the end of the Mass and the return to the village.

Oswald was moved by the beauty of the procession, the music, and the songs. These rituals were followed by a lavish reception, with the local priest as the official host. The Mother Superior from the Mir convent was there, as were his cousins from Bielsko, the only relatives he had in Poland. Although Jewish, they accepted their Catholic cousin. They even photographed the festivities and later shared the pictures with the new priest.

An event of this magnitude did not pass unnoticed by the authorities. Oswald soon learned that *the secret police (UB) protested to the parish priest. They were furious because without a permit a huge religious procession took place. Public religious meetings, unless authorized, were illegal. For this transgression the priest had to pay a fine.*

For five years the monastery had shielded Oswald from the country's political conflicts and the church's problems with the authorities. Only in the sixth year, when Oswald was called on to make public appearances, did he become exposed to Poland's political realities.

Looking back at the Russian presence, Oswald feels that they proceeded in a shrewd way, trying to create the impression that the Poles were in charge and independent. A leader of the peasant party, a former premier of the Polish Government in Exile in London, Stanisław Mikołajczyk, became the vice premier of the postwar government of Poland. Mikołajczyk proved too independent. Soon political maneuvering convinced him of personal danger and he ran away.[7]

After Mikołajczyk's escape the premiership passed on to Józef Cyrankiewicz. He was a Socialist leader (PPS), not a Communist. This last choice too was in part dictated by the desire to appease the population and thus diminish their opposition to the Soviets.[8] While the Russians were making these conciliatory gestures, they were also establishing a tighter grip over the country. Their quest for domination included an attack on the Polish Catholic Church, one of its traditional foes. Anti-church moves involved a curtailment of religious freedoms and confiscation of church property.

Oswald is convinced that governmental confiscation of the church's property indirectly improved the relationship between the clergy and the lay people. Relating this process to his own monastery, he notes, *Sure, land was taken away, but the relation of the local population was never as good as at that time, after we became poor. In the past we had land and forests. We knew that the peasants were economically deprived. They needed wood. There had to be a monk on a horse who guarded the trees so that peasants would not steal. This created conflict between the monastery and the local people, envy, resentment. After the war all this disappeared. Our church was never as full as after we lost everything. Only five hectares of land were left to us and this was enough to live on. The monks understood the change, not that it was God's punishment, but rather some purification. It is not good for a religious order to be rich.*

The curtailment of freedoms, however, was an entirely different matter. Spying on church activities was common. As a result, members of the clergy were frequently called for special interrogations. Some of them were arrested, among them the leader Wyszyński. Some, singled out for special treatment, had perished.[9]

When during the last year of study Oswald became involved with the outside world, he saw no conflict between his religious and secular pursuits. He explains, *I worked in Poland for the church and for the Polish nation. I was also expressing my convictions. I believed in the freedom of man. I was disturbed by the lack of human freedom in the socialist system, freedom of expression, communication, freedom of opinion. These things bothered me.*

Since Oswald was becoming a popular speaker, he was also watched by the authorities. Those in power must have disapproved of his devotion to Catholicism and individual freedom. Yet they did not molest him. Oswald explains this hands-off policy. *During my sermons I took a very patriotic position and therefore I became persona non grata. But I spoke only about religion. I reminded my audiences about the situation. At the same time I was careful not to stir up the masses against the authorities. I spoke about the dignity of man, about education and morality. None of what I said was directed against those in power. I concentrated on religious tolerance. People could interpret my sermons the way they wanted.*

About less personal situations Oswald says that *while the position of the church toward the Soviets was hostile, it did not involve hostile actions. Instead, it expressed itself in keeping up the population's hopes that the present situation will not last. . . . The church, in fact, kept the Poles going, it gave them strength. Without the church, Poles would break down the same way as the Czechs and the Hungarians broke down. A Pole could lean on the church, it gave him solace. The church supported him. All had recognized this.*

Oswald thinks that *by 1956 the Poles had realized that the Russians were a reality and that one cannot throw them out. The church then tried to establish a modus vivendi with the political system, with Wyszyński as its head. Up till then for eleven years, the clergy in Poland was waiting for a political change. Then, in 1956, it realized that this situation will last for a long time and that there is no other way but to accommodate to the Communist presence. This accommodation continues till this very day.*

Though never personally harassed, Oswald became indirectly involved with the government. It happened in the 1950s after the Carmelite order had sent him, another monk, and a lay brother to Szopienice, a village close to the town Katowice, where the Carmelites owned a barn. Oswald and the two others had to transform this barn into a church and a monastery.

At first these new arrivals encountered no opposition and the barn became a popular place of worship. Every Sunday Oswald conducted three Masses. Each time the place was filled to capacity, with most people standing outside. To accommodate the crowd, special loudspeakers were installed. This part of the country was populated by miners, known for their fierce independence. The authorities, no doubt, wanted to avoid a showdown with the strong-minded miners and so initially they chose to tolerate the natives' religious fervor.

As the number of worshipers in this new church continued to grow, reaching into a thousand, the authorities decided to put a stop to this obvious violation. The priest was notified that the architectural changes of the barn were made without an official permit and therefore the place had to be shut down. To Oswald life in Szopienice proved most gratifying and exciting. He was unwilling to give in and searched for solutions.

Oswald knew that the Russian ambassador to Poland was the prominent Belorussian Communist Ponomarenko, the man after whom Oswald's partisan unit was named. He therefore decided to capitalize on the fact that he was a partisan in the Ponomarenko otriad. Dressed as a monk, with his wartime documents and the Soviet medal, Oswald went to the Russian embassy.

The embassy was housed in one of the most beautiful buildings of Warsaw. Father Daniel felt at ease, as he was being shown into a living room that harmonized with the rest of the luxurious surroundings. Here the Persian rugs, crystal lamps, paintings, and the sturdy furniture all created an aura of stable, solid elegance. In an unexpected way too, the old-time Belorussian Communist seemed to fit into this impressive environment. Though a short man, Ponomarenko appeared tall. Impeccably dressed, he projected an aura of quiet self-assurance that put others at ease. When Oswald saw him he classified him as *a sophisticated European type, extremely intelligent and pleasant.*

The ambassador came into the room smiling broadly, with an outstretched hand. Then, with a twinkle in his eyes, he said, "I don't know how to address you. Perhaps the most appropriate way would be brother in Christ? I hope that I can be of help to you. What brought you here?"

These brief sentences were uttered in an appealing, friendly way. Oswald reacted by telling him about Szopienice and the problems with the authorities. He continued by informing his host that he had served in the Russian otriad Ponomarenko and that he received a Soviet medal for his services. Subtly, unobtrusively, he was suggesting that the ambassador might fix his difficulties with the authorities. Ponomarenko needed no elaboration. With a bemused, clever smile, the man said, "For your participation with the Russian partisans you deserve medals but not a church." Then, politely, with a touch of irony, he said that after all Poland was an independent country and he was only a Russian ambassador.

Oswald in turn assured him that he was not asking him to interfere. Still, he added, if the ambassador would only pick up the phone and mention the case to Cyrankiewicz this in itself would solve the problem. (Cyrankiewicz was Poland's prime minister.) Oswald vividly remembers his host's reaction. *So he said: "Cyrankiewicz? Who is Cyrankiewicz?" Nothing came out of it. It only showed what attitude the Russians had to Poland's government. It also showed me how smart Ponomarenko was, exceptionally so.*

Not yet ready to accept defeat, Oswald decided to stay in Warsaw and explore the situation. He explains: *I met a high court judge who happened to be Jewish. He was eager to be of help and advised me to send a petition to the council of the state. This move, he claimed, would allow me to say to the local authorities that I had appealed in the capital and am awaiting an answer. As long as the authorities will not respond to my request, I will be able to remain in Szopienice. In the meantime this judge had arranged within the council that I should not be getting an answer to my plea.*

This is what happened. As Oswald "waited" for an answer, his parish in Szopienice continued to function and flourish. The situation lasted for almost a year. Then members of the secret police arrived at the scene. Without any explanations they demolished the barn, putting an end to the project.

Oswald returned to his former life. Though the monastery became again his home, he continued to dream about settling in Israel. To make his dream come true, he would periodically apply to his superiors for a transfer. All his petitions were turned down. Disappointed, this obedient monk waited for the right moment, convinced that such a time would come.

The wish to settle in Israel did not prevent Oswald from appreciating life in Poland. He found his situation emotionally and spiritually fulfilling yet he did not quite fit into his surroundings. He was different. Most of the others were monks whose lives were confined to the monastery. In contrast, because of his many speaking engagements, Oswald was frequently absent. Also, all the other monks were Polish nationalists who shared a common outlook on life and religion. Father Daniel was outspoken about his Jewishness and his desire to settle in Israel. *There were many similarities among the other monks at Czerna. I was different. I was strange. I disturbed the rest of them. But they disturbed me less. . . . I was a priest, a monk, a Catholic, and a Pole, but I wanted to leave for Israel. I wanted to be home. I felt that in Israel I could be myself. . . . When I did leave Poland it was for positive reasons. I departed not because of anti-Semitism, but in order not to interfere with others and in order to be in my own home.*

However, indirectly Oswald's move to Israel was related to anti-Jewish outbursts. The 1956 estimates of the Jewish population in Poland amount to 50,000. For complex and still widely debated reasons, after October 1956 the country went through a period of extreme anti-Semitic agitation that came together with vocal demands for Jewish emigration. Because of these developments, within a few months the number of Polish Jews was cut in half.[10]

Of those who left the country, many settled in Israel. Among these new immigrants were many mixed marriages and often the partners of these unions wanted to keep their respective religions: Catholic and Jewish. On arrival in Israel some of these Catholics desired the services of Polish-speaking clergymen. For a while a Polish-born priest, with an American passport, lived and worked in Jaffa. He was also an avid anti-Semite. This priest failed to understand that those married to Jews might be disturbed rather than comforted by his anti-Semitic ideology. Eventually he was removed from his post and transferred to Cyprus.

In the anti-Semitic agitations in Poland Oswald saw an opportunity for the fulfillment of his Zionist aspirations. He also thought that by going to Israel he could be of help to the increasing number of Polish-speaking Catholics. Once more Father Daniel submitted an application for a transfer to the Carmelite monestary in Haifa. This time, after a few months, he was granted permission to relocate. With this approval he was ready to apply for a Polish exit visa. Because the Polish government was facilitating Jewish emigration, he was optimistic.

Oswald's case, however, was not as clear-cut. Due to his many outspoken sermons and the incident in Szopienice the authorities looked at him with suspicion. Indeed, after eleven months, without any explanation, his exit visa was denied. Then, by chance, Oswald met the secretary of the Jewish Historical Institute in Warsaw who was also the secretary of the Cultural Association of Jews in Poland. This man was very sympathetic. Eager to help, he gave Oswald a letter of introduction to Hersz Smolar, a high ranking member of the Communist party.

Oswald and Smolar had met in the forest. Already at that time, as an established Communist, Smolar had a high position in the Russian partisan hierarchy. Shared experiences of these former partisans gave their meeting a nostalgic touch. Oswald remembers, *After he read my letter of introduction he began to pace the room. Then he said: "You are a priest and a monk, you also claim that you are a Zionist. You want to go to Israel. I am a Communist and an atheist and an anti-Zionist and I am supposed to help you go to Israel?" I did not react, except with a smile. Then he asked me what I had written in my application for an exit visa. I told him that I wrote about my Zionist upbringing, that I felt well in Poland but because Jews have their country, I considered it my duty to go to Israel. All my life I looked upon Palestine as my future country. To this he said: "Man, who writes such things?! This is stupid! You should have written that you have a brother in Israel and that you want to join him. Zionism for them is equivalent to imperialism to the USA. What should I do with you now? To whom should I send you?"*

Since Oswald had no answer, he remained silent. He felt discouraged, even embarrassed. But, instead of simply getting rid of his unusual visitor, Smolar's parting words were: "Tomorrow you will go to the Central Committee of the Party and see a man by the name of Sława. I will talk to him right away."

In the Central Committee of the Party, Sława was the representative for the minorities. Next day, at that place, Oswald was interrogated by this man's secretary. To her he complained that he had been denied an exit visa, while all other Jews were granted permission to leave.

Oswald recalls: *She said, "But you are a monk and a priest and therefore not a Jew!" So I told her that this is my occupation. But I am a Jew and I have a right like all the other Jews. Then I let her know that I was directed here by Smolar. When she heard who sent me, she asked me to come back the same afternoon. She arranged for me a meeting with the person in charge of passports. After an hour's talk with this director, in someone's presence of course, they gave me permission to leave. Within two weeks I had a passport.*

This passport was offered to Oswald Rufeisen, the Jew. In fact, he was asked to resign his Polish citizenship. Emotionally, Oswald found this hard to do. In the end, however, the desire to see his brother and settle in Israel won. He gave up his Polish citizenship, only to learn that this step did not guarantee a transfer to Israel. Such a move now depended on the Israeli authorities.

And so, this unusual monk met with the Israeli ambassador, Katriel Katz. As a way of introduction Oswald brought with him a book about uprisings in the Jewish ghettos that describes his activities in Mir.

With the preliminary explanations behind him, the ambassador asked, "How do you want to go to Israel—as a missionary? As a tourist?

"I want to go as a Jew" came the answer.

"But you are a Catholic, a priest, a monk?!"

"Being a priest is my profession," Oswald said.

Shaking his head, the ambassador disagreed. Besides, in Israel at the time, there was a crisis that centered around the question of who was a Jew. Katriel Katz explained that he could not make a decision and that this issue will have to be settled by others.

Politely, but firmly, he said, "I cannot give you a visa as a Jew. I advise you to say that you want to keep the Polish passport."

But Oswald had already agreed to resign from his Polish citizenship. Besides, he wanted to go to Israel as a Jew. The ambassador ended their meeting by saying, "I might be able to give you a visa for a year. They will not remove you after a year. Anyway, for that too you would have to apply formally."

Oswald was left without a definite promise of any kind of visa. Nor could he possibly know that permission to go to Israel would come from a meeting in Israel described by his brother, Arieh Rufeisen.

On a Saturday afternoon I hear a knock at the door. I was in shorts and an undershirt. At my hesitant invitation a man came in. A stranger. He introduced himself as Katriel Katz, the Israeli ambassador to Poland. . . . I was surprised. He told me that he came to discuss my brother. He wanted to know how I felt about Oswald and if Israel should allow him to come here or not. He also explained that he happened to be on his way to Safad and therefore decided to stop by. I thought that it was nice of him to do that. To his question I said, "Of course Israel should allow him to come here. Why not?" Then I told him that I don't look at it as a political, national issue. As a brother, of course, I would like him to come. We talked for about fifteen to thirty minutes. When he left I was hopeful. A short while after the ambassador's visit Oswald received permission to come here.

Just as Katz has said, the Israeli visa entitled Oswald to one year's stay.

17

A Catholic Jew?

The closer Oswald's boat came to the Israeli shores, the more obsessed he became with the idea that as a convert to Catholicism he could not count on Jewish acceptance. He knew that the most severe disapproval had to come from the Jewish Orthodox circles, for whom a move to Christianity is equated with death. Others, he realized, though more tolerant, would also react with opposition, ranging from disappointment to social rejection.

As Oswald tried to envision his relationship to those he might soon be facing, he was grateful that his brother was only tenuously attached to religion. From their past correspondence it was clear that Arieh Rufeisen was opposed to and uncomfortable with Oswald's religious fervor. Still, he voiced his objections in a calm and restrained way. Arieh was a soft-spoken, gentle man who tried to have an "open" mind about his brother's "weakness." He did not condemn; he suffered. But precisely because he did not insist or chastise, Oswald found it hard to face him. And as this long-awaited meeting was about to take place, Oswald's apprehension continued to mount, while conflicting thoughts and emotions raced through familiar and unfamiliar grounds. Together and separately, these ideas and feelings moved from family, to friends, to those whose lives he had saved, even to Jews whom he did not yet know, but whom he would be meeting. This traveling monk and priest was both eager and reluctant to face each and all of these people. Who will accept him? What about Israel, the country of his dreams? He was coming home. He knew that he was different. He wanted so much to belong, to the country, to its people!

Oswald wore a brown Carmelite robe. Somehow the fullness of this garment succeeded in covering up its wearer's anxiety. Outwardly, to those who might have watched him, Oswald seemed calm, as his restless imagination began to settle on his brother, the closest and most important relative he had.

Arieh Rufeisen came to the port of Haifa alone; he wanted their first meeting to be private. He remembers feeling apprehensive and excited when he spotted a Carmelite monk among the passengers. A cross hanging from the man's neck seemed to cover his entire chest. Arieh's throat contracted. Something resembling a spasm, or a pain, moved up his head, searching for a way out. This sensation was followed by fleeting questions. Will I cry? Laugh? He disliked uncontrollable outbursts and tried hard to suppress his emotions. Then in the crowd that was meeting the new arrivals Arieh noticed another monk. Even before this stranger made his way toward Oswald he guessed who he was. He came to welcome Oswald. Arieh did not want him there. Quickly he rushed to his brother's side. The two embraced. They looked at each other in silence. It was as if they were embarrassed, or unable to utter a word. When speech did return it bore little resemblance to the strength of their feelings.

Arieh recalls, *I thought it obvious that my brother was coming to stay with us. But he said, "No, I have to go up to the monastery." So I asked him, "Won't you come home with me?" He did. That night we talked. We never went to bed. I asked him over and over again: "Why did you do it? Don't you know what great suffering we had to go through because of Christianity?"*[1]

Oswald's answers failed to satisfy the listener. None made sense. To him they still don't. Similarly, Arieh's arguments had no impact on his brother's determination to move to Stella Maris. And yet the firmness of Oswald's position did not undermine the love Arieh felt for him. Years later, acknowledging sadly the strangeness of it all, the younger brother spoke about their first meeting: "We parted in Poland as two 'Halutzim' (Zionist pioneers). Suddenly, I find a brother a Catholic priest, a monk. Do I justify him? The fact that I tried to persuade him to return to Judaism shows that I do not approve of his actions. But I accept reality as it is."[2]

The rest of the family, Mrs. Rufeisen and her three sons, followed in Arieh's footsteps. In their home Oswald continues to be a frequent and welcomed guest. If anything, over the years, their mutual attachment has become even stronger. For example, a few years ago the Rufeisens gave a party in honor of Oswald's sixtieth birthday. Thirty-five people were invited. Wearing regular clothes, the guest of honor mingled easily with the others. It was a warm, joyous occasion, with much laughter and banter. No outsider could have guessed that a religious and cultural wall was separating Oswald from everyone else. Even now Arieh readily admits, "I talk to my brother, the monk, about any subject except religion and politics."[3]

About this particular party Oswald says, *My sister-in-law at a recent birthday celebration made the following toast: "I wish that our three sons should feel the same brotherly love and strong attachment that exist between Oswald and my husband." I was happy to hear that. I am very fortunate to have such a wonderful family.* Other, more distant relatives show a similar kind of tolerance and acceptance. Oswald notes: *I am on very good terms with all my relatives. Recently I was at the burial of my cousin. She died at eighty. At the cemetery, her husband, who is eighty-four, introduced me to people saying: "He belongs to the Catholic part of our family."*

What about Oswald's friends? Most of those who were there with him in the Zionist movement Akiva, and survived the war, have settled in Israel. One of these friends, Stefi Schanzer, now Spiegel, lives near to the Rufeisens in Bustan Hagalil. In Vilna Stefi and Oswald had shared an apartment and were in contact until he left town. They met again in Israel. Stefi's response to Oswald's religious transformation resembles the reactions of his other friends. She says, *Our relationship was always close. When I heard what had happened to him it shook me up. For all of us, for all his friends, the news that he had converted and become a monk was a great tragedy. . . . But we are still good friends. Of course, I disagree with his religious views. . . . His personality, his person, is one thing, his religion and his religious life is something we do not see eye to eye . . . about Oswald's way of life I cannot approve or identify with. He is in a monastery. He goes to church. This part of his existence we have nothing to do with. But at family festivities and parties we are together. We invite him all the time.*

Like Stefi, Oswald's other old friends include him in their social gatherings: weddings, bar mitzvahs, and funerals. One of these friends, Hilel Seidel, muses, *Maybe because Oswald is lonely he comes to all our functions. He seems to like being with us. Yet he is not fully a part of our group. He is not a part of any group. This must be a problem. Despite his conversion, I appreciate and love him as a human being. I also feel that we should never forget what he had done for others.*

The Jews of Mir whom Oswald had rescued did not disappoint him either. Seidel reports that right after Oswald came to Israel *Mir survivors gathered around him. Many of them were religious Jews. Even though he appeared before them as a monk, they trusted him and they did not stop loving him. They said: "Here comes our savior." The pious among them prayed for his well-being. . . . They were not shocked by his changed religion. Instead of the monk and priest they saw in him the human being. To them he was simply Oswald, the one who had saved their lives.*

This affection is illustrated by an incident described by another friend. Right after Oswald's arrival in Israel Józiek Rakocz went to visit him at Stella Maris. Hours later when the two had finished talking they went to town. Rakocz recalls: *I stopped a taxi, a "sherut" (it picks up a number of passengers at once, and each pays a set price). The driver shouted, "Oswald get in!" There were already other people in the taxi. We got in. Then when the cabbie stopped and we were about to leave, I wanted to pay for the two of us. The driver looked at me as if I had insulted him. He asked, "What? You want to pay me? You come with Oswald and you want to pay me?!" He vehemently refused my money. Later I heard that this was one of the Jews from Mir who was saved by Oswald. You see, all who know him love him. Everyone for a different reason and from different times."*

People with no personal dealings with Oswald, those who did not know him, were hardly as tolerant. The Orthodox Jews, in particular, distrusted this unusual newcomer. Some argued that if he identifies himself as a Jew he should not have become a Catholic. To them this did not make sense. Some were quick to conclude that this religious renegade must have come to this country for the sole purpose of converting Jews to Christianity. Others even accused him of making it easy for such converts to move away from Israel.

Oswald is upset by such accusations. He admits, however, that when he first came to Israel, he did baptize a few Jews who were partners of mixed marriages and that they did leave the country. He is sorry that this happened and has been careful not to repeat the same mistakes. Very recently, his public comments about this touchy subject were: "I am in pain with most Israelis about the lack of Aliyah (immigration) and feel powerless toward the phenomenon of emigration from the country. It is very difficult for me when an Israeli Jew comes asking me to help him leave the country, as if my religion excludes me from the human framework in which I live and endows me with a pseudo foreign status. In such cases, I open the doors and invite the individual to leave my office."[4]

After a while, faced with the truth, the Orthodox Jews stopped accusing him of missionary work, yet this did not mean reconciliation or acceptance. Oswald's relationship to the Orthodox community remains ambiguous. Indirectly, this very ambiguity led him to the High Court of Israel.

According to the Jewish religious law, Halacha, those born to a Jewish mother are Jews, no matter what kind of sins they might have committed. Once a Jew, always a Jew. Taken to its limit, this law suggests that even a person who converted to Christianity can be a Jew.[5]

Though a Catholic, a priest, and a monk, Oswald Rufeisen could leave Poland only as a Jew. When he was about to depart, he spoke to an experienced priest who wanted to know why Oswald was so eager to settle in Israel. He answered that because he is a Jew he wishes to live in his own country, where as a monk and priest he wants to serve God. This prompted the older man to ask whether Oswald had forgotten that not long ago the Jews had lost so many people and only recently succeeded in establishing their own country, a heterogenous community that is still plagued by many unresolved problems. Did Oswald realize that by going to Israel as a Jew and a Catholic, he would be adding to the many difficulties of a struggling nation?[6] The older man's arguments had no effect on his listener. Instead, till this day, when dealing with the concept of Jewish nationality, he prefers to rely on Jesus' saying, "Render . . . unto Caesar the things which are Caesar's; and unto God the things that are God's."[7] Jesus' support for a separation between religion and state appeals directly to Oswald's claim to Jewish identity. And this claim prompted him, in Israel, to invoke the Law of Return and ask to be officially registered as of Jewish nationality. According to this law, any Jew who comes to settle in Israel has a right to an automatic citizenship. But who is a Jew? Traditionally, the term has encompassed both religion and nationality. At times the traditional connection between the two has been widely debated.

For example, when more than forty years ago "cabinet minister Moshe Sharet appeared in the name of the Jewish Agency in front of the special committee of the United Nations that was appointed for the matters of the land of Israel and was asked by one of its members who is viewed by the Jewish Agency as a Jew Sharet answered, 'I would say that technically and legislatively the Jewish religion identifies one as a Jew. What is necessary is that the person should not have transferred to another religion. Such a person does not have to actively follow the Jewish laws to be considered a Jew but if the person were to join another religion, such an individual could not expect to be recognized as a Jew. Yes, I would say that the Jewish religion is the separating line."[8]

In the state of Israel for years the question of who is or is not a Jew continues to be widely discussed. In the late 1950s, many couples of mixed religions, as well as Jews who had converted to Catholicism, were coming to settle in Israel. With these events, the government came to specify the Law of Return by defining the term "Jew." According to the meaning adopted in 1958, "a Jew is a person who declares in good faith that he was a Jew and is not of another religion."[9]

Automatically excluded from this interpretation were Jews who converted to Christianity. But Oswald refused to accept this specification. He continued to object even after the immigration clerk refused to identify him as being of Jewish nationality. Determined to challenge the meaning of the Law of Return, he approached the Ministry of the Interior.

Looking back, Oswald explains: "Already at that time I understood that a move into a theocratic direction might spell misfortune upon the state of Israel. Citizenship had not been the aim of my efforts. I have always known that I would become a citizen one way or another. The Minister of the Interior at that time, Moshe Chaim Shapira, held long talks with me, pleading with me not to go to court and that he would grant me immediate citizenship and absolve me from the waiting time required by law. But I refused to listen to him. My aim was to establish a legal precedent."[10] (Shapira was the head of the Orthodox party of Israel.)

Oswald describes what happened next. "I turned to a known lawyer, who told me: 'The thing is clear, you are a Jew according to the religious Jewish law (Halacha), but I am not interested in representing you.' Without shaking my hand he took me to the door. . . . The Minister of Justice, Pinchas Rosen, told me: 'You will not succeed. Though all the rational factors are on your side, the emotional elements will be against you and you will fail.' "[11]

In different ways and for a variety of reasons, some not even spelled out, those who knew Oswald well tried to discourage him from taking the legal step. Arieh Rufeisen warned his brother that the country was not ready for such a move and that he was born at least fifty years too early. However, when Arieh realized that Oswald was determined to go through with the trial, he stood by him.

Hilel Seidel, at the time a member of the Israeli parliament, says, *Oswald was not prepared to accept the fact that the government would not allow him to put "Jew" in his passport but I wanted to prepare him for this. I knew it. I had discussions about it with different ministers.* Like so many others, Seidel never wavered in his public support.

When Oswald turned to Jacob Greenstein and asked how much aid he was willing to give, his reaction was as follows. *I told him: "I am ready to say the truth but if they will ask me whether the Law of Return should apply to you I will be against it" . . . Why? . . . First of all we have to settle things with Christianity. Second, this is 1962. Our country is young, we have thousands of problems. In fact, we have many difficulties till this day. We did not need to create new issues about Christian Jews. I told him: "Leave it alone, nothing will happen if you will receive the citizenship later." After that our relationship cooled off a bit. . . . He then asked me to give him a written statement. I did. In it I said that in the forest he always considered himself a Jew of a Christian faith, that he was one of the very few who admitted to being a Zionist and that he planned to come to Jerusalem.*

A few years ago on a television program about Oswald's life, Ephraim Sinder, said, "I told him: 'Why do you need this? Either you are a Jew or a Christian.' He said to me: 'What did I come here for? After all, I am a Zionist and I want to be in my own country because I am a Jew.' I answered him: 'You are either a Jew or a Catholic. You cannot be both.' "[12]

While Oswald was coping with Jewish reactions he turned to the Carmelite authorities, asking them for permission to sue the Israeli government. In retrospect he says, *One of the big mistakes I made was to ask my superior at Stella Maris for permission to take my case to the High Court of Israel.*

Actually, it was a question of my own feelings as a person, not as a Catholic or a monk. I knew that I felt like a Jew. I did not need his approval. Because I asked for his consent I had to wait six months for an answer. They did not understand what I was after. In the end a cable arrived from Rome giving me a go ahead. But money I had to find myself.

Oswald was poor. A friend, a Carmelite nun from Haifa, contacted the Mayor of Florence, Giorgio La Pira. Oswald described him as *a supporter of Israel and a great Christian. He saw in my case an important principle and thought that I was right.* La Pira immediately sent money that covered about one-third of the trial's costs, which was $4000. The remainder came from a friend, Joseph Stiassny, the superior of the Ratisbonne monastery in Jerusalem. Stiassny's parents were converted Jews. His own relationship to Judaism is complex. He feels very Jewish but did not accept Israeli citizenship. Till this day he has a French passport.

After the first prominent lawyer refused to represent him, Oswald hired someone who kept the case for a year without bringing it to court. Before Oswald dismissed this lawyer he had to pay him $1000. Eventually he hired two lawyers, Yaron and Kushmir, both members of the leftist political party Mapam. The Israeli Ministry of the Interior was represented by Gideon Hausner, who later became the prosecutor in the Eichman trial. Though they did not know each other, in their youth Hausner and Oswald had belonged to the same Zionist organization, the Akiva. Oswald applied to the High Court of Justice asking that a legal order be issued against a public body, the Ministry of the Interior. No facts were being disputed and the hearings were to be limited to legal arguments alone. The actual participants in this trial were the lawyers who represented each side, and the High Court judges who were to decide on the case.

In applying to the High Court of Justice, Oswald's lawyer used the arguments that: (1) The term nationality is not equal to the term religion. A person who is Jewish by nationality does not have to be a Jew by religion. (2) He is a Jew according to the Jewish code of law (Halacha) because he was born to a Jewish mother. (3) The 1958 decision made by the government that constitutes the basis for the Minister of Interior's refusal to grant him his request has no legal foundation and therefore is not binding. (4) The Minister of the Interior's refusal is arbitrary and based on nonlegal considerations and in fact contains elements that are damaging to the plaintiff's rights and reflects nothing but prejudice against him.[13]

Even before the trial began, the news about the event caught the attention of the entire country and the international community as well. This was the first time in Israeli history that five High Court judges were to decide on a case. The judges were: Moshe Silberg, Moshe Landau, Zvi Berenson, Chaim Cohen, and Eliahu Manni. The public and the media kept careful watch, first over the preparations and later the actual proceedings. All agreed that this was a difficult trial and that its outcome could have far-reaching consequences for the State of Israel and the Jewish people as a whole.

Some had argued that the court had no options; any decision would create problems of its own. A verdict that Oswald Rufeisen was a Jew would no doubt lead to worldwide Jewish opposition, even outrage. On the other hand, if the court concluded that the plaintiff was not a Jew, this too would result in unfavorable reactions from the non-Jews who would then accuse Israel of being a theocratic country. Finally, should the judges state that they cannot make a decision, this would translate into a moral defeat. In this last instance the court and the judges would have been accused of moral weakness.[14]

When the trial began it was clear that the issue the judges were facing was "not whether Rufeisen is a Jew, but more importantly, what is implied in the concept of Jew in the Law of Return, whether it also included a Jew who gave up his religion and converted to Christianity but feels and sees himself as a Jew?"[15] Thus, the summary statement of the proceedings says that "The question which the court now has to decide is: What does the word Jew in the Law of Return mean, does it also include a Jew who has changed his religion, converted to Christianity and was baptized but feels himself and sees himself a Jew in spite of his conversion."[16]

For the trial's duration, in the place reserved for the public, one could see a Carmelite monk. Each day he sat there listening attentively for hours. Oswald thinks that his robe was an expression of his openness, and as such underlined the fact that he was a Christian seeking national recognition as a Jew. He argues that had he come dressed in civilian clothes, he might have been accused of clouding the issues.

To all who had been following the proceedings of this trial, it was clear that the plaintiff enjoyed wide respect, a respect verging on admiration. Mixed in with the approval of Oswald as a person and his wartime deeds was a great deal of ambiguity about the nature and gravity of the issues under deliberation.

While setting forth his arguments, the presiding judge, Moshe Silberg, said, "the great psychological difficulty that we encounter from the beginning of this very unusual trial is . . . as Jews we owe to Oswald Rufeisen our deepest thanks. . . . We see before us a man who in the darkest years of the Holocaust, in Europe, endangered his life many times, countless times, for his Jewish brothers and carried out activities of rescue that were as brave and courageous as literally throwing himself into a lion's den against the Nazis. How can we deny such a person his deepest quest in life to completely fuse with the people that he loves and to become a citizen?

On the other hand, the judge added that "Father Daniel is really asking of us to cross out (nullify) the historical sanctified meaning of the word Jew and to completely turn our backs on the spiritual values for which we have been giving our lives daily. At different periods of our long exile, among the nations."[17]

The tone of Judge Landau's statement was similar when he said, "I appreciate the plaintiff's desire to help us build Israel, I respect his motives and his deeds of courage in the past. But there is still an objective element that makes it impossible for us to grant him his request."[18]

Judge Manni referred to Oswald as "a wondrous man who is not chasing after material gains, his desire for possessions is nonexistent. He was born as a Jew, grew up, suffered as one, and even when he fell into the arms of Christianity he did not despise his people. . . . His deeds of courage proved this and that in his own consciousness he remained a Jew nationally."[19]

In the end, these and other expressions of approval did not add up to a favorable verdict. The only one who accepted Oswald's claim was Judge Chaim Cohen. He said, "If the plaintiff's religion was not Christian nobody would have doubted his Jewishness. Just because he belongs to another religion the government has decreed that he is not Jewish. What one must understand from this declaration is that we have no doubt as to the wholeheartedness of the plaintiff when he announces that he is a Jew and that he is sincere about it. The only stumbling block on his road is the fact that he adheres to another religion. . . . Since the declaration of the plaintiff that he is a Jew was accepted as a sincere wholehearted declaration and was supported by the evidence that was in front of the Minister of the Interior and in front of us . . . it is apparent that the plaintiff is entitled to receive an immigrant's certificate according to the Law of Return and to be written down as having a Jewish nationality in the citizen's census. I would make this court injunction stay and would vote that it is unlawful to withhold from him the citizenship."[20]

Out of the five judges, four voted against Oswald's request. Judge Berenson presented the final opinion stating that "a Jew who changed his religion cannot be counted as a Jew in the sense and the spirit that the Knesset (Parliament) meant in the Law of Return and as it is accepted among our people today. I don't think that we the judges have the permission to be the pioneers in front of this whole nation and decide that which would be happening in the years to come. The law follows in the footsteps of life. Life does not follow in the footsteps of the law."[21]

The issues at stake in this trial were not put to rest. A 1970 law states that a Jew is a person born to a Jewish mother or a person converted to the

Jewish religion and is not affiliated with another religion.[22] Arguments still continue.

Oswald never challenged the court's decision. On the contrary, his voice was conspiciously absent from discussions that disapproved of the verdict. Hilel Seidel, who always stood by his friend, was pleased by the complete lack of bitterness in Oswald's reactions to the trial.

Much later, when Father Daniel was asked to comment on the outcome of his case in a 1984 television program, he said, "I received the decision with pain. But since it is a decision made by the High Court of Israel, I have no choice . . . I cannot ask for things that people will not give me."[23] In a more private conversation he explained, *The fact that I insisted on going to the highest court in Israel was a weakness based on inadequate information. Back then I was surer of myself than now. I went to the High Court convinced that I was right. Today I think that going to court was a mistake.*

Both the trial and the issues it represented made a deep impression on Oswald. Over the years he has been trying to explain and reanalyze this event. Only very recently he wrote, "At the time I had acted like a missionary full of passion, not very reasonably. Such issues and principles should be settled through people's hearts and not through the courts. I refused to see it this way. . . . At the time, out of naivete I did not see in Christianity 'another religion,' neither did I understand that had my position been accepted this would have created a revolution in conventional concepts. Nor did I realize that the courts are not the proper forums for changing social concepts."[24]

Shortly after the trial Oswald Rufeisen became an Israeli citizen. Never again did he publicly claim Jewish nationality. He had accepted the verdict of the High Court without, however, giving up the principle that had prompted him to go to court in the first place.

Recently he wrote, "I am just an Israeli. Jewish national belonging was denied to me, rightly or wrongly. In my identity card, opposite the word 'nationality' it says 'turn to page 10' where the all-powerful official wrote 'Nationality: Not clear.' The same official decides not only who is Jewish and who is not Jewish, but also who is Hungarian, Russian, etc., in accordance with the nationality of the mother, as if the Law of Halacha (Religious Law) is the only factor in the world deciding to which nation a person belongs. The Jewish father, even if he brought his children to Israel to give them a home and a sense of national belonging, is considered irrelevant."[25]

Oswald's legal challenge had some unanticipated but far-reaching consequences. The wide media coverage of the trial propelled Father Daniel into the limelight of Israeli society. He has become both a national personality, a national hero, and a highly sought after lecturer.

18

An Independent Life

The beginnings of the Carmelite order are traced to the twelfth-century crusaders, some of whom settled on the western slopes of Mount Carmel in what is now Israel. Imitating the life of the prophet Elijah, these men lived like hermits in the grottos of that mountain. Both the name and location of the first Carmelite monasteries were associated with Elijah's life. Officially recognized as an order in the thirteenth century, the Carmelites are devoted to the worship of the Virgin Mary and to the memory of the prophet Elijah.

Over the centuries, because of political unrest, several of their cloisters were destroyed. Each recreated structure was located on Mount Carmel, close to and around the site that is said to have witnessed the contest between the prophet Elijah and the prophets of Baal.[1]

Stella Maris, the place Rufeisen came to, was built in the nineteenth century at a spot identified as prophet Elijah's grotto. Part of this monastery became a church and another part is used as living quarters. This building stands at the top of a hill overlooking the harbor of Haifa. To approaching boats it is visible for miles.

Stella Maris welcomes tourists but restricts access to the monks' living quarters. When I expressed an interest in visiting one of the cells, the guide, a Carmelite monk, explained that because I was a woman my request could not be granted. Then he added that the only two women who were permitted into this section of the monastery were the Queen of Belgium and Golda Meir, the prime minister of Israel.

Except for Józiek Rakócz, who came once to Stella Maris, Oswald's other Jewish friends had no direct contact with his religious life. However, lack of factual information had not prevented them from voicing their opinions. For example, Hilel Siedel speculates that: *At first, the local church mistrusted Oswald. They thought that he was working for the Israeli government . . . right now I think that he is number one in the monastery. But it is hard to get out of Oswald personal information. This is the nature of the cloister: not to brag. He does not talk much about his own activities.*

Józiek Rakocz adds: *I am not sure if in the monastery all of them approve of what he is doing. We know that here, among the Catholics, there are many who hate Israel. But he does not tell about this. In general, he does not speak badly about others. Personally, I cannot point to anything about Oswald that I could criticize. Of course, when it comes to religious matters we part company.*

Oswald's other Jewish friends talk about his religious life in similar ways. Rarely, if ever, based on facts, their comments are a mixture of affection, sadness, and a perception of difficulties. It is hard to tell how much of this anticipation of problems comes from an underlying conviction that Jews who turn to Catholicism must face hardships and how much of it is real.

Israeli journalists who had access to Oswald's living quarters at Stella Maris agree that, like other monks, he occupies a modest cell. It is furnished sparingly with a narrow bed, a wooden table, a chair, and a shelf of books. One of the corners holds a sink with cold running water. Everything in his cell is in disarray, books, clothes, papers. One can even find a valise there.[2] A cross hangs over the bed. On another wall is a plaque that says "God give me the patience to fix the things I cannot fix, the courage to fix the things that I can fix, and the wisdom to differentiate between them."[3]

Oswald's friend Stefi sees him as *not materialistic at all. Possessions have no meaning for him. Money was never important to him. He would always give it away.* His civilian clothes, worn for years, attest to a disinterest in luxuries. The simplicity of Oswald's physical surroundings is compatible with his modest needs.

When it comes to freedom of expression and fulfillment through work, he seems much more demanding. The moment Oswald arrived in Stella Maris he made sure everyone around him knew who he was. He introduced himself as a Jew of Catholic religion. Unusual as such a position was, it did not always meet with approval or understanding. Of the fifteen monks who live in the monastery, some view him as odd. To most of them, his ideas seem revolutionary. Still others conclude that anyone making such claims is a heretic. In fact, to this day, one of the monks refuses to return Father Daniel's greetings. (As a priest Oswald is called Father, as a monk, Brother.) When talking about these signs of disapproval, Oswald chuckles. He tends to be amused rather than upset and continues to concentrate on the freedom and independence he has been enjoying at Stella Maris.

At more serious moments, Oswald recognizes that his presence at Stella Maris must be disturbing to some of his Brothers. For this he apologizes, explaining that he had entered the monastery not because he was attracted to this kind of life but rather because he thought that, unhampered by family and other secular obligations, life in a monastery would provide the proper framework for his work. He knows that he is different and believes these differences have led to some tension. He elaborates, *Some of my problems derive from the fact that being a monk, I also work within the framework of the Church. Here, the Church is very traditional, very conservative. It is a church closely associated with Arab circles. . . . My views and the views of the hierarchy are often incompatible. If, for example, the superior in the monastery is strong, if he is a man with a broad outlook, he understands my position, then I have support from him. If, however, there is a superior who comes, let us say, from far away, and thinks that he knows best, then I have difficulties and I try to stay away. Every three years the superior in our monastery changes. Somehow I have to juggle, or there is a struggle.*

I don't have any official function. I am not paid by anyone, not by the church nor the monastery. For all the years here, I have not received a penny. Not from the bishop, not from the monastery, not from the local parish. They each look upon my entire work as a hobby.

Oswald insists that lack of an official function and position was a deliberate choice because *if you are part of the authority structure you must follow a line. You don't have the freedom to act. . . . When I was the first time in the Vatican, at a reception that John Paul II gave for Poles, I felt sorry for him because to me he seemed like a prisoner of a system. Here I thought was a man who loved freedom and movement and he became controlled by a system. I may have more leeway and have a greater impact than someone whose position is set.*

Following a similar line of reasoning, Oswald is convinced that Cardinal Lustiger's effectiveness is limited. He argues that by becoming a cardinal and hence a part of the establishment, Lustiger, a convert who identifies himself as a Jew, gave up his independence and with it the freedom to act, especially on behalf of the Jewish people.[4]

As for his own situation, Oswald says that *with time, between me and my monastery, there developed a silent understanding, a gentlemen's agreement . . . I don't know whether I should be proud of it or not, but I have complete freedom. I act in accordance with my conscience. . . . And, as it sometimes happens, when at issue are the Abbot's orders, we both have another Superior. I do what He asks me to do.*

Oswald starts his day at five o'clock in the morning with a cold water wash. This is followed by prayer and breakfast. At six he might be conducting Mass, either beyond the city of Haifa, or in a local church at the bottom of the hill. In this church Oswald also has an office consisting of a small room with a table, two chairs, and a cabinet that holds an array of books and papers. When Father Daniel does not travel, this is where people can reach him by phone or in person.

In part, Oswald's very presence in this country is associated with certain historical developments and with a special group. He explains, *Before I left Poland, my superior received a letter that told about the necessity of having in Israel someone who knew Polish and who could take care of the spiritual needs of Polish Catholics. At that time in Israel there were thousands of Polish Catholic women and only one priest who spoke Polish. They were lost. When I arrived, I thought that only these Poles were in need of pastoral guidance and I concentrated on their welfare. Later on, I met Bulgarians, Czechoslovakians, Rumanians, and other European Christians who were in a similar predicament. Eventually, as I worked with these people, I found Hebrew as a common language for all of them. From this grew the idea of a Hebrew church. This was a gradual evolutionary development.*

Most of these European Christians were a part of religiously mixed couples. Though married to Jews, some wished to retain their own religion. Oswald's concern about these Catholics heightened when he realized that *the Jewish state did not quite know how to deal with them. The uncertainty that these newcomers were facing interfered with my sense of justice.*

Even now, an ambiguity in the position of these Christians persists. In part, it can be traced to the local Catholic hierarchy. The church in Israel has shown little interest in and concern for such Christians. Rather, the Catholic officials in this country devote their efforts to Arabs. But precisely because no one seemed to care about these special Catholics, Oswald considered it his duty to step in.

When he began to work among them he realized that a monk's robe might offend the Jewish members of these families. He applied to the bishop for permission to wear civilian clothes. As a result, he very rarely puts on the official attire of the Carmelites. Looking back, Oswald notes that *with time the relationship between these Christians and the Jews improved. Of these particular Catholics some have turned to Judaism. Some have left the country. Still others became fully absorbed into the Israeli society. Children born to such mixed couples seem particularly well-suited for life in Israel. Maybe this is the fruit of our labors?*

Oswald's efforts on behalf of Christians with European origin include more than just spiritual and religious guidance. He explains, *Though a non-Jew in this country is not persecuted, he or she has less help from the community than a Jew. I try to fill in the gap. Sometimes these people come to us with their financial problems. When this happens, we send them to governmental institutions.*

If they cannot get a loan there, but the need is real, we lend them the funds. At times, they return what they had borrowed and add some extra money to it. But I never ask for this. Neither do I ask for interest. I don't want to. I am not a bank. If a person cannot pay back, then she or he does not. If, however, a person does not want to return a loan but can, then I go to court. For all the years here, I had to do it only three times. I look upon the funds we have as the property of all our people and upon the entire operation as a communal undertaking. As it is, I am the spiritual guide for all non-Arab Christians who live in the northern part of this country, and I do what I can for them.

Recently I gave a loan to a Polish woman whose husband, a Jew, died, and she did not have enough money for a gravestone in the Jewish cemetery. Or there is a man who breeds goats and sells the milk. He had to buy a new refrigerator. I loaned him $2000 without interest.

Józiek Rakocz is eager to expand on these stories. A dentist in the town of Hedera, he had a patient, a male nurse, who was married to a Catholic woman. Rakocz tells about a conversation he had with this patient who said, *"My wife is a seamstress. In Hedera she has no work. If I could move to a bigger city my wife could find some work." One day he came to tell me the good news: "I live in Haifa now." When I asked how this happened, he said: "There is a Jew here who is also a priest, and he lent us the money to move to Haifa." This man did not even know that I knew Oswald, his benefactor. To give you another example, once I met Oswald with two women in Hedera. So I asked, "What are you doing here." He said: "I am going to the Department of Health." "Why?" He explained: "A Christian woman lived all alone. The neighbors found her a few days after her death. I have to arrange the burial and take care of the formalities." . . . He is only concerned about other people's welfare. . . . There is no end to such stories!*

When he talks to me about the children of mixed marriages, he becomes enthusiastic and says, "I want to make out of them good Israeli citizens and have them contribute to this country." If this was another Catholic priest, a large proportion of these children might have grown up hating Israel. This is the truth. There is no doubt that he identifies with Israel and supports it. His private problem, of course, is his religion. But despite his religion, he is an Israeli patriot and a wonderful friend.

When I asked where the money comes from to cover his charitable activities Oswald told me that since his arrival in Israel neither the church nor the monastery had contributed any funds. In fact, whenever he conducts a mass in Haifa, all parishioner donations go directly to the church. But Oswald found a way of earning money. For more than twenty years, he has been working as a guide for pilgrims and Christian tourists. From what they have been paying him he kept only a fraction, mainly to cover the expenses of his car. Part of the earnings he donated to the monastery. The bulk he kept for his charities and loans.

As Oswald's activities continued to expand, he had to give up the job as a tourist guide. Some of his income has been replaced by private donations. People to whom Oswald had shown Israel send him contributions. One German woman mails one hundred marks each month. Donations continue to arrive, even though Oswald never solicits them. In addition, funds were left from past earnings. Careful accounts are kept and people are asked to sign each loan. Sometimes the yearly sums of these loans reach the $25,000 level.

Oswald's busy schedule takes him also to an old age home, the Dr. Gertrude Luckner Home in Naharyah, named in honor of a German Christian who during World War II risked her life to save Jews and Poles. This home was established with German funds, set aside for non-Jews who were persecuted by the Nazis. Later, contributions also came from the Bishops Conference in Germany and from private sources.

Most of those who live in the Luckner Home are righteous Christians. They come from different European countries: Poland, Hungary, Bulgaria, Holland, and others. Most are women who arrived in Israel with Jewish husbands. When the men died, they felt lonely and were accepted into the home.

These people pay what and if they can. The rest is covered by the Israeli Department of Social Welfare. Run as a family, the home has twelve to fifteen residents. The ages of these residents range from seventy-five to ninety-six. They live within well-kept surroundings and with a bathroom attached to each room.

Every Monday, Oswald comes to conduct Mass, usually in Polish, Hebrew, and German. In addition to the weekly Mass, he offers individual spiritual guidance to all the residents.

For years, Oswald had benefited from the help of Elisheva Hemher, who is also a close friend. A Catholic, Elisheva came to Israel from Germany in 1962. With the title of a pastoral assistant, she is officially employed by the Catholic Church in Israel, but is paid by the bishop from Münster, Germany. Oswald talks about Elisheva's contributions with pride and credits her with the establishment of the Dr. Luckner Home. He was pleased to tell me that recently the German government saw fit to bestow on her a distinguished first class Cross of Merit for services rendered to the country.

Oswald's involvement with the Luckner Home, the non-Arab Christians, and his many speaking engagements keep him away from Stella Maris. He feels indebted to the monastery for his freedom and for his food and shelter. To repay these benefits, three times a year Oswald shows the country to two sets of Stella Maris guests. One is a group of international students who come each year from the seminary in Rome. They stay for approximately two months. Half of the time they spend traveling around the country with Father Daniel as their guide.

The other set of Stella Maris guests are Carmelite Brothers who come to spend part of their sabbaticals, five to six months. Oswald finds these visitors stimulating and enjoys traveling and explaining the country to them.

Though in Oswald's case the monastery offers a wide range of freedoms, he does recognize the overall limitations of a monastic life and points to problems that might be peculiar in his place. *At Stella Maris we come from different countries with different backgrounds. We don't select each other. Only by chance do we come here together. For this reason alone, it is hard to find and develop friendships. In a way too, in a cloister each of us lives a separate life. Maybe each dies alone? A person that has a need for close friendships and attachments finds this kind of a situation confining . . . compared to other features of monastic life, perhaps the social aspects are the most difficult to take. It might be even harder to adjust to these special social conditions than to the basic requirement for worship and obedience. . . . All of us, including myself, enter a monastery and agree to live with people whom we did not choose. . . . In marriage people find each other, they marry out of love, and despite this there are conflicts, crises, divorces.*

When I want to enter a monastery, I am accepted only after a while. During the waiting period I try to adjust. I make an effort to show my good side in order to pass all the tests. Later I may not fit. One may be thrown out, but for this to happen there have to be very serious reasons. . . . At Stella Maris, in particular, there are people with very different values and with very different pasts.

In the monastery in Poland the monks were more homogenous, they did not come from a variety of countries. Some of the monks have lived here for twenty-five years, and they got used to my peculiarities, to my "craziness." But others, the new arrivals, some of whom do come at the age of seventy, might have problems. How can they adjust to this country? To my work? To my special position? . . .

A newspaperman once asked one of our brothers if he had friends in the monastery. He answered that a real monk cannot have friends. But I feel that it is impossible to relate only to God. If you don't like people, then you don't like God either. Oswald loves the world and not only the cross.[5]

Aware that he lives in tolerant times, Oswald, nevertheless, says that for a Jew who becomes a monk, life in a cloister can be especially trying. He knows, for example, that both within the monastery and the church he is still called "the convert." For the reasons he had mentioned, unless a monk has compensations, either in the form of absorbing work or close friendships, his life might be burdensome, at times leading to serious psychological complications.

He does not think that such difficulties apply to him personally, saying, *I feel good in the monastery. I have no problems. I have a great deal of freedom. It is impossible to work continuously as hard as I do. One can get very exhausted. Here I can hide. I can rest. From time to time, I must refill my energy. Stella Maris allows me to do that.*

This overall contentment, however, did not prevent Oswald from admitting during a newspaper interview that, at times, he misses the love of a woman, the love of a child, even sex.[6]

Following up on these themes, I asked, "You were quoted as saying that you longed for a woman, a child, sex. Do you?" The answer was, *Of course I do. Fortunately, I remained a normal person. One part of being normal consists of having sexual desires. In this respect, the vows to the church involve a sacrifice that lasts for years, actually as long as the instinct exists. This is an acceptable sacrifice if I have a compensation for it in the form of a close friendship, a closeness of the soul to God. This can happen with someone of the opposite sex, too. I had such close friendships in Poland and I have them here. Such compensations make the sacrifices easier to bear, but they do not eliminate the problems. Close friendships only ease the situation, including the condition of celibacy.*

Celibacy itself makes sense only if it is for a certain reason, for a goal. I, for example, am not sorry. I don't regret that I decided to be celibate. I don't regret it because celibacy offers me a certain freedom which otherwise I would have never had. I have freedom to act. I come back home almost everyday at 11 or 12 at night. I am continuously among people. I feel good about my way of life. Without celibacy I could not have had this independence. Besides, at the moment I am not even sure I have enough money for gasoline. Somehow, I can rely on God that at the time of need I will receive money. The monastery is not concerned whether I have money or not. No one asks me. But if I had a wife and children, I would have had to worry first of all about them. So I would not have had the kind of freedom that I have. . . . in my case the balance tipped in favor of my inner life, the life of prayer and so forth. But perhaps I have no right to make this last point? Someone living in a marriage can also have this kind of an inner life. There is no impurity in marriage, there is no impurity in sexual life.

I asked, "Why do you think that in your case the Church won?" With a chuckle, Oswald answered, *I am not so sure the Church won . . . there are many Christians who see in me a wolf, an enemy of the Church. I have even "friends," priests of Jewish origin, who are not speaking to me.*

"But," I continued, "in the choice between sex and family on the one hand, and religion, priesthood and the monastery life on the other, obviously the Church won. Why?"

Oswald said: *Like everybody here I am not an exception. What you are asking applies to everybody. Because of the issue of celibacy there is a crisis in the USA. Because of this issue many gave up priesthood, even the Church. Such priests should have continued being priests, under different circumstances. It is more important to retain a person's natural inclinations; it is not right to go against it. Natural inclinations have more rights than promises, than vows. The vows are my selection, my choice, but my nature is given by God. The Church has no right to break human nature.*

So a person, in order not to break his own nature, not to become an abnormal or a pathological type, leaves the order and even priesthood. He does this because he has no other alternative because if he marries he cannot be a priest any more. At that point he leaves everything. This is not right. I don't accept this. In this case, I do not blame the person. I blame the Church. The Church should not forbid such an individual to continue performing the functions of a priest. Of course, if he has special reasons for not wanting to be a priest, this is a different matter. A man should be able to do that. If he does, he should be compensated for all those years he had worked for the Church. First of all there are human rights.

My next question was, "Do you think that this right should apply to others who are so inclined but not to you?"

Oswald's reaction was again preceded by a chuckle: *I am not facing this dilemma . . . in a way, in my case, it was a "package deal." When you make a package deal, you accept things that are also unpleasant because you focus on something else. I am satisfied, both with my celibate state and the situation that exists in my monastery. I must say that my Brothers at Stella Maris show tolerance toward me. I have no real trouble from them even though practically all my life takes place outside of the monastery. Despite this they treat me with consideration.*

In a less serious vein, half-jokingly, Oswald told me that if the bishop would have given him permission, he might have married. But then he added that, for sure, no woman would have him. He explained that his total preoccupation with people and the life around him could not be tolerated by a woman. But even this light comment he finished by emphasizing that he feels free and independent and that only the monastery gives him peace and a proper perspective on life.

Oswald's activities have been guided by two closely related goals. One has to do with the return to Christianity of some of its historically lost features, its universality. The second aims at creating a bridge between Christianity and Judaism, or, as Oswald prefers to say, at repairing the relationship between Jews and Jesus. He is convinced that a group like the Hebrew Christians could play a major part in the fulfillment of these aims. Through these Hebrew Christians, Oswald wants to recreate the early Jewish Church that had strong ties to Judaism.

Who are the Hebrew Christians? Oswald points to a continuity between his ideas and some developments that have been taking place in Israel. When Oswald came to this country, he had met a few theologians, monks, and priests who called themselves the St. James group. St. James was one of the original apostles who later became the head of the first

Judeo-Christian Church. The stated aim of this modern day group was the establishment of a dialogue between Christianity and Judaism. Oswald says that *those who initiated the St. James group did not know about its further developments that instead of remaining Roman Catholic Christians, we will try to restore Hebrew Christianity as it existed at the beginning. In a sense then I entered a stream that was here before me. Some of us have Jewish backgrounds, some are non-Jews. In Israel we try to create a homogenous community made up of Hebrew praying Christians that resembles the early Christian Jews.*

The establishment of this early Christianity, Oswald feels, would ultimately restore to the entire church its universality and unity. *For right now the entire Catholic Church finds itself in a dead-end street. We talk about the unity of Christians but we don't have a key for it. The Jews took the key and put it into their pockets. We talk about Christian universalism, but Israel has the key for this universalism. Every new acculturation has to start with Jerusalem.*

Why? Because early Christianity was Jewish. Then simultaneously, almost simultaneously, after twenty to thirty years, there emerged Greek Christianity. There was a coexistence. There was also a coexistence between early Jewish Christianity and Judaism. The Christians prayed in synagogues. There were Christian cantors. There was no great break between them. The Jews did not see the Christians as dangerous. With time, after perhaps three generations, differences began to emerge. Still there was coexistence. We have in Jerusalem graves where from the same family Jews and Christians are buried (second century). . . . This kind of a church existed till the fourth century.

In the fourth century the non-Jewish Church became so strong, became so connected to the Roman Empire, that it recognized its Greek-Roman form as the only form. In the present Church, right now there is no place for the Jewish Church. A Jew that joins the Church disappears. There is no such thing as a Jewish entity in the Church. The Christianity that exists now is not Jewish but Greek. Indeed, from the fourth century on, Christianity became the religion of the empire. When it felt well integrated into the Greek environment, it eliminated forcefully all the Jewish currents. From the fourth century on, for practical purposes, the Jewish part ceased to exist. This current made its reappearance in Islam, which is an interpretation of the Judeo-Christian form of religion . . . I see in this a tremendous possibility for future dialogue into three directions: Judaism, Islam, and Christianity.

My idea is to fight for a return to pluralism in the Church, with the hope that in Judeo-Christianity there will also be a return to pluralism. Somehow the two tendencies of pluralism will allow for the creation of a church that will have a Jewish character. The Church as it is now is not capable of accepting pluralism.

Oswald equates pluralism with tolerance, with peaceful coexistence. Identifying the Hebrew Christians as the early Jewish Christian Church, recently he wrote, "I see it as our duty to revive this Christianity, notwithstanding all those who oppose it, for the sake of historical justice and also in order to correct a wrong within Christianity, in order to liberate it from the one and almost exclusive cultural embrace of 1600 years."[7]

The problem, Oswald admits, *is will it be possible, after so many centuries, to restore Jewish Christianity, not only in order to save the Jew who is becoming a Christian, but to restore to the Church its universality? Because of the absence of Jewish Christianity, today's Christianity lacks universality and continuity. There is a break between the Hebrew bible and the teachings of the Greek and Latin Fathers (fourth–fifth century).*

Still, Oswald is not quite sure what special characteristics this Christianity should take. He is not certain which Jewish elements should be restored. He is convinced that it should contain a love of human beings and not only the love of the cross.[8] Oswald and his friend Jochanan Elichai, a monk who belongs to the congregation of the Little Brothers of Jesus, agree that the Catholic religion might benefit from some changes. They both feel, for example, that the worship of saints verges on idolatry and is not an essential part of their religion. Jochanan suggests that *anti-idolatry of the Jews could, in fact, be beneficial for Christianity. It would be better for Christianity to give up idolatry.*

The fact that Oswald conducts Mass in Hebrew is already a departure from traditional Catholic worship. He rarely crosses himself and during services refrains from mentioning the Holy Trinity. Though it is customary when conducting Sunday Mass to read the Profession of Faith, Oswald says, *You have to recite the Creed every Sunday. I do not do that. My faith is not in the revealed truths but in the faith in God. I am on the way to restore Jewish Christianity where these things did not exist.*[9] He also thinks that the Church should be more concerned with social justice here on earth. He feels that Catholics focus too much on the second coming of Christ and tend to neglect issues that bear on equity among people. He also believes that Christianity could benefit from the Jewish emphasis on the family and that its present emphasis on celibacy creates a wedge between the clergy and its lay public.

Without imposing its values on any other part, Oswald hopes that a newly recreated Hebrew Church could lead to the reestablishment of Christian universalism. He dreams and argues, *On what does Christian universalism depend? It depends on the fact that in every country Christian religion must feel at home. An African cannot accept the European Christianity. The Church must adapt to the particular surrounding in which it exists. It should not impose on other countries the Roman interpretation. The Church does not have to be centralized. The only binding force can be the early Church. The original Church. This was Jewish Christianity.*

Asked why anyone should welcome the early Jewish Church, he says, *Because Christianity belongs to Judaism. The Jewish Church itself no one has an obligation to accept. And so, Paul fought for the right to accept Christianity not in the Jewish form, without circumcision, without rituals, without Saturdays, without Jewish holidays. The relation of God to the creation of man Paul adopted to the situation in Greece. But why would there be a Roman Catholic Church in South America? There should have been an Aztec or Mayan Church in South America and not a Roman.* He is convinced that this acculturation *would have to start from the initial stage, the source, the one that existed originally: the Jewish stage.*[10]

Right now Oswald guides the Hebrew Christians. He said, "We have registered in Haifa the 'Society of Hebrew Christians in Israel' and the Diaspora whose purpose is stated as being 'the religious and social reconstruction and advancement of the Hebrew Christians in Israel.' The Ministry of Interior approved this registration."[11]

Almost simultaneously, the Hebrew Christians have established their own community center in Haifa. The bishop in Israel was irritated when he heard that the Hebrew Christians were recognized by the government. Oswald feels he objected to the title "Christian." He would have preferred "Catholic" substituted. A more general name was chosen because not all those who belong to the Hebrew Christians are Catholic.

As for the bishop's reaction, Oswald says, *He is not against me personally, only against some of the things I stand for. When I meet him he is friendly. He opposes my line. It does not seem to him orthodox enough. It is all political. If you agree and accept the concept of Hebrew Christians, you must consider the return of the Jews to this country. . . . We, as a group, take seriously the fact that we have presently three times as many Jews as in the time of Jesus. . . . The bishop would prefer to have here an Arab society and Jews as strangers. After all, the bishop is an Arab and it would be better for all of us to have someone else.*

Still, the local church never took any steps against the Hebrew Christians or Oswald. Perhaps this noninterference can be explained by Father Daniel's ties to the Vatican. John Paul II and Oswald had met in Cracow after the war. Oswald's attitudes toward this Pope are a mixture of admiration and occasional patches of criticism. For example, he regrets that, as a conservative, the present Pope might be reluctant to institute necessary Church reforms. When it comes to the Church's position toward the Jews and Israel, Oswald's reactions are consistent. Arieh Rufeisen knows that his brother *is convinced that the time has come for the Vatican to recognize Israel. At the same time, he sees the Polish Pope as a holy father, more pro-Israel than those who were before him.*

When a few years ago the Pope was to meet with Arafat, Oswald had sent a cable begging John Paul II not to receive him. He argued that such a meeting would inevitably be detrimental to Israel. This plea remained unanswered. Not only did the pontiff receive Arafat, but he embraced him in public. Despite this rebuff and the Vatican's persistent refusal to recognize

Israel, Oswald continues to say that this Pope will improve the Church's relationship to the Jews and Israel. Whenever he is confronted with a Vatican anti-Jewish or anti-Israel move, he argues that this Pope would have liked to act differently, but for reasons beyond his power cannot.

On the other hand, Oswald is not afraid to disagree with the pontiff publicly. For instance, he recalls that John Paul II once said that " 'the Church breathes with two lungs: with Eastern and Western lungs.' If this is how it is, then I don't have a place in this Church. This is the case not only for me but also for Africans, for the Japanese, etc. I have my own lungs that breathe."[12]

And yet one of the most significant highlights in Father Daniel's life was a 1984 visit to the Vatican and an audience with John Paul II. In the course of their conversation, Israel came up only once and at the explicit suggestion of the pontiff. In this connection, Oswald reports asking *"Isn't it strange that three years after the Jews were almost totally eliminated, the Jewish nation came into being? Don't you see in this an expression of higher justice that eventually somehow evens out everything?" To this the Pope said: "No doubt." I continued: "If the Church teaches about this justice on earth based on the bible, isn't it sad that the same Church, as a state, will be the last country that will recognize the Jews' right to a state?" To this there was silence. Only the secretary who was present said, "But it moves in this direction."*

About the meeting itself Oswald says, *The Pope would not have spoken to me for an hour and a half if he would not have found it interesting. Heads of States he receives for only twenty or forty minutes. I was not alone. His secretary was also present. . . . I told him about things that for sure no Pope had heard for eighteen centuries. In a nice way, in a loyal way, but in a way that a free man communicates with another free man. It was almost a communication between partners. I was representing another Church. I was representing the Hebrew Church, which does not exist yet officially, but which did exist, which was the mother of this Church. Actually, it is also mine. When could I have dreamed about such a situation?*

What did Oswald expect from the conservative John Paul II? *I went to the Pope with different Church matters, not to ask him for anything, only to inform him. He should know. He listened to me. He did not excommunicate me for these ideas . . . I expect nothing from him. I don't ask him for anything. The changes will come from us, not from him. We have to do it. The Pope cannot tell us what is good here. We must find a way and then he can try and decide what to do with us. This is his business. It is clear that we are right. I have no doubt that we are. The problem is to find a balance in this process, not to hurt anyone, not to become conceited. Initially, the early Jewish Church suffered from some conceit. They were somewhat elitist.*

Recognizing that, as a group, the Hebrew Christians are tolerated in the church rather than accepted, Oswald would certainly welcome an official approval by the church. This becomes clear from his following statement. *In the fourth century, this early Christianity was suppressed. I am not accusing anyone. However, a new situation emerged now. With the establishment of the state of Israel, we have a right to receive back our position within the Church. Only then could we become the bridge. Only we, because here we have the Jewish connection. We speak the same language. The Church is incapable of talking to the Jews because it does not share the same theological language and the culture we do. That is why all kinds of things are happening at the Vatican in relation to Jews. They take a step forward and then two steps backward only because they do not know the language. They think that they speak in a language accepted by Jews, yet at the same moment, they insult them. We are the ones who could develop a dialogue, but no one asks us now because we do not mean very much. This is something that worries me. We do not mean much because we are not a part of the establishment, we are not a part of the hierarchy.*

As if to counteract his own pessimism, Oswald says that *the Vatican now, for the first time, said that in the flock of the new patriarch here (last year a new patriarch was elected), 15% are not of Arabic origin. This amounts to about 10,000. But not all belong to the Hebrew Church. Some do, some do not. There might be 8000 of those who do not feel this new phenomenon. But you see, up till now, the Vatican thought that our group of Hebrew Christians consists only of a few hundred people. There might be 2000 who actually belong to our group. They could function as a starting point for the establishment of a dialogue with Judaism.*

Oswald emphasizes over and over that the Hebrew Christians do not proselytize and that the appropriate home for their brand of Christianity is Israel. Asked if there is any resemblance or connection between the Hebrew Christian and the Jews for Jesus he says, *Those Jews for Jesus are today's Jews in the U.S. with present-day ideas about Jesus as represented by the different Protestant not churches but sects. And I am neither an American Jew nor a Protestant Jew. I am a universal Christian. I have to find a way to restore Christianity that was and still is Jewish. This was another kind of Christianity. This is our problem here, in this country.* Oswald was reluctant to talk about Jews for Jesus.[13]

Oswald's objections and criticism apply to the Jewish religion as well. He is convinced that Judaism, like Christianity, could benefit from a pluralistic approach to religion. He feels *sad, sad that the born-again Jew today can only be a Yeshiva man. I would want more (alternatives), more possibilities. Either the Jewish religion will reform itself or it will ruin this country. I don't want this country to be ruined. Go to the parliament and listen to what is going on there. What is the connection between airplane flights on Saturday and Judaism?*

He insists that *Israel as a country cannot continue with the present religious form that developed in an abnormal situation in the Diaspora. This form of Judaism strangles us all the time, it destroys us. For example, the religious people have to give their approval about operating on heart patients, whether to give them a heart of another person!*

Oswald becomes upset whenever some ultrareligious elements engage in what he sees as outrageous acts. This happened when a group of Orthodox Jews removed the body of a Christian woman who was buried in a Jewish cemetery. The woman, Teresa Angielewicz, was buried as a Jew. When these religious fanatics discovered that she was Christian, they took it on themselves to unearth her.[14]

All such criticisms and objections are easily overshadowed by Oswald's love for Israel. Whenever he shows the country to Christian tourists, he always refers to the Israelis as "we," never "they." About his Israeli ties, he says, "I love this country, from the problem of its water resources and the joy of its blessed winter, to the issues of employment and the Lavy. (He is referring to the cancellation of a large project to build a sophisticated plane that created economic hardships.) Willingly do I present my Israeli passport abroad. Everything here is mine. Once a Jew who was listening to the talk I was giving to a group of pilgrims about the view from Mount Muhraka said, 'One can feel that you love this country.' This was one of the sweetest compliments that I have heard."[15]

While Oswald objects to the excesses of some religious Jews, he is quick to emphasize that this is not what Israel stands for. The government, he insists, does not support such violations of civil liberties. On the contrary, he sees Israel as a tolerant society. For proof, he turns to his own situation and how he is being constantly invited to schools to talk to Jewish children about his life. He argues, *Can you imagine if this were the other way around, Catholics inviting a Jew? I always say that the Israelis are very tolerant people, but they don't know it. I am a Catholic priest, an apostate, and they invite me to Jewish schools to teach Jewish children about Christianity. Twice I gave lectures about Christianity to Israeli guides, for money. Each lecture was sponsored by the Tourist Department. Later these guides were told: "Be careful, because he is very persuasive. Don't accept all he is saying." And yet they keep inviting me.*

Oswald is grateful for the tolerance he is treated with and recognizes that his involvement with Israel and its people adds meaning and excitement to his life. Only after considerable prodding did he offer a glimpse of these special activities. *Last night I was invited to a kibbutz to a meeting attended by a rabbi, a Moslem, and myself to discuss the importance of Jerusalem to the three religions. I tried to get out of it because as a Christian I have no special relation to Jerusalem. I don't need Jerusalem for my faith. You can say it openly because there are different voices in the Church that disagree with me. As a Christian, I don't even need a Christian presence in Jerusalem. I can be a very good Christian without it. So I did not want to participate in this meeting, but they wanted me to come. On*

Sunday, I have a lecture in a school with Jewish youngsters. I was invited by the director of the school. I have to tell them about my life.

Next day, I will be in another kibbutz, Dalia, where I will participate in a discussion with a professor of the Tel-Aviv University and a member of the kibbutz, who belonged once to a religious collective farm. We will talk about the relationship between Christianity and Judaism. Try to find another priest in Israel who has these kinds of meetings, in the collective farms and in schools. My situation is good here. I have interesting work. I am content. Not that I am satisfied with myself, but I am grateful to God that I have such fascinating work.

Where does he think he fits best right now? *In the monastery, I am a friendly outsider. But in the State of Israel, I am not a friendly outsider. I am an insider.* At times he muses that his past might have given him the strength to face up to grave demands. About his life and himself, he says, *Sometimes I am alone. I feel lonely. But I like challenges. I am fascinated by difficult problems. I feel good with it. I want to have an interesting life. I don't want to be a plain bread eater. What I do now is most fascinating and, in a sense, more difficult than in the wartime period. Because during the war it was a question of using the opportunities as they came along. Here, now, it is a question of ideological directions and the consequences can be enormous.*

Though Oswald has a wide range of involvements, he insists that *in the center of my interest lies the success of Israel. I don't see any other future for the Jewish nation, only Israel.* His friend Seidel sees Oswald as *a Jew among Christians and not as a Christian among Jews.* He is also convinced that Oswald will return to Judaism. When I repeated this to Oswald, he smiled and said, *But how can I return? I never left!* To a journalist who also raised the issue of returning to Judaism, Oswald said, "I am all the time on my way back. Back to the source, to the beautiful period, in the faraway past before we split and removed ourselves from each other. I am sure that we will meet again."[16]

Notes

Notes to Acknowledgments

1. Oswald Rufeisen belongs to a select group of Jews who, while passing for Christians, had connections to those in power and used these connections against the Nazis for the benefit of potential victims. Besides Oswald Rufeisen, I know of four such cases. Two of them were discovered by the Nazis and murdered. See Betti Ajzensztajn, ed., *Ruch Podziemny W Ghettach I Obozach (Materiały I Dokumenty)* (*Underground Movements in Ghettoes and Camps [Materials and Documents]*) (Warsaw: Centralna Żydowska Komisja Historyczna, 1946), pp. 109–119. This collection of documents refers to two cases of Jews who during the war pretended to be German or half German and who were in a position of power. Both were known for their help to others. Of the two, one is Oswald Rufeisen, the other is Klinger (no first name mentioned). Klinger was a commandant of the German police in Łuck. His protection of Jews led to suspicion. Eventually he was recognized as a Jew by a Volksdeutsche and shot in the courtyard of his home. As two of his Jewish workers carried him into the house, he said, "Avenge my death because I am a Jew." This information comes from a testimony by Rozenfeld, No. 74 in the Jewish Historical Institute in Warsaw.

Another was a young Jew from Łódź, Zygmunt Grossbart. In 1941, he lived in the Ukraine in the region of Humania where he became an associate of the Nazi authorities. He was also a member of a partisan group. He would supply the local underground with important information and documents that served as protection for all kinds of potential victims. This case was described by Stefan Krakowski, "Partyzancki Oficer Wywiadu" (A Partisan Intelligence Officer) *Nasz Głos* Addition to *Folks Sztyme,* August 10, 1966. (In Israel Krakowski uses as his first name Shmuel and not Stefan.)

Salomon Strauss-Marko, who survived the war as a Ukrainian, was recognized by a Nazi special commission as being of pure Aryan blood. He had an important position in a camp for prisoners of war but was helping other prisoners and engaging in underground activities. After the war, he published his autobiography, *Czysta Krew* (*Pure Blood*) (Łódz: Wydawnictwo Łódzkie, 1966). He lives in Israel.

Oscar Glick posed as a Volksdeutsche in Vilna. Thanks to his initiative, a labor camp "Khailis" was created outside the ghetto that gave employment to many Jews. Glick became the manager of the camp. When Glick's Jewish identity was discovered in 1942, he and his wife were shot by the Nazis. This case is mentioned in Itzhak Arad, *Ghetto in Flames: The Struggle and Destruction of the Jews in Vilna in the Holocaust* (New York: Holocaust Library, 1982.), pp. 148–149.

2. Hilel Seidel, *Adam Bmivhan* (*The Testing of a Man*) (Tel-Aviv: Published privately by the author, 1973), pp. 88–133.

Notes to Chapter 1

1. Though his Hebrew name was Shmuel, he is known as Oswald, even in official documents. I checked the spelling of all those I interviewed and whenever it differs from the accepted form I use their personal preference. For example, Hilel Seidel's first name is usually spelled with two ls, but he writes it with one l only.

2. Of the three occupying powers Russia applied the most oppressive policies. Convinced that maintaining the Poles in a backward state would be to its advantage, Russia actively opposed any attempts by the Polish leaders to improve the country's educational, economic, and cultural life. As a result, with the exception of a relatively few rich landowners who were allowed to benefit from the status quo, as an inducement not to disturb it, most Poles in the Russian-held regions remained poor and backward. One favored device employed by the successive Tzarist regimes to help distract the mass of Poles from their deplorable plight, and deflect blame from themselves, was to lay at the feet of Poland's Jews responsibility for all the nation's problems. Together with other forces that continued to stoke the traditionally strong Polish anti-Semitism, these accusations led to periodic pogroms, which in turn brought about the destruction of Jewish life and property in eastern Poland.

In contrast to Russia, the policies of Austria and Prussia over the lands they controlled were more liberal, allowing room for Polish participation in political and cultural life. Of the two, Austria offered Poles greater freedom. Though neither the parts of Poland occupied by Austria nor those occupied by Prussia were ever free of anti-Semitism, it is nevertheless true that in these two sectors violence against the Jews was not state organized or sanctioned. In these parts of Poland there were no pogroms.

3. For interesting discussions about Poland's historical situation prior to World War II, see: Norman Davies, *Heart of Europe: A Short History of Poland* (New York: Oxford University Press, 1984); Jan Karski, *The Great Powers and Poland 1919–1945: From Versailles to Yalta* (New York: University Press of America, Inc., 1985); Antony Polonsky, *Politics in Independent Poland, 1921–1939* (Oxford: Oxford Claredon Press, 1972); Edward J. D. Wynot, *Polish Politics in Transition* (Athens: University of Georgia Press, 1974).

4. *Miasta Polskie W Tysiącleciu* (Polish Towns During a Millennium) (Kraków: Zakład Narodowy Imienia Ossolinskich, 1965), Vol I, pp. 683–684.

5. I was told this during an interview conducted with Oswald Rufeisen's cousin, Ernest Seifter, in Baltimore, in 1986.

6. From now on, whenever I quote someone without giving a footnote it means that I have interviewed this individual directly. Interviews took place between 1983–1989.

7. Arieh is his Hebrew name. While he lived in Poland, he used the name Leon. I met him in Israel as Arieh and will be referring to him by this name.

8. In an article about Oswald Rufeisen, the author, a nun, says that while he attended the school in Zadziele, he did not identify himself as a Jew. When I asked Oswald about it, he categorically denied that this was the case. Then, with a chuckle, he said that, as a good Catholic, the nun had a special need to say this. He added that in those days he always identified himself religiously as a Jew, nationally as a Pole. See S. Maria Lucyna Mistecka Cr., "Droga Oswalda Rufeisena Do Kapłańistwa" (Oswald's Road to Priesthood), *Chrześcijanin W Świecie, Zeszyty Odiss*, Vol. 69, September, 1978, p. 55.

9. This situation might be common. As a young Jewish girl in Poland, I had similar experiences. Though I lived in a Christian part of town, all my friends were Jewish. I became aware of this fact only much later, after the war. See Nechama Tec, *Dry Tears: The Story of a Lost Childhood* (New York: Oxford University Press, 1984).

10. There are different spellings of the city of Vilna: Wilno, Vilnius, Wilna. The Polish name for the city is Wilno. Here I use the frequently used version, Vilna. See Norman Davies, *God's Playground: A History of Poland* (New York: Columbia University Press, 1984), Vol II, p. 505.

Notes to Chapter 2

1. Jan Karski, *The Great Powers and Poland, 1919–1945: From Versailles to Yalta* (New York: University Press of America, Inc., 1985), p. 357.

2. Norman Davies, *Heart of Europe: A Short History of Poland* (New York: Oxford University Press, 1984), p. 129.

3. Jan Karski, *The Great Powers and Poland, 1919–1945*, pp. 391–393.

4. Ibid., pp. 72–74.

5. Norman Davies, *God's Playground: A History of Poland* (New York: Columbia University Press, 1984), Vol. 2, p. 505.

6. Yehuda Bauer, *A History of the Holocaust* (New York: Franklin Watts Inc., 1982), p. 282.

7. Norman Davies, *God's Playground*, p. 443.

8. Yitzhak Arad, *Ghetto in Flames: The Struggle and Destruction of the Jews in Vilna in the Holocaust* (New York: Holocaust Library, 1982), p. 18.

9. O. Halecki, *A History of Poland* (New York: David McKay Company, Inc., 1976), p. 315.

10. Yitzhak Arad, *Ghetto in Flames*, p. 18.

11. Yehuda Bauer, *A History of the Holocaust*, p. 283.

12. Sara Neshamit, "Rescue in Lithuania During the Nazi Occupation," p. 289 in *Rescue Attempts During the Holocaust*, Proceedings of the Second Yad Vashem International Historical Conference, 1974 (Jerusalem: Yad Vashem, 1977); "Vilna," p. 148 in *Encyclopedia Judaica* (Jerusalem: Keter Publishing House, 1971).

13. Yitzhak Arad, *Ghetto in Flames*, p. 18; Yehuda Bauer, *A History of the Holocaust*, p. 283.

14. Ibid., p. 145.

15. Those parts of Poland that were not annexed to Germany and left after the Russian occupation were referred to as General Gouvernment. The spelling of this term varies.

16. Yitzhak Arad, *Ghetto in Flames*, pp. 20–21.

17. For discussions about such forced deportations to Russia, see: Norman Davies, *God's Playground*, pp. 448–451; Jan Karski, *The Great Powers and Poland, 1919–1945*, pp. 403–463; "Lithuania," Vol. 16, pp. 385–386 in *Encyclopedia Judaica;* Franciszek J. Proch, *Poland's Way of the Cross, 1939–1945* (New York: Polish Association of Former Political Prisoners of Nazi and Soviet Concentration Camps, 1986), p. 123–139.

18. "Vilna," p. 148 in *Encyclopedia Judaica*.

19. Yitzhak Arad, *Ghetto in Flames*, p. 23.

20. Yehuda Bauer, *A History of the Holocaust*, p. 284.

21. Yitzhak Arad, *Ghetto in Flames*, p. 25.

22. Ibid., p. 24.

23. Ibid., p. 29.

24. Yitskhok Rudashevski, *The Diary of the Vilna Ghetto, June 1941–April 1943* (Israel: Ghetto Fighter's House, 1973), pp. 24–25.

25. Yitzhak Arad, *Ghetto in Flames*, pp. 31–35.

26. Raul Hilberg, *The Destruction of the European Jews* (New York: Franklin Watts, Inc., 1973), pp. 257–267; Filip Friedman, "Zagłada Żydow Polskich W Latach, 1939–1945" (Jewish Extermination in Poland, 1939–1945), *Biuletyn Głównej Komisij Badania Zbrodni Niemieckiej W Polace*, no. 6, pp. 165–208.

27. Sarah Neshamit, "Rescue in Lithuania During the Nazi Occupation," p. 293.

28. Raul Hilberg, *The Destruction of the European Jews*, p. 205.

29. Sarah Neshamit, "Rescue in Lithuania During the Nazi Occupation," p. 293.

30. Yitzhak Arad, *Ghetto in Flames*, pp. 35–38, 41.

31. Ibid., pp. 46–58.

32. Yitskhok Rudashevski, *The Diary of the Vilna Ghetto*, pp. 28–29.

Notes to Chapter 3

1. Yitzhak Arad, *Ghetto in Flames: The Struggle and Destruction of the Jews in Vilna in the Holocaust* (New York: Holocaust Library, 1982), p. 75.

2. Martin Gilbert, *The Holocaust: A History of the Jews of Europe During the Second World War* (New York: Holt, Rinehart and Winston, 1985), p. 207.

Notes to Chapter 4

1. The idea that Polish Jews were not assimilated and could easily be identified either by their speech or behavior is generally agreed on by those who have dealt with the subject. A few examples of sources where this assertion is made are: Michael Borwicz, *Les Vies Interdites* (*Forbidden Lives*) (Paris: Casterman, 1969); Celia S. Heller, *On the Edge of Destruction* (New York: Columbia University Press, 1977); Anthony Polonsky, *Politics in Independent Poland, 1921–1939* (Oxford: The Claredon Press, Oxford University, 1972); Nechama Tec, *When Light Pierced the Darkness: Christian Rescue of Jews in Nazi-Occupied Poland* (New York: Oxford University Press, 1987).

2. In those days it was common for Jews to carry their important documents with them all the time.

3. For a reproduction of this law, see: Lucy Dawidowicz, ed., *A Holocaust Reader* (New York: Behrman House Inc., 1976), pp. 67–68; for a discussion of some of the implications of this law, see: Nechama Tec, *When Light Pierced the Darkness,* pp. 25–85.

4. For a discussion about the implications of the different working passes in the Vilna ghetto, see: Yitzhak Arad, *Ghetto in Flames: The Struggle and Destruction of the Jews in Vilna in the Holocaust* (New York: Holocaust Library, 1982), pp. 143–163. A Jewish adolescent in Vilna described the issuance of these passes as follows: "Fate suddenly split the people of the ghetto into two parts. One part possesses the yellow certificate. They believe in the power of this little paper. It bestows the right to life. The second part, lost, despairing people who sense their doom, and do not know where to go. We do not have a yellow certificate. Our parents are running around like hundreds of others, as though in fever." Yitskhok Rudashevsky, *The Diary of the Vilna Ghetto, June 1941–April 1943* (Israel: Ghetto Fighter's House, 1973), p. 36.

5. Nechama Tec, *When Light Pierced the Darkness,* pp. 40–51.

Notes to Chapter 5

1. "Lithuania," pp. 385–386 in *Encyclopedia Judaica* (Jerusalem: Keter Publishing House, 1971).

2. Norman Davies, *God's Playground: A History of Poland* (New York: Columbia University Press, 1984), Vol. 2, p. 448.

3. Kazimierz Plater Żyberk, "In Defense of Poles in the USSR," *Polish Ex-Combatant Association,* 1982, pp. 3–19.

4. At first Oswald thought that Serafimowicz reached the rank of a sergeant. Later he was not sure, thinking that he might have been only a corporal.

Notes to Chapter 6

1. Dr. N. M. Gelber, "Tsu Der Geschikhte Fun Mirer Yidn" ("Towards A History of Mir Jews), pp. 449–464 in *Mir,* ed. N. Blumenthal (Jerusalem: Memorial Books Encyclopedia of the Diaspora, 1962).

2. "Mir," pp. 70–72 in *Encyclopedia Judaica* (Jerusalem: Keter Publishing House, 1971); S. Maria Lucyna Mistecka Cr., "Droga Oswalda Rufeisena Do *Kapłaństwa*" ("Oswald's Road to Priesthood), *Chrześcijanin W Świecie, Zeszyty Odiss,* Vol. 69, September, 1978, p. 55.

3. Gelber, "Towards A History of Mir Jews," pp. 449–464 in *Mir,* ed. N. Blumenthal: Noach Miszkowski, "Main Shtetl Mir" (My Town Mir), pp. 466–475 in *Mir,* ed. N. Blumenthal.

4. "Mir," p. 70 in *Encyclopedia Judaica;* Josef Rolnik, "Die Ieshive" (The Yeshiva), pp. 475–481 in *Mir,* ed. N. Blumenthal; M. Tiktinsky, "Mir, The City of the Torah," pp. 17–26 in *Mir,* ed. N. Blumenthal.

5. Yisrael Gutman and Shmuel Krakowski, *Unequal Victims: Poles and Jews During World War II* (New York: Holocaust Library, 1986), pp. 35–36.

6. Ibid., pp. 10–25; Celia S. Heller, *On the Edge of Destruction* (New York: Columbia University Press, 1977), p. 50; Paweł Korzec, "Anti-Semitism in Poland

as an Intellectual, Social and Political Movement," p. 87 in *Studies on Polish Jewry,* ed. Joshua A. Fishman (New York: YIVO, Jewish Institute of Social Research,1974); Edward D. Wynot, Jr., "A Necessary Cruelty: The Emergence of Official Anti-Semitism in Poland, 1926–1939," *The American Historical Review 76,* no. 4 (October 1971), pp. 1035–1058.

7. Jacob Lestchinsky, "Economic Aspects of Jewish Community Organization in Independent Poland," *Jewish Social Studies 9,* no. 1–4 (1947), pp. 319–338; L. Lifschutz, "Selected Documents Pertaining to Jewish Life in Poland, 1919–1938," pp. 277–294 in *Studies on Polish Jewry,* ed. Fishman; Simha Resnik, "Mir Before the Destruction," pp. 33–40 in *Mir,* ed. Blumenthal; Emmanuel Ringelblum, *Polish-Jewish Relations During the Second World War* (Jerusalem: Yad Vashem, 1974), pp. 10–22.

8. Resnik, "Mir Before the Destruction," pp. 38–40 in *Mir,* ed. N. Blumenthal.

9. Norman Davies, *God's Playground: A History of Poland* (New York: Columbia University Press, 1984), Vol. 2, p. 443; Gutman and Krakowski, *Unequal Victims,* pp. 36–37; Jan Karski, *The Great Powers and Poland, 1919–1945: From Versailles to Yalta* (New York: University Press of America, Inc., 1985), p. 403; Witold Sworakowski, "The Poles In the Soviet Union, Facts and Figures," *The Polish Review,* Vol. 19, nos. 3–4, pp. 143–150; Kazimierz Plater Żyberk, "In Defense of Poles in the USSR," *Polish Ex-Combatant Association* (1982), p. 3–19.

10. "Mir," pp. 70–72 in *Encyclopedia Judaica.*

11. The Judenrat during the Nazi occupation represents a tragic and controversial chapter in Jewish history. A most extensive and balanced study of this topic is *The Judenrat* (New York: The Macmillan Co., 1972) by Isaiah Trunk.

12. "Di Erste Groyse Shkhite, 9.11, 1941" (The First Big Slaughter), pp. 611–618 in *Mir,* ed. N. Blumenthal.

13. This incident was described in a letter written by Bruria Rosenblum, Secretary of the Association of the Jews of Mir. She was among those who were saved that day. About 35 Jews were spared because the priest allowed them into different parts of the convent. This letter was received by Father Daniel. I had heard about it in May 1987.

14. "Mir," pp. 70–72 in *Encyclopedia Judaica.*

15. Nohm Alter Salutsky, "Erster Khurbn" (First Destruction), pp. 621–626 in *Mir,* ed. N. Blumenthal.

16. The Nazi police system, a complex bureaucratic structure, was made up of separate and overlapping compartments. Unclearly defined functions plus internal struggles for power resulted in continuous changes and internal readjustments.

To simplify what in reality were complex and sometimes confusing arrangements, by 1941 the Nazi police was divided into two main parts: the regular police (Ordnungspolizei) and the secret police (Siecherheitspolizei). Each of these major branches was further subdivided. The first, the regular police, consisted of two main sections, the Schutzpolizei and the Gendarmerie. The Schutzpolizei was assigned to cities. One of their functions was to guard Jewish ghettos. The second, the Gendarmerie, stayed in rural areas where it performed different police functions, including the implementation of the policies of Jewish annihilation.

The secret police, the Siecherheitspolizei, was also subdivided into two main sections. One of them, Sipo or Gestapo, dealt with matters related to the security of the state. This was the political police. The second section, Kripo, handled criminal rather than political matters. Penetrating into, and superimposed on, all these police sections was the SS (Schutzstaffel). Perceived as the expression of the Führer's will, the SS eventually assumed control over all police branches.

See Lucy S. Dawidowicz, *The War Against the Jews, 1939–1945* (New York: Holt, Rinehart and Winston, 1975), p. 79; *Encyklopedia II Wojny Światowej* (*World War II Encyclopedia*) (Warszawa: Wydawnictwo Ministerstwa Obrony Narodowej, 1975), pp. 561, 563; Raul Hilberg, *The Destruction of the European Jews* (New York: Franklin Watts, Inc., 1973) pp. 134, 150.

17. Lider-Świrnowski, "In the Jewish Quarter," pp. 607–612 in *Mir,* ed. N. Blumenthal.

18. Oswald is not sure whether his name was Adolf or Karol. I will refer to him as Karol.

19. I will return to a discussion of this event in a later chapter.

Notes to Chapter 7

1. Nicolas P. Vakar, *Belorussia, The Making of a Nation* (Cambridge: Harvard University Press, 1956), p. 178.

2. Some have described Oswald as blond, tall, and "Nordic" looking. In reality, he is short with dark hair and hardly the Nordic type. Two examples of people who knew him personally and saw him as tall and blond are: Mike Breslin, "The SS Man Who Was a Jewish Partisan," *Weekender* (Supplement to the Weekend Argus, April 25, 1987), p. 3; Jacob Greenstein, "The Story of the Amazing Oswald," pp. 246–252 in *They Fought Back: The Story of the Jewish Resistance in Europe,* ed. Yuri Suhl (New York: Shocken Books, 1975).

3. Nechama Tec, *When Light Pierced the Darkness: Christian Rescue of Jews in Nazi-Occupied Poland* (New York: Oxford University Press, 1987), pp. 27–84.

4. Statement made by Fani Bilecki during an Israeli television program about Oswald, May 8, 1984.

5. For some discussion of Jewish circumcision and the effects it had on safety, see: Nechama Tec, *Dry Tears: The Story of a Lost Childhood* (New York: Oxford University Press, 1984); Nechama Tec, "Sex Distinctions and Passing as Christians During the Holocaust," *East European Quarterly 18,* no. 1 (March 1984): 113–123.

6. Most of those interested in the Rufeisen story had assumed that he was passing for a Volksdeutsche or a German. Among those who did are: Shlomo Charchas Testimony No. 727, Jewish Historical Institute in Warsaw; Simha Resnik and Moshe Rovni, "Sipuro Hanifla Shel Oswald Rufeisen" ("The Remarkable Story of Oswald Rufeisen"), pp. 315–328 in *Mir,* ed. N. Blumenthal (Jerusalem: Memorial Books Encyclopedia of the Diaspora, 1962); Hilel Seidel, *Adam Bmivhan* (*The Testing of a Man*) (Tel-Aviv: Published privately by the author, 1973); Breslin even refers to him as an SS man. See "The SS Man Who Was a Jewish Partisan." Similarly, Moshe Kalhcheim refers to his friend Oswald as someone who was passing for a Gestapo man. See Moshe Kalhcheim, "Mein Haver Der Galech Daniel—Rufeisen Oder A Gilgul Fun A Yidischer Neshome" (My Friend the Priest Daniel Rufeisen or the Wanderings of a Jewish Soul), *Di Zionistische Shtime* (Paris, December 12, 1957).

7. Rufeisen and Resnik have each described this meeting independently in a number of places. See Dov Resnik Testimony No. 543/II, Jewish Historical Institute in Warsaw. Resnik also writes about it in "Der Kampf Kegen Die Deutschen" (The Fight Against the Germans), pp. 631-643 in *Mir,* ed. N. Blumenthal. Oswald repeated the story several times to me. It is also a part of his official testimony in Israel. See Oswald

Rufeisen Yad Vashem Archives No. 03/2302; Oswald categorically and consistently denies a version of this event told by Shlomo Charchas. Charchas claims to have been the one who established contacts in Mir with Rufeisen. See Charchas Testimony No. 727, Jewish Historical Institute. This alleged meeting was also described by Charchas on May 8, 1984, during an Israeli television program about Rufeisen. Charchas' version was accepted by many who have written about Oswald. See Shalom Cholawski, "B'Yarketei Ya-ar" (In the Depth of the Forest) pp. 465–498 in *Sefer Hapartisanim Hayehudim* (*The Jewish Partisan Book*), ed. M. Gefen, et al. (Merchavia: Sifriat Poalim) 1958; the same is true for Maria Lucyna Mistecka Cr, "Droga Oswalda Rufeisena Do Kapłańnstwa" ("Oswald's Road to Christianity"), *Chrzścijnanin W. Świecie Zeszyty, Odiss*, Vol. 69, September, 1978, pp. 54–71.

8. Oswald insists that in Mir he met with Jews only when it was absolutely necessary. Charchas' version of their encounter suggests that Rufeisen had visited his home. Oswald denies that he had any direct contact with Charchas in Mir. Oswald thinks that at the time, as a prominent Jewish leader in Mir, Charchas might have felt that it was safer for him not to meet with Oswald. Again, such meetings are described by those who rely on Charchas' testimony.

Notes to Chapter 8

1. Ester Krynicki Gorodejski Berkowitcz, "Sichrojnes Fun Der Deitscher Okupacje" (Memoirs from the German Occupation), pp. 587–602 in *Mir*, ed. N. Blumenthal (Jerusalem: Memorial Books, Encyclopedia of the Diaspora, 1962); Simcha Resnik and Moshe Rovni, "Sipuro Hanifla Shel Oswald Rufeisen" (The Remarkable Story of Oswald Rufeisen), pp. 315–328 in *Mir*, ed. N. Blumenthal.

2. Berl Resnik, "Der Kampf Kegen Die Deutschen" (The Fight Against the Germans), pp. 631–643 in *Mir*, ed. N. Blumenthal.

3. This is written in the testimony of Shlomo Charchas, No. 727, Jewish Historical Institute, Warsaw. Also in: Shalom Cholawski, "B'yarketei Ya-r" (In the Depth of the Forest), pp. 465–498 in *Sefer Hapartisanim Hayehudim*, ed. M. Gefen, et al. (Merchavia: Sifriat Hapoalim, 1958), and Isaiah Trunk, *Jewish Responses to Nazi Persecution* (New York: Stein & Day Publishers, 1974), p. 291.

4. The Kołdyczewo Camp is described in Betti Ajzensztajn, ed., *Ruch Podziemny W Ghettach I Obozach* (Materiały I Dokumenty) (*Underground Movement in Ghettos and Camps*) (Cracow Central Jewish Historical Commission in Poland, 1946), pp. 179–180; Joseph A. Foxman, "The Escape from Kołdyczewo Camp," pp. 172–175 in *They Fought Back: The Story of Jewish Resistance in Nazi-Occupied Europe*, ed. Yuri Suhl (New York: Schocken Books, 1975).

5. Władysław Bartoszewski, *1859 Dni Warszawy* (*1859 Warsaw Days*) (Kraków: Wydawnictwo Znak, 1974); Władysław Bartoszewski, *Straceni Na Ulicach Maistra* (*Perished in the Streets of the City*) (Warszawa: Książka I Wiedza, 1970); Lucy Dawidowicz, *The War Against the Jews* (New York: Holt, Rinehart and Winston, 1975), pp. 394–395; Nechama Tec, *When Light Pierced the Darkness: Christian Rescue of Jews in Nazi-Occupied Poland* (New York: Oxford University Press, 1987), p. 52.

6. For some discussions about Belorussian nationalism, see: Thomas Fitzsimmons, Peter Molaf, John C. Fiske, *USSR* (New Haven: Hraf Press, 1960), p. 17; Jerzy Tomaszewski, *Rzeczpospolita Wielu Narodów* (*Country of Many Nations*) (Warsaw: Czytelnik, 1985), pp. 105–134; Nicholas P. Vakar, *Belorussia, The Making of a Nation* (Cambridge: Harvard University Press, 1956), pp. 191–193.

7. Oswald is not sure if this was Hein's own or adopted son.

8. Resnik and Rovni, "The Remarkable Story of Oswald Rufeisen," pp. 315–328 in *Mir,* ed. N. Blumenthal.

9. Ephraim Sinder, statement made during an Israeli television program about Rufeisen, May 8, 1984.

Notes to Chapter 9

1. Nicholas P. Vakar, *Belorussia, The Making of a Nation* (Cambridge: Harvard University Press, 1956), pp. 170–174.

2. Reuben Ainsztein, *Jewish Resistance in Occupied Eastern Europe* (New York: Barnes & Noble, 1974), p. 243.

3. Nicholas P. Vakar, *Belorussia,* pp. 174–175.

4. Reuben Ainsztein, *Jewish Resistance,* p. 279.

5. Nicholas P. Vakar, *Belorussia,* p. 192.

6. Shmuel Krakowski, *The War of the Doomed: Jewish Armed Resistance in Poland, 1942–1944* (New York: Holmes & Meier Publishers, Inc., 1984), p. 28.

7. Reuben Ainsztein, *Jewish Resistance,* pp. 307–338; Yehuda Bauer, *A History of the Holocaust* (New York: Franklin Watts, 1982), p. 271; Bryna Bar-Oni, *The Vapor* (Chicago: Visual Impact, Inc., 1976); Shalom Cholawski, *Soldiers from the Ghetto* (New York: The Herzel Press, 1982), p. 147.

8. Thomas Fitzsimmons, Peter Malof, and John C. Fiske, *USSR* (New Haven: Hraf Press, 1960), pp. 17, 50; Nicholas P. Vakar, *Belorussia,* p. 185.

9. Filip Friedman, "Zagłada Żydow Polskich W Latch, 1939–1945" (Destruction of Polish Jewry, 1939–1945), *Biuletyn Głównej Komisji Badań Zbrodni Niemieckiej W Polsce,* no. 6 (1946): pp. 196–208.

10. Jacob Lestchinsky, "Economic Aspects of Jewish Community Organization in Independent Poland," *Jewish Social Studies 9,* nos. 1–4 (1947): pp. 319–338; Jacob Lestchinsky, "The Industrial and Social Structure of the Jewish Population of Interbellum Poland," *YIVO Annual of Jewish Social Science 2* (1956–1957): pp. 243–269; Antony Polonsky, *Politics in Independent Poland, 1921–1939* (New York: Oxford, The Claredon Press, 1972).

11. Yitzhak Arad, *The Partisan from the Valley of Death to Mount Zion* (New York: Holocaust Library, 1979), pp. 160–163; Yehuda Bauer, *The Jewish Emergence from Powerlessness* (Toronto: The University of Toronto Press, 1979), p. 30; Yisrael Gutman and Shmuel Krakowski, *Unequal Victims, Poles and Jews During World War II* (New York: Holocaust Library, 1986), pp. 103–139; Shmuel Krakowski, *The War of the Doomed,* pp. 27–42.

12. Nicholas P. Vakar, *Belorussia,* p. 192.

13. Józef Marchwinski, Yad Vashem Testimony *No. 03/3568.* See also references in Note 7. These are only a small fraction of the sources supporting this association.

14. Nicholas P. Vakar, *Belorussia,* p. 193.

15. Ibid., pp. 191–192.

Notes to Chapter 10

1. Konrad Wallenrod served as a grand master of the Teutonic Order for three years, from 1391–1394. At the end of his rule, in a battle with the Lithuanians, he led his order into defeat. History is silent about the motives for and the special ways

in which this battle was fought. Konrad Wallenrod became an important legendary hero because of a publication by Poland's foremost poet. See Adam Mickiewicz, *Konrad Wallenrod: Powieść Historyczna Z Dziejów Litewskich I Pruskich* (*Konrad Wallenrod: A Historical Novel About Lithuanian and Prussian Events*), pp. 69–136, in Adam Mickiewicz, *Powieści Poetyckie* (Warszawa: Czytelnik, 1983).

Konrad Wallenrod had accomplished his goal but died in this battle. Since the publication of Mickiewicz's work, the image of this tragic knight left a tremendous imprint on the Polish culture. Norman Davies thinks that in its more precise meaning, Konrad Wallenrod's actions represent a "two-faced attitude, characterized by apparent servility towards an enemy whom one intends to betray and destroy." See Norman Davies, *Heart of Europe: A Short History of Poland* (New York: Oxford University Press, 1984), p. 218.

2. If a member of the SS showed some disapproval of SS crimes, he was asked to perform a criminal task that tied him more firmly to the SS. See Leo Alexander, "War Crimes and Their Motivation," *Journal of Criminal Law and Criminology*, 39, no. 3 (September 1948): 298–326.

3. At different times, Oswald referred to this woman as sister and wife. When confronted with this inconsistency, he felt that it was probably the wife.

4. She survived as a member of the Bielski family camp. See Yitzhak Arad, "Jewish Family Camps in the Forests: An Original Means of Rescue," pp. 333–353 in *Rescue Attempts During the Holocaust*, Proceedings of the Second Yad Vashem International Historical Conference, April 1974, eds. Yisrael Gutman and Efraim Zuroff (Jerusalem: Yad Vashem, 1977).

5. Ester Marchwinska, Yad Vashem Archives No. 03/3567; Dov Resnik, "Hacala Wmeri Shel Yehudei Mir" (Rescue and Resistance of the Mir Jews), pp. 329–346 in *Mir*, ed. N. Blumenthal (Jerusalem: Memorial Books, Encyclopedia of the Diaspora, 1962).

6. Ibid., p. 331.

7. Berl Resnik, "Der Kampf Gegen Die Deutschen" (The Fight Against the Germans), pp. 631–644 in *Mir*, ed. N. Blumenthal.

8. Shlomo Charchas, Testimony No. 727, Jewish Historical Institute in Warsaw.

9. This name and story have been reconfirmed by Simcha Resnik and Moshe Rovni, "Sipuro Hanifla Shel Oswald Rufeisen" (The Remarkable Story of Oswald Rufeisen), pp. 315–328 in *Mir*, ed. N. Blumenthal.

10. Told to me by Oswald Rufeisen, this story is reconfirmed in several sources. See Berl Resnik, "The Fight Against the Germans," pp. 631–644 in *Mir*, ed. N. Blumenthal; Shlomo Charchas, Testimony No. 727, Jewish Historical Institute. Also described in Isaiah Trunk, *Jewish Responses to Nazi Persecution: Collective and Individual Behavior in Extremes* (New York: Stein & Day, 1979), p. 292. Only the number of young Jews who were supposedly involved in this underground group varies, ranging from thirty to eighty.

11. Resnik reconfirms Oswald's version of this event. See Berl Resnik Testimony No. 2/543, Jewish Historical Institute in Warsaw.

12. Ester Marchwinska, Yad Vashem Archives No. 03/3567.

13. Ibid.

14. Dov Resnik, "Rescue and Resistance of the Mir Jews," pp. 329–346 in *Mir*, ed. N. Blumenthal.

15. The same incident is also described in Berl Resnik, "The Fight Against the Germans," pp. 631–641 in *Mir*, ed. N. Blumenthal.

16. Ephraim Sinder, statement made during an Israeli television program about Oswald Rufeisen, May 8, 1984.

17. Born in 1921, Cila Kapelowicz was a ghetto inmate in Mir. She survived the war in the Bielski partisan unit and now lives in South Africa. I interviewed her during her visit to Israel in June 1987.

18. Fani Bilecki, statement made during an Israeli television program about Oswald Rufeisen, May 8, 1984.

19. This story is repeated in Charchas Testimony No. 727, Jewish Historical Institute.

20. Resnik and Rovni, "The Remarkable Story of Oswald Rufeisen," pp. 315–328 in *Mir,* ed. N. Blumenthal.

21. Fani Bilecki, Israeli television, May 8, 1984.

Notes to Chapter 11

1. Simcha Resnik and Moshe Rovni, "Sipuro Hanifla Shel Oswald Rufeisen" (The Remarkable Story of Oswald Rufeisen), pp. 315–328 in *Mir,* ed. N. Blumenthal (Jerusalem: Memorial Books, Encyclopedia of the Diaspora, 1962).

2. Fani Bilecki, statement made during an Israeli television program about Oswald Rufeisen, May 8, 1984.

3. Shlomo Charchas Testimony No. 727, Archives of the Jewish Historical Institute, Warsaw.

4. Resnik and Rovni, "The Remarkable Story of Oswald Rufeisen" pp. 315–328 in *Mir,* ed. N. Blumenthal.

5. Hilel Seidel wrote that a Jewish locksmith made a copy of the key to this cupboard. See Hilel Seidel, *Adam Bmivhan* (*The Tesing of a Man*) (Tel-Aviv: Published privately by the author, 1973). Oswald said that he had easy access to the keys and weapons.

6. Shlomo Charchas Testimony No. 727, Archives of the Jewish Historical Institute.

7. This quantity of arms is independently reported by Charchas, Resnik, and Rufeisen.

8. Charchas says that with Oswald's prodding, they indeed changed their plans and decided to leave the ghetto. See Charchas Testimony No. 727; this is reconfirmed by Berl Resnik, "Der Kampf Gegen Die Deutschen" (The Fight Against the Germans), pp. 631–643 in *Mir,* ed. N. Blumenthal.

9. Ibid. This is repeated in the above two sources.

10. Resnik Testimony No. 543/II, Archives of the Jewish Historical Institute in Warsaw.

11. Israeli television program about Oswald Rufeisen, May 8, 1984.

12. Dov Resnik, "Hacala Wmeri Shel Yehudei Mir" (Rescue and Resistance of the Mir Jews), pp. 329–346 in *Mir,* ed. N. Blumenthal. Among the few young women accepted into the ghetto underground was Ester Marchwinska, Yad Vashem Archives No. 03/3567.

13. Ephraim Sinder, statement made during an Israeli television program about Oswald Rufeisen, May 8, 1984.

14. Dov Resnik, "Rescue and Resistance of the Mir Jews," pp. 329–346 in *Mir,* ed. N. Blumenthal; "Nieświeź," pp. 966–967, *Encyclopedia Judaica* (Jerusalem: Keter Publishing House Ltd, 1971). For a more detailed description of the resistance and

escape from Niéswież, see Shalom Cholawski, *Soldiers from the Ghetto* (New York: The Herzel Press, 1980), pp. 69–71.

15. Charchas and Resnik describe these events in their respective testimonies. See Note 6.

16. Dov Resnik, "Rescue and Resistance of the Mir Jews," pp. 329–346 in *Mir*, ed. N. Blumenthal.

17. During a television statement on May 8, 1984, Fani Bilecki said that Rufeisen made sure that not even one policeman was left in Mir. Oswald categorically denies this, saying that four men were left behind, but were told to stay inside the building.

18. There are descriptions of the atmosphere in the ghetto and the events that took place there. See, for example, Resnik and Rovni, "The Remarkable Story of Oswald Rufeisen," pp. 315–328 in *Mir*, ed. N. Blumenthal.

19. Personal communication, Celia Kapelowicz, Israel, 1987. Her observations are confirmed by those who wrote about these events in *Mir*, ed. N. Blumenthal.

20. Ibid.

21. Ephraim Sinder, statement made during an Israeli television program about Oswald Rufeisen, May 8, 1984.

22. Ester Marchwinska, Yad Vashem Archives No. 03/3567.

23. Shlomo Charchas Testimony No. 727, Jewish Historical Institute. The following articles describe the last night in the ghetto. All are a part of the book *Mir*, ed. N. Blumenthal. Shimon Kagan, "Fun Partizaner Leben" (About Partisan Life), pp. 620–626; Devora Rakovitch, "Der Letster Tog in Geto" (The Last Day in Ghetto), pp. 627–630; Berl Resnik, "The Fight Against the Germans," pp. 631–643.

24. Dov Resnik also survived in the Bielski camp as did 1200 other Jews. See Yitzhak Arad, "Jewish Family Camps in the Forests: An Original Means of Rescue," pp. 333–353 in *Rescue Attempts During the Holocaust*, Proceedings of the Second Yad Vashem International Historical Conference, April 1974, eds. Yisrael Gutman and Efraim Zuroff (Jerusalem: Yad Vashem, 1977).

25. Dov Resnik Testimony No. 543/II, Jewish Historical Institute.

26. Based on children's stories of B. Gurewicz, E. Vranikof, Z. Szreiber, E. Szkolonwitz, and D. Sinder, written up as "Iladim Partisanim" (Partisan Children), pp. 347–353 in *Mir*, ed. N. Blumenthal.

27. Ibid.

28. Ibid.

29. For a description of the resistance in Nieświeź, see Cholawski, *Soldiers from the Ghetto*, pp. 69–71.

Notes to Chapter 12

1. Reports about the number of Jewish runaways from the Mir ghetto vary with different sources. From Bielanowicz, and later from Wanda, Oswald heard that 300 had escaped and that on August 13, 500 Jews were executed. He feels that the figure 300 comes very close to the actual number. In contrast, Charchas testified that 210 Jews escaped from the Mir ghetto. However, at the same page of his testimony, he says that 500 Jews remained in the ghetto (page 10). It is generally assumed that altogether at that time in Mir there were a little over 800 Jews (805). Charchas' figures do not add up to this number. See Shlomo Charchas Testimony No. 727, Jewish Historical Institute in Warsaw; Berl (Dov) Resnik says that 180 Jews

succeeded in escaping. See his Testimony No. 543/2, Jewish Historical Institute in Warsaw. A Pole who was with the Russian partisans, Józek Marchwinski, says that 100 Jews ran away from the Mir ghetto. See his Testimony No. 03/3568, Yad Vashem Archives. In still another source it is stated that from the Mir ghetto 200 had succeeded in running away. See "Mir" in *Encyclopedia Judaica,* Vol. 12 (Jerusalem: Keter Publishing House Ltd., 1971), pp. 70–72.

2. Charchas mentions Hein's visit to the ghetto. See Shlomo Charchas Testimony No. 727, Jewish Historical Institute. The information about Hein's behavior in the ghetto had to come from the few who had survived the last Aktion. Before the August 13 executions, six young girls succeeded in hiding within the ghetto. When it was over, they sneaked out of the castle. One of them was Masha Sinder, the sister of Ephraim Sinder. I am grateful for this information to Chaja Bielski (Haifa, Israel, 1987).

3. Both Charchas and Resnik feel that Stanisławski denounced Oswald because he wanted to save his own life. For references, see Note 1. Fani Bilecki thinks that he might have also wanted to save the lives of others. She made this statment during an Israeli television program about Oswald Rufeisen, May 8, 1984.

4. When talking to Oswald, I have continuously returned to the events of this day. In 1986, the chief archivist of the Jewish Historical Institute in Poland, Jan Krupka, sent me document No. 2827 from the Institute's archives in Warsaw. This is a 1948 handwritten statement by Oswald Rufeisen. It focuses on his experiences as they touch on his confrontation with Meister Hein. I did not know about the existence of this document and am grateful to Jan Krupka for sending it to me.

Notes to Chapter 13

1. St. Luke 10:25–37, in *The New Testament* (The Authorized King James Version) (Nashville: The Gideons International, 1985).

2. For a discussion about these miraculous cures, see "Lourdes," p. 352 in *Encyclopedia Britanica* (Chicago: Encyclopedia Britanica, 1974), Vol. 6; "Lourdes," pp. 1031–1033 in *New Catholic Encyclopedia* (New York: McGraw-Hill Book Co., 1967); Patrick Marnham, *Lourdes: A Modern Pilgrimage* (New York: Coward, McCann & Geoghegan, Inc., 1981); "Mysteries of the Unexplained," *Readers Digest* (New York: Reader's Digest, 1987), pp. 266–267, 274, 281.

3. Oswald's meeting with Pope John Paul II is discussed in a later chapter.

4. For a discussion about the Nazi law against the harboring of Jews and the death of those who defied this law, see Tatiana Berenstein, et al, eds., *Exterminacja Żydów Na Ziemiach Polskich: Zbiór Dokumentów* (*Extermination of Jews on Polish Soil During the German Occupation*) (Warsaw: Jewish Historical Institute, 1957), p. 123; Lucy Dawidowicz, ed., *A Holocaust Reader* (New York: Behrman House, Inc., 1976), p. 67; Nechama Tec, *When Light Pierced the Darkness: Christian Rescue of Jews in Nazi-Occupied Poland* (New York: Oxford University Press, 1986), pp. 52–69.

5. Oswald refuses to reveal the names of the nuns who were opposed to his stay in the convent.

6. Talking about the affection Hein had for Oswald, Fani Bilecki emphasized that, in general, people found it easy to love him. This statement she made during a television program about Oswald Rufeisen in Israel, May 8, 1984. During an interview I conducted with Cila Kapelowicz, a former Mir ghetto inmate, she insisted

that Oswald had a reputation of a good person and that everybody liked him. Young girls in particular, she feels, were attracted to him.

7. Oswald's efforts at paying respect to this nun were unsuccessful. At the time when he tried to see her, she was too sick to receive visitors.

Notes to Chapter 14

1. The underground in wartime Poland had an intricate and varied history. Its complexity extends to the internal structures of the many anti-Nazi subgroupings and to their loose, frequently hostile relationships. Though important and potentially fascinating, an overall, comprehensive study of the many complex anti-Nazi operations has not yet been published. Though the literature contains valuable discussions about different underground movements in wartime Poland, none of them represents a fully integrated, comprehensive examination of the different kinds of subgroupings and their relationship to each other. For a few different examples, see Reuben Ainsztein, *Jewish Resistance in Nazi-Occupied Eastern Europe* (New York: Barnes & Noble, 1974); Gustaw Alef Bolkowiak, *Gorące Dni* (*Hot Days*) (Warsaw: Wydawnictwo Ministerstwa Obrony Narodowej, 1959); Jan Karski, *Story of a Secret State* (Boston: Houghton Mifflin Co., 1944); Tadeusz Bor-Komorowski, *The Secret Army* (London: Victor Gollancz, Ltd., 1950); Stefan Korboński, *The Polish Underground State: A Guide to the Underground, 1939–1945* (Boulder: East European Quarterly, 1978); Shmuel Krakowski, *The War of the Doomed: Jewish Armed Resistance in Poland, 1942–1944* (New York: Holmes & Meier Publishers, Inc., 1984); Chaim Lazar, *Murawska 7: The Warsaw Ghetto Rising* (Tel-Aviv: Massada P.E.C., 1966); Dov Levin, *Fighting Back: Lithuanian Jewry's Armed Resistance to the Nazis, 1941–1945* (New York: Holmes & Meier, 1985); Teresa Prekerowa, *Konspiracyjna Rada Pomocy Żydom W Warszawie, 1942–1945* (*Illegal Help to Jews in Warsaw*) (Warsaw: Państwowy Instytut Wydawniczy, 1982); Nicolas P. Vakar, *Belorussia, The Making of a Nation* (Cambridge: Harvard University Press, 1956).

2. Jacob Greenstein, personal interviews conducted in 1984, 1986, and 1987 in Israel; Józef Marchwinski, Yad Vashem Archives No. 03/3568.

3. Marchwinski, a Polish partisan, commandant, and former Communist, was a part of the Russian partisan movement in this area. Marchwinski differs with Greenstein about the size of this Polish unit, referring to 600 men. See Józef Marchwinski, Yad Vashem Archives No. 03/3568.

4. The National Armed Forces NSZ, a Fascist underground group, joined the dominant Polish underground in 1943. See Yisrael Gutman and Shmuel Krakowski, *Unequal Victims: Poles and Jews During World War II* (New York: The Holocaust Library, 1986), pp. 109–127; "National Democrats," p. 622 in *Wielka Encyklopedia Powszechna* (*The Great Popular Encyclopedia* (Warsaw: Wydawnictwo Naukowe, 1964).

5. These killings were independently reported by Greenstein and Marchwinski. For reference, see Note 4; Cholawski, a partisan who was in the Nolibocki forest, writes that, in 1943, Poles in the woods received orders to attack Jews and Russians. He specifically refers to an attack on a Jewish group of partisans by Polish partisans in the summer of 1943. See Shalom Cholawski, *Soldiers from the Ghetto* (New York: The Herzel Press, 1980), p. 162. Killings of Jewish partisans by Polish partisans in the Nalibocki forest are also mentioned in Gutman and Krakowski, *Unequal Victims*, p. 131.

6. He is referring to 4300 Polish officers murdered by the Soviets and buried

in a common grave. In addition, more than 10,000 Polish officers and soldiers, taken prisoners by the Russians, were never accounted for. Oswald also refers to the deliberate Red Army halt at the gate of Warsaw while the Germans were decimating the Polish underground fighters and civilians. Two outstanding studies on these topics are Janusz K. Zawodny, *Death in the Forest: The Story of the Katyn Massacre* (New York: Hippocrene Books, Inc., 1988); Janusz K. Zawodny, *Nothing But Honor: Story of the Uprising of Warsaw* (Stanford: Hoover Institution, 1978).

7. The Polish-Russian antagonism has a long history. During World War II, it had to do with the fight for Poland's independence. For a discussion of these issues, see Norman Davies, *God's Playground: A History of Poland* (New York: Columbia University Press, 1984), Vol. 2, pp. 464–491; Jan Karski, *The Great Powers and Poland 1919–1945: From Versailles to Yalta* (New York: University Press of America, Inc., 1985), pp. 388–440.

8. Published and unpublished sources are filled with reports about the murder of Jews who tried to survive in the forests. Partisans of different nationalities are accused of such killings and harassments. For a selected number of examples, see Ainsztein, *Jewish Resistance in Eastern Europe*, pp. 307–338, 333–335; Yitzhak Arad, *The Partisan from the Valley of Death to Mount Zion* (New York: Holocaust Library, 1979), pp. 160–163; Yehuda Bauer, *The Jewish Emergence from Powerlessness* (Toronto: The University of Toronto Press, 1979), p. 28; Shmuel Krakowski, *The War of the Doomed*, pp. 42, 54, 67, 86.

9. Yitzhak Arad, "Jewish Family Camps in the Forest—An Original Means of Rescue," pp. 333–353 in *Rescue Attempts During the Holocaust*, eds. Yisrael Gutman and Efraim Zuroff (Jerusalem: Yad Vashem, 1977); Shmuel Krakowski, "Jewish Partisan Leadership in Poland During the Holocaust" (1988, unpublished paper), pp. 1–10.

10. Ephraim Sinder statement made during an Israeli television program about Oswald Rufeisen, May 8, 1984.

11. Ibid.

12. NKVD is the National Commissariat of Internal Affairs. By 1943, this unit had a special responsibility for all the areas freed from the German occupation. See Norman Davies, *God's Playground*, p. 471.

13. Statements made during an Israeli television program about Oswald Rufeisen, May 8, 1984.

14. Most Jewish partisans report being attacked or threatened with attacks by non-Jewish partisans. A few examples of personal accounts are Ester Krynicki Gorodejski Berkowicz, "Sichrojnew Fun Der Deitscher Okupacje" (Memoirs from the German Occupation), pp. 587–602 in *Mir*, eds., N. Blumenthal (Jerusalem: Memorial Books, Encyclopedia of the Diaspora, 1962); Cila Kapelowicz was a ghetto inmate in Mir who survived the war in the Bielski partisan unit and lives now in South Africa. I interviewed her during her visit to Israel in June 1987; Ester Marchwinska, Yad Vashem Archives No. 03/3567; Dov Resnik, "Hacala Wmeri Shel Yehudei Mir" ("Rescue and Resistance of the Mir Jews"), pp. 329–346 in *Mir*, ed. N. Blumenthal.

15. I interviewed Jehuda Rytman in 1983 at his farm in Connecticut.

16. The special welcome M.D.s received by the partisans is a frequently repeated theme. For one such interesting example, see Michael Temchin, M.D., *The Witch Doctor: Memoirs of a Partisan* (New York: The Holocaust Library, 1983).

17. This story is repeated in Shlomo Charchas' Testimony No. 727, Jewish Historical Institute in Warsaw.

18. Fani Bilecki, statement made during an Israeli television program about Oswald Rufeisen, May 8, 1984.

Notes to Chapter 15

1. Jacob Greenstein survived the war as a partisan in the Ponomarenko otriad. I have interviewed him several times from 1984 to 1988 in Israel.

2. Bela Greenstein survived the war as a partisan in the Ponomarenko otriad. I spoke with her on and off between 1984–1988 in Israel.

3. Cwi Henryk Issler, M.D., Tad Vashem Archives No. 1706/113-1c. Dr. Issler was a member of the Bielski otriad. His testimony offers an excellent description of this family camp and, particularly, its medical care.

4. Moshe Bairach survived the war as a partisan in the Bielski unit. I interviewed Bairach in 1987 in Israel.

5. This refers to a telephone conversation I had with Tuvia Bielski in 1984. In 1987, a month before he died, I interviewed him in his home in Brooklyn, New York.

6. For an excellent account of the Polish uprising in Warsaw, see Janusz K. Zawodny, *Nothing But Honor, Story of the Uprising of Warsaw* (Stanford: Hoover Institute, 1978).

7. Raul Hilberg, *The Destruction of the European Jews* (New York: Franklin Watts, Inc., 1973), pp. 628–635.

8. Father Daniel met Wanda Juszkiewicz in Poland in September 1987. At his suggestion, she wrote to me from Chicago. I then spoke to her by phone. Wanda told me that her sister Jadwiga is in a mental institution and that they both had no contact with Serafimowicz. She was annoyed whenever I asked questions about her brother-in-law. Those other family members that were deported by the Russians disappeared without a trace. In Poland, a few years after the war, Oswald reestablished contact with the Balicki sisters. By then they were all married.

Notes to Chapter 16

1. S. Maria Lucyna Mistecka C.R., "Droga Oswalda Do Kapłańštwa" (Oswald's Road to Priesthood), *Chrześcijanin W Świecie, Zeszyty Odiss*, September 1978, Vol. 69, p. 55.

2. Mrs. Rufeisen was active in the Jewish underground in Cracaw. For a description of this underground, see Gusta Dawidson-Draengerowa, *Pamiętnik Justyny (Justyna's Diary)* (Cracaw: Żydowska Komisja Historyczna, 1946); *Hechalutz Halochem (The Fighting Haultz)* (Israel: Organ of the Chalutz Underground Movement in Occupied Cracaw, August–October 1943, The Ghetto Fighters House, 1984).

3. Hilel Seidel told me this when I interviewed him in Israel, 1983–1987. He also wrote about this meeting with the nun in his book. See Hilel Seidel, *Adam Bmivhan (The Testing of a Man)* (Tel-Aviv: Published privately by the author, 1973), pp. 88–133.

4. I asked Oswald a number of times about the meeting between Seidel and the Mother Superior. Each time he denied that it took place. Seidel, on the other hand, stood by his story. I was not able to resolve the difference. It is possible that

Seidel met with another nun. It was clear to me from Oswald's reaction that he did not like the story. He felt that it was out of character, that the Mother Superior would have never made the statement that was attributed to her.

5. Postwar Poland was a dangerous place for Jews. On July 4, 1946, Poles attacked the Jewish survivors in Kielce, killing 42 in one day. See Martin Gilbert, *The Holocaust: A History of the Jews of Europe During the Second World War* (New York: Holt, Rinehart & Winston, 1985), pp. 816–819.

6. His fears were justified; see ibid. Borwicz writes that after the war in 1945, 353 Jews were murdered in Poland. See Michael Borwicz, "Polish-Jewish Relations, 1944–47," pp. 190–198 in Chimen Abramski, et al., eds., *The Jews in Poland* (Oxford: Basil Blackwell, 1986).

7. Norman Davies, *Heart of Europe, A Short History of Poland* (New York: Oxford University Press, 1984), p. 5; Jan Karski, *The Great Powers and Poland 1919–1945: From Versailles to Yalta* (New York: University Press of America, Inc., 1985), pp. 621–624.

8. Norman Davies, *God's Playground, A History of Poland* (New York: Columbia University Press, 1984), Vol. II, pp. 571–572. Cyrankiewicz was also a former inmate in the concentration camp at Auschwitz where he became an underground leader. See Krzysztof Dunin-Wąsowicz, *Resistance In The Nazi Concentration Camps, 1933–1945* (Warsaw: PWN-Polish Scientific Publishers, 1982), p. 102.

9. Davies, *God's Playground*, p. 580.

10. Lukasz Hirszowicz, "The Jewish Issue in Post War Communist Politics," pp. 199–208 in Abramski, et al., eds., *The Jews in Poland*.

Notes to Chapter 17

1. Arieh Rufeisen spoke to me about his first meeting during a 1984 interview in Israel. He has also described it during an Israeli television show about Oswald Rufeisen on May 8, 1984.

2. Quoted in an article by Gidon Levi, "Haglima" (The Robe), *Haaretz*, January 26, 1982, pp. 5–7.

3. Ibid. Opposed to religious control over the secular life of a country, Oswald has always voted for the political left.

4. Daniel Oswald Rufeisen, "And Is Not of Another Religion," *Politika*, October 19, 1987, pp. 20–23. This is an Israeli political magazine, and this entire issue is devoted to the subject of who is an Israeli. I am grateful to my friend Arieh Gelblum for sending me his own translated version of this article.

5. Who is and is not a Jew is an issue that continues to be widely debated from religious, legal, political, and social perspectives. For discussion of these complex issues, see Avner H. Shaki, *Mi Hu Yehudi Bdiney Medinat Israel* (*Who Is a Jew in the Laws of the State of Israel*) (Tel-Aviv: Law Faculty, Tel-Aviv University, 1976), Volume I, Chapter 6, pp. 143–172. For an English translation of this material, I want to thank my friend Geuli Arad. This question has been periodically discussed in more popular sources. See Thomas L. Friedman, "Uproar in Israel Over Converts' ID's," *The New York Times*, June 25, 1986, p. 11; "Israeli Court Upholds a Convert," *The New York Times*, December 3 1986, p. 3; Elie Kadurie, "Who Is a Jew?" *Commentary*, Vol. 85, no. 6, June 1988, pp. 25–30. The definition of a Jew reemerged as a central issue right after the November 1988 elections in Israel. For some discussions about this

topic see: Celestine Bohlen, "U.J.A. Is Thriving But Also Being Challenged," *The New York Times,* November 28, 1988, p.21; Joel Brinkley, "Two Major Parties in Israel Reopen Coalition Talks," *The New York Times,* November 29, 1988; pp. 1,5; Yosef Goell, "While Politicians Close Their Eyes," *The Jerusalem Post,* November 22, 1988, p.4.

6. Jerzy Turowicz, "Chrześcijanie I Żydzi W Israelu" (Z.O. Danielem Rozmawia Jerzy Turowicz (Christians and Jews in Israel), *Tygodnik Powszechny* (Katolickie Pismo Społeczno Kulturalne), Cracaw, September 1983, no. 39, pp. 1, 4, 5.

7. St. Matthew 22:21 in *The New Testament* (The Authorized King James Version) (Nashville: The Gideons International, 1985).

8. This statement is a part of the transcript of Oswald's trial. In translation, the title of this transcript reads as follows: *Oswald Rufeisen versus the Ministry of the Interior at the Supreme Court of Justice in Israel (1962)*, pp. 2428–2455. From now on, I will refer to this document as Transcript.

9. Rufeisen, "And Is Not of Another Religion."

10. Ibid. In addition to writing, Oswald repeated these ideas during an Israeli television program about Oswald Rufeisen, May 8, 1984.

11. Ibid. In addition to the television program, Oswald repeated this story to me on several occasions.

12. Statement made by Ephraim Sinder on an Israeli television program about Oswald Rufeisen, May 8, 1984.

13. This is a free translation of parts of the Transcript.

14. The press at the time was filled with discussions about the dilemma inherent in the case. A few such examples are Max Lerner, "Daniel Come to Judgment," *Jerusalem Post,* December 13, 1962; H. Rosenblum, "Ach Daniel" (Brother Daniel) *Yiediot Achronot,* November 11, 1962; "Hamishpat Shel Daniel" (The Trial of Daniel) Maariv, November 20, 1962.

15. Transcript.

16. Ibid.

17. Ibid.

18. Ibid.

19. Ibid.

20. Ibid.

21. Ibid.

22. Avner H. Shaki, *Who Is a Jew,* Vol. I, Chapter 6, pp. 143–172.

23. Statement made by Oswald on an Israeli television program about Oswald Rufeisen, May 8, 1984.

24. Daniel Oswald Rufeisen, "If Not of Another Religion."

25. Ibid.

Notes to Chapter 18

1. "Carmel Mount," pp. 113–114 in *New Catholic Encyclopedia* (New York: MaGraw-Hill Book Co., 1967), Vol. 3; "Elijah," pp. 632–642 in *Encyclopedia Judaica* (Jerusalem: Keter Publishing House, 1971), Vol. 6.

2. Amos Nvo, "Bein Shnei Olamot" (Between Two Worlds), *Ydiot Achronot,* March 16, 1984, pp. 17–18.

3. Gidon Levi, "Haglima" (The Robe), *Haaretz*, January 26, 1982, pp. 5–7.

4. Ibid.

5. Ibid.

6. Amos Nvo, "Between Two Worlds."

7. Daniel Oswald Rufeisen, "And Is Not of Another Religion," *Politika*, October 19, 1987, pp. 20–23.

8. Goga Kogan, "Yehudi Shedato Nozrit," (A Jew Whose Religion is Christian), *Al Hamishmar*, May 23, 1975; Amos Nvo, "Between Two Worlds." Similar ideas were expressed by Oswald during his interview with Hanah Rosenthal, "Ani Shaiach Gam Lkan Vgam Lkan" ("I Belong Here and There"), *Al Hamishmar*, April 25, 1986, pp. 20–21.

9. *Today's Missal*, Vol. 55, no. 3, 1988, p. 48.

10. Frequently expressed in the course of Oswald's interviews, these ideas also reappear in print in Daniel Oswald Rufeisen, "And Is Not of Another Religion"; Oswald Daniel Rufeisen OCD, "Kann Ein Jude In Der Kirche Seine Identität Bewahren? Sur Frage Der Inkulthuration Des Christentums In Israel" (Can A Jew Retain His Identity in the Church? Towards The Question of Christian Acculturation in Israel) *Judaica*, Vol. 38, no. 1, March 1982, pp. 24–28.

11. Daniel Oswald Rufeisen, "And Is Not of Another Religion."

12. Oswald had told me that he made a similar statement during an interview that appeared as an article in a Polish weekly magazine. After the journalist decided to eliminate this comment, feeling that it was too provocative, Oswald objected. The article is Jerzy Turowicz, "Chrześcijanie I Żydzi W Israelu" (Z.O. Danielem Rozmawia Jerzy Turowicz) (Christians and Jews in Israel) *Tygodnik Powszechny* (Katolickie Pismo Społeczno Kulturalne), Cracow, September 1983, no. 39, pp. 1, 4, 5.

13. I am very grateful to my friend Alice Eckardt, professor of religion, for discussing the idea of Jews for Jesus and directing me to the voluminous literature on the topic. From her I learned about the complexities of the concept. Indeed, in one of her enlightening letters, she wrote: "There are a variety of designations that Jews who have converted to Christianity but wish to insist on their Jewish identity also use: Hebrew-Christian (for which there is an International Alliance with a publication [which we receive]), Jewish-Christians, and the specific movements of recent times, "Jews for Jesus," and "Messianic Jews." Oh yes, the "Children of God" movement is led by a converted Jew and has other converted Jews as members. There is a long and complicated history of this type of movement, beginning, of course, very early." Because of the complexity of this topic, I am not qualified to deal with it. What follows are a few select examples from the vast literature on the subject. Nancy Silver Cochran, "The Journey," *The Hebrew Christian*, Vol. 40, no. 4, December 1987–February 1988, pp. 103–107; Karen Dolan, "Jew Preaches Message of Christ in Passover in LV," *The Globe Times*, March 26, 1987, p. 3; John Fischer, *The Olive Tree Connection: Sharing Messiah with Israel* (Downers Grove, Ill.: InterVarsity Press, 1983) (review in *Theology Today*, XLI, 3, October 1984), pp. 287–289; Arnold Fruchtenbaum, *Hebrew Christianity, Its Theology, History and Philosophy* (Washington, D.C.: Canon Press, 1974); Jan Hoffman, "Inside Jews for Jesus," *New York*, Vol. 19, no. 17, April 28, 1986, pp. 42–48; Arthur Katz, "Odyssey of a Modern Jew," *Logos Journal*, Vol. 39, no. 9, September–October 1971, pp. 8–13; Roland B. Gittelsohn, "Jews for Jesus—Are They Real?" *Midstream*, May 1979, pp. 41–45; Stephen Sharot, "A Jewish Christian Adventist Movement," *The Jewish Journal of Sociology*, Vol. 10, no. 1, June 1968, pp. 35–45; Joseph

Shiff, "Jews for Jesus: Facing the Realities," *SHMA* (A Journal of Jewish Responsibility), Vol. 50, no. 3, March 16, 1973.

14. Amos Nvo, "Between Two Worlds."
15. Daniel Oswald Rufeisen, "And Is Not of Another Religion."
16. Gidon Levi, "The Robe."

Index